ESSENTIAL PRINCIPLES
OF COMMUNICATIONS LAW

Essential Principles of Communications Law

DONALD E. LIVELY

New York
Westport, Connecticut
London

Library of Congress Cataloging-in-Publication Data

Lively, Donald E.,
    Essential principles of communications law / Donald E. Lively.
        p.   cm.
    Includes bibliographical references (p.   ) and index.
    ISBN 0–275–93912–X (alk. paper)
    1. Mass media—Law and legislation—United States. 2. Press law—
United States. 3. Telecommunication—Law and legislation—United
States. I. Title.
    KF2750.L58   1992
    343.7309′9—dc20
    [347.30399]   91–6303

British Library Cataloguing in Publication Data is available

Library of Congress Catalog Card Number: 91–6303
ISBN: 0–275–93912–X

First published in 1992

Praeger Publishers, One Madison Avenue, New York, NY 10010
An imprint of Greenwood Publishing Group, Inc.

Printed in the United States of America

The paper used in this book complies with the
Permanent Paper Standard issued by the National
Information Standards Organization (Z39.48–1984).

10 9 8 7 6 5 4 3 2 1

Copyright Acknowledgments

Grateful acknowledgment is given for permission to reprint "Why Cable Costs Too
Much" by John Barnes, June 1989. Reprinted with permission from *The Washington
Monthly*. Copyright by The Washington Monthly Company, 1611 Connecticut Avenue,
N.W., Washington, D.C. 20009. (202) 462-0128.

Also for permission to reprint an excerpt from Coase's "The Federal Communications
Commission," *Journal of Law and Economics*, vol. 1, 1–7, 35–40. Copyright 1959 by
University of Chicago Press. Reprinted by permission of the publisher.

Also for permission to reprint an excerpt from Fowler and Brenner's "A Marketplace
Approach to Broadcast Regulation." Originally published in 60 *Texas Law Review* 207
(1982). Copyright 1982 by the Texas Law Review Association. Reprinted by permission.

TO PAM AND RICO

Contents

Preface

The coursing of the law in general, as Justice Holmes once observed, is a function of logic and experience. Communications law, as a discrete body of legislative enactment, administrative regulation, and constitutional and statutory jurisprudence, reflects logic and experience that are especially fluid and reactive to new and rapidly evolving realities. The quickening and consequences of technology have generated media forms and legal issues that were barely conceivable when the twentieth century commenced, much less when the First Amendment was formulated.

Given an area of law so susceptible to continuous and even sudden redefinition, many textbooks that have occupied the field increasingly risk obsolescence. A primary aim of this book is to facilitate the study of communications law in the most comprehensive and contemporary sense. Coverage includes not only a focus upon print and broadcasting but extensive treatment of cable and unprecedented attention to common carriage.

As its title suggests, the book is intended to relate basic concepts and principles. Notwithstanding that fundamental aim, the text comprises materials carefully chosen to afford opportunity for in-depth discussion and sophisticated understanding of significant themes and topics.

A work of this nature, although attributed to the author, reflects the cumulative influences of some excellent teachers and colleagues in the academic world, some thoughtful practitioners in the professional world, and some insightful friends, acquaintances, and family in the real world. The research assistance of Barbara McCalla and Esther Jacobo-Rubio was particularly valuable and appreciated. Special thanks are owed to Carmen Gonzalez, who displayed a virtuoso touch in processing the manuscript and whose contributions were as multifold as they were significant.

Part One

THE NATURE AND LAW OF MEDIA

The terms of the First Amendment were constitutionally fixed two centuries ago. Since then, the means for communicating information have multiplied in exponential fashion. Nearly 150 years after the First Amendment was ratified, the Supreme Court depicted the press in terms of newspapers, periodicals, pamphlets, and leaflets. Even that characterization is underinclusive and hence obsolete for modern purposes, given the subsequent development of broadcasting, cable, satellites, telecommunications, and computers.

Media law commences with the deceptively simple premise that "Congress shall make no law...abridging the freedom of speech, or of the press." Governance has become detailed, complex, and even contradictory as the media have been progressively redefined and augmented. Until this century, mass communication primarily was a function of the printing press. Technology in general and electronification in particular have accelerated the processing and movement of information. What until recently were recognized as unique and legally significant capabilities and characteristics of various media, and the basis for media-specific regulation, increasingly are suspect as methodologies of processing and disseminating information become increasingly fungible.

Communications law is as dynamic as the field it governs. Recent history has demonstrated that premises must be continuously scrutinized to guard against obsolescence. Until a few years ago, the notion that broadcasting used a scarce resource was the central premise for making the medium uniquely susceptible to official content control, as discussed in Chapter 10. Competing against and increasingly prevailing over the scarcity premise is the evolving reality of new and rival communications technologies, with the consequent implication that each medium is an element of a media universe composed of functional equivalents.

As the First Amendment approached the end of its second century, dominant concerns with the press included concentration of ownership and effects of the media especially upon children. Commencement of a third constitutional century intimated the prospect of decentralization and fragmentation of information processing and transmission attributable to computer networking, desktop publishing, telefacsimile, and other technological options. Such democratization of the information marketplace conceivably may accentuate or alleviate concern with the media's impact. Metamorphosis that is continual, rather than periodic or occasional, at minimum indicates that society's formulation of media policy remains no less critical than it was when the First Amendment itself was composed.

Chapter 1

The Origins and Nature of the First Amendment

[T]he best test of truth is the power of the thought to get itself accepted in the competition of the market.

Abrams v. United States, 250 U.S. 616, 630 (1919)
(Holmes, J., dissenting)

The relationship between communications and the law is characterized generally by its variability. It is defined specifically by time, circumstance, and the nature of the message, medium, or both. Freedom of speech and of the press represents the extension of ideology that has evolved over almost an entire millennium. Constitutionalization of the principle, although now replicated in the charter documents of many other nations, is an originally American notion.

An explicit guarantee of expressive freedom by itself does not ensure that speech and press will be immune to official control or influence. Even in the United States, expression is routinely and constitutionally abridged for reasons considered compelling or substantial. As the English experience illustrates, an enumerated guarantee is not essential to the existence of significant expressive liberty. Constitutional enshrinement of principle nonetheless illuminates a culture's professed values and purported character. Even more revealing, when such formalization exists, may be the exceptions and qualifications that ultimately define the real nature and extent of constitutional freedom.

It is an elemental precept of American constitutional law, dating back to *Marbury v. Madison*, that the judiciary has the final responsibility for determining "what the law is." The actual contours of the First Amendment thus are defined by accumulated jurisprudence that charts the boundary between expressive liberty and official control. Insofar as the First Amendment responds to new problems and is a basis for challenging official action that directly or indirectly affects expression, its actual meaning will remain a function of evolution rather than specific ordination.

I. PRELUDE TO THE FIRST AMENDMENT

A. SEMINAL CONCEPTS

Freedom of the press represents a relatively fresh and still-developing aspect of the media's existence. For most of the press's history, official suppression and control have been normative rather than exceptional governmental responses. Even before the advent of movable type, English law proscribed spoken criticism of the state. Seditious libel was criminalized in the thirteenth century, long before the capacity existed for mass dissemination of information and thought. The printing press thus was introduced in the late fifteenth century against a backdrop of official intimidation calculated to deter rather than facilitate technological maximization, expressive initiative, and viewpoint diversity.

The emergence of the printing press and its capacity to function as a mass medium presented both an opportunity and a risk for the established order. While the press afforded political and religious institutions an enhanced means to propagate their expectations and sentiments, it also possessed potential for effectively disseminating competing views and criticism. To account for such possibilities in England, the Crown introduced a system of licensing. The linchpin of official control was the creation of a special company to which all printing was assigned. Publication thus was a special privilege conferred upon a select few. Official control was effectuated not only by government franchise but by pre-publication review, harsh penalties for criticism of church or state, and proscription of obscene or immoral expression.

As media technology and usage evolved, regulation became increasingly sophisticated. By the seventeenth century, the methodology of suppression had expanded to include taxation and a well-developed system of previous restraint. Official efforts to control the flow and content of information were increasingly confounded, however, by a confluence of entrepreneurial initiative, emerging political ideology, and a quickening sense of the utility of instrumentalities for mass communication. Central to the philosophy of natural law, which propounded the existence of rights fundamental to human nature and transcending positive law, were notions of expressive freedom. Principles of natural justice, although eventually regarded as problematic because they are reducible to debatable moral ideology, were critical factors in inspiring charter documents of the American nation and its several states. A primary exponent of natural law was the seventeenth-century English philosopher John Locke, who advanced the premise that government's legitimacy rests upon the consent of the governed. Locke's theories, which especially emphasized freedom of expression as a key to discovery of truth, proved to be a significant influence upon the movement toward independence. He also echoed sentiments sounded by John Milton in his *Areopagitica* in 1644. Milton posited that

the liberty to know, to utter, and to argue freely according to conscience, [is] above all liberties.... Though all the winds of doctrine were let loose to play upon the earth, so Truth be in the field, we do injuriously by licensing and prohibiting to misdoubt her strength. Let her and falsehood grapple; whoever knew Truth put to the worse in free and open encounter.

Milton in the midseventeenth century thus introduced the basic imagery of a marketplace of ideas and a preferred position for expressive liberty that even now helps define First Amendment jurisprudence. Within their own time, Milton's and Locke's works provided intellectual stimulation that contributed to England's abandonment of official licensing by the end of the seventeenth century.

The repeal of licensing did not foreclose a significant role for the state in controlling the nature and flow of information. Criminal libel laws continued to deter criticism of church and state. The introduction of revenue laws in the eighteenth century imposed new burdens upon publishers and were a special source of antagonism in the American colonies. Media control, instead of disappearing, assumed new incarnations as concepts of press freedom increasingly vied for attention. The prominent English jurist William Blackstone sought to resolve the apparent contradiction by asserting that "liberty of the press is ... essential to the nature of a free state, ... [but] consists in laying no previous restraints upon publications and is by no means infringed or violated ... [w]here blasphemous, immoral, treasonable, schematical, seditious or scandalous libel are punished by the English law." The distinction was a significant antecedent for modern jurisprudence, which remains especially hostile to systems of prior restraint but countenances subsequent punishment of expression. Notwithstanding more expansive notions of press liberty since, official content control now, as then, remains a question not of whether it is permissible but of when and how.

B. COLONIAL EVENTS

Concepts of press freedom in the American colonies were shaped not only by the English experience and legacy but by a mutually reinforcing progression of prerevolutionary ideology and events. The eighteenth century, prior to the American Revolution, was characterized by entrepreneurial and expressive initiative that merged into new challenges to official suppressive tendencies. Early colonial publications competed for public attention and acceptance by offering a menu of news, essays, poetry, and advertising. Publishing was subject to developmental realities, however, that influenced the nature and quality of coverage. Given practical problems of inadequate printing supplies and deficient lighting, production processes and aesthetics were subject to uncontrollable disadvantages. Underdeveloped means of distribution diminished or limited timeliness and influence. The law itself was generally unfriendly toward criticism of public officials and thus a significant impediment to meaningful appraisal of government. Contrary to modern principles, truth was an aggravating factor of defamation rather than a defense against it. Further complicating the publishing environment were official attitudes not yet conditioned to media criticism and accustomed instead to enforcing penal sanctions against unruly publishers.

Notwithstanding the compounding of suppressive forces, publishing played a crucial role in facilitating revolution and affording an experience from which constitutional principle would be extracted. A particularly significant event in the movement toward expressive freedom was the trial and acquittal of John Peter Zenger in 1735. Although Zenger's name is indelibly etched in First Amendment lore, his place in history is attributable more to fortuitous circumstances than to any ideology or agenda that he personally conceived. As a New York publisher hard pressed to find work, Zenger became a hired hand for critics of Governor William Cosby. The actual editorial content of Zenger's New York *Journal* was the work of a prominent attorney, James Alexander, who, like many of his contemporaries, was disaffected by Cosby's greed, corruption, and imperious ways.

Well-aimed criticisms and barbs were not the *Journal*'s only stock in trade. Alexander's pointed commentary was effective in catalyzing public support for a change in administration. Anticipating the inevitable legal action his editorial crusade would engender, Alexander also devoted attention to the general philosophy of and case for freedom of expression as a curb against official tyranny. When the governor finally sued Zenger as the publisher of allegedly seditious libel, therefore, a critical conditioning process already had commenced that effectively sensitized the public generally and the jury specifically to the virtues of expressive liberty and the vices of official oversight.

Governor Cosby's initial effort to secure a grand jury indictment presaged the outcome of the trial itself. The grand jury, presented with several claims of seditious libel, responded to popular opinion instead and rendered a no bill. Given the refusal to indict, Cosby exercised the power of his office to have Zenger arrested and charged with the same offense. Under then-existing defamation law, the prosecution was obligated only to prove the fact of publication. As noted previously, proof that a statement was true did not constitute a defense and actually enhanced the severity of the libel. The reality of publication was undeniable, and thus material issues of fact were not even controverted. Zenger's litigation strategy conceded what was irrefutable and legally sufficient to convict him. His counsel appealed directly to the jury instead to consider the truth of what had been published and evaluate not merely the undisputed fact but the law itself. Consistent with what is the still-honored prerogative of jury nullification, the trial jury effectively negated the law's operation under the circumstances. It promptly returned a verdict in Zenger's favor and thereby vindicated the interests of expressive freedom.

The Zenger verdict was significant not because it formally rewrote defamation law or established an official precedent. General jury verdicts articulate no legal principle and have no precedential value. The decision nonetheless is notable as a significant way station in the development of popular sentiment that eventually would help define the First Amendment. It served as an effective role model for future challenges to colonial law and evinced the increasing pertinence of libertarian ideology. The trial's outcome did not eliminate official efforts to control or muzzle the press. As the Revolution approached, however, the Zenger experience became a point of reference and inspiration for a subsequent generation of partisan editors whose publishing aims and activities were tied to the cause of independence.

The role of the colonial press in the decade preceding the Revolution is difficult to exaggerate. Although prerevolutionary media were composed of approximately two dozen weekly newspapers, they provided a significant forum for articulating grievances against British rule, arguing the case for independence, and mobilizing sentiment that, if not consensual, at least was sufficient to effect a political rupture. A period characterized by increasingly candid and vitriolic rhetoric, however, also disclosed the often-treacherous context within which freedom of expression operates. Even if it was regarded as a natural right by the new republic's instigators, freedom of the press in reality visibly deviated from theory. Liberty of the press for purveyors of pro-British sentiment effectively was denied by mob action and intimidation. Even the struggle to secure expressive liberty thus was waged with tactics that included denial of such freedom to exponents of competing viewpoints. The very process of attaining this liberty thereby afforded a preview of the enduring tension between society's documental commitment and frequent inclinations nonetheless toward intolerance.

II. THE EMERGENCE AND EVOLUTION OF THE FIRST AMENDMENT

Independence from British rule created at least as many political problems as it solved. Effectuation of independence did not by itself establish rules of governance or secure freedom of expression or any other fundamental right. To the contrary, the postrevolutionary period was characterized by societal chaos, instability, and systemic enfeeblement inimical to well-defined and enforceable principles. Several years of governance under the Articles of Confederation were notable for sectional friction, trade barriers, and national weakness that precluded the reality of a viable union and any defining common morality. Responding to these deficiencies, delegates from the various states convened in Philadelphia in 1787 and fashioned what became and has served since as the nation's constitution. As originally framed and circulated for ratification, the document represented a blueprint for the allocation and exercise of governmental power. Although it created and assigned power to three federal branches and bifurcated responsibility between national and state governments, the charter as first conceived made no reference to individual rights or liberties. The omission, instead of representing any antagonism toward the freedoms eventually formalized by the Bill of Rights, reflected a sense that they were self-evident to the point that their recital was superfluous. Further militating against any itemization of basic rights and liberties were perceptions that they were adequately accounted for by state constitutions and not imperiled by a federal government of limited power.

As the various states contemplated ratification, and anxiety intensified with respect to the risks of national power, opposition coalesced over the document's omission of enumerated rights. Incorporation of the Bill of Rights, cataloging liberties including freedom of speech and of the press, thus proved critical for tipping the balance of sentiment toward ratification. Formalization of the First Amendment, like other itemized guarantees, represented in part a principle of convenience necessary to accomplish the overarching priority of ratification. Consistent with original concern regarding the dangers of federal power, the First Amendment dictates that "*Congress* shall make no law . . . abridging the freedom of speech, or of the press" (emphasis added). Subsequent jurisprudential glosses have expanded the guarantee's purview so that it responds to governmental action, regardless of whether it is federal or state and whether it is legislative, executive, judicial, or administrative. Freedom of the press, moreover, has been extended to reckon with media and realities entirely beyond the purview of the framers' vision.

The decade immediately following the First Amendment's adoption is instructive for purposes of appreciating the frailty of a system of freedom of expression. Particularly revealing of the treacherous circumstances in which the First Amendment functions is how its meaning first was imperiled by the generation responsible for its creation. Notwithstanding original concern with invasion of liberty by the federal government and a consequent documental focus upon Congress, ratification operated as a transition rather than a termination point for competing political agendas. Rival ideologies that had surfaced over the course of ratification were renewed and intensified as attention turned to elections and the actual exercise of legislative and executive power. The critical medium for debate was a highly partisan press devoted primarily to political advocacy and characterized by overt favoritism. The nation's seminal experience with robust and uninhibited discourse, that between Hamiltonian Federalists and Jeffersonian Republicans, proved neither happy nor promising. In 1798, a Federalist-dominated Congress enacted and Federalist President Adams executed the Sedition Act in an effort to silence and neutralize their ideological rivals. The law held freedom of expression captive to political convenience by making it a crime to

write, print, utter or publish...any false, scandalous and malicious writing or writings against the government of the United States, or either house of the Congress of the United States, or the President of the United States, with intent to defame the said government, or either house of the said Congress, or the said President, or to bring them, or either of them, into contempt or disrepute, or to excite against them or either or any of them, the hatred of the good people of the United States, or to stir up sedition within the United States.

Violation was punishable by two years' imprisonment and a $2,000 fine. Not surprisingly, targeted defendants were politicians and publishers of Republican persuasion. The Sedition Act lapsed after two years. Although it was never challenged as an invasion of First Amendment freedom, it represented an initial but hardly final challenge to First Amendment values.

Operation of such a draconian scheme within a decade of the First Amendment's ratification also suggested that there was more (or less) to the guarantee than met the eye. Nearly two-thirds of the nation's history would pass, nonetheless, before the First Amendment would become a subject of serious jurisprudential reckoning. Until then, it was at most a matter of passing reference. First amendment issues were presented but not directly litigated, in the first half of the nineteenth century, when southern states attempted to prohibit dissemination of abolitionist literature. While upholding slavery in *Scott v. Sandford*, the Supreme Court adverted to the First Amendment and other enumerated guarantees for purposes of exemplifying a general constitutional scheme curtailing federal power. Shortly after ratification of the Fourteenth Amendment, the Court in the *Slaughter-House Cases* mentioned without amplification the First Amendment "right to peaceably assemble and petition for redress of grievances." Even as society entered the twentieth century, and media never contemplated by the Constitution's architects emerged into prominence, First Amendment questions initially were bypassed. When censorship of motion pictures was first considered by the Court in 1915, film's significance was explicitly discounted. In *Mutual Film Corp. v. Industrial Commission of Ohio*, the medium was denominated a mere "spectacle" unworthy of press status. Not until the middle of this century did the Court make clear that motion pictures were within the First Amendment's field of interest.

Meaningful inquiry into the nature and scope of the First Amendment finally manifested itself toward the end of World War I. Early decisions concerned broadly structured federal and state laws devised and employed to silence persons who agitated against, dissented from, or even criticized government or official policy. The federal Espionage Act, which among other things prohibited interference with military activities, including recruiting and enlistment processes, provided prison sentences of up to twenty years for violations. Initial decisions concerning convictions of persons who denounced American participation in the war and advocated draft resistance in part revealed judicial deference to government action during wartime. They also set a tone, however, that even after the cessation of hostilities was inhospitable to political criticism venturing beyond mainstream opinion. Particularly illustrative of the limited tolerance for and serious criminal consequences of speech criticizing government was the case of Eugene Debs. As a prominent Socialist and critic of American involvement in World War I, Debs was convicted and sentenced to ten years in prison under an Espionage Act provision prohibiting interference with military recruiting. As the Socialist candidate for president in 1920, Debs received nearly one million votes while he was incarcerated. Debs was released in two years by presidential order. Professor Kalven equated his fate with the notion of putting "George McGovern . . . in prison for his criticism of the [Vietnam] war." The decision in *Debs v. United States*, combined with other formative contributions to First Amendment jurisprudence, offered an early warning that trading in unorthodox or radical political ideas may be a dangerous enterprise regardless of constitutional enumerations.

In its search for constitutional meaning during the postwar era, the Court proceeded from the assumption that the First Amendment did not afford unqualified immunity for all expression. For the most part, early cases were decided on the basis of whether the expression at issue had conceivably dangerous propensities. Although operative standards proved unforgiving, and lengthy prison sentences were affirmed for antiwar leafleting intended "to cripple or hinder" the war effort, some significant principles were sounded that eventually would furnish a predicate for doctrine more friendly toward expressive diversity.

The original incarnation of the clear and present danger test, for instance, was enunciated in *Schenck v. United States*. Although the Court upheld convictions for Espionage Act violations based upon dissemination of antidraft leaflets found obstructive of military recruiting, it determined that but for wartime circumstances the expression would have been constitutionally protected. Articulating the clear and present danger doctrine in its initial configuration, Justice Holmes observed that

[t]he most stringent protection of free speech would not protect a man in falsely shouting fire in a theater and causing a panic.... The question in every case is whether the words are used in such circumstances and are of such a nature as to create a clear and present danger that they will bring about the substantive evils the Congress has a right to prevent. It is a question of proximity and degree.

Notwithstanding what has proved to be enduring constitutional imagery, the Court invested in standards concerned with conceivably "bad tendencies" of expression regardless of the actual proximity or degree of harm. Dissenting from the majority opinion in *Abrams v. United States*, Holmes observed that expression should not be suppressed unless it "so imminently threaten[s] immediate interference with the lawful and pressing purpose of the law that an immediate check is required to save the country." Advocating and amplifying the concept of clear and present danger, Holmes noted that "the ultimate good is better reached by free trade in ideas and that the best test of truth is the power of thought to get itself accepted in the competition of the market."

Holmes thereby introduced into First Amendment jurisprudence sentiments originally expressed by John Milton nearly three centuries earlier. Despite the transition from war to peace and Holmes's counsel, however, the Court continued to apply the bad tendency standard. In *Gitlow v. New York*, it upheld convictions of persons who had been prosecuted under a state criminal anarchy statute for disseminating literature advocating political strikes. The *Gitlow* decision is of long-term constitutional significance, notwithstanding its obsolete standard of review, because the Court found freedom of speech and of the press to be incorporated into the Fourteenth Amendment and thus secured against state as well as federal abridgment. The Court, in *Whitney v. California*, next affirmed a conviction based upon violation of a state criminal syndicalism act. Dismissing the defendant's argument that she had advocated peaceful political change through the democratic process, the Court emphasized that she belonged to and assisted an organization while knowing its illegal aim of overthrowing the government. Justice Brandeis, joined by Holmes, authored a concurring opinion in *Whitney* that would become a cornerstone of modern review. They noted that

even advocacy of violation, however reprehensible morally, is not a justification for denying free speech where the advocacy falls short of incitement and there is nothing to indicate that the advocacy would be immediately acted on. . . . [N]o danger flowing from speech can be deemed clear and present, unless the incidence of the evil apprehended is so imminent that it may befall before there is opportunity for full discussion.

The confluence of the Cold War and McCarthyism at the midpoint of this century commenced another cycle of repression that similarly tested First Amendment boundaries. Official concern with subversive influences engendered legislation prohibiting the Communist party and membership therein. Numerous congressional investigations were conducted to identify insurrectionary forces that might be at work in government and industry. Consistent with the prevailing sense of apprehension, the Court, despite professed subscription to clear and present danger criteria, adjudged cases pursuant to less forgiving terms. The constitutionality of the Smith Act, which was the basis of convictions for conspiring to organize the Communist party, was measured by "whether the gravity of the evil discounted by its improbability, justifies such invasion of free speech as is necessary to avoid danger." Instead of focusing upon the likelihood and imminence of harm, analysis in *Dennis v. United States* was reduced to a balancing test that afforded regulatory latitude according to the relative magnitude of danger. Insofar as insurrection was advocated, a plurality of the Court considered it unnecessary for "Government to wait until the catalyst is added" or for indications that the "putsch is about to be executed." Notwithstanding how the standard of review was depicted, analysis reflected the operation of criteria first advanced in 1917 as an alternative to the clear and present danger test. Primary attention to the "gravity of the evil" had been advanced by Judge Learned Hand in *Masses Publishing Co. v. Patten*. From Hand's perspective, no meaningful distinction existed between incitement and persuasion, and expression that "counsel[ed] the violation of law" was categorically unprotected. The *Dennis* decision thus was the product of analysis pitched directly toward content rather than toward its immediate or likely effect.

Nearly half a century passed before the Court responded fully to the prompting of Holmes and Brandeis. In *Brandenburg v. Ohio*, it considered a state criminal syndicalism law comparable to the statute it had upheld in *Whitney*. Reversing the convictions of several Ku Klux Klan members who had been prosecuted under the law, the Court moved beyond criteria concerned only with content or bad tendency. Despite an incongruous citation to *Dennis* as a precedent, it embraced the clear and present danger test as originally formulated by Brandeis and Holmes. Government, as a consequence, is precluded from "forbid[ding] or proscrib[ing] advocacy of the use of force or of law violation except where such advocacy is directed to inciting or producing imminent lawless action and is likely to incite or produce such action."

The modern clear and present danger formula at least theoretically affords more constitutional breathing room to unorthodox political expression insofar as it demands a showing of imminent harm. It has yet to be tested in circumstances comparable to the Red Scare of the 1920s or the McCarthyism of the 1950s, when distorted societal perception and official overreaction are normative. For some critics, moreover, the standard of review is not protective enough. Justices Black and Douglas, although concurring in the *Brandenburg* result, asserted that the First Amendment afforded no room for a clear and present danger test. Their concern, rooted in First Amendment history, was with its vulnerability to manipulation as a function of society's mood swings. From Black's and Douglas's perspective, clear and present danger criteria, no matter how elegantly or pointedly styled, always would be at constitutional risk.

The political process is the crucible from which much First Amendment profundity has originated. Even before the Court announced the modern clear and present danger test, it constructed a constitutional immunity to defamation laws for falsehoods pertaining to public officials. The exemption forthrightly defers to First Amendment interests, particularly the "profound national commitment to the principle that debate on public issues should be uninhibited, robust and wide-open." The decision, in *New York Times Co. v. Sullivan*, concerned criticism of Alabama police officials for their treatment of civil-rights protesters during the early 1960s. Jurisprudential response disclosed not only the Court's valuation of political speech but its sensitivity to processes that would inhibit it.

Despite special attention to political speech, the First Amendment has proved responsive to other expressive interests. At the midpoint of this century, several forms of expression were deemed beyond the First Amendment's concern and thus entirely unprotected. Defamation, obscenity, and fighting words, as noted in *Chaplinsky v. New Hampshire*, had been regarded as "certain well-defined and narrowly limited classes of speech, the prevention and punishment of which have never been thought to raise any constitutional problem." Such expression was perceived as having little or no social value and thus being unworthy of First Amendment consideration. Doctrine commencing in the early 1940s also was indifferent to regulation of commercial advertising. By the 1960s, as noted previously, defamation was afforded qualified protection insofar as it was considered necessary to preserve the vitality of political debate. The categorical significance of fighting words largely has been eclipsed by doctrines of vagueness and overbreadth, which preclude regulation that is ambiguous, confusing with respect to its coverage, or capable of impairing protected expression. Commercial expression by the 1970s became recognized for its significant social utility and was afforded First Amendment status. Unlike other categories of expression that have evolved from unprotected to protected status, obscenity remains beyond the Constitution's ken.

The latter part of the twentieth century also has witnessed the conferral of First Amendment status upon media that were not even imaginable two centuries ago. Motion pictures, broadcasting, and cable are accorded constitutional protection that, as discussed in the next chapter, varies depending upon each medium's special characteristics. Despite the First Amendment's expanding amplitude, the existence and operation of a speech and press classification system demonstrates that expressive liberty is not of infinite breadth. Actual perimeters of freedom of speech and of the press, insofar as constitutional terms are not read in literal or expansive terms, are a function instead of the theory and values that inspire First Amendment doctrine.

III. FIRST AMENDMENT THEORY

A. THE VALUATION AND CLASSIFICATION OF EXPRESSION

Defining the First Amendment's meaning has proved a highly competitive process. Rival theories have debated not only why but what speech should be protected. Freedom of expression often has been esteemed for facilitating democratic processes dependent upon open debate and as the linchpin of liberty generally. The First Amendment, in *Palko v. Connecticut*, thus was described as "the matrix, the indispensable condition of nearly every other form of freedom." In the midnineteenth century, John Stuart Mill itemized several values accounted for by free trade in ideas regardless of the truth or falsity of expression.

First, if any opinion is compelled to silence, that opinion for aught we can certainly know, be true. To deny this is to assume our own infallibility. Secondly, though this silenced opinion be in error, it may and very commonly does, contain a portion of the truth, and since the generally prevailing opinion of any subject is rarely or never the whole truth, it is only by the collision of adverse opinion that the remainder of the truth had any chance being supplied. Thirdly, even if the received opinion be not only true but the whole truth; unless it is suffered to be, and actually is vigorously and earnestly contested, it will, by most of those who receive it, be held in the manner of a prejudice, with little comprehension or feeling of its rational grounds. And not only this, but fourthly, the meaning of the doctrine itself will be in danger of being lost or enfeebled.

Modern theorists have expounded upon Mill's basic premises and have conceptualized First Amendment values in both complementary and competing ways. The theory that has proved most influential to the modern course of First Amendment standards has been Alexander Meiklejohn's notion that expression relating to the democratic process is the guarantee's real or primary concern. Investment in the Meiklejohn theory is evidenced by the jurisprudential sense that "speech relating to self-government" has paramount value and so merits utmost constitutional attention. Such appraisal tends to measure value and significance from a dominant societal rather than individual perspective. Rival notions contest both the predicate and the result. Instead of focusing upon collective interests, alternative reference points would value expression according to its capacity to advance personal knowledge, engender self-development, and facilitate self-realization. Various other theories, which are not necessarily mutually exclusive, emphasize specific utilities, including the capacity of speech to promote participation in decision-making processes, facilitate societal adaptability and stability, operate as a checking mechanism against official action, and function as a social safety valve. A primary reference point of societal rather than personal utility has significant consequences for the First Amendment's reach. To the extent that value and constitutional status are not determined from an individualized perspective, the breadth of protected expression is narrower than it otherwise might be. Especially insofar as particular speech forms are devalued, autonomous selection may be compromised in favor of authoritative determination of fitness for public consumption.

The classification of expression as an extension of selected values creates significant problems and anomalies. Categorization has translated not only into diminished protection for some speech variants but into exclusion of others altogether from the First Amendment's protective ambit. Obscenity, as mentioned previously and as discussed further in Chapter 3, is constitutionally devalued and dismissed on grounds that it entirely lacks social value. Explaining obscenity's unprotected status, the Court has observed that "modern civilization does not leave disposal of garbage and sewage to free will." Appraisal might yield different results if, instead of being calibrated to societal interest, it was performed with an eye to personal utility. When obscenity is examined on the basis of possible worth to the individual rather than according to general or dominant norms, constitutional respect may be warranted to the extent that it affords personal pleasure, helps establish sexual identity, or promotes autonomous selection. No category of expression is more susceptible to jurisprudential disparagement than obscenity. Intractable definitional problems and at least arguable merit pursuant to alternative valuation systems, however, disclose the potential for analytical treachery that is magnified as expression with more universally acknowledged worth becomes implicated.

Value-driven constitutional line drawing and resultant imprecision of classifications present risks even to the most esteemed variants of expression. Charting a line between political speech and supposedly less worthy expression may be neat in theory but is perilous in practice. Commercial speech, for instance, has been defined as expression proposing an economic transaction or relating to economic self-interest. Neither depiction is exact enough, however, to avoid sometimes ensnaring political expression and in the process diminishing its status. Political fund-raising and advocacy inspired by economic considerations, for example, have significant commercial dimensions. The actual denomination of the expression, as discussed in Chapter 3, is critical to whether it is more or less protected.

The risk of classifying speech in singular terms when expression may have multidimensional characteristics is evident too in jurisprudence that identifies and devalues indecent expression. Political speech, at least when it is clearly discernible, is jurisprudentially revered to the point that vilification and even falsehood may be countenanced in deference to the imperatives of "uninhibited, robust and wide-open" debate. Political or social commentary presented in a way that offends dominant sensitivity or taste, however, may be subject to devaluation. Speech, even if it is protected, has been subject to nuisance analogies when perceived as "a right thing in the wrong place—like a pig in the parlor instead of the barnyard."

With respect to sexually explicit but not obscene expression, the Court has observed that "few of us would send our sons and daughters off to war to preserve the citizen's right to see specified 'Sexual Activities' exhibited in the theaters of our choice." Neither the appraisal nor the prediction, even if accurate, accounts for the possibility that allegedly indecent expression may be mixed with higher-priority speech. Such merged expression has been protected insofar as it is used for purposes of political protest, but it has been found regulable to the extent that it is broadcast as a social satire. The divergence reveals a procrustean classification system premised not only upon the medium but upon the message.

The selection of values that inspire First Amendment doctrine influences also whether purportedly content-neutral criteria are impartial in reality. The Court has enunciated the general principle that "above all else, the First Amendment means that government has no power to restrict expression because of its message, its ideas, its subject matter, or its content." Time, place, and manner controls are permissible, however, provided they are reasonable. Determining governance that is reasonable and thus permissible requires consideration of whether the regulation is "narrowly tailored to serve a significant governmental interest,... leave[s] open ample alternative channels of communication," and is unrelated to content. As the classification process has evolved, time, place, and manner analysis effectively has functioned pursuant to a sliding-scale scheme of valuation. The point has been emphasized by dissenting justices that a majority of the Court has yet to coalesce in support of a formal classification for indecent expression. For practical purposes, however, it is difficult to imagine the Court allowing a zoning ordinance to impose the same restrictions upon political expression that are tolerated upon speech classified as indecent. Consideration of what constitutes reasonable regulation in reality may factor out or diminish the significance of neutrality considerations insofar as the worth of expression is perceived to be slight. Official control, which supposedly is not permitted if it is related to content, thus may operate precisely because of content.

The ultimate acceptability of classification processes and consequences depends upon the validity and strength of presumptions underlying speech differentiation. The premise that political speech is of paramount importance, however, is at least controvertible. If actual electoral participation is a touchstone, political expression has limited rather than comprehensive societal pertinence. Participation in the economic marketplace, by contrast, is much more a universal phenomenon. The Court itself has observed that "interest in the free flow of commercial information... may be as keen, if not keener by far, than... interest in the day's most urgent political debate." Assignment of the highest constitutional ranking to political expression reflects an exercise that, regardless of the reason, delimits autonomous selection and development.

Even if political speech merits utmost constitutional attention, the argument exists that its significance is a basis for close rather than relaxed regulatory attention. Justice White has observed that false speech, even of a political nature, presents serious-enough dangers to merit stricter control. White suggests that if expression is valued for facilitating informed decisions relating to self-government, falsehood may undermine that paramount aim to the extent that it misinforms the public and pollutes the stream of information. Strengthening White's position is the concern that misleading expression breeds cynicism within the citizenry and alienates persons who otherwise would participate in the political process. Such considerations, as detailed in Chapter 3, challenge traditional notions that the First Amendment assumes the risk of the public being duped, manipulated into unwise decisions, or even apathetic.

Somewhat akin to the classification of speech on the basis of perceived value, the press is categorized pursuant to the notion that "each [medium] tends to present its own peculiar problems." Radio and television have been subject to a comprehensive system of federal regulation requiring broadcasters to function as public trustees. Contrary to traditional First Amendment expectations, content regulation actually became normative to the extent that it was considered necessary to facilitate fairness and balance, protect impressionable children from adverse influences, and control the media's pervasive and intrusive character. Uniting these rationales, at least with respect to governance of broadcasting, is the statutory obligation to serve the public interest. An early observer commented that the criterion "means about as little as any phrase that . . . drafters . . . could have used." It at least introduces to freedom of the press analysis, as discussed in Chapter 10, problems of appraisal and subjectivity that continue to plague freedom of speech review.

B. The "Preferred" Position of the First Amendment

The high value attached to expressive freedom has influenced the status of the First Amendment in the broader constitutional order. A sense that freedom of speech and of the press was crucial to the vitality of other basic rights and liberties engendered notions that the First Amendment's status was unique among other guarantees, and that judicial review should reflect its special role. The Court, in *Murdock v. Pennsylvania*, ventured the notion that "freedom of press [and] freedom of speech . . . are in a preferred position."

The concept, if fully and persistently subscribed to, would have profound implications for a system of freedom of expression. Recognition that the First Amendment is not merely an end in itself, but a means of facilitating the general liberty experience, directs attention not merely to the specific guarantee but to values and emanations pertinent to personal freedom generally. Rights of the public to access the media for purposes of self-expression, or for the press to obtain as well as disseminate information, may be rational extensions of the First Amendment insofar as they help accommodate expressive freedom, individual autonomy, and democratic robustness. Modern jurisprudence in significant part has repudiated the predicate of a preferred status and has accordingly delimited analytical potential. To the extent that the Court insists upon compelling justification for speech regulation, presumes the invalidity of prior restraints, relaxes standing to sue, and is otherwise particularly attentive to expressive interests, however, the First Amendment continues to possess a special, if not preferred, status in constitutional law.

C. THE FIRST AMENDMENT AS AN ABSOLUTE

If the First Amendment were regarded as an absolute, it would beget a neat, tidy, and concise body of law. Like other constitutional rights and liberties, it has evolved as a relative guarantee that requires a selection from competing values for doctrinal moorage. The notion that the First Amendment is an absolute and must be strictly construed is identified most closely with Justice Black and to a slightly lesser extent with Justice Douglas. Although the Court never has subscribed to absolutism, Black adhered persistently to the notion that "the First Amendment's unequivocal command that there shall be no abridgment of the rights of free speech . . . shows the men who drafted the Bill of Rights did all the 'balancing' that was to be done." Black's unremitting subscription to absolutism reflected his sense that more flexible analytical methodologies weakened constitutional guarantees. If rights could be expanded, he observed, they also could be diluted.

Even absolutism affords no escape from an eventual need to chart First Amendment perimeters. The term "speech" is not defined by the Constitution. Because it can be read broadly to include symbolic expression or narrowly to include only verbal communication, amplification beyond the specific terms of the First Amendment eventually was required. The wearing of black arm bands to protest the Vietnam War, for instance, was recognized by a majority of the Court in *Tinker v. Des Moines Independent Community School District*, as within the purview of speech. Justice Black, in *Cox v. Louisiana*, described "standing, patrolling, or marching" even to make a political statement as beyond the ambit of speech. In *Cohen v. California*, he would have found an antiwar statement inscribed on a piece of clothing to be unprotected conduct. By concluding that speech and conduct were conceptually and constitutionally separate, Black offered a distinction that was at least debatable and thus represented participation in active, competitive line drawing necessary to vitalize the First Amendment and delineate its reach.

Denomination of a right or liberty as conditional permits the introduction of analytical reference points that would be precluded if the guarantee were absolute. The practical meaning of a qualified freedom is defined not by what the Constitution commands but by what is found tolerable despite the Constitution. To the extent that it does not speak entirely for itself, the First Amendment, like other open-ended constitutional terms, is dependent upon external values for inspiration and actuation. The consequent law of the First Amendment is primarily a function of jurisprudentially selected ideals that have engendered a classification process and consequent ordering of speech and press variants. If it were edited to account for such interpretation, the First Amendment would have a more detailed and equivocal cast than appears documentally. In pertinent part, the First Amendment as inscribed provides that "Congress shall make no law . . . abridging the freedom of speech, or of the press." As qualified by accumulated expoundment and gloss, the guarantee for modern and practical purposes would read:

No branch of government, federal, state, or local, shall legislate or act in a way that abridges freedom of speech or of the press except (1) when expression categorically excluded from the First Amendment is implicated; (2) when expression presents a direct, imminent, and probable danger of inciting unlawful conduct; (3) to protect reputational interest, provided claims by public officials and public figures are subject at least to an actual malice standard; (4) to safeguard privacy interests under specified circumstances; and (5) to effectuate legitimate and substantial governmental interests pursuant to narrowly drawn regulation of commercial expression. Nothing in this guarantee should be construed as exempting otherwise protected expression from reasonable time, place, and manner restriction. Protection also may be dependent upon or vary according to the context of expression, especially insofar as government's special interest in protecting children is implicated and unique characteristics of a particular medium require special attention.

An accurate understanding of the law of the First Amendment requires recognition that the meaning of the guarantee transcends a single clause or sentence. Broad statements of principle tend to be susceptible to exception and displacement depending upon circumstances. First Amendment maxims disclaiming "paternalistic approach[es] . . . which restrict what people may hear" or asserting "right conclusions are more likely to be gathered from a multitude of tongues, than through any kind of authoritative selection" are notable as much for their circumstantial inoperativeness as their lofty ring. Problematical cases and results notwithstanding, the persistence and vitality of debate over the First Amendment's meaning constitute evidence of the guarantee's vitality, pertinence, and significance.

REFERENCES

CASES

Abrams v. United States, 250 U.S. 616 (1919).
Brandenburg v. Ohio, 395 U.S. 444 (1969).
Chaplinsky v. New Hampshire, 315 U.S. 568 (1942).
Cohen v. California, 403 U.S. 15 (1971).
Cox v. Louisiana, 379 U.S. 559 (1965).
Debs v. United States, 249 U.S. 211 (1919).
Dennis v. United States, 341 U.S. 494 (1951).
Gitlow v. New York, 268 U.S. 652 (1925).
Marbury v. Madison, 5 U.S. (1 Cranch) 137 (1803).

Masses Publishing Co. v. Patten, 244 F. 535 (S.D.N.Y.), rev'd, 246 F. 24 (2d Cir. 1917).
Murdock v. Pennsylvania, 319 U.S. 105 (1943).
Mutual Film Corp. v. Industrial Commission of Ohio, 236 U.S. 230 (1915).
New York Times Co. v. Sullivan, 376 U.S. 254 (1964).
Palko v. Connecticut, 302 U.S. 319 (1937).
Schenck v. United States, 249 U.S. 47 (1919).
Scott v. Sandford, 60 U.S. (19 How.) 393 (1857).
Slaughter-House Cases, 83 U.S. (16 Wall.) 36 (1872).
Tinker v. Des Moines Independent Community School District, 393 U.S. 503 (1969).
Whitney v. California, 274 U.S. 357 (1927).

PUBLICATIONS

Blackstone, Commentaries on the Laws of England (1872).
Blasi, *The Checking Value in First Amendment Theory*, 1977 Am. B. Found. Res. J. 521.
Emerson, The System of Freedom of Expression (1970).
Kalven, *Ernst Freund and the First Amendment Tradition*, 40 U. Chi. L. Rev. 235 (1973).
Levy, Legacy of Suppression: Freedom of Speech and Press in Early American History (1960).
Meiklejohn, Free Speech and Its Relation to Self-Government (1948).
Meiklejohn, Political Freedom: The Constitutional Powers of the People (1960).
Meiklejohn, *The First Amendment Is an Absolute*, 1961 Sup. Ct. Rev. 245.
Mill, On Liberty (1859).
Milton, Areopagitica, A Speech for the Liberty of Unlicensed Printing to the Parliament of England (1644).
Redish, Freedom of Expression (1984).
Shiffrin, The First Amendment, Democracy, and Romance (1990).

Chapter 2

Freedom of the Press: Basic Operational Terms and Conditions

[L]iberty of the press...has meant, principally although not exclusively, immunity from previous restraints or censorship.

Near v. Minnesota, 283 U.S. 697, 716 (1931)

I. DEFINING THE PRESS

Freedom of the press is an elusive concept that has not proved amenable to objectification. Charting the contours of press liberty is further complicated by the difficulty of establishing a satisfactory definition of the institution itself. Efforts to define the press have traveled three basic avenues. The press has been described respectively in institutional, functional, and registry terms. None of these approaches, however, is without significant problems.

An institutional definition advanced by Justice Stewart essentially would regard the press as the industry whose business it is to publish. Stewart suggested that

the Free Press guarantee is, in essence, a *structural* provision of the Constitution. Most of the other provisions in the Bill of Rights protect specific liberties or specific rights of individuals: freedom of speech, freedom of worship, the right to counsel, the privilege against compulsory self-incrimination, to name a few. In contrast, the Free Press Clause extends protection to an institution. The publishing business is, in short, the only organized private business that is given explicit constitutional protection.

Stewart's depiction of the press in a structural sense avoids, at least in part, conceptualization of freedom of the press synonymously with freedom of expression. Although publishers, like all other persons, are guaranteed the latter pursuant to the free speech clause, Stewart maintained that interpretation of freedom of speech and of the press as coextensive would be a constitutional redundancy. The institutional definition of the press clearly identifies speech and media as distinct notions and predicates constitutional protection of the media upon a discrete footing. However, the focus upon structure has been criticized as dangerously narrow. Excluded from the purview of an institutional press may be the artist, the scientist, and the novelist. Even the individual pamphleteer whose partisan works may have fit squarely within the ambit of the press at the time the Constitution was framed might not qualify for institutional standing. Especially insofar as classification of the press may determine special rights of access or privilege, the constitutional status of an individual or entity is of considerable threshold significance. Distinguishing speech and press thus may have more than merely semantic import.

An alternative view of the press regards it as any methodology for communicating information or opinion to the public. Largely in response to the institutional definition's potential for "conferring special [constitutional] status on a limited group," former Chief Justice Burger found

no difference between the right of those who seek to disseminate ideas by way of a newspaper and those who give lectures or speeches and seek to enlarge the audience by publication and wide dissemination. . . . [T]he First Amendment does not "belong" to any definable category of persons or entities: It belongs to all who exercise its freedoms.

Not surprisingly, given Burger's adoption of a functional definition of the press, he was hostile toward recognition of any special freedom or rights of the institutional media. Oddly, however, it was Justice Stewart who supported an opinion denying the press a right of access to prisons and Chief Justice Burger who afforded the press access rights that were special in effect if not in letter. Unlike the institutional definition, which is criticized for its narrowness, the focus upon function is objected to for its expansiveness. Because of its breadth, the functional definition of the press may be indistinguishable from speech. By thus making the freedom of speech and press clauses redundant, it tends to effectuate what the institutional concept endeavors to avoid.

The difficulty, if not the impossibility, of satisfactorily identifying the common character and associative traits of the press may enhance the appeal of merely itemizing the media that constitute the press. In discussing liberty of the press some years ago, the Supreme Court described the press itself in terms of newspapers, periodicals, pamphlets, and leaflets. Although the characterization was presented in a sweeping rather than a restrictive tone, the rendition demonstrated the significant dangers inherent in what amounts to a registry definition. Conspicuously missing from the Court's list were motion pictures, which effectively had been denied press status at the time, and radio and television, whose status for constitutional purposes was then largely uncertain. The problem with composing a definition akin to a laundry list, therefore, is the absence of any standard for determining qualification and the consequent risk of subjectivity.

Justice Brennan, in an extrajudicial commentary, has suggested that both structural and functional conceptualizations are relevant but that the utility of either depends upon circumstances. Insofar as the press operates in a "public spokes[person]" role, Brennan would find that it "readily lends itself to the rhetoric of absolutism." He cautioned against exclusive reliance upon a spokesperson model, however, because it creates the mistaken impression that the First Amendment is merely concerned with speech and protects only self-expression. Brennan suggested that the Constitution "also protects the structure of communications necessary for the existence of our democracy." As a consequence, it is necessary to protect the press not only when it speaks out but when it performs associated tasks of collecting and disseminating news. Unlike a focus upon the public spokesperson function, analysis of the structural role would require balancing of informational capability against competing societal interests. Whether the press can be regulated because of what it says or with respect to its news-gathering role requires two distinct forms of review, Brennan counseled, with the former tending toward absolutism and the latter always requiring balancing.

No matter how the press is defined, exclusion from any official denomination of it has profound consequences. The original depiction of motion pictures as "a business pure and simple, ... not to be regarded ... as part of the press," effectively left the medium without any First Amendment protection. The further failure of the Court to recognize a constitutional interest in film as a medium is a forceful example of the free press clause's independent significance, as well as an illustration of the importance of definition. Government, as a consequence, was free to regulate the medium in ways that would be intolerable if the same expression were communicated by print. Censorship boards in the South, for instance, capitalized upon the constitutional void and banned films at odds with laws and customs that did not countenance scenes of racial mixing or suggesting equality.

More recently, the question of what the press comprises arose in the context of whether an investment newsletter constituted a bona fide publication that would be immune from regulation by the federal securities laws. Such a publication conceivably fits within the bounds of the institutional, functional, and registry models. If an investment news-letter is the output of a publishing business, it falls within the institutional definition. Its role in informing the public also satisfies the criteria of the functional definition. Determination of bona fide status, however, represents a subjectivity problem akin to that associated with whether any medium falls within a registry definition of the press. Uncertainty of standards and unpredictability of results suggest that the analytical process remains capable of treacherous consequences.

II. ORIGINS AND NATURE OF REGULATORY CONCERN

The transformation of the press from an essentially print medium run by individual entrepreneurs to a concentrated and diversified in-formation industry has profoundly affected public perceptions of the press and consequent policy toward it. Early concern with the role and influence of mass media was articulated in the late nineteenth century by Louis Brandeis. If the print media's technological capabilities had been more developed at the time of the Constitution's drafting, they too conceivably might have been subject to official attitudes now reserved for newer media. The advent of photojournalism drastically altered the performance and perceptions of the media by the beginning of the twentieth century, as newspapers and magazines increasingly became regarded as instrumentalities of intrusion, impropriety, and indecency. For Brandeis, the media that in 1789 were primarily vehicles for partisan debate had become purveyors of idle gossip catering to prurient tastes. He thus expressed revulsion over increasing journalistic commitment to sensationalism and entertainment. Such emphasis troubled Brandeis who considered the dedication of space that otherwise might be afforded to "matters of genuine community concerns" an inversion of public priorities. His advancement of a right of privacy in significant part con-stituted a proposed regulatory solution for controlling perceived media excesses.

Brandeis's concern over the functioning of the press has proved to be anything but unique and seems reducible in large part to a matter of taste. To enforce preferences and protect sensibilities with which he identified, Brandeis's right of privacy would have operated to place cer-tain subject matter off limits. Although he declared gossip to be the primary target of his enmity, the constitutional problems in effectuating official control of it are manifest. Gossip as a category of expression probably is impossible to define without encountering problems of vagueness and overbreadth. Reports of a married politician's extramar-ital liaisons, for instance, might qualify both as intrusive gossip that titillates and political speech that facilitates informed voting. Still, the type of qualitative concerns expressed by Brandeis has been a consistent source of regulatory rationales and even jurisprudence supporting official control calculated to civilize the level of public discourse. The proposal of a right of privacy thus may be regarded as one of the first important responses to changes in the nature, focus, and influence of the mass media.

Less than half a century after Brandeis articulated his distress over the modern media's direction, Congress enacted a broad regulatory scheme for radio and television that required broadcasters to operate in the public interest. The concept of broadcasters as public trustees might be viewed in part as an extension and formalization of Brandeis's notion that the media should focus upon matters of "genuine community concern." In a speech to the National Association of Broadcasters in the early 1960s, Federal Communications Commission Chairman Newton Minow characterized television as "a vast wasteland" and defined the public interest in terms of promoting the "character, citizenship and intellectual capacity of the people." More recently, the broadcast of indecent and offensive language has been subject to less charitable constitutional review than would be the norm for other media or speech. Contemporary depictions of programming as being akin to allowing "a pig [in] the parlor" and characterizations to the effect that it is "disgusting" or "garbage" suggest too an effort to elevate the quality of or sanitize public discourse. Such an objective, no matter how well intentioned, invites criticism that it is elitist and insensitive to the realities and imperatives of cultural pluralism. Public interest can be defined synonymously with popularity or tolerance as easily as it can be tied to notions of what is healthy or educational. It is the subjective spin of Brandeis and his philosophical progeny that enables a concept such as the public interest to operate as an intrusive regulatory predicate. For critics, a gloss of that nature may call to mind Alexis de Tocqueville's warning that the greatest threat to democratic institutions is well-intentioned policies with poorly foreseeable consequences.

Even before the emergence of broadcasting as a dominant mass medium, the sentiments expressed by Brandeis had seeped into communications jurisprudence. In *Mutual Film Corp. v. Industrial Commission of Ohio*, the Supreme Court considered a challenge to a state law providing for censorship of motion pictures. Although the motion picture company alleged only violations of state speech and publication guarantees, the Court's observations and opinion applied logically to First Amendment interests as well. Although the Court acknowledged the role of film as a means for expressing opinion, disseminating information, and educating, it focused upon what it perceived as the medium's potential for being a dangerous influence. The resultant opinion accordingly is suffused with references reflecting anxiety with, rather than constitutional attentiveness to, the new medium.

[C]ounsel have gone into a very elaborate description of moving picture exhibitions and their many useful purposes as graphic expressions of opinion and sentiments, as exponents of policies, as teachers of science and history, as useful, interesting, amusing, educational and moral. And a list of the "campaigns," as counsel call them, which may be carried on is given. We may concede the praise. ... But they may be used for evil, and against that possibility the statute was enacted. Their power of amusement and, it may be, education, the audiences they assemble, not of women alone nor of men alone, but together, not of adults only, but of children, make them the more insidious in corruption by a pretense of worthy purpose. Indeed, we may go beyond that possibility. They take their attraction from the general interest, eager and wholesome it may be, in their subjects, but a prurient interest may be excited and appealed to. Besides, there are some things which should not have pictorial representation in public places and to all audiences. And not only the State of Ohio but other States have considered it to be in the interest of the public morals and welfare to supervise moving picture exhibitions. We would have to shut our eyes to the facts of the world to regard the precaution unreasonable or the legislation to effect it a mere wanton interference with personal liberty....

It cannot be put out of view that the exhibition of moving pictures is a business pure and simple, originated and conducted for profit, like other spectacles, not to be regarded, nor intended to be regarded by the Ohio constitution, we think, as part of the press of the country or as organs of public opinion. They are mere representations of events, of ideas and sentiments published and known, vivid, useful and entertaining no doubt, but, as we have said, capable of evil, having power for it, the greater because of their attractiveness and manner of exhibition. It was this capability and power, and it may be in experience of them, that induced the State of Ohio, in addition to prescribing penalties for immoral exhibitions as it does in its Criminal Code, to require censorship before exhibition, as it does by the act under review. We cannot regard this as beyond the power of government.

Like many well-intentioned ideas, notions that the media should address matters of genuine community concern or otherwise function in the public interest have a dangerous potential. What may be advanced as culturally uplifting by Brandeis may, from a competing perspective, rate as culturally imperialistic. Brandeis's displeasure with and expectations of the media in large part translate into an expression of subjective preference. Such claims to the public interest, however, are no more or less legitimate than a definition attuned to competing cultural values or synonymous with raw popularity. Pursuant to any such standard of subjectivity, interests of diversity and pluralism may be endangered. Whether expression is denominated as gossip, sensationalism, or indecency, its classification as a prelude to regulation involves vagueness and overbreadth problems. Standards for elevating or purifying public discourse necessitate an enforcement mechanism. To the extent that perimeters of acceptability are officially set, and regardless of regulatory motive, editorial autonomy is put at risk.

III. STATE ACTION

All media are governed by one of three distinct regulatory models. The press that existed at the time the First Amendment was drafted receives the fullest measure of constitutional protection. Freedom of the press is closest to absolute, therefore, for the print media. At the opposite pole, common carriage is subject to policies that facilitate universal service on equal terms. Nondiscriminatory access, rather than editorial autonomy, is the focus of common-carrier regulation. Between the extremes of maximum and nonexistent editorial autonomy exists the regulatory structure for what is now the dominant medium. Governance of broadcasting, as well as cablecasting, borrows from both the print and common-carrier models. Although broadcasters may be obligated to serve the public interest and thus satisfy an array of subsidiary requirements as a condition for licensing, they also maintain a measure of editorial freedom. Cablecasters too may be required, as part of their franchising agreement, to fulfill obligations that legally could not be imposed upon the print media.

All newer media are subject to regulatory schemes that insinuate the government into the editorial function. Some also are subject to official charting of technical, financial, character, and other structural standards. The pervasive nature of such regulation in broadcasting has prompted arguments that radio and television are essentially governmental instrumentalities. Acceptance of the notion that broadcasting or perhaps cablecasting represents state action would have significant consequences for even the qualified editorial freedom that presently exists for these media. The First Amendment is a restraint not on private persons but on government. As the Court has observed, were it to find government action, "few licensee decisions on the content of broadcasts or the process of editorial evaluation would escape constitutional scrutiny." Because government is prohibited from discriminating on the basis of content, a finding of state action might require media operators to afford the public access to facilities and transmission. Since equal access is a hallmark of common carriage, state action is a less significant issue with respect to telephone or telegraph service. Precisely because such a requirement would reduce cable to the status of a common carrier, the Court invalidated regulations that would have effectuated access terms.

A general finding of state action nonetheless might set as a constitutional requirement what is mostly impermissible now as a regulatory objective.

In *Columbia Broadcasting System, Inc. v. Democratic National Committee,* the Court considered the notion that editorial decisions of broadcasters constitute state action. The court of appeals had determined that broadcasters were instrumentalities of the government because they were awarded use of the public domain and regulated as "proxies" or "fiduciaries of the people." Although it recognized the significant government controls upon broadcasting, a plurality opinion authored by Chief Justice Burger rejected the state action argument and expressed serious concern with the implications of a contrary finding. The Burger plurality noted broadcasting's emergence as "a vital [and dominant] part of our system of communications." It also intimated reluctance to undermine further the qualified First Amendment freedom of broadcasters, given Congress's adoption of a regulatory scheme reflecting "a desire to maintain for licensees, so far as consistent with necessary regulation, a traditional journalistic role." The opinion identified mixed responsibilities that officially charged broadcasters with public trustee obligations for fairly and objectively informing the public and delegated to government the function of " 'overseer' and ultimate arbiter and guardian of the public interest." It nonetheless refused to equate the association with a partnership, symbiotic relationship, or any other tie that would rise to the level of state action.

Justice Brennan, in contrast, adverted to prior determinations that "[c]onduct that is formally 'private' may become so entwined with government policies or so impregnated with a government character as to become subject to the constitutional limitations placed upon [government] actions." In pressing the case for state action, Brennan emphasized "the public nature of the airwaves, the governmentally created preferred status of broadcast licensees, the pervasive federal regulation of broadcast programming, and the [Federal Communications] Commission's specific approval of the challenged broadcaster policy." More particularly, he noted that ownership and ultimate control of the electromagnetic spectrum is vested in the public, and that consequent regulatory power is an established denotation of governmental involvement. The centrality of the government's role was further evinced, from Brennan's perspective, by the dependence of licensees upon an official grant of broadcasting rights and privileges. Although he recognized that regulation of an industry by itself is not sufficient to establish state action, he noted the "elaborate," "automatic," "continuing," and "pervasive" nature of broadcast controls and reiterated the court of appeals' observation that "[a]lmost no other regulated private business—is so intimately bound by government."

Although a majority was not formed in support of or in opposition to the principle that broadcasting constituted state action, Justice Douglas identified the consequences that would follow if it were found to exist. Douglas noted that public broadcasting in particular is a creature of Congress, managed by a directorate chosen by the president and the Senate and thus comparable to having "the United States own[ing] and manag[ing] a prestigious newspaper like the New York Times, Washington Post, or Sacramento Bee." Acknowledging prior jurisprudential rejection of his position that licensing was a premise for state action, he maintained that public broadcasters at least had no "free[dom] to pick and choose news items as [they] desired," were obligated to provide access to the public, and could let "[p]olitics, ideolog[y]..., [and] rightist or leftist tendencies... play no part in [their] design of programs."

Douglas's position even with respect to public broadcasting never has been embraced by a majority. The trend in constitutional law in recent years appears to be against finding state action. The concept in fact is malleable and manipulable insofar as its discernment depends upon "sifting the facts and weighing the circumstances." Given the opportunity to analyze the issue on a case-by-case basis and the draconian consequences if state action actually were discerned, the likelihood seems slim that broadcasting will be designated the functional equivalent of official action.

Even more improbable is the possibility that cablecasting would be denominated as state action. Cable operators are subject to a bifurcated system of regulation. Under the Cable Communications Policy Act of 1984, local government may award cable franchises, while various functions are subject to federal control. A cable system thus seems analogous, for state action purposes, to a public utility providing gas or electricity. In *Jackson v. Metropolitan Edison Co.*, the Court determined that a utility's termination of customer service did not constitute state action. Although licensing and regulation evinced a relationship between the utility and government, the connection was not considered significant enough to establish a symbiotic relationship or joint venture. The Court also rejected the notion that the utility's services themselves constituted a public function. It left open the possibility, however, that a practice commanded, encouraged, or sanctioned by government might amount to state action. Although the Court specifically found that discontinuance of electric service was not so ordained, the language of *Jackson* suggests that a specific practice dictated by government could have constitutional implications. It is difficult to conclude with certainty what activity might qualify on such grounds. Presumably, given the recent disinclination to find state action, a claim would have to make a strong showing that the action in question was a function of official prescription and not private discretion. It seems unlikely that compliance with general regulatory policy or provisions alone would qualify as state action.

Extensive regulation of an industry does not appear to translate into state action. A state action theory must be tied to the contention that government uniquely commands or encourages a broadcaster's action. It then might be argued that a broadcaster's decision not to allow the public to speak for itself on radio or television is the result of a specific federally prescribed fiduciary function for licensees. When such a claim is measured against the Court's recent trends in the area of state action, it would seem necessary to establish (1) the deprivation of a constitutional right by a state-created rule of conduct or by a person for whom the state is responsible, and (2) a function that fairly may be denominated a state action because the otherwise private party has acted together with or been significantly aided by state officials or conduct otherwise attributable to the state. Satisfying the first prong of the test would appear to be easier than fulfilling the second. Because the Court has established in broadcasting a First Amendment right of the public to receive access to diverse views and voices, it is arguable that an official charge that disserves diversity interests constitutes a deprivation chargeable to the state. Ample evidence in fact exists that fairness regulation has undercut the diversity aims underlying the public's First Amendment rights. Still, the second prong appears to require a showing of a partnership, symbiotic relationship, or other entwining of function and roles that the modern Court seems less inclined to recognize. Finally, it is questionable as a matter of sheer policy and practical consequence, given the role of broadcasting in modern society, whether the Court would craft a decision that might entirely remove the most dominant contemporary medium from the First Amendment's protective ambit.

IV. MEDIA-SPECIFIC FIRST AMENDMENT STANDARDS

For constitutional purposes, not all media are the same. It may be argued that all elements of the press, regardless of how they are individually labeled, have the overarching purpose of disseminating information and thus should be treated the same under the First Amendment. The Court has focused upon structural differences among media, however, and thereby created varying degrees of constitutional protection for media that did not exist when the First Amendment was drafted.

Media-specific analysis for newer forms of communication became entrenched at the same time the Court determined that motion pictures had First Amendment status. In *Joseph Burstyn, Inc. v. Wilson*, the Court rejected its earlier determination to the contrary and concluded that "expression by means of motion pictures is included within the . . . guaranty of the First and Fourteenth Amendments." Although the *Wilson* case generally was hailed as a major First Amendment victory for new media, it actually constitutionalized their qualified standing within a press hierarchy. While the Court expanded the reach of the First Amendment, it also affirmed a scheme of constitutional relativity.

An accommodation that afforded First Amendment status at the price of regulation has proved to be the model for defining the constitutional protection for all new media. As the Court observed in *Wilson*, First Amendment recognition "is not the end of [the] problem" but the beginning. No uniform criteria determine the scope and contours of a medium's freedom. Rather, the Court favors individualized evaluation and standards pursuant to the premise that "each tends to present its own peculiar problems." Such analysis borrows substantially and substantively from Justice Jackson's concurring opinion in *Kovacs v. Cooper* supporting an ordinance banning loud and raucous sound trucks from public streets. Jackson observed that approval of the regulation did not necessarily obligate the Court to allow like controls of other communications methodologies. Rather, he concluded, "[t]he moving picture screen, the radio, the newspaper, the handbill, the sound truck and the street orator have differing natures, values, abuses, and dangers. Each, in my view, is a law unto itself."

Applying Jackson's media-specific formula to motion pictures, in *Wilson*, the Court initially rejected rationales upon which it earlier had relied to deny film First Amendment status. It thus acknowledged that motion pictures were "a significant medium for the communication of ideas... [that] may affect public attitudes and behavior in a variety of ways, ranging from direct espousal of a political or social doctrine to the subtle shaping of thought which characterizes all artistic expression." The Court abandoned any distinction upon grounds that film may entertain more than inform, noting that the line between information and entertainment is too elusive. An earlier determination that motion pictures represented a mere business product also was dropped because that reality did not truly set them apart from the print media that likewise produce and sell their output for profit. The medium's potential for evil, especially in connection with children, was not recognized in *Wilson* as a basis for denying First Amendment protection altogether, as previously had been the case. The Court nonetheless found that "capacity for evil... may be relevant in determining the permissible scope of community control." Consistent with the concerns recognized in the *Wilson* decision, censorship boards could continue to function provided their focus was calibrated to considerations acknowledged by the Court and valid and proper administrative procedures were followed.

Rationales for content regulation of radio and television have been diverse and problematic. Some measure of government control generally has been conceded as necessary because technical factors require administration to prevent interference between or among signals. Arguments that electronic media should be regulated more tightly than the print media surfaced in *Banzhaf v. Federal Communications Commission*. The court of appeals in that case suggested that broadcasting is distinguishable from a written press characterized by "a rich variety of outlets for expression and persuasion, . . . which are available to those without technical skills or deep pockets." It also found a difference on grounds that "[w]ritten messages are not communicated unless . . . read, and reading requires an affirmative act. Broadcast messages, in contrast, are 'in the air.'" Because the electronic media were pervasive and their effect difficult to calculate, the court found it reasonable to conclude that their impact was greater.

Both the scarcity and magnitude of effect rationales, however, are problematic. In reality, dissemination of information to a mass audience may be prohibitively costly regardless of the medium chosen. For practical purposes, the opportunity to own or operate any mass medium is primarily a function of capital. Most persons would be denied an opportunity to become a broadcaster primarily because of inadequate resources and thus would never even reach the point of being considered for a license. Nor is a medium's relative impact a persuasive basis for differentiating its First Amendment status. As recognized in freedom of speech cases, relative influence is an impermissible basis for regulation. If it were a permissible reference point, the First Amendment would protect only ineffective or inconsequential expression.

The Supreme Court subsequently advanced the concept of spectrum scarcity as a basis for requiring broadcasters to comply with special content controls upon their programming. In *Red Lion Broadcasting Co. v. Federal Communications Commission*, the Court observed that "only a tiny fraction of [the public] can hope to communicate if intelligible communication is to be had, even if the entire radio spectrum is utilized in the present state of commercially acceptable technology." The scarcity premise, as will be discussed in Chapter 10, has been widely criticized, has been abandoned by broadcasting's primary regulator, and has been subjected to increasing judicial criticism. Among other things, it does not account for competition among media, as opposed to within a medium itself, and ignores the reality that the primary barrier to broadcasting, as to any other mass medium, is financial. It also fails to distinguish broadcasting meaningfully from a newspaper industry that suffers from an even more obvious scarcity problem in terms of raw numbers.

Shortly after the *Red Lion* decision, Chief Justice Burger suggested that it was proper "to take into account the reality that in a very real sense listeners and viewers constitute a 'captive audience.'" Burger's opinion, in *Columbia Broadcasting System, Inc. v. Democratic National Committee*, further developed the pervasiveness theory advanced in the *Banzhaf* decision and tied it to early regulatory concerns with the advent of radio. Thereafter, in *Federal Communications Commission v. Pacifica Foundation*, the pervasiveness concern was combined with privacy interests and worries about the presence of children in the audience to justify particularized controls upon indecent and offensive programming. In addition to the scarcity rationale, media-specific regulation of broadcasting was grounded upon (1) broadcasting's "uniquely pervasive presence in the lives of all Americans," (2) "the privacy of the home, where the individual's right to be left alone plainly outweighs the First Amendment rights of an intruder," and (3) "the ease with which children may obtain access to broadcast material."

Pursuant to these concerns, broadcasting has been afforded the most limited First Amendment protection of any medium. The rationales for diminished constitutional status are not unassailable. It is not clear, for instance, why children must be protected from broadcasting but not from the same content in other media or other surroundings. Although broadcast transmission to the home is subject to official control to weed out indecent expression, common carriage, cable transmission, and the electronic playback of recordings on the same audio or video system are not. Equally problematic is why an expletive is any less objectionable when it is printed and publicly displayed than when it is communicated electronically. The same vulgarity, constitutionally protected when it is expressed publicly, is regulable when it is broadcast.

Another troubling point is why the special privacy interest of the home cuts in favor of instead of against regulation. Just as an indecent or offensive guest can be ordered to leave the home, so too can a radio or television be switched to a different channel or turned off. Traditional concepts of privacy, and particularly privacy that translates into personal autonomy, arguably are more affronted by governance that determines what individuals can see and hear in their home. It also remains to be explained why the interests of offended persons require depriving the rest of the public of what it might choose if it were free to make autonomous selections. Consent to the risk of being offended might be presumed from the decision to place a radio or television in the home. The option also exists for viewers and listeners to obtain knowledge of available programming and avoid it. Problems of exposure are not unique to a given medium. Each has the potential for presenting material to which the reader, viewer, or listener objects. None is so powerful or pervasive, however, as to operate beyond the ultimate control of the individual.

From a viewer's perspective, it is unlikely that cable and broadcasting are significantly distinguishable. Because the obligation exists to identify differences in the characteristics of new media, courts nonetheless have endeavored to identify differentiating traits. In so doing, they have divided over whether cable is more akin to the print or the broadcast media. Some courts have focused upon cable's capacity to carry a multitude of channels and have consequently distinguished it from broadcasting's ability to transmit only a limited number of signals. They also have noted that cable, unlike broadcasting, is not saddled with the problem of "physical interference and scarcity requiring an umpiring role for government." A competing determination holds that constraints upon competition in the cable industry create scarcity analogous to what has been identified in broadcasting. Monopoly status for many cable operators exists as a consequence of franchising and capital costs. Yet the scarcity theory also has been discounted by reference to the Supreme Court's observation that economic scarcity does not justify "intrusions into First Amendment rights."

It may be that the problems of equating cable satisfactorily with newspapers or radio and television emphasize the deficiencies of media-specific analysis. If so, casual public perceptions that would fit more neatly with media-comprehensive than media-specific assessments may prove more sensible than distinctions that may be technical or legalistic. Cable, like broadcasting and the print media, provides information, disseminates original or retransmitted data, and has an interest in editorial discretion. If cable were afforded freedom comparable to that of the print media, denying such liberty to broadcasters would seem even more difficult to justify. At least with respect to the portion of a broadcaster's programming that is identical to a cablecaster's, imposition of content restrictions on one but not the other would seem anomalous. Alternatively, regulation of cable by a scheme akin to what governs broadcasting actually might endanger broader freedoms of the print media. Subjecting the electronic but not the printed edition of a newspaper to content regulation might engender more than a problem of inconsistency. Insofar as cable was equated with broadcasting for purposes of control, but the analogy between cable and print was apt, a predicate would exist for conditioning the liberty of all media. A focus on functional similarity rather than structural difference would favor uniformity rather than disparity of standards. Even then, it would be necessary to decide whether media should be subject to constitutional standards governing old or new media. Especially as the capabilities of traditional and evolving media merge and because qualified constitutional protection for media is well established, any such choice between regulatory models seems destined to be the function of a highly competitive process.

V. PRIOR RESTRAINT

A. Direct Restraint

Restraint of expression prior to its articulation or publication generally is considered to be at serious odds with the First Amendment. Until

1694, publishing in England was subject to the approval of the church and the state. Following the demise of the licensing system, impermissibility of prior restraint was advanced as a central meaning of press freedom. William Blackstone, the prominent English jurist, thus observed that

[t]he liberty of the press...consists in laying no previous restraints upon publication....To subject the press to the restrictive power of a licenser...is to subject all freedom of sentiment to the prejudices of one man, and to make him the arbitrary and infallible judge of all controverted points in learning, religion and government.

A prior restraint in simplest terms is an official restraint upon expression prior to its dissemination. It is possible to identify several variants of such a restriction. A prior restraint exists, for instance, when government forbids expression without approval or a permit. Censorship boards, park and street permits, and even a radio or television license, which precludes broadcasting by an unsuccessful applicant, exemplify such official prohibition. Prior restraint also may be effectuated by the judiciary if it prohibits publication by means of an injunction. Media subject to official action, calculated to silence criticism or block the release of government information have relied upon the First Amendment for relief. Statutes or regulations requiring compliance with specific legal standards or demands also constitute a variant of prior restraint.

Prior restraints, regardless of the form they take, traditionally have been regarded with special concern and as a particularly grave threat to First Amendment interests. Professor Emerson has observed that "the most significant feature of systems of prior restraint is that they contain within themselves forces which drive irresistibly toward unintelligent, overzealous, and usually absurd administration." Because the function of any censor is to censor, the perceived problem is that institutional impulses and First Amendment interests cannot harmoniously coexist. It is the fundamental mission of the Securities and Exchange Commission, for instance, to protect investors and the integrity of the investment marketplace. Registration materials, including promotional information for dissemination to the public, are edited by attorneys who function as official censors. If it is assumed that they identify with agency goals and have normal interests in career advancement, they are more likely than not to perform their tasks energetically. It is improbable that a staff attorney who edited sparsely out of concern for freedom of expression, rather than full disclosure, would be rewarded for having effectively served agency goals. Pursuant to career and institutional objectives, the common tendency would be to maximize challenges and revisions. Under such circumstances, it would seem that the incentive exists to censor more rather than less.

Prior restraint also tends to be considered especially worrisome because, unlike a system of subsequent punishment, suppression is thought to be more effective. Even if harsh criminal sanctions seemingly could operate as forcefully and effectively as prior restraint, postpublication punishment is not a certainty. Although the government sought to restrain publication of the *Pentagon Papers* and an article on how to make a hydrogen bomb, subsequent punishment did not follow despite arguments that pertinent laws had been violated. At least in theory, prior restraint is considered categorically more serious because it operates as a more significant deterrent than subsequent punishment.

Near v. Minnesota represents the seminal case on prior restraint. In *Near*, the Court examined a public nuisance statute that enabled the state to secure an injunction barring publication of any "malicious, scandalous and defamatory newspaper, magazine or other periodical." The statute was directed toward a weekly newspaper, the *Saturday Press*, that had a forthright anti-Semitic bias. Specifically targeted as a basis for prosecution were the following articles.

"Facts Not Theories"

" 'I am a bosom friend of Mr. Olson,' snorted a gentleman of Yiddish blood, 'and I want to protest against your article,' and blah, blah, blah, ad infinitum, ad nauseam.

"I am not taking orders from men of Barnett faith, at least right now. There have been too many men in this city and especially those in official life, who HAVE been taking orders and suggestions from JEW GANGSTERS, therefore we HAVE Jew Gangsters, practically ruling Minneapolis.

"It was buzzards of the Barnett stripe who shot down my buddy. It was Barnett gunmen who staged the assault of Samuel Shapiro. It is Jew thugs who have pulled practically every robbery in this city. It was a member of the Barnett gang who shot down George Rubenstein (Ruby) while he stood in the shelter of Mose Barnett's ham-cavern on Hennepin Avenue. It was Mose Barnett, himself who shot down Roy Rogers on Hennepin Avenue. It was at Mose Barnett's place of business that the '13 dollar Jew' found a refuge while the police of New York were combing the country for him. It was a gang of Jew gunmen who boasted that for five hundred dollars they would kill any man in the city. It was Mose Barnett, a Jew, who boasted that he held the chief of police of Minneapolis in his hand—had bought and paid for him.

"It is Jewish men and women—pliant tools of the Jew gangster, Mose Barnett, who stand charged with having falsified the election records and returns in the Third ward. And it is Mose Barnett himself, who, indicted for his part in the Shapiro assault, is a fugitive from justice today.

"Practically every vendor of vile hooch, every owner of a moonshine still, every snake-faced gangster and embryonic yegg in the Twin Cities is a JEW.

"Having these examples before me, I feel that I am justified in my refusal to take orders from a Jew who boasts that he is a 'bosom friend' of Mr. Olson.

"I find in the mail at least twice per week, letters from gentlemen of Jewish faith who advise me against launching an attack on the Jewish people. These gentlemen have the cart before the horse. I am launching, nor is Mr. Guilford, no attack against any race, BUT:

"When I find men of a certain race banding themselves together for the purpose of preying upon Gentile or Jew; gunmen, KILLERS, roaming our streets shooting down men against whom they have no personal grudge (or happen to have); defying OUR law; corrupting OUR officials; assaulting business men; beating up unarmed citizens; spreading a reign of terror through every walk of life, then I say to you in all sincerity, that I refuse to back up a single step from that 'issue'—if they choose to make it so.

"If the people of Jewish faith in Minneapolis wish to avoid criticism of these vermin whom I rightfully call 'Jews' they can easily do so BY THEMSELVES CLEANING HOUSE.

"I'm not out to cleanse Israel of the filth that clings to Israel's skirts. I'm out to 'hew to the line, let the chips fly where they may.'

"I simply state a fact when I say that ninety percent of the crimes committed against society in this city are committed by Jew gangsters.

"It was a Jew who employed JEWS to shoot down Mr. Guilford. It was a Jew who employed a Jew to intimidate Mr. Shapiro and a Jew who employed JEWS to assault that gentleman when he refused to yield to their threats. It was a JEW who wheedled or employed Jews to manipulate the election records and returns in the Third ward in flagrant violation of law. It was a Jew who left two hundred dollars with another Jew to pay to our chief of police just before the last municipal election, and:

"It is Jew, Jew, Jew, as long as one cares to comb over the records.

"I am launching no attack against the Jewish people AS A RACE. I am merely calling attention to a FACT. And if the people of that race and faith wish to rid themselves of the odium and stigma THE RODENTS OF THEIR OWN RACE HAVE BROUGHT UPON THEM, they need only to step to the front and help the decent citizens of Minneapolis rid the city of these criminal Jews.

"Either Mr. Guilford or myself stand ready to do battle for a MAN, regardless of his race, color or creed, but neither of us will step one inch out of our chosen path to avoid a fight IF the Jews want to battle.

"Both of us have some mighty loyal friends among the Jewish people but not one of them comes whining to ask that we 'lay off' criticism of Jewish gangsters and none of them who comes carping to us of their 'bosom friendship' for any public official now under our journalistic guns."

"Gil's [Guilford's] Chatterbox"

"I headed into the city on September 26th, ran across three Jews in a Chevrolet; stopped a lot of lead and won a bed for myself in St. Barnabas Hospital for six weeks. . . .

"Whereupon I have withdrawn all allegiance to anything with a hook nose that eats herring. I have adopted the sparrow as my national bird until Davis' law enforcement league or the K.K.K. hammers the eagle's beak out straight. So if I seem to set crazy as I ankle down the street, bear in mind that I am merely saluting MY national emblem.

"All of which has nothing to do with the present whereabouts of Big Mose Barnett. Methinks he headed the local delegation to the new Palestine-for-Jews-only. He went ahead of the boys so he could do a little fixing with the Yiddish chief of police and get his twenty-five percent of the gambling rake-off. Boys will be boys and 'ganefs' will be ganefs."

"Grand Juries and Ditto"

"There are grand juries, and there are grand juries. The last one was a real grand jury. It acted. The present one is like the scion who is labelled 'Junior.' That means not so good. There are a few mighty good folks on it—there are some who smell bad. One petty peanut politician whose graft was almost pitiful in its size when he was a public official, has already shot his mouth off in several places. He is establishing his alibi in advance for what he intends to keep from taking place.

"But George [a grand juror], we won't bother you. We are aware that the gambling syndicate was waiting for your body to convene before the big crap game opened again. The Yips had your dimensions, apparently, and we always go by the judgment of a dog in appraising people.

"We will call for a special grand jury and a special prosecutor within a short time, as soon as half of the staff can navigate to advantage, and then we'll show you what a real grand jury can do. Up to the present we have been merely tapping on the window. Very soon we shall start smashing glass."

Despite the anti-Semitic nature of the articles, they identified persons who controlled local organized crime and tied the police chief and other city officials to corruption. Even if the *Saturday Press* was identifiable as malicious, scandalous, and defamatory, therefore, it performed an important role in exposing serious corruption in local government. Suppression thus was the consequence of published allegations of official misconduct. If such reporting was declared a nuisance, and future publication was enjoined, the publisher would have been vulnerable to contempt for any subsequent allegation of public corruption or misdeed. Such a result would have been unfortunate, the Court observed, because the increasing complexity of government and multiplying opportunities for corruption and malfeasance necessitate "a vigilant and courageous press." From the Court's perspective, that imperative was not diminished by the possibility or even reality that liberty of the press might be abused. Because the statute afforded excessive protection to officials who otherwise could sue for defamation, and suppression would ensue unless the publisher proved truth, good motive, and justifiable ends, the Court found that the law facilitated an intolerable system of censorship.

In declaring the nuisance statute unconstitutional, the Court concluded that "it has been generally, if not universally, considered that it is the chief purpose of [freedom of the press] to prevent previous restraints upon publication." Adverting to Blackstone's commentary upon liberty of the press, the Court further observed that "[e]very freeman has an undoubted right to lay what sentiments he pleases before the public; to forbid this, is to destroy the freedom of the press; but if he publishes what is improper, mischievous or illegal, he must take the consequence of his own temerity." Even if the First Amendment did not countenance prior restraint, at least under the circumstances, the possibility of subsequent punishment was not foreclosed. A libel action might be available, for instance, to those who claimed that they had been defamed by the newspaper.

Although the Court refused to restrain publication of the *Saturday Press,* it observed that the guarantee against censorship is not absolute. It further noted that any exception to the rule must be justified by extraordinary interests. The Court mentioned several exceptional cases that would justify prior restraint. Thus

government [during wartime] might prevent actual obstruction to its recruiting service or the publication of the sailing dates of transports or the number and location of troops. On similar grounds, the primary requirements of decency may be enforced against obscene publications. The security of the community life may be protected against incitements to acts of violence and the overthrow by force of orderly government. The constitution [citation omitted] does not "protect a man from an injunction against uttering words that may have all the effect of force"

From the Court's qualification of the general rule against prior restraint in *Near,* an exception based upon national security could be logically inferred. Four decades later such a reservation was further developed. In *New York Times Co. v. United States,* the Court determined that the *Washington Post* and the *New York Times* should not be restrained from publishing a classified report on American policy-making in Vietnam eventually known as the *Pentagon Papers.* In a per curiam opinion, the Court determined that "[a]ny system of prior restraint . . . bear[s] a heavy presumption against its constitutionality," and the "Government . . . carries a heavy burden of showing justification for the prior restraint." Although it dismissed temporary restraining orders entered by a lower court, the Court's enduring contributions to the law of prior restraint were dispersed among nine opinions. Justices Black and Douglas, who asserted that prior restraint was categorically impermissible, effectively combined with Justices Brennan, Stewart, White, and Marshall to deny an injunction against publication of the *Pentagon Papers.* However, the determination of Justices Burger, Harlan, and Blackmun that an injunction against the newspapers was inappropriate under the circumstances, combined with the suggestion of Justices Stewart, White, and Marshall that prior restraint was permissible when statutorily authorized, would have favored a different outcome under altered circumstances. Although the First Amendment's antagonism toward prior restraint was affirmed, the elements of the *Pentagon Papers* decision may have helped enlarge the category of exceptions to the rule against prior restraint and represented a retreat from the fullest implications of the *Near* decision.

In seeking the injunction, President Nixon had claimed an inherent power to protect against harm to national security. Justices Black and Douglas not only rejected the chief executive's argument but staked out a position even more absolutist than that of the Court in *Near*. Black characterized the government's case as a request "to hold that the First Amendment does not mean what it says, but rather means that the Government can halt the publication of current news of vital importance to the people in this country." Thus Black regarded the president's claim of inherent power as "a threat that would wipe out the First Amendment," which he saw as having been conceived primarily to outlaw "injunctions like those sought here." Finally, he warned that national security is a vague term capable of being manipulated and misused at the expense of basic freedoms and informed representative government.

Justice Douglas expressed his preference for resolving the issue pursuant to the literal terminology of the First Amendment. From his perspective, the guarantee that " 'Congress shall make no law ... abridging the freedom ... of the press,' [left] no room for governmental restraint of the press." He noted, moreover, that no relevant statute barred publication of the official study. Douglas also emphasized that the presidential claim of inherent power to obtain an injunction had been repudiated by *Near*, and that governmental secrecy in the end was antidemocratic.

Justice Brennan found error in the granting of injunctive relief under the circumstances. Unlike Black and Douglas, however, Brennan concluded that judicial restraints on the press might be permissible in certain instances. The primary flaw in the government's case, from his viewpoint, was its predication "upon surmise or conjecture that untoward consequences may result." Adverting to a primary exception to the rule against prior restraint cited by the *Near* Court, Brennan concluded that "only governmental allegation and proof that publication must inevitably, directly and immediately cause the occurrence of an event kindred to imperiling the safety of a transport already at sea can support even the issuance of an interim restraining order." In effect, Brennan engrafted the modern clear and present danger test upon the categorical exclusion identified in *Near*. Pursuant to his analysis, it would be enough for the government not merely to assert the exception but to demonstrate significant, direct, and imminent harm.

Justice Stewart, although concurring that an injunction was inappropriate under the circumstances, observed that the president nonetheless had plenary power to conduct foreign affairs and maintain national defense. Thus he maintained that the president also had a "largely unshared duty to determine and preserve the degree of internal security to exercise that power successfully." Stewart had no doubt that confidentiality and secrecy were essential at times for successful diplomacy and effective defense. He emphasized that truly effective security is characterized by maximum possible disclosure, however, because secrecy works only when credibility is maintained. Stewart noted both the executive and congressional powers respectively to promulgate rules and enact legislation to protect confidentiality, but found no such provision applicable to the case. Although he believed that the president was correct about the consequences flowing from publication of some of the documents, Stewart, like Brennan, could not conclude that disclosure would "surely result in direct, immediate, and irreparable damage to our Nation or its people."

Both Justices White and Marshall concurred in the judgment but might have decided otherwise if Congress had authorized a prior restraint of the materials at issue. Justice White, like Stewart, was confident that "revelation of these documents will do substantial damage to public interests." Having determined that the government had not met its heavy burden for restraint and Congress had not enacted pertinent authorizing legislation, he too refused to ban publication. White's denial of the requested relief was grudging, however, and apparently reached only because of the infrequency of prior-restraint cases and his sense that security already had been breached and damage done if the information was available for publication.

Chief Justice Burger and Justices Harlan and Blackmun dissented from the judgment. Burger favored at least temporary relief because the Court did not really know all the facts and thought that the issue was being resolved "in unseemly haste." He thus chastised the *Times*, which had spent three to four months studying purloined documents, for pressing the Court for a decision in a matter of hours. For Black and Douglas, each moment that a prior restraint operated constituted offense to the First Amendment. Burger, however, would have factored in the interests of "the effective functioning of a complex modern government and specifically the effective exercise of certain constitutional powers of the Executive." He thus would have allowed whatever time was necessary for "deliberated and reasonable judicial treatment."

Justice Harlan also complained about a rush to judgment, suggesting "that the Court ha[d] been almost irresponsibly feverish." Harlan's concern was that the quick decision required bypassing several pertinent issues, including whether (1) the Justice Department could bring the suits in the name of the United States, (2) the First Amendment allowed injunctions against publication that endangered national security, (3) national security would be harmed regardless of the documents' content,

(4) unauthorized disclosure would impair national security, (5) the newspapers could use stolen documents, and (6) national security interests should prevail despite First Amendment policy and the possibility that security already had been compromised. Beyond his sense that the case required more deliberation, Harlan dissented from the judgment on grounds that judicial review of executive power in the field of foreign affairs was "very narrowly restricted." Thus he would have permitted judicial inquiry only to determine whether the subject matter fell within the president's power and whether a finding of irreparable harm to national security had been made by the head of the relevant executive department.

Justice Blackmun criticized the judgment as paying too high a tribute to the First Amendment, which he characterized, "after all, [as] only one part of an entire Constitution." What Blackmun found missing was a balancing, pursuant to properly developed standards, "of the broad right of the press to print and of the very narrow right of the Government to prevent." Like Burger and Harlan, Blackmun favored more extensive deliberation before passing judgment. Extensive personnel changes and jurisprudential developments since the opinions were rendered leave open the possibility that, if it were faced with a like issue, the Court's review at least might be more protracted.

Despite the highly fragmented nature of the *Pentagon Papers* decision, several important principles emerge clearly from the case. The Court unanimously embraced the general notions that prior restraints have a presumption of unconstitutionality and that government carries a heavy burden in justifying them. Majority support also exists for the propositions that the president does not possess inherent power to secure a prior restraint on national security grounds and that even if publication is not enjoined, subsequent criminal prosecution may be appropriate. Finally, when the three dissenting opinions are added to Justices White's, Stewart's, and Marshall's concurrences, support seemingly would have existed for a contrary result if Congress had enacted legislation specifically authorizing restraint under the circumstances.

The presence of a pertinent statute seems to have been critical to a lower court's decision to restrain publication of an article explaining how to construct a hydrogen bomb. In *United States v. The Progressive, Inc.*, a federal district court determined that national security outweighed competing First Amendment interests. Although it acknowledged the heavy presumption against the constitutionality of a prior restraint, it was convinced that the government had demonstrated that publication would gravely, directly, immediately, and irreparably injure the national interest. The trial court found unpersuasive arguments that because the article contained material available in the public domain, dissemination could not violate a statutory prohibition against disclosing restricted data.

Rather, it concluded that the article could facilitate development of a weapon more efficiently by less developed nations and enable them to bypass what otherwise might be blind alleys. The district court proceeded to distinguish the case from the *Pentagon Papers* decision on three basic grounds. First, it noted that the documents at issue in the *New York Times* case were historical documents. Second, the government then had offered no cogent reason to block publication except that it might embarrass the United States. Third, a precise statute prohibited communication, including publication, of restricted data concerning the production of nuclear weapons.

The trial court portrayed the essential question as a confrontation between First Amendment freedom and national security interests implicating "the right to life itself." Typifying the balancing of competing interests that courts must perform when confronted with freedom of the press and national security concerns is the following analysis by the *Progressive* court.

What is involved here is information dealing with the most destructive weapon in the history of mankind, information of sufficient destructive potential to nullify the right to free speech and to endanger the right to life itself.

Stripped to its essence then, the question before the Court is a basic confrontation between the First Amendment right to freedom of the press and national security.

The Court believes that each of us is born seized of a panoply of basic rights that we institute governments to secure these rights and that there is a hierarchy of values attached to these rights which is helpful in deciding the clash now before us.

Certain of these rights have an aspect of imperativeness or centrality that make them transcend other rights. Somehow it does not seem that the right to life and the right to not have soldiers quartered in your home can be of equal import in the grand scheme of things. While it may be true in the long-run, as Patrick Henry instructs us, that one would prefer death to life without liberty, nonetheless, in the short-run, one cannot enjoy freedom of speech, freedom to worship or freedom of the press unless one first enjoys the freedom to live.

Faced with a stark choice between upholding the right to continued life and the right to freedom of the press, most jurists would have no difficulty in opting for the chance to continue to breathe and function as they work to achieve perfect freedom of expression.

Is the choice here so stark? Only time can give us a definitive answer. But considering another aspect of this panoply of rights we all have is helpful in answering the question now before us. This aspect is the disparity of the risk involved.

The destruction of various human rights can come about in differing ways and at varying speeds. Freedom of the press can be obliterated overnight by some dictator's imposition of censorship or by the slow nibbling away at a free press through successive bits of repressive legislation enacted by a nation's lawmakers. Yet, even in the most drastic of such situations, it is always possible for a dictator to be overthrown, for a bad law to be repealed or for a judge's error to be subsequently rectified. Only when human life is at stake are such corrections impossible. . . .

The Court is faced with the difficult task of weighing and resolving these divergent views.

A mistake in ruling against *The Progressive* will seriously infringe cherished First Amendment rights. If a preliminary injunction is issued, it will constitute the first instance of prior restraint against a publication in this fashion in the history of this country, to this Court's knowledge. Such notoriety is not to be sought. It will curtail defendants' First Amendment rights in a drastic and substantial fashion. It will infringe upon our right to know and to be informed as well.

A mistake in ruling against the United States could pave the way for thermonuclear annihilation for us all. In that event, our right to life is extinguished and the right to publish becomes moot.

In the *Near* case, the Supreme Court recognized that publication of troop movements in time of war would threaten national security and could therefore be restrained. Times have changed significantly since 1931 when *Near* was decided. Now war by foot soldiers has been replaced in large part by war by machines and bombs. No longer need there be any advance warning or any preparation time before a nuclear war could be commenced.

In light of these factors, this Court concludes that publication of the technical information on the hydrogen bomb contained in the article is analogous to publication of troop movements or locations in time of war and falls within the extremely narrow exception to the rule against prior restraint.

Because of this "disparity of risk," because the government has met its heavy burden of showing justification for the imposition of a prior restraint of publication of the objected-to technical portions of the Moorland article, and because the Court is unconvinced that suppression of the objected-to technical portions of the . . . article would in any plausible fashion impede the defendants in their laudable crusade to stimulate public knowledge of nuclear armament and bring about enlightened debate on national policy questions, the Court finds that the objected-to portions of the article fall within the narrow area recognized by the Court in *Near v. Minnesota* in which a prior restraint on publication is appropriate.

Although the trial court alluded to a test of "immediate, direct and irreparable harm" to justify a prior restraint, akin to Justice Brennan's formula in the *Pentagon Papers* case, it is evident that the trial court's application of the standard varied from its precise terms. The decision to restrain publication essentially was grounded in the magnitude of possible harm rather than in any proof of actual or imminent damage. Thus a restraint of publication was premised upon speculation rather than certainty of consequence. The case ultimately evidenced the acuity of Justice White's observation that once security is breached at its origin, prior restraint may be an ineffective response. While the issue was on appeal, other newspapers published the article that the *Progressive* had been enjoined from printing. Thereafter, the case was dismissed.

Development of the law of prior restraint has not been restricted to the context of national security. Censorship issues have arisen in an array of circumstances and have the potential to surface whenever an official interest exists in regulating speech. In *Organization for a Better Austin v. Keefe*, the Supreme Court affirmed the notions that a system of prior restraint is presumptively invalid and requires a heavy burden of justification. It thus lifted a lower-court order prohibiting the peaceful distribution of leaflets that promoted integration and criticized alleged blockbusting and panic-arousing tactics of a real-estate agent. Later, in *Linmark Associates, Inc. v. Township of Willingboro*, it invalidated an ordinance barring placement of For Sale signs by homeowners. Even interests in minimizing white flight and maintenance of integrated neighborhoods thus did not satisfy the heavy burden of justifying a prior restraint.

Chief Justice Burger, who had dissented from the judgment in the *Pentagon Papers* case, a few years later authored an opinion that vindicated First Amendment interests otherwise constrained by constitutional concern for a fair trial. The decision, in *Nebraska Press Association v. Stuart*, lifted a gag order entered by a state court restraining publication of a defendant's statements before a criminal trial. The trial court had entered the restraining order pursuant to its determination of "a clear and present danger that pre-trial publicity could impinge upon the defendant's right to a fair trial." The lower court obviously had departed from the modern requirements for finding a clear and present danger, as evidenced by its conclusion that harm could, rather than likely would, result. Although Burger noted that the restraining order would have postponed rather than prohibited publication, as in the *New York Times* case, he determined that officially imposed delay was intolerable because prompt reporting of criminal proceedings was more imperative.

The Court identified three pertinent factors for determining whether a gag order was appropriate. It considered "(a) the nature and extent of pretrial news coverage; (b) whether other measures would be likely to mitigate the effects of unrestrained pretrial publicity; and (c) how effectively a restraining order would operate to prevent the threatened danger." Although it recognized that the trial judge reasonably could have concluded that pretrial publicity would be pervasive and intensive and might impair the right to a fair trial, the Court found error in his speculation of harm. In emphasizing an obligation to consider less restrictive alternatives, the Court noted that possibilities included change of venue, postponement of trial, searching voir dire of prospective jurors, clear jury instructions, and sequestration. Finally, the Court doubted the efficacy of a restraining order under the particular circumstances, given the limited territorial jurisdiction of the trial court and a small town in which information traveled swiftly by word of mouth anyway.

The *Nebraska Press Association* decision is not without problems both on fair-trial and First Amendment grounds. Each of the less restrictive alternatives identified by the Court may burden a defendant. Given the pervasiveness of modern media and the expansion of markets effectuated by the emergence of cable and satellites, venues not exposed to publicity may be difficult to locate. Postponement to let public sentiment abate may create speedy-trial problems. Extensive questioning of jurors may expose the jury to negative information for the first time or condition it against the defendant. Individuals also may be unlikely to recognize or acknowledge prejudice. Even clear jury instructions may not overcome the natural difficulty of compartmentalizing information, and sequestration may foster juror resentment. The ruling in favor of First Amendment interests, despite these problems, also contains some language that is potentially incongruous with freedom of the press. The Court observed that "[t]he extraordinary protections afforded by the First Amendment carry with them something in the nature of a fiduciary duty to exercise the protected rights responsibly." Although the fiduciary duty was not amplified beyond an announced expectation that the press would exercise some effort to protect rights of the accused to a fair trial, it is reminiscent of the public trustee standard used to impose special content obligations upon broadcasters. It is a philosophical predicate, whether developed or not, for a fair rather than a free press.

Despite concurring in the Court's judgment, Justice Brennan would have gone farther in accounting for First Amendment interests. Brennan would have held that prior restraint is never a permissible means of securing the right to a fair trial. Furthermore, he would have found that deprivation of the Sixth Amendment right to an impartial jury never could rise to the level of harm required for prior restraint. Brennan maintained that because a defendant always has a right to appeal, harm could never be irreparable.

Like all general principles of law, jurisprudential intolerance of prior restraint is subject to exception. The seminal opinion on the subject, *Near v. Minnesota*, contemplated the possibility of censorship not only when national security interests were at stake but insofar as speech was calculated to incite violence and insurrection or was obscene. The *Pentagon Papers* decision further amplified the national security exception to the general prohibition against prior restraint. The line of cases culminating in *Brandenburg v. Ohio*, discussed in Chapter 1, did likewise with respect to expression inciting violent overthrow of the government. Insofar as expression is entirely unprotected, normative standards regarding censorship do not operate. The Court accordingly is more tolerant of prior restraints impacting upon obscenity. As evidenced by the Court's affirmance of an injunction in *Kingsley Books, Inc. v. Brown*, censorship may be accommodated even before the ultimate question of obscenity is determined and despite the consequent risk to what may prove to be protected speech.

When the media themselves are a party to litigation, proscriptions against prior restraint may not operate. A gag order against a media defendant in a defamation action thus was upheld in *Seattle Times Co. v. Rinehart.* The newspaper was prohibited from disclosing information obtained in the course of discovery on grounds that the protective order was supported by "good cause," liberal pretrial discovery presents significant potential for abuse, and discovery is not a traditional public source of information. In *Butterworth v. Smith*, the Court invalidated a state law prohibiting grand jury witnesses from revealing their testimony. A reporter who had appeared before the grand jury challenged the statute, and the Court discerned a constitutional right to relate truthful information he possessed and otherwise could communicate freely.

The status of commercial speech as a constitutionally protected form of expression is a relatively recent development. Although the Court accorded commercial expression First Amendment protection during the mid–1970s, it observed that normal presumptions against prior restraint would not necessarily operate. In *Lowe v. Securities and Exchange Commission*, the Court considered whether the Commission could enjoin an investment adviser from publishing and selling investment newsletters. The court of appeals had upheld the Commission's authority to restrain publication as a permissible sanction against an individual who had violated the federal securities laws. A dissenting judge noted the First Amendment dangers of the regulatory scheme, however, since the newsletters contained expression on political, economic, and social issues that "could appear in our favorite local newspaper." He observed that the prohibition against publishing was akin to the English licensing system abandoned in 1694. Although the Supreme Court reversed the appeals court decision, only Justice White, joined by Chief Justice Burger and Justice Rehnquist, confronted the constitutional issue. In a concurring opinion, they concluded that "to prevent petitioner from publishing at all is inconsistent with the First Amendment."

The Court refused to review a temporary order barring the airing of telephone conversations between a criminal defendant and his attorneys. In *Cable News Network, Inc. v. Noriega*, it thus allowed a prior restraint to operate at least until the district court evaluated the tapes and determined whether it was necessary to protect the right to a fair trial. Justices Marshall and O'Connor dissented on grounds the Court's denial of review deviated from precedent and allowed suppression to operate minus any threshold showing of impairment to fair trial interests or consideration of other means for averting harm. The district court, having satisfied itself that airing the tapes would not compromise a fair trial, lifted the ban several days later. The procedure, coupled with the Court's refusal to intervene, suggests the possibility that judges under certain circumstances may impose short term restraints free of normal presumptions of invalidity. Even allowing for a relaxation of normative criteria, it would be reasonable to expect that any temporary restraint should operate no longer than necessary for a court to ascertain whether dissemination would cause intolerable harm.

The presumption against prior restraint has been less firm in relationship to newer media, or the justifications for it have been more readily accepted. Licensing of radio and television stations, for instance, is based upon past experience when unrestrained competition resulted in chaos, confusion, and massive signal interference. Less convincing is the Court's rationale for allowing censorship boards to review films and determine whether they are suitable for public viewing. Arguments that motion pictures have a special capacity for evil although they are consistent with the notion that each medium presents unique problems, never have been subjected to rigorous examination. Even if the rationale is usable as a basis for other regulatory action, it does not seem to comport with the heavy burden of actually proving the need for a prior restraint. Despite the diminished protection afforded motion pictures, the Court has insisted upon procedural safeguards for any censorship system. Thus administrative review must be prompt, the burden of proof is upon the censor to demonstrate that the expression is unprotected, and an opportunity must exist for speedy judicial review.

The special concern that the Court has evinced toward prior restraint rests in large part upon a perception that the regulatory methodology imposes "an immediate and irreversible sanction." While recognizing that subsequent punishment may chill expression, the Court has observed that prior restraint freezes it. The disparity in constitutional attitude toward prior restraint and subsequent punishment has been criticized, however, for a failure to explain why an injunction justifies special constitutional disfavor. Despite a dominant sense that prior restraint is peculiarly intolerable when timeliness of information is a pertinent factor, one commentator has suggested that jurisprudence is a function of "a remote and usually unarticulated premise underlying a broad and uncritical acceptance of the conventional rhetoric of prior restraint." In so doing, he has noted that the doctrine of prior restraint too often focuses on an inconsequential form that diverts attention from critical substantive issues of First Amendment coverage. The *Near* decision, which could have rested on grounds that the statute at issue was vague, overbroad, and inconsistent with basic First Amendment principles of robust and open debate, thus is regarded as having elevated form or substance in a way that may deny government a sometimes proper means for vindicating valid interests. Even if principles operating against prior restraint may divert attention from substantive First

Amendment and competing interests, categorical repudiation of them may assume the risk, especially in national security cases, that judges may overpredict harm if they are merely allowed to balance harms. Perhaps that danger is offset by the prospect that when confidentiality is breached, the flow of information cannot effectively be controlled anyway.

B. INDIRECT RESTRAINT

Criticism of the doctrine of prior restraint to the effect that it is overly inclusive is not pertinent to the court's analysis of official clearance procedures for employee publications. In *Snepp v. United States*, the Court disregarded how an employment contract requiring a former CIA agent to submit a book to the agency for prepublication approval had at least the same functional effect as a prior restraint. Per curiam, it found that the employee had violated not only his contract with the government but his fiduciary duty even though the book at issue contained no classified information. Given a breach of the employment agreement, the Court ordered the channeling of profits from the book into a constructive trust.

The Court thus upheld an official preclearance procedure as a legitimate means for government to determine whether publication would be harmful to intelligence interests and the safety of agents. Justice Stevens, in dissent, criticized the Court for "enforc[ing] a species of prior restraint on a citizen's right to criticize his government." In part, the decision rested upon analysis tied to the law of contracts. The Court, however, did not address the possibility that the contract at issue might be unconscionable. Although some contracts are void because they violate public policy, the Court also did not appear to consider whether the employment agreement might be invalid as a contravention of First Amendment policy.

C. COMPULSORY PROPAGATION

When government commands rather than prohibits publication, the Court has recognized a form of restraint that does "not fall into familiar or traditional patterns." In *Miami Herald Publishing Co. v. Tornillo*, the Court declared unconstitutional a statutory right for political candidates to obtain equal space in response to newspaper criticisms of their record. Such compulsion, it observed, exacted a penalty "in terms of the cost in printing and composing time and materials and in taking up space that could be devoted to other material the newspaper may have preferred to print." The practical effect of the law thus was considered identical to a forthright restraint. Because the choice of what is to be published and decisions concerning newspaper size and content are at the heart of editorial control and judgment, the Court concluded that regulation of that process was inconsistent with free press guarantees.

Similarly, a federal appeals court found regulations requiring cable operators to carry the signals of local broadcasters inconsistent with the First Amendment. Adverting to the *Tornillo* decision, it concluded that "[f]orcing an editor to print that which he otherwise would not . . . was a restraint the First Amendment would not tolerate." Nor would it make any difference from the appeals court's standpoint if the intrusion into editorial autonomy was not extensive. A contrary result was reached when the Supreme Court examined personal attack and political editorial rules and the fairness doctrine as they applied to broadcasting. Rejecting any suggestion that such restraints were inconsistent with the First Amendment, the Court in *Red Lion Broadcasting Co. v. Federal Communications Commission* found that the regulations were justified by the medium's scarce nature. Because "there are substantially more individuals who want to broadcast than there are frequencies to allocate, [the Court found it] idle to posit an unabridgeable First Amendment right to broadcast comparable to the right . . . to . . . publish." The continuing viability of that distinction is questionable, given (1) the Court's indication that it is prepared to reevaluate the scarcity principle and (2) the Federal Communications Commission's abandonment of the fairness doctrine (discussed in Chapter 10). The operation of prior restraint as a normative phenomenon in some instances, nonetheless, discloses a constitutional barrier that is semipermeable rather than entirely impenetrable.

REFERENCES

CASES

Banzhaf v. Federal Communications Commission, 405 F.2d 1082 (D.C. Cir. 1968), cert. denied, 396 U.S. 842 (1969).

Brandenburg v. Ohio, 395 U.S. 444 (1969).

Butterworth v. Smith, 110 S.Ct. 1376 (1990).

Cable News Network, Inc. v. Noriega, 111 S. Ct. 451 (1991).

Columbia Broadcasting System, Inc. v. Democratic National Committee, 412 U.S. 94 (1973).

Federal Communications Commission v. Pacifica Foundation, 438 U.S. 726 (1978).

First National Bank of Boston v. Bellotti, 435 U.S. 765 (1978).

Jackson v. Metropolitan Edison Co., 419 U.S. 345 (1974).

Joseph Burstyn, Inc. v. Wilson, 343 U.S. 495 (1952).

Kingsley Books, Inc. v. Brown, 354 U.S. 436 (1957).

Kovacs v. Cooper, 336 U.S. 79 (1949).

Linmark Associates, Inc. v. Township of Willingboro, 431 U.S. 85 (1977).

Lowe v. Securities and Exchange Commission, 472 U.S. 181 (1985).

Miami Herald Publishing Co. v. Tornillo, 418 U.S. 241 (1974).

Mutual Film Corp. v. Industrial Commission of Ohio, 236 U.S. 230 (1915).

Near v. Minnesota, 283 U.S. 697 (1931).

Nebraska Press Association v. Stuart, 427 U.S. 539 (1976).

New York Times Co. v. United States, 403 U.S. 713 (1971).

Organization for a Better Austin v. Keefe, 402 U.S. 418 (1971).

Quincy Cable TV, Inc. v. Federal Communications Commission, 768 F.2d 1434 (D.C. Cir. 1985), cert. denied, 476 U.S. 1169 (1986).

Red Lion Broadcasting Co. v. Federal Communications Commission, 395 U.S. 367 (1969).

Seattle Times Co. v. Rinehart, 467 U.S. 20 (1984).

Snepp v. United States, 444 U.S. 507 (1980).

United States v. The Progressive, Inc., 467 F. Supp. 990 (W.D. Wis. 1979), appeal dismissed, 610 F.2d 819 (7th Cir. 1979).

PUBLICATIONS

Blackstone, Commentaries on the Laws of England (1872).

Blasi, *Toward a Theory of Prior Restraint: The Central Linkage*, 66 Minn. L. Rev. 11 (1981).

Brandeis & Warren, *The Right to Privacy*, 4 Harv. L. Rev. 193 (1890).

Brennan, *Address*, 32 Rutgers L. Rev. 173 (1979).

Emerson, *The Doctrine of Prior Restraint*, 20 Law & Contemp. Probs. 648 (1955).

Entin, *United States v. Progressive, Inc.: The Faustian Bargain and the First Amendment*, 75 Nw. U.L. Rev. 171 (1980).

Jeffries, *Rethinking Prior Restraint*, 92 Yale L.J. 409 (1983).

Lange, *The Speech and Press Clauses*, 23 U.C.L.A. L. Rev. 77 (1975).

Linde, *Courts and Censorship*, 66 Minn. L. Rev. 171 (1981).

Lively, *Fear and the Media: A First Amendment Horror Show*, 69 Minn. L. Rev. 1071 (1985).

Lively, *Old Media, New Dogma*, 30 Ariz. L. Rev. 257 (1988).

Nimmer, *Introduction—Is Freedom of the Press a Redundancy? What Does It Add to Freedom of Speech?* 26 Hastings L.J. 639 (1975).

Stewart, *Or of the Press*, 26 Hastings L.J. 631 (1975).

de Tocqueville, Democracy in America (1956).

Chapter 3

Freedom of the Press and Competing Considerations

> Debate on public issues should be uninhibited, robust, and wide-open, and...may well include vehement, caustic, and sometimes unpleasantly sharp attacks on government and public officials.
>
> *New York Times Co. v. Sullivan*, 376 U.S. 254, 270 (1964)

The First Amendment, notwithstanding its unqualified terms, operates, like other basic guarantees, in relative rather than absolute fashion. Absolutism was propounded consistently by Justice Black and to a slightly lesser extent by Justice Douglas. Despite the assertion that the framers performed "all the 'balancing' that was to be done in this field," the Court has rejected the notion that the guarantee must prevail in all instances or be construed literally. When freedom of the press collides with a competing constitutional provision, statute, or policy, therefore, the question is which interest must give way or how the conflicting concerns can be accommodated. Prominent rival constitutional interests implicate the Fourth, Fifth, Sixth, and Fourteenth Amendments. Nonconstitutional concerns that may delimit press freedom include defamation, privacy, public morals, and copyright.

I. CONSTITUTIONAL CONCERNS

A. FOURTH AMENDMENT: SEARCH AND SEIZURE

The Supreme Court for the most part has refused to confer upon the press any special privilege in or immunity from the criminal justice process. In *Zurcher v. Stanford Daily*, the Court upheld the seizure of evidence from a newsroom pursuant to a valid search warrant. The search had been judicially authorized upon probable cause that the newspaper possessed photographs revealing the identities of persons who allegedly had assaulted police officers during a demonstration. The Court found the procedure constitutional even though the newspaper was not suspected of a crime. It rejected an argument that First Amendment interests require, when practicable, use of a subpoena duces tecum. For the Court, the critical element of a reasonable search was not that the owner or holder of property is suspected of a crime but that reasonable cause exists to believe that evidence of a crime is located upon the premises. Rather than create any special rule for obtaining evidence from the press, the Court observed that the standards for a search warrant must be applied with particular exactitude when First Amendment interests are implicated. Any unique consideration for the press with respect to searches and seizures thus appears limited to urging of special caution to ensure that the media's ability to gather, analyze, and disseminate news is not compromised.

The Court's decision at least coincides with some practical realities. Most prosecutors, as elected officials, are unlikely to risk unnecessarily antagonizing the media. Although a subpoena may be less intrusive than a search warrant, it also may be less effective if evidence disappears. Justice Stewart in dissent noted that the procedure upheld by the Court would enable police to ransack news files and thus chill sources and the flow of information. Whether or not his worries would have proved well founded, Congress enacted legislation restricting the ability of federal and state police to obtain evidence from the news media by means of search warrants.

The resultant Privacy Protection Act of 1980, 42 U.S.C. §2000aa, limits newsroom searches and seizures to specified circumstances. Government generally may not search for or seize the work product of reporters. An exception exists if a person possessing the evidence has committed the crime and reason exists to believe that immediate seizure is essential to avoid death or serious injury. Other materials in the media's possession are subject to the same conditions for search and seizure governing work product plus exceptions when (1) notice by subpoena would result in loss or concealment of evidence and (2) a judicial order to produce evidence is resisted and appeals are exhausted or delay would undermine the interests of justice.

B. FIFTH AMENDMENT: GRAND JURY

Consistent with the determination that the First Amendment confers no special immunity from the needs of the criminal justice system, the

Supreme Court has concluded that it also creates no privilege against testifying in a grand jury proceeding. In *Branzburg v. Hayes,* the Court rejected the argument that the First Amendment authorized a reporter's refusal to identify confidential sources. It responded at least partially to the concern, however, that confidentiality requires protection if the flow of information to the public is not to be impaired. Thus the Court observed that "[o]nly where news sources themselves are implicated in crime or possess information relevant to the grand jury's task need they or the reporter be concerned about grand jury subpoenas." Such a notation may suggest the need for a relevancy requirement that does not otherwise attach to grand jury requests for information. Still, the Court evinced a reluctance to single out the media for special treatment, noting that they were not immune from the general principle that the criminal justice system is entitled to receive "every man's evidence." The Court emphasized too the significant function of the grand jury.

The prevailing constitutional view of the newsman's privilege is very much rooted in the ancient role of the grand jury that has the dual function of determining if there is probable cause to believe that a crime has been committed and of protecting citizens against unfounded criminal prosecutions. Grand jury proceedings are constitutionally mandated for the institution of federal criminal prosecutions for capital or other serious crimes, and "its constitutional prerogatives are rooted in long centuries of Anglo-American history." The Fifth Amendment provides that "[n]o person shall be held to answer for a capital or otherwise infamous crime unless on a presentment or indictment of a grand Jury." The adoption of the grand jury "in our Constitution as the sole method for preferring charges in serious criminal cases shows the high place it held as an instrument of justice." . . . Although state systems of criminal procedure differ greatly among themselves, the grand jury is similarly guaranteed by many state constitutions and plays an important role in fair and effective law enforcement in the overwhelming majority of the States. Because its task is to inquire into the existence of possible criminal conduct and to return only well-founded indictments, its investigative powers are necessarily broad. "It is a grand inquest, a body with powers of investigation and inquisition, the scope of whose inquiries is not to be limited narrowly by questions of propriety or forecasts of the probable result of the investigation, or by doubts whether any particular individual will be found properly subject to an accusation of crime." Hence, the grand jury's authority to subpoena witnesses is not only historic . . . but essential to its task. Although the powers of the grand jury are not unlimited and are subject to the supervision of a judge, the longstanding principle that "the public . . . has a right to every man's evidence," except for those persons protected by a constitutional, common-law, or statutory privilege . . . is particularly applicable to grand jury proceedings. . . .

Thus, we cannot seriously entertain the notion that the First Amendment protects a newsman's agreement to conceal the criminal conduct of his source, or evidence thereof, on the theory that it is better to write about crime than to do something about it. Insofar as any reporter in these cases undertook not to reveal or testify about the crime he witnessed, his claim of privilege under the First Amendment presents no substantial question. The crimes of news sources are no less reprehensible and threatening to the public interest when witnessed by a reporter than when they are not. . . .

The argument that the flow of news will be diminished by compelling reporters to aid the grand jury in a criminal investigation is not irrational, nor are the records before us silent on the matter. But we remain unclear how often and to what extent informers are actually deterred from furnishing information when newsmen are forced to testify before a grand jury. The available data indicate that some newsmen rely a great deal on confidential sources and that some informants are particularly sensitive to the threat of exposure and may be silenced if it is held by this Court that, ordinarily, newsmen must testify pursuant to subpoenas, but the evidence fails to demonstrate that there would be a significant constriction of the flow of news to the public if this Court reaffirms the prior common-law and constitutional rule regarding the testimonial obligations of newsmen. Estimates of the inhibiting effect of such subpoenas on the willingness of informants to make disclosures to newsmen are widely divergent and to a great extent speculative. . . .

Accepting the fact, however, that an undetermined number of informants not themselves implicated in crime will nevertheless, for whatever reason, refuse to talk to newsmen if they fear identification by a reporter in an official investigation, we cannot accept the argument that the public interest in possible future news about crime from undisclosed, unverified sources must take precedence over the public interest in pursuing and prosecuting those crimes reported to the press by informants and in thus deterring the commission of such crimes in the future. . . .

We are admonished that refusal to provide a First Amendment reporter's privilege will undermine the freedom of the press to collect and disseminate news. But this is not the lesson history teaches us. As noted previously, the common law recognized no such privilege, and the constitutional argument was not even asserted until 1958. From the beginning of our country the press has operated without constitutional protection for press informants, and the press has flourished. The existing constitutional rules have not been a serious obstacle to either the development or retention of confidential news sources by the press. . . .

At the federal level, Congress has freedom to determine whether a statutory newsman's privilege is necessary and desirable and to fashion standards and rules as narrow or broad as deemed necessary to deal with the evil discerned and, equally important, to refashion those rules as experience from time to time may dictate. There is also merit in leaving state legislatures free, within First Amendment limits, to fashion their own standards in light of the conditions and problems with respect to the relations between law enforcement officials and press in their own areas. It goes without saying, of course, that we are powerless to bar state courts from responding in their own way and construing their own constitutions so as to recognize a newsman's privilege, either qualified or absolute. . . .

Finally, as we have earlier indicated, news gathering is not without its First

Amendment protections, and grand jury investigations if instituted or conducted other than in good faith, would pose wholly different issues for resolution under the First Amendment. Official harassment of the press undertaken not for purposes of law enforcement but to disrupt a reporter's relationship with his news sources would have no justification. Grand juries are subject to judicial control and subpoenas to motions to quash. We do not expect courts will forget that grand juries must operate within the limits of the First Amendment as well as the Fifth.

The *Branzburg* decision is problematic on more than one count. Although only a qualified privilege was sought, the Court depicted the claim as "virtually impenetrable" in nature. In dismissing the First Amendment argument as an imposition on the criminal justice system and even on a criminal defendant's rights, the Court failed to mention that several interests of a nonconstitutional order justify a like burden. Attorney-client, physician-patient, accountant-client, and other privileges are allowed to operate because they are perceived as advancing significant policy interests. Intentionally or not, the *Branzburg* decision suggests that First Amendment interests are less important than these other concerns.

Despite its firm tone, the *Branzburg* decision's dismissal of a First Amendment privilege may not be as complete as it appears. In a concurring opinion, Justice Powell observed that if "a newsman believes that the grand jury investigation is not being conducted in good faith he is not without remedy." Essentially, Powell would have assessed a grand jury subpoena against a standard of good faith, relevancy, and need. The implication of such a test is that a grand jury may not seek information from the media unless it first exhausts other alternatives. Powell's criteria, combined with the dissenting opinions, therefore, actually may provide support for a qualified privilege.

The *Branzburg* decision by its terms was limited to the criminal justice context. Left unanswered was whether and to what extent a First Amendment privilege may exist in other settings. Some courts have found the holding inapplicable in the civil arena on grounds that the interest at stake there is less compelling. Relevance and need as a result have helped determine whether discovery should be permitted against the media. Pertinent too has been whether the press was a party or a witness.

In the wake of *Branzburg,* several states passed shield laws designed to create a statutory privilege for news reporters. Such enactments are consistent with the Court's observation that Congress and the states may create press immunity laws that are absolute or qualified. Regardless of how they are framed, such measures do not necessarily constitute an impregnable defense. Some courts have balanced statutory privileges against both federal and state constitutional guarantees. Despite the presence of an unequivocal shield law, in *Matter of Farber*, the New Jersey Supreme Court assessed a privilege claim pursuant to a relevancy, less intrusive means, and need test.

C. FIFTH, SIXTH, AND FOURTEENTH AMENDMENTS: FAIR TRIAL AND RELATED RIGHTS

1. Access to Judicial Proceedings

Fair trial and free press interests most frequently come into conflict in connection with the issue of prejudicial publicity. News coverage of a crime, of pretrial proceedings, or of a trial itself has presented demonstrable problems of fairness in the adjudicative process. The media's role, when combined with poor judgment of prosecutors or judges, may facilitate something less than an impartial criminal justice system. Reporting also may undermine the fairness of a trial by influencing jurors to the point that guilt is decided on grounds other than the evidence presented. If this occurs, not only the guarantee to a fair trial but also the Sixth Amendment right to an impartial jury is compromised.

Prejudice to rights of the accused may result from reporting of information concerning a case or from the media's presence at an adjudicative event. In *Nebraska Press Association v. Stuart*, the trial court attempted to minimize the danger of pretrial publicity by enjoining the media from publishing certain information. As noted previously, such a restraint is an impermissible intrusion on freedom of the press, at least absent exhaustion of less restrictive avenues for securing a defendant's fair trial rights. Equally if not more suppressive in its effect would be a judicial decision to close a proceeding entirely to the press and public. Despite consequences that were practically indistinguishable from a prior restraint, and a procedure arguably more burdensome to First Amendment interests, the Court in *Gannett Co., Inc. v. DePasquale* upheld closure of a pretrial hearing. The decision rested primarily upon the Sixth Amendment guarantee of a public trial, which the Court identified as a right of the defendant's and not assertable by the press or public. Closure also was tied to the mutual assent of the prosecutor, judge, and defendant. In denying a right of access on Sixth Amendment grounds, the Court noted that interests associated with open proceedings were not being sacrificed. After the danger of prejudice had abated, a transcript of the proceeding had been available to the press.

The *Gannett* decision invited criticism on multiple grounds. Although the facts of the case concerned a suppression hearing, the language of the decision mixed references to pretrial proceedings and trials. Contrary to the strict conditions imposed on issuance of a gag order, moreover, the Court determined that a trial judge might close a pretrial proceeding despite the availability of other options. Support for closure was premised substantially upon the consequences of freedom afforded the press to publish information legally acquired.

A year later, in *Richmond Newspapers, Inc., v. Virginia,* the Court determined that the First Amendment established a right to attend trials. Emphasizing the traditional openness of trials to the public and the risk of abuse, including collusion and misconduct, if such proceedings are conducted in secret, the Court narrowed the power of a trial judge to order closure. Although the opinions were splintered, a majority supported a right of access premised upon the First Amendment. Soon thereafter, the Court reinforced the notion that the press and public had a right of access to criminal trials not only because they historically have been open but "to ensure [the] constitutionally protected 'discussion of governmental affairs' is an informed one." In *Globe Newspaper Co. v. Superior Court,* a state law requiring exclusion of the press and public from the courtroom during a young sex offense victim's testimony was invalidated. The key flaw in the statute was its mandatory nature. Although the statute was intended to protect victims from further injury and embarrassment and to encourage testimony, the Court concluded that an absolute requirement was too demanding and that a trial judge should factor in age, maturity, family desires, nature of the crime, and whether testimony could be elicited without closure. A denial of access thus must rest upon demonstration of "a compelling governmental interest... narrowly tailored to serve that interest." Although child sex abuse cases may present special problems with respect to further traumatization of victims, they also may have the potential for overzealousness and misconduct by prosecutors more interested in headlines than justice.

Critical to the *Globe Newspaper* decision was the notion that "[t]he First Amendment is... broad enough to encompass those rights that, while not unambiguously enumerated in the very terms of the Amendment, are nonetheless necessary to the enjoyment of other First Amendment rights." A right of access to criminal trials thus was regarded as essential for protecting "free discussion of public affairs." Justice Brennan, in authoring the majority opinion, adverted also to the nature of the criminal justice system itself as a reason for recognizing a constitutional right of access.

Two features of the criminal justice system... together serve to explain why a right of access to criminal trials in particular is properly afforded protection by the First Amendment. First, the criminal trial historically has been open to the press and general public. "[A]t the time when our organic laws were adopted, criminal trials both here and in England had long been presumptively open."

And since that time, the presumption of openness has remained secure. Indeed, at the time of this Court's decision in re Oliver, 333 U.S. 257 (1948), the presumption was so solidly grounded that the Court was "unable to find a single instance of a criminal trial conducted in camera in any federal, state, or municipal court during the history of this country." This uniform rule of openness has been viewed as significant in constitutional terms not only "because the Constitution carries the gloss of history," but also because "a tradition of accessibility implies the favorable judgment of experience."

Second, the right of access to criminal trials plays a particularly significant role in the functioning of the judicial process and the government as a whole. Public scrutiny of criminal trials enhances the quality and safeguards the integrity of the fact finding process, with benefits to both the defendant and to society as a whole. Moreover, public access to the criminal trial fosters an appearance of fairness, thereby heightening public respect for the judicial process. And in the broadest terms, public access to criminal trials permits the public to participate in and serve as a check upon the judicial process—an essential component in our structure of self-government. In sum, the institutional value of the open criminal trial is recognized in both logic and experience.

The Court's insistence upon alternatives that are less restrictive than closure, and refusal to exclude a category of cases entirely from public view, strike a balance among competing interests that is largely congruent with open governance. The *Gannett* decision as a consequence was effectively narrowed to reach only pretrial proceedings. Since the Court in *Gannett* found no evidence supporting the notion that the public historically had a right to attend pretrial proceedings as opposed to trials, a basis for distinguishing the two circumstances persisted. It appears, however, that the Court will forgo such a distinction.

In *Press-Enterprise Co. v. Superior Court,* the Court identified a First Amendment right of access to a preliminary hearing. Besides recognizing a traditional practice of openness in the particular jurisdiction, the Court emphasized the widespread preference of modern practice for open proceedings. It also accounted for a reality that seemed to have been disregarded or discounted in *Gannett.* Although the Court in *Richmond Newspapers* had stressed the importance of openness in a critical proceeding such as a trial, pretrial proceedings for many defendants are the dispositive event in the criminal justice system. Because the vast majority of cases result in pleas without a trial, the pretrial phase for practical purposes may be the most crucial. If public access is to operate as a check upon the process's abuse, therefore, its extension to the pretrial context is well justified.

The *Press-Enterprise* decision responded to the preliminary hearing context but refers generally to criminal proceedings. Although concern was expressed that the determination might apply also to grand juries, it seems unlikely that the Court will extend its logic that far. The opinion itself suggested that the grand jury's investigative function requires secrecy, and confidentiality is supported by a long history of such practice. Closure also remains a possibility for pretrial proceedings if the appropriate standard is satisfied. Thus, when the right to a fair trial is asserted, exclusion of the press and public is permissible "if specific findings are made that first, there is a substantial probability that the defendant's right to a fair trial will be prejudiced by publicity that closure would prevent and second, reasonable alternatives to closure cannot adequately protect the defendant's free trial rights." Although the standard was enunciated in the context of a preliminary hearing, it presumably would be relevant for other proceedings, including a trial. Even if the showing necessary for closure is made, it would seem that a transcript must be made available as soon as the threat of prejudicial publicity abates.

2. Cameras in the Courtroom

Prejudice to a defendant's right of a fair trial and associated guarantees may be attributed to consequences of the media's general function of disseminating information or to specific difficulties created by its presence at a judicial proceeding. Of particular concern to the Court has been the influence of broadcasting upon the fairness of the criminal justice system. From 1937 until fairly recently, the American Bar Association Canons of Judicial Ethics provided that a judge should prohibit cameras from the courtroom because they detracted from the dignity of the proceeding. When the Court was first confronted with the effect of television coverage, it reversed a murder conviction on grounds that pretrial publicity had contributed to the jury's verdict. Thereafter, it found a due process violation attributable to the broadcast of a defendant's confession prior to trial. Given what it characterized as the public's pervasive exposure to a spectacle, moreover, the Court assumed a constitutional deprivation instead of requiring proof that the jury actually was prejudiced. The mere presence of cameras in the courtroom, over the defendant's objection, convinced a plurality of the Court that due process was denied. In *Estes v. Texas*, it was observed that the presence of the electronic media "involves such a probability of prejudice that it is deemed inherently lacking in due process." The Court's fears about the effect of television were based upon possibilities that jurors might be distracted, parties, witnesses, counsel, and judges might have their attention diverted, and the quality of legal representation might be undermined.

Only Justice Harlan's concurring opinion precluded the *Estes* decision from operating as a constitutional prohibition of the electronic media from the courtroom. Harlan expressed serious concerns about the constitutional compatibility of cameras in the courtroom, especially in connection with cases attracting widespread interest, but noted that technological advances ultimately might make the media's presence less of a threat to the imperatives of a fair criminal justice system.

As television acquired the capacity to cover events in a less intrusive fashion, working with available light, minimal cable, and miniaturized equipment, some states became more willing to accommodate electronic coverage of court proceedings. In *Chandler v. Florida*, the Court upheld a state law permitting broadcast coverage of a criminal proceeding even if the defendant objected. The unanimous decision found no satisfactory evidence that the presence of cameras in the courtroom inherently denies due process. Critical to the determination appears to have been the presence of guidelines obligating judges to safeguard the rights of the accused. A defendant still may assert that media coverage may adversely affect any of the trial participants to the point that due process is compromised. A showing of actual prejudice rather than mere "juror awareness" of the media's presence and interest is essential, however, to establish a due process deprivation.

To demonstrate prejudice in a specific case a defendant must show something more than juror awareness that the trial is such as to attract the attention of broadcasters. *Murphy v. Florida*, 421 U.S. 794, 800 (1975). No doubt the very presence of a camera in the courtroom made the jurors aware that the trial was thought to be of sufficient interest to the public to warrant coverage. Jurors, forbidden to watch all broadcasts, would have had no way of knowing that only fleeting seconds of the proceeding would be reproduced. But the appellants have not attempted to show with any specificity that the presence of cameras impaired the ability of the jurors to decide the case on only the evidence before them or that their trial was affected adversely by the impact on any of the participants of the presence of cameras and the prospect of broadcast.

Although the Court conclusively abandoned previous intimations that the presence of the electronic media amounted to a constitutional violation per se, it emphasized that its decision did not establish a right of access to broadcast court proceedings. Such a determination in practical terms arguably puts broadcasters at a constitutional disadvantage, given recognition of a right of access to trials for the press and public. Although such a result is justifiable on legalistic grounds, insofar as radio and television have been regarded as the least protected medium, it does not conform especially well with the holding that cameras in the courtroom do not inherently compromise due process. The Judicial Conference of the United States has structured a three-year experiment through 1994 with television and radio access to federal district and appeals courts. Considerable movement toward accommodating the electronic media already has been evidenced at the state level, where most jurisdictions with the endorsement of the American Bar Association have revised their laws to permit cameras in the courtroom. Typically, such statutes permit electronic coverage provided it is unobtrusive and subject to guidelines that help avoid interference with the defendant's rights. Pursuant to *Chandler*, the only issue concerning admission of cameras into the courtroom is whether, under the particular circumstances of a given case, their presence and operation cause a due process deprivation.

3. Prejudicial Influences

The press, apart from any problems attributable to a particular medium, is generally capable of upsetting fair-trial guarantees. In *Sheppard v. Maxwell*, the Court found a denial of due process resulting from the combined effect of massive pretrial publicity and disruptive conduct by all elements of the press. Prior to the trial, a newspaper had printed numerous articles about the defendant that were inflammatory and erroneous. It had also published the identity of jurors, thereby conferring celebrity status upon them and making them susceptible to public pressure. Further compounding the peril to due process was the fact that the presiding judge was in the midst of a reelection campaign. In reviewing the defendant's claim that he was denied a fair trial, the Court depicted circumstances that disclosed a media circus rather than orderly administration of justice.

Marilyn Sheppard, petitioner's pregnant wife, was bludgeoned to death in the upstairs bedroom of their lakeshore home in Bay Village, Ohio, a suburb of Cleveland. On the day of the tragedy, July 4, 1954, Sheppard pieced together for several local officials the following story: He and his wife had entertained neighborhood friends, the Aherns, on the previous evening at their home. After dinner they watched television in the living room. Sheppard became drowsy and dozed off to sleep on a couch. Later, Marilyn partially awoke him saying that she was going to bed. The next thing he remembered was hearing his wife cry out in the early morning hours. He hurried upstairs and in the dim light from the hall saw a "form" standing next to his wife's bed. As he struggled with the "form" he was struck on the back of the neck and rendered unconscious. On regaining his senses he found himself on the floor next to his wife's bed. He rose, looked at her, took her pulse and "felt that she was gone." He then went to his son's room and found him unmolested. Hearing a noise he hurried downstairs. He saw a "form" running out the door and pursued it to the lake shore. He grappled with it on the beach and again lost consciousness. Upon his recovery he was lying face down with the lower portion of his body in the water. He returned to his home, checked the pulse of his wife's neck, and "determined or thought that she was gone." He then went downstairs and called a neighbor, Mayor Houk of Bay Village. The mayor and his wife came over at once, found Sheppard slumped in an easy chair downstairs and asked, "What happened?" Sheppard replied: "I don't know but somebody ought to try to do something for Marilyn." Mrs. Houk immediately went up to the bedroom. The Mayor told Sheppard, "Get hold of yourself. Can you tell me what happened?" Sheppard then related the above-outlined events. After Mrs. Houk discovered the body, the Mayor called the local police, Dr. Richard Sheppard, petitioner's brother, and the Aherns. The local police were the first to arrive. They in turn notified the Coroner and Cleveland police. Richard Sheppard then arrived, determined that Marilyn was dead, examined his brother's injuries, and removed him to the nearby clinic operated by the Sheppard family. When the Coroner, the Cleveland police and other officials arrived, the house and surrounding area were thoroughly searched, the rooms of the house were photographed, and many persons, including the Houks and the Aherns, were interrogated. The Sheppard home and premises were taken into "protective custody" and remained so until after the trial.

From the outset officials focused suspicion on Sheppard. After a search of the house and premises on the morning of the tragedy, Dr. Gerber, the Coroner, is reported—and it is undenied—to have told his men, "Well, it is evident the doctor did this, so let's go get the confession out of him." He proceeded to interrogate and examine Sheppard while the latter was under sedation in his hospital room. On the same occasion, the Coroner was given the clothes Sheppard wore at the time of the tragedy together with the personal items in them. Later that afternoon Chief Eaton and two Cleveland police officers interrogated Sheppard at some length, confronting him with evidence and demanding explanations. Asked by Officer Shotke to take a lie detector test, Sheppard said he would if it were reliable. Shotke replied that it was "infallible" and "you might as well tell us all about it now." At the end of the interrogation Shotke told Sheppard: "I think you killed your wife." Still later in the same afternoon a physician sent by the Coroner was permitted to make a detailed examination of Sheppard. Until the Coroner's inquest on July 22, at which time he was subpoenaed, Sheppard made himself available for frequent and extended questioning without the presence of an attorney.

On July 7, the day of Marilyn Sheppard's funeral, a newspaper story appeared in which Assistant County Attorney Mahon—later the chief prosecutor of Sheppard—sharply criticized the refusal of the Sheppard family to permit his immediate questioning. From there on headline stories repeatedly stressed Sheppard's lack of cooperation with the police and other officials. Under the headline "Testify Now In Death, Bay Doctor Is Ordered," one story described a visit by Coroner Gerber and four police officers to the hospital on July 8. When Sheppard insisted that his lawyer be present, the Coroner wrote out a subpoena and served it on him. Sheppard then agreed to submit to questioning without counsel and the subpoena was torn up. The officers questioned him for several hours. On July 9, Sheppard, at the request of the Coroner, re-enacted the tragedy at his home before the Coroner, police officers, and a group of newsmen, who apparently were invited by the Coroner. The home was locked so that Sheppard was obliged to wait outside until the Coroner arrived. Sheppard's performance was reported in detail by the news media along with photographs. The newspaper also played up Sheppard's refusal to take a lie detector test and "the protective ring" thrown up by his family. Front-page newspaper headlines announced on the same day that "Doctor Balks At Lie Test; Retells Story." A column opposite that story contained an "exclusive" interview with Sheppard headlined: " 'Loved My Wife, She Loved Me' Sheppard Tells News Reporter." The next day, another headline story disclosed that Sheppard had "again late yesterday refused to take a lie detector test" and quoted an Assistant County Attorney as saying that "at the end of a nine hour questioning of Dr. Sheppard, I felt he was now ruling [a test] out completely." But subsequent newspaper articles reported that the Coroner was still pushing Sheppard for a lie detector test. More stories appeared when Sheppard would not allow authorities to inject him with "truth serum."

On the 20th, the "editorial artillery" opened fire with a front-page charge that somebody is "getting away with murder." The editorial attributed the ineptness of the investigation to "friendships, relationships, hired lawyers, a husband who ought to have been subjected instantly to the same third-degree to which any other person under similar circumstances is subjected...." The following day, July 21, another page-one editorial was headed: "Why No Inquest? Do It Now, Dr. Gerber." The Coroner called an inquest the same day and subpoenaed Sheppard. It was staged the next day in a school gymnasium; the Coroner presided with the County Prosecutor as his advisor and two detectives as bailiffs. In the front of the room was a long table occupied by reporters, television and radio personnel, and broadcasting equipment. The hearing was broadcast with live microphones placed at the Coroner's seat and the witness stand. A swarm of reporters and photographers attended. Sheppard was brought into the room by police who searched him in full view of several hundred spectators. Sheppard's counsel were present during the three-day inquest but were not permitted to participate.

When Sheppard's chief counsel attempted to place some documents in the record, he was forcibly ejected from the room by the Coroner, who received cheers, hugs and kisses from ladies in the audience. Sheppard was questioned for five and one-half hours about his actions on the night of the murder, his married life, and a love affair with Susan Hayes. At the end of the hearing the Coroner announced that he "could" order Sheppard held for the grand jury, but did not do so.

Throughout this period the newspapers emphasized evidence that tended to incriminate Sheppard and pointed out discrepancies in his statements to authorities. At the same time Sheppard made many public statements to the press and wrote feature articles asserting his innocence. During the inquest on July 26, a headline in large type stated: "Kerr [Captain of the Cleveland Police] Urges Sheppard Arrest." In the story, Detective McArthur "disclosed that scientific tests at the Sheppard home have definitely established that the killer washed off a trail of blood from the murder bedroom to the downstairs section," a circumstance casting doubt on Sheppard's accounts of the murder. No such evidence was produced at trial. The newspapers also delved into Sheppard's personal life. Articles stressed his extramarital love affairs as a motive for the crime. The newspapers portrayed Sheppard as a Lothario, fully explored his relationship with Susan Hayes, and named a number of other women who were allegedly involved with him. The testimony at trial never showed that Sheppard had any illicit relationships besides the one with Susan Hayes.

On July 28, an editorial entitled "Why Don't Police Quiz Top Suspect" demanded that Sheppard be taken to police headquarters. It described him in the following language:

"Now proved under oath to be a liar, still free to go about his business, shielded by his family, protected by a smart lawyer who has made monkeys of the police and authorities, carrying a gun part of the time, left free to do whatever he pleases..."

A front-page editorial on July 30 asked: "Why Isn't Sam Sheppard in Jail?" It was later titled "Quit Stalling—Bring Him In." After calling Sheppard "the most unusual murder suspect ever seen around these parts" the article said that "[e]xcept for some superficial questioning during Coroner Sam Gerber's inquest he has been scot-free of any official grilling...." It asserted that he was "surrounded by an iron curtain of protection [and] concealment."

That night at 10 o'clock Sheppard was arrested at his father's home on a charge of murder. He was taken to the Bay Village City Hall where hundreds of people, newscasters, photographers and reporters were awaiting his arrival. He was immediately arraigned—having been denied a temporary delay to secure the presence of counsel—and bound over to the grand jury.

The publicity then grew in intensity until his indictment on August 17. Typical of the coverage during this period is a front-page interview entitled: "DR. SAM: 'I Wish There Was Something I Could Get Off My Chest—but There Isn't.'" Unfavorable publicity included items such as a cartoon of the body of a sphinx with Sheppard's head and the legend below: "'I Will Do Everything In My Power to Help Solve This Terrible Murder.'—Dr. Sam Sheppard." Headlines announced, inter alia, that: "Doctor Evidence is Ready for Jury," "Corrigan Tactics Stall Quizzing," "Sheppard 'Gay Set' Is Revealed By Houk," "Blood Is Found In Garage," "New Murder Evidence Is Found, Police Claim," "Dr. Sam Faces Quiz At Jail On Marilyn's Fear Of Him." On August 18, an article appeared under the headline "Dr. Sam Writes His Own Story." And reproduced across the entire front page was a portion of the typed statement signed by Sheppard: "I am not guilty of the murder of my wife Marilyn. How could I, who have been trained to help people and devoted my life to saving life, commit such a terrible and revolting crime?" We do not detail the coverage further. There are five volumes filled with similar clippings from each of the three Cleveland newspapers covering the period from the murder until Sheppard's conviction in December 1954. The record includes no excerpts from newscasts on radio and television but since space was reserved in the courtroom for these media we assume that their coverage was equally large.

With this background the case came on for trial two weeks before the November general election at which the chief prosecutor was a candidate for common pleas judge and the trial judge, Judge Blythin, was a candidate to succeed himself. Twenty-five days before the case was set, 75 veniremen were called as prospective jurors. All three Cleveland newspapers published the names and addresses of the veniremen. As a consequence, anonymous letters and telephone calls, as well as calls from friends, regarding the impending prosecution were received by all of the prospective jurors. The selection of the jury began on October 18, 1954.

The courtroom in which the trial was held measured 26 by 48 feet. A long temporary table was set up inside the bar, in back of the single counsel table. It ran the width of the courtroom, parallel to the bar railing, with one end less than three feet from the jury box. Approximately 20 representatives of newspapers and wire services were assigned seats at this table by the court. Behind the bar railing there were four rows of benches. These seats were likewise assigned by the court for the entire trial. The first row was occupied by representatives of television and radio stations, and the second and third rows by reporters from out-of-town newspapers and magazines. One side of the last row, which accommodated 14 people, was assigned to Sheppard's family and the other to Marilyn's. The public was permitted to fill vacancies in this row on special passes only. Representatives of the news media also used all the rooms on the courtroom floor, including the room where cases were ordinarily called and assigned for trial. Private telephone lines and telegraphic equipment were installed in these rooms so that reports from the trial could be speeded to the papers. Station WSRS was permitted to set up broadcasting facilities on the third floor of the courthouse next door to the jury room, where the jury rested during recesses in the trial and deliberated. Newscasts were made from this room throughout the trial, and while the jury reached its verdict.

On the sidewalk and steps in front of the courthouse, television and newsreel cameras were occasionally used to take motion pictures of the participants in the trial, including the jury and the judge. Indeed, one television broadcast carried a staged interview of the judge as he entered the courthouse. In the corridors outside the courtroom there was a host of photographers and television personnel with flash cameras, portable lights and motion picture cameras. This group photographed the prospective jurors during selection of the jury. After the trial opened, the witnesses, counsel, and jurors were photographed and televised whenever they entered or left the courtroom. Sheppard was brought to the courtroom about 10 minutes before each session began; he was surrounded by reporters and extensively photographed for the newspapers and television. A rule of court prohibited picture-taking in the courtroom during the actual sessions of the court, but no restraints were put on photographers during recesses, which were taken once each morning and afternoon, with a longer period for lunch.

All of these arrangements with the news media and their massive coverage of the trial continued during the entire nine weeks of the trial. The courtroom remained crowded to capacity with representatives of news media. Their movement in and out of the courtroom often caused so much confusion that, despite the loud-speaker system installed in the courtroom, it was difficult for the witnesses and counsel to be heard. Furthermore, the reporters clustered within the bar of the small courtroom made confidential talk among Sheppard and his counsel almost impossible during the proceedings. They frequently had to leave the courtroom to obtain privacy. And many times when counsel wished to raise a point with the judge out of the hearing of the jury it was necessary to move to the judge's chambers. Even then, news media representatives so packed the judge's anteroom that counsel could hardly return from the chambers to the courtroom. The reporters vied with each other to find out what counsel and the judge had discussed, and often these matters later appeared in newspapers accessible to the jury.

The daily record of the proceedings was made available to the newspapers and the testimony of each witness was printed verbatim in the local editions, along with objections of counsel, and rulings by the judge. Pictures of Sheppard, the judge, counsel, pertinent witnesses, and the jury often accompanied the daily newspaper and television accounts. At times the newspapers published photographs of exhibits introduced at the trial, and the rooms of Sheppard's house were featured along with relevant testimony.

The jurors themselves were constantly exposed to the news media. Every juror, except one, testified at voir dire to reading about the case in the Cleveland papers or to having heard broadcasts about it. Seven of the 12 jurors who rendered the verdict had one or more Cleveland papers delivered in their home; the remaining jurors were not interrogated on the point. Nor were there questions as to radios or television sets in the jurors' homes, but we must assume that most of them owned such conveniences. As the selection of the jury progressed, individual pictures of prospective members appeared daily. During the trial, pictures of the jury appeared over 40 times in the Cleveland papers alone. The Court permitted photographers to take pictures of the jury in the box, and individual pictures of the members in the jury room. One newspaper ran pictures of the jurors at the Sheppard home when they went there to view the scene of the murder. Another paper featured the home life of an alternate juror. The day before the verdict was rendered—while the jurors were at lunch and sequestered by two bailiffs—the jury was separated into two groups to pose for photographs which appeared in the newspapers.

While the Court noted the significance of First Amendment interests, it emphasized that freedom of discussion must be coordinated with the fair and orderly administration of justice. Paramount in the weighing of these interests was ensuring the resolution of cases based solely on evidence adduced in open court. In striking a proper balance between competing constitutional concerns, the Court suggested several avenues of recourse. They included rules governing the media's behavior and numbers in the courtroom, judge-directed voir dire to ensure that juror impartiality had not been compromised by pretrial publicity, sequestration to maintain such objectivity, change of venue or postponement, and orders prohibiting parties, witnesses, police, judicial employees, and counsel from divulging information that might be prejudicial. The Court also observed that "there is nothing that proscribes the press from reporting events that transpire in the courtroom." Not surprisingly, given the Court's emphasis upon the trial judge's duty to take steps necessary to protect the adjudicative process from prejudice, restraining orders barring the media from publishing certain information became increasingly common. Eventually, such orders became subject to the strong presumption against a prior restraint's constitutionality and to the requirement that they could not be entered unless alternatives less burdensome to First Amendment interests were exhausted.

II. NONCONSTITUTIONAL CONCERNS

A policy interest need not be of a constitutional order to prevail over the First Amendment. Defamation, privacy, obscenity, and copyright laws operate either because the expression they regulate is constitutionally unprotected or because the harm they address is considered significant enough to require control of speech and press.

A. DEFAMATION

Until fairly recently, defamation was a category of expression that, like obscenity, was considered to be outside the First Amendment's protective ambit. Defamation comprises libel and slander, which traditionally implicated injury to reputation respectively by the written and the spoken word. Given the merged characteristics of modern media, and unless contrary to peculiar circumstantial requirements, simplicity and accuracy are served by using the term defamation when considering harm to reputational interests caused by the press.

In *Beauharnais v. Illinois*, the Court upheld a criminal statute designed to prohibit and punish group libel. Essentially, the state law criminalized any publication portraying "depravity, criminality, unchastity, or lack of virtue of a class of citizens, of any race, color, creed or religion, [subjecting a group] to contempt, derision, or obloquy or which is productive of breach of the peace or of riots." Pursuant to that statute, a person disseminating leaflets warning of "the need to prevent the mongrelization of the white race" was convicted. (*See* Peoples Exhibit 3.)

In affirming the conviction, the Court determined that "[l]ibelous utterances [are not] within the area of constitutionally protected speech" and thus may be proscribed. Only if regulation represented a deliberate and irrational restraint unrelated to the peace and well-being of the community would the Court have found a constitutional issue. The Court in *Beauharnais* thus recognized that speech promoting racial tension and strife is subject to official control. Because the decision never has been expressly overruled, it conceivably might still be relevant for contemporary institutional policy-making that attempts to factor racial and religious sensitivity into standards of acceptable conduct and discourse. Justice Black, in dissent, identified significant risks that inhere in such a regulatory approach. Black not only found the group libel statute at direct odds with the terms of the First Amendment but noted the vulnerability created for the media in general and the special danger presented to minority interests. When used by the majority against a minority, such a regulation has particularly oppressive potential. Thus Black observed that if "there be any minority groups who hail this holding as their victory, they might consider the possible relevancy of this ancient remark: 'Another such victory and I am undone.' "

Black's worries became fully realized a decade later when the police commissioner of Montgomery, Alabama, sued civil-rights activists and the *New York Times* in response to an advertisement criticizing the way

PRESERVE and PROTECT WHITE NEIGHBORHOODS!

FROM THE CONSTANT AND CONTINUOUS INVASION, HARASSMENT AND ENCROACHMENT BY THE NEGROES

(WE WANT TWO MILLION SIGNATURES OF WHITE MEN AND WOMEN)

PETITION
To The Honorable Martin H. Kennelly
and City Council of the City of Chicago.

WHEREAS, the white population of the City of Chicago, particularly on the South Side of said city, are seething, nervous and agitated because of the constant and continuous invasion, harassment and encroachment by the Negroes upon them, their property and neighborhoods and —

WHEREAS, there have been disastrous incidents within the past year, all of which are fraught with grave consequences and great danger to the Peace and Security of the people, and

WHEREAS, there is great danger to the Government from communism which is rife among the Negroes, and
WHEREAS, we are not against the negro; we are for the white people and the white people are entitled to protection: —

We, the undersigned white citizens of the City of Chicago and the State of Illinois, hereby petition the Honorable Martin H. Kennelly, Mayor of the City of Chicago and the Alderman of the City of Chicago, to halt the further encroachment, harassment and invasion of white people, their property, neighborhoods and persons, by the Negro — through the exercise of the Police Power; of the Office of the Mayor of the City of Chicago, and the City Council.

WANTED

ONE MILLION SELF RESPECTING WHITE PEOPLE IN CHICAGO TO UNITE UNDER THE BANNER OF THE WHITE CIRCLE LEAGUE OF AMERICA to oppose the National Campaign now on and supported by TRUMAN'S INFAMOUS CIVIL RIGHTS PROGRAM and many Pro Negro Organizations to amalgamate the black and white races with the object of mongrelizing the white race!

THE WHITE CIRCLE LEAGUE OF AMERICA is the only articulate white voice in America being raised in protest against negro aggressions and infiltrations into all white neighborhoods. The white people of Chicago MUST take advantage of this opportunity to become UNITED. If persuasion and the need to prevent the white race from becoming mongrehized by the negro will not unite us, then the aggressions . . . rapes, robberies, knives, guns and marijuana of the negro, SURELY WILL.

The Negro has many national organizations working to push him into the midst of the white people on many fronts. The white race does not have a single organization to work on a NATIONAL SCALE to make its wishes articulate and to assert its natural rights to self-preservation. THE WHITE CIRCLE LEAGUE OF AMERICA proposes to do the job.
WE ARE NOT AGAINST THE NEGRO! WE ARE FOR THE WHITE PEOPLE!
We must awaken and protect our white families and neighborhoods before it is too late. Let us work unceasingly to conserve the white man's dignity and rights in America.

THE WHITE CIRCLE LEAGUE OF AMERICA, INC. - Joseph Beauharnais, Pres. - FR 2-8633, Suite 808, 82 W. Washington St. VOLUNTEERS NEEDED TO GET 25 SIGNATURES ON PETITION! COME TO HEADQUARTERS!

I wish to be enrolled as a member in THE WHITE CIRCLE LEAGUE OF AMERICA and I will do my best to secure ten (10) or more members.

THE FIRST LOYALTY OF EVERY WHITE PERSON IS TO HIS RACE. ALL THE COMBINED PRO NEGRO FORCES HAVE HURLED THEIR ULTIMATUM INTO THE FACES OF THE WHITE PEOPLE. WE ACCEPT THEIR CHALLENGE.

THEY CANNOT WIN!

IT WILL BE EASIER TO REVERSE THE CURRENT OF THE ATLANTIC OCEAN THAN TO DEGRADE THE WHITE RACE AND ITS NATURAL LAWS BY FORCED MONGRELIZATION.

THE HOUR HAS STRUCK FOR ALL NORMAL WHITE PEOPLE TO STAND UP AND FIGHT FOR OUR RIGHTS TO LIFE, LIBERTY AND THE PURSUIT OF HAPPINESS.

JOSEPH BEAUHARNAIS.

APPLICATION FOR 1950 MEMBERSHIP
THE WHITE CIRCLE LEAGUE OF AMERICA, INC.
(Not For Profit)

Mail To —

THE WHITE CIRCLE LEAGUE OF AMERICA Inc.
82 W. Washington St.
Chicago 2, Illinois
Tel. FR 2-8533

DATE_____19___

☐ Membership _____$1.00
☐ Subscription to Monthly Magazine (WHITE CIRCLE NEWS) per year _____$3.00
☐ Voluntary Contribution $_____
☐ I can volunteer some of my time to aid the WHITE CIRCLE in getting under way.

(SIGNED) (Print Name) _____
NAME _____
ADDRESS _____ PHONE_____
CITY _____ STATE_____
(Note: Tear Off and Mail to Headquarters with Your Remittance)

police handled a civil-rights demonstration ("Heed Their Rising Voices"). The advertisement did not mention the plaintiff by name. It also contained some minor inaccuracies, although none pertained to the plaintiff's character. Nonetheless, a state court awarded half a million dollars in damages pursuant to a jury's finding that the advertisement was false and pertained to the plaintiff. The damage amount was based not upon any proof of actual loss but upon the state's doctrine of presumed damages.

In *New York Times Co. v. Sullivan*, the Supreme Court reversed the Alabama decision and significantly recontoured defamation law. For the first time, the Court declared that even defamatory expression implicated First Amendment interests. Regulation of it, moreover, was to be measured against "a profound national commitment to the principle that debate on public issues should be uninhibited, robust, and wide-open, and that it may well include vehement, caustic, and sometimes unpleasantly sharp attacks on government and public officials." Given the competing concerns presented, namely the reputational interests of public officials and expressive freedom, the Court recognized a need to create breathing space that would countenance even vilification and falsehood. Such a result reflects investment in the theory that expression relating to self-government deserves maximum constitutional security.

The general proposition that freedom of expression upon public questions is secured by the First Amendment has long been settled by our decisions. The constitutional safeguard, we have said, "was fashioned to assure unfettered interchange of ideas for the bringing about of political and social changes desired by the people." ... "The maintenance of the opportunity for free political discussion to the end that government may be responsive to the will of the people and that changes may be obtained by lawful means, and opportunity essential to the security of the Republic, is a fundamental principle of our constitutional system." ... "[I]t is a prized American privilege to speak one's mind, although not always with perfect good taste, on all public institutions," *Bridges v. California*, 314 U.S. 252, 270, and this opportunity is to be afforded for "vigorous advocacy" no less than "abstract discussion." ...

The First Amendment, said Judge Learned Hand, "presupposes that right conclusions are more likely to be gathered out of a multitude of tongues, than through any kind of authoritative selection. To many this is, and always will be, folly; but we have staked upon it our all." *United States v. Associated Press*, 52 F. Supp. 362, 372 (D.C.S.D.N.Y. 1943). Mr. Justice Brandeis, in his concurring opinion in *Whitney v. California*, 274 U.S. 357, 375–376, gave the principle its classic formulation:

> "Those who won our independence believe ... that public discussion is a political duty; and that this should be a fundamental principle of the American government. They recognized the risks to which all human institutions are subject. But they knew that order cannot be secured merely through fear of punishment for its infraction; that it is hazardous to discourage thought, hope and

Heed Their Rising Voices

"The growing movement of peaceful mass demonstrations by Negroes is something new in the South, something understandable....

Let Congress heed their rising voices,

for they will be heard."

—*New York Times* editorial
Saturday, March 19, 1960

As the whole world knows by now, thousands of Southern Negro students are engaged in wide-spread non-violent demonstrations in positive affirmation of the right to live in human dignity as guaranteed by the U. S. Constitution and the Bill of Rights. In their efforts to uphold these guarantees, they are being met by an unprecedented wave of terror by those who would deny and negate that document which the whole world looks upon as setting the pattern for modern freedom....

In Orangeburg, South Carolina, when 400 students peacefully sought to buy doughnuts and coffee at lunch counters in the business district, they were forcibly ejected, tear-gassed, soaked to the skin in freezing weather with fire hoses, arrested en masse and herded into an open barbed-wire stockade to stand for hours in the bitter cold.

In Montgomery, Alabama, after students sang "My Country, 'Tis of Thee" on the State Capitol steps, their leaders were expelled from school, and truck-loads of police armed with shotguns and tear-gas ringed the Alabama State College Campus. When the entire student body protested to state authorities by refusing to re-register, their dining hall was pad-locked in an attempt to starve them into submission.

In Tallahassee, Atlanta, Nashville, Savannah, Greensboro, Memphis, Richmond, Charlotte, and a host of other cities in the South, young American teen-agers, in face of the entire weight of official state appa-ratus and police power, have boldly stepped forth as protagonists of democracy. Their courage and amaz-ing restraint have inspired millions and given a new dignity to the cause of freedom.

Small wonder that the Southern violators of the Constitution fear this new, non-violent brand of freedom fighter ... even as they fear the upwelling right-to-vote movement. Small wonder that they are determined to destroy the one man who, more than any other, symbolizes the new spirit now sweeping the South—the Rev. Dr. Martin Luther King, Jr., world-famous leader of the Montgomery Bus Protest. For it is his doctrine of non-violence which has inspired and guided the students in their widening wave of sit-ins; and it is this same Dr. King who founded and is president of the Southern Christian Leadership Con-ference—the organization which is spearheading the surging right-to-vote movement. Under Dr. King's direction the Leadership Conference conducts Stu-dent Workshops and Seminars in the philosophy and technique of non-violent resistance.

Again and again the Southern violators have answered Dr. King's peaceful protests with intimida-tion and violence. They have bombed his home almost killing his wife and child. They have assaulted his person. They have arrested him seven times—for "speeding," "loitering" and similar "offenses." And now they have charged him with "perjury"—a *felony* under which they could imprison him for *ten years*. Obviously, their real purpose is to remove him physi-cally as the leader to whom the students and millions of others—look for guidance and support, and thereby to intimidate *all* leaders who may rise in the South. Their strategy is to behead this affirmative movement, and thus to demoralize Negro Americans and weaken their will to struggle. The defense of Martin Luther King, spiritual leader of the student sit-in movement, clearly, therefore, *is* an integral part of the total struggle for freedom in the South.

Decent-minded Americans cannot help but applaud the creative daring of the students and the quiet heroism of Dr. King. But this is one of those moments in the stormy history of Freedom when men and women of good will must do more than applaud the rising-to-glory of others. The America whose good name hangs in the balance before a watchful world, the America whose heritage of Liberty these Southern Upholders of the Constitution are defending, is *our* America as well as theirs ...

We must heed their rising voices—yes—but we must add our own.

We must extend ourselves above and beyond moral support and render the material help so urgently needed by those who are taking the risks, facing jail, and even death in a glorious re-affirmation of our Constitution and its Bill of Rights.

We urge you to join hands with our fellow Amer-icans in the South by supporting, with your dollars, this Combined Appeal for all three needs—the defense of Martin Luther King—the support of the embattled students—and the struggle for the right-to-vote.

Your Help Is Urgently Needed . . . NOW!!

We in the south who are struggling daily for dignity and freedom warmly endorse this appeal

COMMITTEE TO DEFEND MARTIN LUTHER KING AND THE STRUGGLE FOR FREEDOM IN THE SOUTH
312 West 125th Street, New York 27, N. Y. UNiversity 6-1700

Chairmen: A. Philip Randolph, Dr. Gardner C. Taylor; Chairmen of Cultural Division: Harry Belafonte, Sidney Poitier; Treasurer: Nat King Cole; Executive Director: Bayard Rustin; Chairmen of Church Division: Father George B. Ford, Rev. Harry Emerson Fosdick, Rev. Thomas Kilgore, Jr., Rabbi Edward E. Klein; Chairmen of Labor Division: Morris Iushewitz

Please mail this coupon TODAY!

- -

Committee To Defend Martin Luther King
and
The Struggle For Freedom In The South
312 West 125th Street, New York 27, N. Y.
UNiversity 6-1700

I am enclosing my contribution of $............
for the work of the Committee.

Name ....
(PLEASE PRINT)

Address ....

City .... Zone ...... State ......

[ ] I want to help   [ ] Please send further information

Please make checks payable to:
Committee To Defend Martin Luther King

imagination; that fear breeds repression; that repression breeds hate; that hate menaces stable government; that the path of safety lies in the opportunity to discuss freely supposed grievances and proposed remedies; and that the fitting remedy for evil counsels is good ones. Believing in the power of reason as applied through public discussion, they eschewed silence coerced by law—the argument of force in its worst form. Recognizing the occasional tyrannies of governing majorities, they amended the Constitution so that free speech and assembly should be guaranteed."

Thus we consider this case against the background of a profound national commitment to the principle that debate on public issues should be uninhibited, robust, and wide-open, and that it may well include vehement, caustic, and sometimes unpleasantly sharp attacks on government and public officials.

The present advertisement, as an expression of grievance and protest on one of the major public issues of our time, would seem clearly to qualify for the constitutional protection. The question is whether it forfeits that protection by the falsity of some of its factual statements and by its alleged defamation of respondent.

Authoritative interpretations of the First Amendment guarantees have consistently refused to recognize an exception for any test of truth—whether administered by judges, juries, or administrative officials—and especially one that puts the burden of proving truth on the speaker. The constitutional protection does not turn upon "the truth, popularity, or social utility of the ideas and beliefs which are offered." As Madison said, "Some degree of abuse is inseparable from the proper use of every thing; and in no instance is this more true than in that of the press." In *Cantwell v. Connecticut*, 310 U.S. 296, 310, the Court declared:

> "In the realm of religious faith, and in that of political belief, sharp differences arise. In both fields the tenets of one man may seem the rankest error to his neighbor. To persuade others to his own point of view, the pleader, as we know, at times, resorts to exaggeration, to vilification of men who have been, or are, prominent in church or state, and even to false statement. But the people of this nation have ordained in the light of history, that, in spite of the probability of excesses and abuses, these liberties are, in the long view, essential to enlightened opinion and right conduct on the part of the citizens of a democracy."

Th[e] erroneous statement is inevitable in free debate, and . . . must be protected if the freedoms of expression are to have the "breathing space" that they "need . . . to survive." . . . Judge Edgerton spoke for a unanimous court which affirmed the dismissal of a Congressman's libel suit based upon a newspaper article charging him with anti-Semitism in opposing a judicial appointment. He said:

> "Cases which impose liability for erroneous reports of the political conduct of officials reflect the obsolete doctrine that the governed must not criticize their governors. . . . The interest of the public here outweighs the interest of appellant or any other individual. The protection of the public requires not merely discussion, but information. Political conduct and views which some respectable people approve, and others condemn, are constantly imputed to Congressmen. Errors of fact, particularly in regard to a man's mental states and processes, are inevitable. . . . Whatever is added to the field of libel is taken from the field of free debate."

Injury to official reputation affords no more warrant for repressing speech that would otherwise be free than does factual error. Where judicial officers are involved, this Court has held that concern for the dignity and reputation of the courts does not justify the punishment as criminal contempt of criticism of the judge or his decision. This is true even though the utterance contains "half-truths" and "misinformation." Such repression can be justified, if at all, only by a clear and present danger of the obstruction of justice. If judges are to be treated as "men of fortitude, able to thrive in a hardy climate," surely the same must be true of other government officials, such as elected city commissioners. Criticism of their official conduct does not lose its constitutional protection merely because it is effective criticism and hence diminishes their official reputations.

A rule compelling the critic of official conduct to guarantee the truth of all his factual assertions—and to do so on pain of libel judgments virtually unlimited in amount—leads to a comparable "self-censorship." Allowance of the defense of truth, with the burden of proving it on the defendant, does not mean that only false speech will be deterred. Even courts accepting this defense as an adequate safeguard have recognized the difficulties of adducing legal proofs that the alleged libel was true in all its factual particulars.... Under such a rule, would-be critics of official conduct may be deterred from voicing their criticism, even though it is believed to be true and even though it is in fact true, because of doubt whether it can be proved in court or fear of the expense of having to do so. They tend to make only statements which "steer far wider of the unlawful zone." *Speiser v. Randall,* 357 U.S., at 526. The rule thus dampens the vigor and limits the variety of public debate. It is inconsistent with the First and Fourteenth Amendments.

The constitutional guarantees require, we think, a federal rule that prohibits a public official from recovering damages for a defamatory falsehood relating to his official conduct unless he proves that the statement was made with "actual malice"—that is, with knowledge that it was false or with reckless disregard of whether it was false or not.

Prior to the *New York Times* decision, the primary defense against a defamation claim was truth. A standard that afforded broader latitude for erroneous criticism of public officials thus represented a significant accommodation of First Amendment interests. Liability does not exist, as the Court observed, unless a defamatory statement directly relates to a public official, who then has the burden of proving it was false and made with "actual malice." The "actual malice" standard operates as a term of art rather than in a literal sense. Although translating for general purposes into spite or ill will, actual malice for purposes of a defamation action means "knowledge that [the statement] was false or . . . reckless disregard of whether it was false or not." The resultant privilege is analogous to the immunity afforded a public official when sued for defamation. Statements by such persons are absolutely privileged insofar as they are made within the scope of their official duties. As subsequent application of the *New York Times* standard has revealed, liability cannot be based upon a showing of negligence or pursuant to criteria of strict liability.

The Court has observed that although the notion of reckless disregard "cannot be fully encompassed in one infallible definition, ... we have made clear that the defendant must have made the false publication with a 'high degree of awareness of probable falsity, ...' or must have 'entertained serious doubts as to the truth of his publication.' " The Court emphasized in *Harte-Hanks Communications, Inc. v. Connaughton* that proof of actual malice must be established by "clear and convincing" evidence. It further noted that the clear and convincing standard operates independently to guide appellate review which is limited, however, to examination of evidence that was undisputed or not rejected by the trier of fact.

The *New York Times* decision qualified the actionability of defamatory expression concerning public officials. Litigation immediately focused upon pertinent terms, such as "official conduct" and "public official" itself, which the Court did not fully define. Allegations of criminality, regardless of whether they directly relate to service in office, have been protected by the actual malice standard. It would appear, therefore, that the relevant scope of "official conduct" is to be regarded broadly rather than narrowly to include any comment pertaining to official qualification. The term "public official" so far has included an array of persons possessing the common trait of having significant responsibility or discretion for the transaction of official affairs. It has been read to include candidates for public office. The term also applies retroactively to protect comments upon past official action by a former public servant. Beyond litigation concerning these terminological issues, the *New York Times* decision has tended to minimize disputes over material facts and has facilitated resolution pursuant to summary judgment motions.

For a decade after the *New York Times* decision, the Court worked upon expanding the actual malice test beyond public officials. Chief Justice Warren, noting that speech concerning self-government transcends the acts of public officials, initially advanced the notion that certain roles and prominence should be regarded as akin to official status. In *Curtis Publishing Co. v. Butts*, Warren thus introduced the concept of public figures, whom he defined as persons "intimately involved in the resolution of important public questions or [who], by reason of their fame, shape events in areas of concern to society at large." Thereafter a plurality in *Rosenbloom v. Metromedia, Inc.*, supported a further extension of theory emphasizing the value of speech pertaining to self-government. It thus declared that the actual malice standard should govern any allegedly defamatory statement concerning a matter of public interest. Justice Black's insistence upon an unconditional liberty of expressive freedom ironically helped preclude emergence of a standard protecting "statements concerning matter[s] of general or public interest."

The Court eventually abandoned development of a public interest standard on grounds that it unreasonably interfered with legitimate state interests in protecting private reputation. It also expressed concern about committing to judges responsibility to decide on an ad hoc basis what does and does not implicate the general or public interest. Although the Court has expressed legitimate concern about the manipulability of such terms and their susceptibility to subjective delineation, it has not been hesitant to draw lines in other First Amendment areas possessing equally treacherous potential. Incongruously, Justice Powell, who rejected the *Metromedia* standard, later reintroduced the concept of public concern as a standard for determining the availability of damages.

In *Gertz v. Robert Welch, Inc.*, the Court limited the actual malice standard to defamation actions brought by public officials and figures. The relevant inquiry for determining the standard's operability is the status of the plaintiff rather than the nature of the controversy. Arguably, a focus upon the qualitative aspects of the expression instead of the defendant's denomination would be more pertinent to the predicate of "the profound national commitment to . . . uninhibited, robust and wide-open debate" on public issues set forth in the *New York Times* decision. Instead, the Court broadened the actual malice standard less expansively to include public figures but not private persons.

Some tension necessarily exists between the need for vigorous and uninhibited press and the legitimate interest in redressing wrongful injury. As Mr. Justice Harlan stated, "some antithesis between freedom of speech and press and libel actions persists, for libel remains premised on the content of speech and limits the freedom of the publisher to express certain sentiments, at least without guaranteeing legal proof of their substantial accuracy." In our continuing effort to define the proper accommodation between these competing concerns, we have been especially anxious to assure to the freedoms of speech and press that "breathing space" essential to their fruitful exercise. . . . To that end this Court has extended a measure of strategic protection to defamatory falsehood.

The *New York Times* standard defines the level of constitutional protection appropriate to the context of defamation of a public person. Those who, by reason of the notoriety of their achievements or the vigor and success with which they seek the public's attention, are properly classed as public figures and those who hold governmental office may recover for injury to reputation only on clear and convincing proof that the defamatory falsehood was made with knowledge of its falsity or with reckless disregard for the truth. This standard administers an extremely powerful antidote to the inducement to media self-censorship of the common-law rule of strict liability for libel and slander. And it exacts a correspondingly high price from the victims of defamatory falsehood. Plainly many deserving plaintiffs, including some intentionally subjected to injury, will be unable to surmount the barrier of the *New York Times* test. Despite this substantial abridgment of the state law right to compensation for wrongful hurt to one's reputation, the Court has concluded that the protection of the *New York Times* privilege should be available to publishers and broadcasters of defamatory falsehood concerning public officials and public figures. We think that these decisions are correct, but we do not find their holdings justified solely by reference to the interest of the press and broadcast media in immunity from liability. Rather, we believe that the *New York Times* rule states an accommodation between this concern and the limited state interest present in the context of libel actions brought by public persons. For the reasons stated below, we conclude that the state interest in compensating injury to the reputation of private individuals requires that a different rule should obtain with respect to them....

[W]e have no difficulty in distinguishing among defamation plaintiffs. The first remedy of any victim of defamation is self-help—using available opportunities to contradict the lie or correct the error and thereby to minimize its adverse impact on reputation. Public officials and public figures usually enjoy significantly greater access to the channels of effective communication and hence have a more realistic opportunity to counteract false statements than private individuals normally enjoy. Private individuals are therefore more vulnerable to injury, and the state interest in protecting them is correspondingly greater.

More important than the likelihood that private individuals will lack effective opportunities for rebuttal, there is a compelling normative consideration underlying the distinction between public and private defamation plaintiffs. An individual who decides to seek governmental office must accept certain necessary consequences of that involvement in public affairs. He runs the risk of closer public scrutiny than might otherwise be the case. And society's interest in the officers of government is not strictly limited to the formal discharge of official duties. As the Court pointed out in *Garrison v. Louisiana*, 379 U.S., at 77, the public's interest extends to "anything which might touch on an official's fitness for office.... Few personal attributes are more germane to fitness for office than dishonesty, malfeasance, or improper motivation, even though these characteristics may also affect the official's private character."

Those classed as public figures stand in a similar position. Hypothetically, it may be possible for someone to become a public figure through no purposeful action of his own, but the instances of truly involuntary public figures must be exceedingly rare. For the most part those who attain this status have assumed roles of especial prominence in the affairs of society. Some occupy positions of such persuasive power and influence that they are deemed public figures for all purposes. More commonly, those classed as public figures have thrust themselves to the forefront of particular public controversies in order to influence the resolution of the issues involved. In either event, they invite attention and comment.

Even if the foregoing generalities do not obtain in every instance, the communications media are entitled to act on the assumption that public officials and public figures have voluntarily exposed themselves to increased risk of injury from defamatory falsehood concerning them. No such assumption is justified with respect to a private individual. He has not accepted public office or assumed an "influential role in ordering society."... He has relinquished no part of his interest in the protection of his own good name, and consequently he has a more compelling call on the courts for redress of injury inflicted by defamatory false-hood. Thus, private individuals are not only more vulnerable to injury than public officials and public figures; they are also more deserving of recovery.

For these reasons we conclude that the States should retain substantial latitude in their efforts to enforce a legal remedy for defamatory falsehood injurious to the reputation of a private individual. The extension of the *New York Times* test proposed by the *Rosenbloom* plurality would abridge this legitimate state interest to a degree that we find unacceptable. And it would occasion the additional difficulty of forcing state and federal judges to decide on an ad hoc basis which publications address issues of "general or public interest" and which do not—to determine, in the words of Mr. Justice Marshall, "what information is relevant to self-government." *Rosenbloom v. Metromedia, Inc.*, 403 U.S., at 79. We doubt the wisdom of committing this task to the conscience of judges. Nor does the Constitution require us to draw so thin a line between the drastic alternatives of the *New York Times* privilege and the common law of strict liability for defam-atory error. The "public or general interest" test for determining the applicability of the *New York Times* standard to private defamation actions inadequately serves both of the competing values at stake. On the one hand, a private individual whose reputation is injured by defamatory falsehood that does concern an issue of public or general interest has no recourse unless he can meet the rigorous requirements of *New York Times*. This is true despite the factors that distinguish the state interest in compensating private individuals from the analogous interest involved in the context of public persons. On the other hand, a publisher or broadcaster of a defamatory error which a court deems unrelated to an issue of public or general interest may be held liable in damages even if it took every reasonable precaution to ensure the accuracy of its assertions. And liability may far exceed compensation for any actual injury to the plaintiff, for the jury may be permitted to presume damages without proof of loss and even to award punitive damages.

The Court in *Gertz* made clear that public figure status could result not just from widespread fame but from injection of oneself into a particular public controversy for purposes of influencing the outcome. Diminished protection for public figures was justified on grounds that they invited public comment and commanded greater access to the me-dia. An arguable counterpoint, however, may be that any such advantage is offset by a greater potential for reputation damage or loss. The ra-tionale also invites criticism along the lines expressed by Justice Brennan in dissent, that no evidence supports the notion of disparate access. A competitive medium actually may be quick to identify flaws in a rival's account of events.

Given the criteria for a public figure, it may have been reasonable for the Court to determine that Gertz fit them. He was an attorney who had brought a wrongful-death action on behalf of the family of a young man shot by a police officer. Gertz had been described in a publication of the

John Birch Society as the "architect [of a] communist frame-up," a "Communist-fronter," and possessor of a criminal record. The Court determined that he had not advanced himself into the public eye beyond serving as an attorney and, although also active in community affairs, was not a general or limited public figure in the context of the case. Conceivably, as a member of various government commissions and boards and as an officer of the court, Gertz also could have been denominated a public official. Such a determination, however, would have removed an entire profession from the normal protection of defamation laws. In Gertz's case, moreover, the falsehoods did not pertain to his official extralegal positions.

Having determined that Gertz's status was that of a private person, the Court refused to extend the actual malice standard to that category of plaintiffs. Rather, it concluded that "so long as they do not impose liability without fault, the States may define for themselves the appropriate standard of liability for a publisher or broadcaster of defamatory falsehood injurious to a private individual." The Court thus did not announce a uniform standard for scienter that must be established in a defamation action by a private person. Provided that strict liability is not the operative criterion, states have latitude to choose the relevant standard. As a consequence, the law among the states varies from actual malice to negligence, sometimes coupled with the public interest standard rejected as a constitutional requirement in *Gertz*. The consequent disparity of standards for liability may be of special concern to any medium disseminating information across state lines, including broadcasters whose signals may be picked up by satellite or cable and carried outside their immediate markets.

Actual malice also remains pertinent in defamation actions brought by private persons insofar as punitive or presumed damages are sought. Recoverable damages otherwise are limited to "actual damages," which the Court depicted as "not only out-of-pocket loss [but]...impairment of reputation and standing in the community, personal humiliation, and mental anguish and suffering." Such a rule appears to have been designed to protect the media from the prospect of bankrupting judgments but has elicited criticism for its potential to convert defamation into an action for mental distress.

Concern that the concept of damages delineated by *Gertz* might invite claims for mere emotional distress may have abated, given the decision in *Hustler Magazine v. Falwell*. The Court determined "that public figures and public officials may not recover for the tort of intentional infliction of emotional distress by reason of publication such as the one at issue without showing in addition that the publication contains a false statement of fact which was made with 'actual malice.'" At issue was a characterization of the plaintiff, a well-known evangelist, in a parody of liquor advertisements in which celebrities describe their "first time." The mock advertisement, accompanied by a disclaimer and notice not to take it seriously, featured an interview in which "he states that his 'first time' was during a drunken incestuous rendezvous with his mother in an outhouse." Given its sense that the law does not generally favor the tort of intentional distress, the Court found that the operation of such claims presented unacceptable risks to First Amendment interests. The consequences were considered particularly undesirable "in the world of debate about public affairs, [where] many things are done with motives that are less admirable and protected by the First Amendment." Voicing its concern with the risks that otherwise would be presented to satire, parody, and other well-established forms of social criticism, the Court resolved that the Constitution prohibits reference to bad motive in charting the perimeters of debate about public officials and public figures. The decision, however, did not discuss whether the interests underlying the disfavored tort would be more competitive against First Amendment concerns minus the presence of public interest.

Justice White criticized the *Gertz* decision for reasons that were polar opposites to concerns with the dangerous potential of an emotional distress claim. From his perspective, the modern press was vigorous and robust enough to accept responsibility for defamation of private citizens even on terms of strict liability. Protection of the media from chilling libel judgments, in White's view, was facilitated satisfactorily by the Court's restrictions on punitive and presumed damages. Given Justice Brennan's competing criticism that the decision promotes self-censorship on matters of public interest concerning persons not clearly within the public official category, the *Gertz* decision has been denounced on grounds both that it is overly sympathetic and that it is too insensitive to First Amendment needs.

If the Court, by adopting a public figure criterion, had sought to avoid the fine and potentially subjective exercises that made the public interest standard unacceptable, it soon became evident that the definition of a public figure would be an equally treacherous process. In *Time, Inc. v. Firestone*, the Court applied the public figure test in a narrow fashion. The plaintiff was not held to the actual malice standard governing a public figure, despite being a prominent Palm Beach socialite, employing a press agent, maintaining a news-clipping service, and conducting news conferences in the course of a divorce proceeding that was the subject of the defamatory article. The magazine had erred by stating that a divorce was granted on grounds of extreme cruelty and adultery, when in fact the full basis had not been set forth explicitly in the judge's order. The Court found that the plaintiff did not have special prominence in the resolution of public questions and had not voluntarily injected herself into "the forefront of any particular public controversy in order to influence the resolution of the issues involved in it." It also emphasized that the plaintiff, to obtain a divorce, had no choice but to avail herself of a public process.

The Court discounted the significance of the plaintiff's press conferences pursuant to its sense that they were not calculated to influence the outcome of the legal dispute. Such a characterization may be criticized as too narrow, legalistic, and perhaps reflective of an instinctual rather than a well-reasoned reaction to the subject matter and focus of the article. It arguably disregards or discounts acts that may have been designed to influence perceptions in the court of public opinion. The observation that a divorce proceeding was not the type of public controversy meriting special constitutional attention may reveal precisely the type of subjectivism that worried the Court when it chose governing standards in *Gertz*. At minimum, the result demonstrates the divergence of outcomes possible pursuant to public figure or public interest criteria.

Further limiting the definition of a public figure was the Court's determination in *Wolston v. Reader's Digest Association* that characterization of the plaintiff as a Soviet agent was not protected by the actual malice standard. Sixteen years prior to publication of the actionable statement, the plaintiff had failed to respond to a grand jury subpoena, claiming illness, and had been cited for contempt. Although his refusal to appear had been extensively reported at the time, the plaintiff since had not been in the public eye. Thus the Court concluded that failure to respond to the subpoena could not represent a voluntary injection of oneself into a controversy over foreign espionage unless it was calculated to protest the investigation and influence public opinion. The *Wolston* decision reiterated the principle set forth in *Firestone* that qualification as a public figure requires affirmative entry into a public controversy with intent to shape public sentiment on a precise issue. Status as a limited public figure in one context will not suffice to establish such standing in an unrelated setting. As the Court has noted, moreover, the category of involuntary figures is an extremely limited one. The concept in fact has yet to be fleshed out in a meaningful way. Nor is it a likely classification for development, since recognition of involuntary public figures could reach so far as potentially to create a de facto public interest standard.

Further hardening of the public figure category seems to have occurred in *Hutchinson v. Proxmire*. The plaintiff had been named in connection with a U.S. senator's dubious Golden Fleece of the Month award for a government research grant on animal behavior. Although the trial court considered the recipient of the research grant a public figure because of his long record of publicly funded research, local media coverage of his work, and public interest in government spending, the Supreme Court reversed. It found instead that mere receipt of a public grant does not result in public figure standing. More importantly, a person's access to the media, which was a key attribute in *Gertz* of such status, must be regular and continuing to qualify him or her as a public figure. Since such access is limited to very few persons, and perhaps none that could not qualify as general-purpose public figures, a possible basis exists for reading limited-purpose public figures out of existence for practical purposes.

Because the *Gertz* decision applies by its nature to media defendants, the possibility remains that a different standard may apply for nonmedia defendants. Arguments have been advanced that the operation of the actual malice standard against media defendants presumes the presence of some minimal public concern that is not necessarily present in private communications. Creation of a different standard for media and non-media defendants, however, would elevate the press above the public for constitutional purposes, contrary to the Court's general reluctance to accord it special intra–First Amendment status. The possibility of such a result also has elicited criticism to the effect that it would afford maximum protection to those capable of causing the most damage. Despite the Court's inclination to set standards on the basis of a plaintiff's status rather than the nature of the pertinent expression, it appears that the public concern standard rejected in *Gertz* has not been buried entirely. In *Dun & Bradstreet, Inc. v. Greenmoss Builders, Inc.*, Justice Powell, who authored the *Gertz* opinion, found it significant that the defamatory statement at issue was a "purely private" rather than a "public concern." Because an erroneous credit report was a private rather than a public matter, Powell with Justices O'Connor and Rehnquist concluded that reputational interests supported the availability of presumed and punitive damages even absent actual malice. The plurality left undetermined whether such damages might be available without proof of fault. Also unclear is whether the three-justice plurality would allow a public official or figure to collect presumed or punitive damages when a defamation was not tied to a matter of public concern.

Concern with the impact of multimillion-dollar damage awards has prompted arguments that they cross not only First Amendment concerns but the Eighth Amendment guarantee against "excessive Fines." In *Browning-Ferris Industries of Vermont, Inc. v. Kelso Disposal, Inc.*, the Court found that a six-million-dollar punitive damages award did not violate the Eighth Amendment. Left open was the possibility, however, that the size of a punitive damages award may be at odds with due process guaranteed by the Fourteenth Amendment.

Resurrection of a public concern standard would invite the risks of subjectivity and ad hoc judgment that worried the Court in *Gertz*. Possible hostility to the press's interest in the *Firestone* divorce proceeding and subsequent delimitation of the public figure standard suggest the pertinence of these concerns. A public interest standard is highly malleable and risks significant judicial meddling in the editorial process. So too is a public figure determination, however, that dismisses the relevance of public concern entirely if the plaintiff is identified as a private person.

The evolution of constitutional standards reveals a significant rethinking on the part of the Court in its valuation of false expression. In *New York Times v. Sullivan*, the Court proclaimed the merits of false speech without regard to whether it constituted fact or idea. Within a decade, it observed in *Gertz* that "there is no such thing as a false idea . . . , but there is no constitutional value in false statements of facts." A decade later, in *Keeton v. Hustler Magazine, Inc.*, the Court noted that false statements not only injure a specific victim but harm the public. Consistent with that determination, Justice White, who joined in formulating the actual malice standard, now urges its abandonment. His concern is that false expression misinforms the public, creates misleading impressions and pollutes the flow of information. In *Dun & Bradstreet, Inc. v. Greenmoss Builders, Inc.*, he thus asserted that "the Court struck an improvident balance in the *New York Times* case between the public's interest in being informed about public officials and public affairs and the competing interests of those who have been defamed in vindicating their reputation." White complains that the actual malice standard lets "the lie" stand and the public remain misinformed about public matters. His preferred methodology for protecting reputation from defamation and the press from intimidation would be to retain common-law standards of negligence and strict liability but to limit the amount of damages available. Given such revisionist thought, the uncertain operation of a public concern standard, and unknown sentiments of newer Court appointees, the constitutional law of defamation has the potential for considerable instability.

B. PRIVACY

Facts and circumstances supporting a defamation action also may support a privacy claim. The claims tend to be comparable except for the type of injury suffered. In a defamation case, the harm asserted is reputational damage. Injury in a privacy action is the actual breach of privacy itself. In examining the law of privacy, it is imperative to recognize that significant disparity may exist between the law as it appears to exist and as it likely would be applied today. That reality is the result of developments in privacy law prior to *Gertz* that coursed along a public concern rather than a public figure track. Especially in false light privacy cases, which mirror defamation actions except with respect to the actual injury claimed, it is essential to understand the law as it was enunciated earlier but to recognize that subsequent developments in defamation law likely would be relevant to future privacy jurisprudence.

Rights of privacy exist pursuant to state statute or common law. Essentially, four subcategories of actionability exist: right of publicity, unreasonable intrusion into a person's privacy, unreasonable publicity of a person's private life, and false light privacy.

1. Right of Publicity

A right of publicity protects a person's interest in the availability and exploitation of name, likeness, and image. Thus a person may seek to enjoin unauthorized profiting from such qualities of self or require compensation as a condition for such usage. Actions based on appropriation are a rarity, at least so far as the media are concerned. Even so, the Supreme Court has emphasized that unauthorized use of an entertainer's performance impairs a protectable proprietary interest. In *Zacchini v. Scripps-Howard Broadcasting Co.*, the Court determined that a television news presentation of the plaintiff's performance as a human cannonball at a county fair appropriated his entire act. The Court thus concluded that

[t]here is no doubt that entertainment, as well as news, enjoys First Amendment protection. It is also true that entertainment itself can be important news. *Time, Inc. v. Hill.* But it is important to note that neither the public nor respondent will be deprived of the benefit of petitioner's performance as long as his commercial stake in his act is appropriately recognized. Petitioner does not seek to enjoin the broadcast of his performance; he simply wants to be paid for it. Nor do we think that a state-law damages remedy against respondent would represent a species of liability without fault contrary to the letter or spirit of *Gertz v. Robert Welch, Inc.*, 418 U.S. 323 (1974). Respondent knew that petitioner objected to televising his act but nevertheless displayed the entire film.

We conclude that although the State of Ohio may as a matter of its own law privilege the press in the circumstances in this case, the First and Fourteenth Amendments do not require it to do so.

It is questionable, as Justice Powell noted, whether the fifteen-second clip minus prelude and fanfare truly constituted the whole act. Also uncertain is whether a different result would be reached if a lesser part of an act were appropriated. If type of use and significance of the presentation are critical, review amounts to both a qualitative and quantitative appraisal. Even if liability is established, damages may be difficult to calculate and perhaps nonexistent if publicity results in larger crowds for and enhanced profits from future performances. In any event, the Court concluded that laws protecting publicity interests, like copyright statutes, protect creative activity and thus do not offend the First Amendment.

2. Intrusion

Actions asserting invasion of a legally protected zone of privacy, such as a home or office, also are infrequent. Typical defendants in instances when they do occur, however, are the media. Actionable intrusion may result from the use of video or audio technology enabling a reporter to snoop into private space and obtain information that otherwise would be confidential. Unlike other actions for privacy, the intrusion itself is sufficient to complete the wrong, and no publication is required. Nor is newsworthiness necessarily a defense against such a claim. In *Dietemann v. Time, Inc.*, reporters from a magazine used false representations to obtain entry into the plaintiff's home. With use of a hidden camera and recording equipment, they elicited information demonstrating that the plaintiff was a medical quack. Nonetheless, the plaintiff prevailed on his privacy claim because the First Amendment afforded no protection against liability that might arise in the course of news gathering. The wrong was not publication of the story but the intrusion effectuated by false pretenses. Investigative journalists and undercover reporters should be especially alert that intrusion as a consequence of misrepresentation is hazardous. A mitigating reality may be that if wrongdoing is revealed and the public interest is advanced by the actionable procedure, sympathy for the ends may be a factor in a jury's damage award punishing the means.

The use of purloined documents or leaked information may present ethical questions but does not create a legal problem, at least for the media. Those who steal or reveal information, however, may themselves be subject to criminal or civil liability.

3. Disclosure of Intimate Details

Publication of accurate facts that are damaging does not give rise to a defamation action, since truth is a defense, but still may support a privacy claim. In *Cox Broadcasting Corp. v. Cohn*, the Court determined that the media could not be held liable by statute or common law for publishing damaging or embarrassing information contained in records open to the public. The plaintiff had sued the television station for identifying his deceased daughter as a murder-rape victim. Although the Court curtailed the reach of the tort, it did not eliminate the availability of an action altogether. Left open was the possibility that a privacy claim based on truthful but damaging statements can be asserted when information was not obtained from a public record. If the Court is not willing to provide comprehensive protection for the media, it becomes necessary to determine how far a newsworthiness defense or privilege might reach and whether liability should vary, as in a defamation action, according to the plaintiff's status.

The Court refused an opportunity to clarify the ambit of First Amendment interest in such instances when it denied review in *Virgil v. Time, Inc.* The case concerned a story about a surfer who was interviewed but revoked his consent upon learning that the article would address some of his bizarre personal ways as well as his surfing. The court of appeals refused to accept the argument that truth affords complete defense against a privacy claim premised on true but harmful facts. Such a holding prevents the First Amendment from swallowing an entire category of tort. At the same time, the determination that a defense requires a showing that the story is newsworthy and not just an appeal to the public's idle curiosity complicates the process of achieving principled results. Separating the public's idle curiosity from the public interest implicates the same exercises that plagued early suggestions to have the media focus upon matters of "genuine community concern" and early decisions suggesting a constitutional line between information and entertainment. As eventually became manifest, "the line between the informing and the entertaining is too elusive for the protection of that basic right [a free press].... What is one man's amusement, teaches another's doctrine." Nonetheless, it is the type of line, evidenced by the Court's observation that a divorce proceeding was not the type of controversy it had in mind when it set the qualifications of a public figure, that it still seems inclined to draw, even if subjectively and unpredictably.

The *Cohn* decision and its aftermath did not determine the general question of whether publication of truthful information ever could be punished consistent with the First Amendment. Nor was the more specific issue of whether truthful publication ever could give rise to criminal or civil liability for invading a zone of privacy resolved. Although the Court was recently afforded the opportunity to consider either proposition, it again declined to issue a comprehensive statement. In *The Florida Star v. B.J.F.*, it concluded "that the sensitivity and significance of the interests presented in clashes between the First Amendment and privacy rights counsel relying on limited principles that sweep no more broadly than the appropriate context of the [immediate] case." The Court thus determined that a newspaper could not be held liable for publication of a rape victim's identity when it obtained her name from a publicly released police report.

The state in *The Florida Star* case had made it unlawful only for an "instrument of mass communication" to disclose the name of a sex-offense victim. The statute was premised upon interests of securing the privacy of victims, protecting them from retaliation, and encouraging reporting of crimes without fear of exposure. The Court observed, however, that publication of lawfully obtained information concerning "a matter of public significance" could not be punished "absent a need to further a state interest of the highest order." Taking into account that the information was contained in a government news release (indicating that government had failed to police itself), the law established negligence *per se* from which liability automatically followed, and the statute was underinclusive insofar as it reached only the mass media, the Court found a failure to further an "interest of the highest order."

Despite its holding, the Court emphasized that it did not find truthful publication categorically and automatically protected, or that publication of a sex-offense victim's name never could be punished. It also disregarded the warning in *Gertz*, unheeded also in *Dun & Bradstreet*, against drawing lines pursuant to such subjective standards as public concern or public significance.

4. False Light Privacy

A false light privacy action is most evocative of, and may be intertwined with, a defamation claim. Liability arises insofar as false portrayal of a person may invade privacy regardless of whether the falsehood is actionable as defamation. In *Time, Inc. v. Hill*, the plaintiff had stated a false light privacy claim on grounds that the magazine had inaccurately depicted what had occurred to him and his family when they were taken captive by a group of escaped convicts. In real life, they had been held hostage and never harmed. The magazine's reporting of a play showing similar circumstances but including violence and verbal abuse presented photographs of actors reenacting events at the plaintiff's home and purporting to recount the incident there.

Although state law did not provide a newsworthiness defense, the Court introduced a standard of that ilk. It held that liability could not be established if (1) the plaintiffs were implicated in a matter of public interest and (2) unless the article was published with knowledge of its falsity or with reckless disregard of the truth. The determination essentially transferred the actual malice standard from the defamation context to the related false light privacy setting and extended its reach beyond public officials and public figures. For false light privacy purposes, the Court embraced a standard that subsequently would not command a majority in the defamation setting. As noted previously, the Court in the latter context has evolved immunity standards pitched toward the status of the defendant rather than the nature of the expression.

The rerouting of defamation law from a public interest to a public figure focus suggests that a false light privacy claim today would be analyzed pursuant to the standards of *Gertz* rather than *Hill*. In *Cantrell v. Forest City Publishing Co.*, the Court affirmed liability on a false light privacy theory for publication of an article mischaracterizing a family's living conditions and causing mental distress and humiliation. Jury instructions were framed in terms of having to prove actual malice, and reckless disregard was established. The Court thus considered it inapt to determine whether, in an action by a private figure, a lesser showing of scienter could have sufficed. Given the identical nature of defamation and false light privacy actions in all aspects but the technical nature of the injury, it would be surprising if the standards for scienter were to be as asymmetrical as established case law otherwise might suggest.

C. Public Morals

1. Obscenity

Unlike defamation, expression denominated as obscene has not been welcomed into the protective fold of the First Amendment. Obscenity is a form of expression that the Court consistently has found to have "no essential part of any exposition of ideas, and [to be] of such slight social value as a step to the truth that any benefit derived from [it] is clearly outweighed by the social interest in morality." Even before any formal pronouncement, the Court appears to have assumed that obscenity was not safeguarded by the First Amendment. In *Near v. Minnesota*, the Court noted that the state's interest in regulating obscenity constituted one of the few exceptions justifying departure from the normal rule against prior restraint. Because any definition of obscenity is unlikely to be consensual, much of the Supreme Court's energy has been devoted to constructing standards that will be broadly subscribed to and workable. The effort itself has succeeded largely in demonstrating how invariably subjective the concept is. Nonetheless, criteria persist both for identifying obscenity and punishing its dissemination.

Despite multiple allusions in dicta to the unprotected nature of obscenity, it was not until 1957 that the Court made that status official. In *Roth v. United States*, the Court found "implicit in the history of the First Amendment . . . rejection of obscenity as utterly without redeeming social importance."

The guaranties of freedom of expression in effect in 10 of the 14 States which by 1792 had ratified the Constitution, gave no absolute protection for every utterance. Thirteen of the 14 States provided for the prosecution of libel, and all of those States made either blasphemy or profanity, or both, statutory crimes. As early as 1712, Massachusetts made it criminal to publish "any filthy, obscene, or profane song, pamphlet, libel or mock sermon" in imitation or mimicking of religious service. . . . Thus, profanity and obscenity were related offenses.

In light of this history, it is apparent that the unconditional phrasing of the First Amendment was not intended to protect every utterance. This phrasing did not prevent this Court from concluding that libelous utterances are not within the area of constitutionally protected speech. *Beauharnais v. Illinois*, 343 U.S. 250, 266. At the time of the adoption of the First Amendment, obscenity law was not as fully developed as libel law, but there is sufficiently contemporaneous evidence to show that obscenity, too, was outside the protection intended for speech and press.

The protection given speech and press was fashioned to assure unfettered interchange of ideas for the bringing about of political and social changes desired by the people. This objective was made explicit as early as 1774 in a letter of the Continental Congress to the inhabitants of Quebec:

> "The last right we shall mention, regards the freedom of the press. The importance of this consists, besides the advancement of truth, science, morality, and arts in general, in its diffusion of liberal sentiments on the administration of Government, its ready communication of thoughts between subjects, and its consequential promotion of union among them, whereby oppressive officers are shamed or intimidated, into more honorable and just modes of conducting affairs." 1 Journals of the Continental Congress 108 (1774).

All ideas having even the slightest redeeming social importance—unorthodox ideas, controversial ideas, even ideas hateful to the prevailing climate of opinion—have the full protection of the guaranties, unless excludable because they encroach upon the limited area of more important interests. But implicit in the history of the First Amendment is the rejection of obscenity as utterly without redeeming social importance. This rejection for that reason is mirrored in the universal judgment that obscenity should be restrained, reflected in the international agreement of over 50 nations, in the obscenity laws of all of the 48 States, and in the 20 obscenity laws enacted by the Congress from 1842 to 1956. This is the same judgment expressed by this Court in *Chaplinsky v. New Hampshire*, 315 U.S. 568, 571–572:

> "There are certain well-defined and narrowly limited classes of speech, the prevention and punishment of which have never been thought to raise any Constitutional problem. These include the lewd and obscene...It has been well observed that such utterances are no essential part of any exposition of ideas, and are of such slight social value as a step to truth that any benefit that may be derived from them is clearly outweighed by the social interest in order and morality..." (Emphasis added by Court).

We hold that obscenity is not within the area of constitutionally protected speech or press.

Having carved out a special category of expression immune from constitutional norms, the Court turned to the still-daunting task of defining it. In *Roth*, the Court depicted obscenity as "material which deals with sex in a manner appealing to prurient interest." The term "prurient" is at best imprecise and was not particularly well fleshed out, as the Court's dictionary references to "[i]tching; longing; uneasy with desire or longing [and so on]" suggest. Given a concept that did not lend itself to a clearly articulable and objectifiable definition, the Court provided for individualized assessments of whether "to the average person, applying contemporary standards, the dominant theme of the material taken as a whole appeals to prurient interest."

Although the *Roth* decision largely formalized what previously had been assumed with respect to obscenity and the Constitution, it had significant and enduring implications. Without any First Amendment status, expression denominated as obscene can be freely regulated. As the Court noted, it is unnecessary in a particular instance to identify a competing interest or even prove harm as a basis for regulation. The *Roth* case disclosed both extremes in the spectrum of philosophies and attitudes that continues to characterize the debate over obscenity. Contrary to the Court's notion that such expression is categorically unprotected, Justices Douglas and Black argued that obscenity could be suppressed only if "so closely brigaded with illegal action as to be an inseparable part of it." Their dissent raised questions and concerns that largely have been avoided by analysis consisting of categorical exclusion and consequent deference to regulatory premise. As Douglas and Black observed, it was an assumption rather than provable fact that "the arousing of sexual thoughts and desires [which] happens every day in normal life in dozens of ways" is worthless. Nonetheless, the Court has never seriously or openly questioned the premise and even has gone out of its way to dismiss any need for requiring a causal connection between obscenity and illegality or harm. Some years later, the Court pointed out that "[f]rom the beginning of civilized societies, legislators and judges have acted on various unprovable assumptions." Such an observation contrasts with its demands for compelling reasons for official encroachment upon a constitutional interest and strong proof that the regulatory action taken truly advances the legitimate and pressing governmental concern. The Court, however, was untroubled by the absence of conclusive proof of linkage between obscene material and antisocial behavior and was willing to countenance presumption of such a connection.

Since *Roth*, the Court has evinced little interest in examining any empirical uncertainties or considering any alternatives to obscenity's entirely unprotected status. The law of obscenity thus has evolved as a function of the Court's conscious inclination to assume rather than to establish that such expression has no value and so does not implicate constitutional concerns. Such broad assumptions preclude even the possibility of considering whether, in a given instance, prurient materials might be valuable because they afford pleasure or release, contribute to formation of sexual identity, or safeguard against imposition of "politically correct sex." The categorical exclusion of obscenity diverges from traditional libertarian wisdom that favors decision making by, rather than for, individuals and does not lightly brook interference with personal thoughts and beliefs. The analysis ultimately assumes that official definition of acceptable expression is less dangerous than the exercise of individual judgment. Critics would argue that if the individual cannot be trusted to make decisions regarding one type of expression, especially when lack of value is presumed rather than proved, it may be difficult to establish meaningful limiting principles against the expansion or transferability of such thinking.

Jurisprudence satisfied with assumption rather than proof has relegated to a level of marginal relevance official or scholarly efforts to discern harm attributable to obscenity. President Nixon appointed a special commission to identify any linkage between obscenity and antisocial behavior. It found no evidence that exposure to explicit sexual materials caused delinquent or criminal conduct. A subsequent study, commissioned by President Reagan, concluded that a relationship exists between exposure to sexually degrading material and aggression toward women. Insofar as the law concerning obscenity continues to rest on assumptions, the findings of either report have no real constitutional influence. The continuing debate, however, discloses an interest in jurisprudence that at least has the appearance of being informed rather than presumptive. Even if evidence shows a causal connection between obscenity and a definable harm, the question likely will remain as to whether the problem should be solved by policies of official control or individual autonomy.

Roth and its progeny have supported Justice Harlan's observation that obscenity is an elusive concept. Justice Stewart eventually depicted classification efforts as "trying to define what may be indefinable" and conceded that he could do no better than "know it when I see it." Justice Brennan, who authored the *Roth* opinion, later maintained that formulation of a viable description was impossible and a threat to First Amendment values. Nonetheless, the Court has pressed forward in a largely frustrating and confounding effort to distill the essence of obscenity and uphold governmental power to regulate it. Following a lower-court determination that the book *Fanny Hill* was obscene, a fragmented Court reversed. A plurality of three led by Justice Brennan in *A Book Named "John Cleland's Memoirs of a Woman of Pleasure" v. Attorney General of Massachusetts*, concluded that the work was not "*utterly* without redeeming social value" and accordingly was not beyond the First Amendment's purview. The *Roth* decision had emphasized prurience and had assumed that obscenity was utterly without redeeming social importance. The Brennan plurality depicted the latter reference point as an independent standard that must be affirmatively satisfied and demanded a showing that the subject matter must offend contemporary community standards. The tripartite criteria focusing upon speech appealing to prurient interests, offending contemporary community standards, and entirely lacking redeeming social value obligated prosecutors to satisfy not just any but each of the standards. Proof that material was without any redeeming social value whatsoever constituted an exacting standard. It became evident, however, that it would not operate as a consistent bar to successful prosecution. In *Ginzburg v. United States*, the Court concluded that forthright pandering to prurient interests was sufficient to support an obscenity conviction. The defendant overtly had marketed his publication in a way that emphasized its sexually provocative nature and manifested an intent to capitalize upon "an unrestricted license allowed by law in the expression of sex and sexual matters." By itself, a conscious and forthright appeal to prurient interests proved to be adequate grounds for conviction regardless of whether the materials themselves might have had redeeming social value. The latter question was preempted by the former determination.

Until 1973, a majority of the Court was unable to coalesce behind a unifying set of principles for analyzing obscenity issues. As a consequence, the Court for several years followed a rather unusual practice of reversing per curiam whenever five or more justices considered materials less than obscene. Eventually, in *Miller v. California*, a majority fashioned a formula to the effect that obscenity is to be discerned according to

(a) whether "the average person, applying contemporary community standards" would find that the work, taken as a whole, appeals to the prurient interest, (b) whether the work depicts or describes, in a patently offensive way, sexual conduct specifically defined by the applicable state law, and (c) whether the work taken as a whole, lacks serious literary, artistic, political, or scientific value.

Although the *Miller* opinion emphasized that the First Amendment's meaning "does not vary from community to community," the decision to measure prurient interest and patent offensiveness pursuant to local standards created the possibility that reality would diverge from theory. Even if the consequences might be rationalized on grounds that a finding of obscenity eliminates the First Amendment as a pertinent concern, the variability of results pursuant to disparate community standards would transform the guarantee into a relative rather than a consistent safeguard. Reliance on community standards not only extended an invitation for prosecutorial forum shopping but, as was soon evidenced, presented a problem for actuating rights transcending a given community. In *Jenkins v. Georgia*, the Court reversed a jury determination that the relatively mainstream film *Carnal Knowledge* was obscene. Although the Court's assignment of the prurient interest and patent offensiveness questions to juries probably reflected to a considerable extent its own frustration with an "intractable ... problem," the *Jenkins* decision demonstrates that local community standards will not be allowed to operate unchecked. Because the Court has not rescinded its assignment to the trier of fact, however, future oversight for practical purposes may be a function of its own subjective predilections.

The *Miller* decision itself concerned jury instructions denominating the relevant community as the state. It has become evident, however, that a trial judge would not necessarily err by using a community standard without any geographically qualifying reference point. An exception arguably might arise in the event that a national standard was prescribed when a local standard would be more tolerant. The Court's adoption of the community standard approach recognized "that the people of Maine or Mississippi [need] not accept public depiction of conduct found tolerable in Las Vegas or New York City." Arguably, the converse would be true with respect to allowing local norms to operate unimpaired by less tolerant outside standards.

Patent offensiveness, as the second part of the *Miller* test, also must be measured against contemporary community standards. Whatever is punishable as patently offensive, however, must depict or describe sexual conduct that the law specifically defines. Examples of statutory definitions satisfying the *Miller* criteria were

(a) Patently offensive representation or descriptions of ultimate sexual acts, normal or perverted, actual or simulated. (b) Patently offensive representations or descriptions of masturbation, excretory functions and lewd exhibition of the genitals.

As the Court subsequently emphasized, such recitations were examples rather than exhaustive guidelines. The models themselves do not afford clear notice of what is proscribed, and the Court effectively has acceded to inevitable imprecision by noting that the "specifically defined" requirement can be satisfied by a regulation "as written or authoritatively construed." Given the nature of the subject and the invariable need to rely upon such subjective terms as "normal," "perverted," and "lewd," any expectations of precise guidelines probably would have been misplaced. Constitutional shelter for expression relating to what the Court might consider normal or healthy sexual desires suggests that the dividing line between "materials depict[ing], or describ[ing] patently offensive 'hard core' sexual conduct" and protected characterizations at bottom is subjective. That likelihood in itself creates a strong incentive for media in general to exercise caution in the selection and presentation of sexually oriented materials.

The final component of the *Miller* test, obligating prosecutors to demonstrate that material "lacks serious literary, artistic, political, or scientific value," altered preceding terminology that "a work must be 'utterly without redeeming social value.'" It is doubtful whether the modification has profound significance, although the Court has intimated that it is a distinguishing characteristic of the *Miller* test. It also has held that determinations of literary, artistic, political, or scientific value are to be made pursuant to a reasonable-person rather than community standard. Such attempted objectification is premised upon the notion that value is not a function of local popularity or acceptability. The amplified standard has the potential, if it is ever used vigorously, for neutralizing the influence of community standards operating in connection with the first two parts of the test. Notwithstanding its operation, the standard does not entirely eliminate the problem of subjectivity, because all reasonable persons do not subscribe to like values or have the same sensitivities.

The status of obscenity as unprotected expression has deterred, if not preempted, any serious inquiry into whether concerns underlying regulation could be effectuated in a fashion that is more deferential to individual autonomy. In *Stanley v. Georgia*, the Court determined that a person could not be punished for mere possession of obscenity in the privacy of the home. The possibility that the law of obscenity might be contoured along the lines of individual rather than authoritative selection, however, essentially has been aborted. The Court cut short potential jurisprudential development in that direction when, in *Paris Adult Theatre I v. Slaton*, it ruled against a theater owner who posted signs warning about the nature of the films being exhibited and whose audience was limited to consenting adults. Although the Court found state regulation of obscenity permissible, even pursuant to "unprovable assumptions," it identified several reasons for official control of the expression at issue.

We categorically disapprove the theory, apparently adopted by the trial judge, that obscene, pornographic films acquire constitutional immunity from state regulation simply because they are exhibited for consenting adults only. This holding was properly rejected by the Georgia Supreme Court. Although we have often pointedly recognized the high importance of the state interest in regulating the exposure of obscene materials to juveniles and unconsenting adults, . . . this Court has never declared these to be the only legitimate state interest permitting regulation of obscene material. The States have a long recognized legitimate interest in regulating the use of obscene material in local commerce and in all places of public accommodation, as long as these regulations do not run afoul of specific constitutional prohibitions. . . . "In an unbroken series of cases extending over a long stretch of this Court's history, it has been accepted as a postulate that 'the primary requirements of decency may be enforced against obscene publications. . . . ' " These include the interest of the public in the quality of life and the total community environment, the tone of commerce in the great city centers, and, possibly, the public safety itself. The Hill-Link Minority Report of the Commission on Obscenity and Pornography indicates that there is at least an arguable correlation between obscene material and crime. Quite apart from sex crimes, however, there remains one problem of large proportions aptly described by Professor Bickel:

"It concerns the tone of the society, the mode, or to use terms that have perhaps greater currency the style and quality of life, now and in the future. A man may be entitled to read an obscene book in his room, or expose himself indecently there.... We should protect his privacy. But if he demands a right to obtain the books and pictures he wants in the market, and to foregather in public places— discreet, if you will, but accessible to all—with others who share his tastes, then to grant him his right is to affect the world about the rest of us, and to impinge on other privacies. Even supposing that each of us can, if he wishes, effectively avert the eye and stop the ear (which, in truth, we cannot), what is commonly read and seen and heard and done intrudes upon us all, want it or not."

As Mr. Chief Justice Warren stated, there is a "right of the Nation and of the States to maintain a decent society."

Amplification of regulatory justifications, including neighborhood quality and aesthetics, improving the quality of commerce, and pro- moting public safety, technically was unnecessary given obscenity's un- protected status. The Court itself emphasized that obscenity regulation need not be predicated upon any demonstrable harm.

From the beginning of civilized societies, legislators and judges have acted on various unprovable assumptions. Such assumptions underlie much lawful state regulation of commercial and business affairs.... The same is true of the federal securities and antitrust laws and a host of federal regulations.... On the basis of these assumptions both Congress and state legislatures have, for example, drastically restricted associational rights by adopting antitrust laws, and have strictly regulated public expression by issuers of and dealers in securities, profit sharing "coupons," and "trading stamps," commanding what they must and must not publish and announce.... Understandably those who entertain an absolutist view of the First Amendment find it uncomfortable to explain why rights of association, speech, and press should be severely restrained in the marketplace of goods and money, but not in the market place of pornography.

Likewise, when legislatures and administrators act to protect the physical en- vironment from pollution and to preserve our resources of forests, streams and parks, they must act on such imponderables as the impact of a new highway near or through an existing park or wilderness area. Thus, § 18(a) of the Federal- Aid Highway Act of 1968, 23 U.S.C. § 138, and the Department of Transpor- tation Act of 1966, as amended, 82 Stat. 824, 49 U.S.C. § 1653(f), have been described by Mr. Justice Black as "a solemn determination of the highest law- making body of this Nation that the beauty and health-giving facilities of our parks are not to be taken away for public roads without hearings, fact findings, and policy determinations under the supervision of a Cabinet officer...." The fact that a congressional directive reflects unprovable assumptions about what is good for the people, including imponderable aesthetic assumptions, is not a sufficient reason to find that statute unconstitutional....

It is argued that individual "free will" must govern, even in activities beyond the protection of the First Amendment and other constitutional guarantees of privacy, and that government cannot legitimately impede an individual's desire to see or acquire obscene plays, movies, and books. We do indeed base our society on certain assumptions that people have the capacity for free choice.

Most exercises of individual free choice—those in politics, religion, and expression of ideas—are explicitly protected by the Constitution. Totally unlimited play for free will, however, is not allowed in our or any other society. We have just noted, for example, that neither the First Amendment nor "free will" precludes States from having "blue sky" laws to regulate what sellers of securities may write or publish about their wares. See *supra*, at 61–62. Such laws are to protect the weak, the uninformed, the unsuspecting, and the gullible from the exercises of their own volition. Nor do modern societies leave disposal of garbage and sewage up to the individual "free will," but impose regulation to protect both public health and the appearance of public places. States are told by some that they must await a "laissez-faire" market solution to the obscenity-pornography problem, paradoxically "by people who have never otherwise had a kind word to say for laissez-faire," particularly in solving urban, commercial, and environmental pollution problems.

While the Court delineated a virtually unbridled power to regulate obscenity, Justice Brennan used the *Paris Adult Theatre* decision as his point of departure from the jurisprudential course he had commenced in *Roth*. Although he acknowledged significant regulatory interests, he concluded that problems in defining obscenity and applying vague standards "cannot justify the substantial damage to constitutional rights and to this Nation's judicial machinery." Brennan thus argued for reading the First Amendment as a bar to categorical exclusion of sexually oriented materials except to protect juveniles and unconsenting adults. Brennan's position thus would combine the implications of the *Stanley* decision with those of *Ginsberg v. New York* and make them the central body of obscenity law. The Court in *Ginsberg* recognized a government's special interest in children, given their impressionability, and thus constructed an obscenity standard that is more encompassing when they are a concern. So far, however, Brennan's urgings that the Court alter and narrow its focus have been officially unheeded.

Jurisprudential and critical ferment suggests abiding concern with the *Miller* test, if not a consensus for a replacement standard. Consistent with Justice Brennan's sense that obscenity cannot be defined with sufficient precision, Justice Scalia has observed that "[j]ust as there is no use arguing about taste, there is no use litigating about it." Some theorists advocate moving jurisprudence beyond the notion that obscenity has no value to the more assertive premise that it harms women and reinforces their societal subordination. They would redefine obscenity to account for speech depicting women as sex objects, characterizing them in a diminished position, or reinforcing harmful ways of thinking about women. Although the court of appeals acknowledged the validity of such concerns in *American Booksellers Association Inc. v. Hudnut*, it found that freedom of speech assumes the risk that insidious expression may "influence the culture and shape our socialization." It further warned that "if a process of [social] conditioning were enough to permit governmental regulation, that would be the end of freedom of speech." In *Pope v. Illinois*, meanwhile, Justices Stevens, Marshall, and Brennan suggested that constitutional protection should be afforded if "*some reasonable people* would consider [the expression] as having serious literary, artistic, political, or scientific value [emphasis in original]." Even if the precise direction is uncertain, the potential at least exists for some movement beyond existing standards.

2. Indecency

The absence of any constitutional concern for sexually oriented expression characterized as obscene may have helped condition and facilitate less tolerant attitudes toward speech that, even if it is not obscene, is depicted as offensive or indecent. Although not categorically denied First Amendment status altogether, sexually explicit expression even if it does not fit the *Miller* definition of obscenity may be afforded diluted constitutional protection. So far, the Court has not formally defined indecency in terms of an official speech classification. Regulation of sexually explicit speech nonetheless has been upheld pursuant to considerations of context. Such attention has proved particularly significant for broadcasting, which, as the Court has observed, has the most limited First Amendment protection of all media. In *Federal Communications Commission v. Pacifica Foundation*, the Court concluded that civil and criminal liability could attach to the broadcast of indecent or profane language. The First Amendment thereby was not violated by standards for sexually oriented expression that were less exacting than the *Miller* formula.

The *Pacifica* decision referenced its holdings to what was described as radio and television's pervasive presence, intrusive nature, and unique accessibility to children. Permeating the opinions, however, was a subjective revulsion to the nature of the expression. The deprecating references to a satire upon attitudes toward several commonly used expletives are reminiscent of obscenity-related review in that they reflect a sense that "modern civilization does not leave disposal of garbage and sewage to free will."

A majority of the Court has never formally endorsed the notion that indecent expression constitutes a distinct and less protected speech form. For practical purposes, however, it is difficult not to recognize that a practical speech classification exists subject to variable standards tied largely to taste. That sense is magnified by the observation in *Young v. American Mini Theatres, Inc.*, that "few of us would send our sons and daughters off to war to preserve the citizen's right to see [explicit sex portrayals] exhibited in the theaters of our choice." Such commentary in support of a zoning ordinance regulating the location of adult bookstores and movie houses accurately may reflect the notion that many persons do not cherish or revere sexually provocative expression. Even if the observation is accurate, a competing reality is that there are many people for whom political expression is so irrelevant that they might not consider it worth fighting for. A more pertinent argument may be that it is the full ambit and dynamics of a pluralistic system of free expression, rather than any segment of it, and the opportunity to select autonomously from a diverse menu of expression that evoke and merit defense. Conclusions that a particular form of expression is unworthy of protection not only endanger that variant of speech but narrow the range of diversity and choice. The constitutional challenge, if devaluation is to be brooked in discrete instances, is to ensure that the process functions as an isolated and well-justified exception rather than a norm.

D. COMMERCIAL SPEECH

Commercial speech is a form of expression characterized by an especially high degree of constitutional instability. Until the 1970s, the level of protection afforded commercial speech attracted little discussion because the Court had set it outside the First Amendment's purview. A challenge to a city's prohibition of for-hire advertising on trucks, therefore, elicited more equal protection than First Amendment interest. Eventual recognition that commercial speech merited constitutional protection has been compounded by subsequent holdings and observations tending to diminish its First Amendment status. A key problem that flows from the determination that commercial expression is a protected speech variant, and that has been a focus of litigation since, is the proper standard of review for regulation and the interests and concerns justifying government control. Even more fundamental is what such speech comprises.

Nearly half a century ago, in *Valentine v. Chrestensen*, the Court determined that the First Amendment did not preclude regulation of "purely commercial advertising." Notwithstanding the unprotected nature of commercial speech at the time, the decision was problematic and revealed an analytical treachery that has endured. The Court in *Chrestensen* affirmed the conviction of an entrepreneur who violated a municipal ordinance by distributing a handbill advertising a commercial exhibition on one side and protesting the city's denial of a public show place on the other. It classified the leaflet in singular terms as commercial speech, although the content also had a political dimension.

The consequences of selective classification are significant when expression may have multiple dimensions, because characterization determines relative constitutional status and consequent vulnerability to regulation. Ever since the Court determined that commercial expression falls within the First Amendment's ambit, it has tended to classify complex expression in singular terms. By focusing upon what is perceived to be the primary purpose of speech or merely denominating expression as commercial without further elaboration, review essentially discounts or disregards what may be significant secondary attributes. Such analysis is reminiscent of the Court's inclination in *Chrestensen* not to "indulge nice appraisal based on subtle distinctions."

The evolution of commercial speech into a constitutionally protected variant of expression commenced during the early 1970s. In *Capital Broadcasting Co. v. Mitchell*, the Court upheld a federal law prohibiting cigarette advertising on radio and television. Although the net result was indistinguishable from that in *Chrestensen*, the lower-court decision affirmed without opinion suggested limits upon government's regulatory power. The observation that the state may restrict truthful advertising of lawful activities determined by the legislature to be harmful intimated a qualifying predicate that would have been unnecessary if the expression at issue categorically was unprotected.

Shortly thereafter, in *Pittsburgh Press Co. v. Pittsburgh Commission on Human Relations*, the Court by its own words moved a step further toward altering the constitutional status of commercial speech. In upholding an ordinance prohibiting a newspaper's segregation of help-wanted advertisements by gender, the Court determined that states may prohibit advertising of illegal activities. A logical inference from the decision was that commercial expression concerning a lawful activity was entitled to some measure of constitutional protection.

The implication of the *Pittsburgh Press* decision was stated more affirmatively in *Bigelow v. Virginia*, when the Court held that the government may not prohibit touting of a lawful activity. The *Bigelow* opinion was characterized by a rather vain effort to reconcile evolving commercial-speech doctrine with the *Chrestensen* decision. The Court depicted its original ruling as affirming a reasonable time, place, and manner restriction rather than insulating all regulation of commercial speech from constitutional challenge. Reconciliation of emerging principle with *Chrestensen*'s exclusion of commercial speech from the First Amendment soon was abandoned in favor of official discrediting. What emerged as a predicate for the newly recognized status of commercial speech was a candid recognition that the value of such expression for many was "as keen, if not keener by far, than [any] interest in the day's most urgent political debate." In *Virginia State Board of Pharmacy v. Virginia Citizens Consumer Council*, the Court thus recognized the public's interest in the flow of commercial expression and forthrightly conferred upon it First Amendment status.

We begin with several propositions that already are settled or beyond serious dispute. It is clear, for example, that speech does not lose its First Amendment protection because money is spent to project it, as in a paid advertisement of one form or another.... Speech likewise is protected even though it is carried in a form that is "sold" for profit, and even though it may involve a solicitation to purchase or otherwise pay or contribute money....

Our question is whether speech which does "no more than propose a commercial transaction,"... is so removed from any "exposition of ideas,"... and from " 'truth, science, morality, and arts in general, in its diffusion of liberal sentiments on the administration of Government,' " that it lacks all protection. Our answer is that it is not....

Generalizing, society also may have a strong interest in the free flow of commercial information. Even an individual advertisement, though entirely commercial, may be of general public interest....

Moreover, there is another consideration that suggests that no line between publicly "interesting" or "important" commercial advertising and the opposite kind could ever be drawn. Advertising, however tasteless and excessive it sometimes may seem, is nonetheless dissemination of information as to who is producing and selling what product, for what reason, and at what price. So long as we preserve a predominantly free enterprise economy, the allocation of our resources in large measure will be made through numerous private economic decisions. It is a matter of public interest that those decisions, in the aggregate, be intelligent and well informed. To this end, the free flow of commercial information is indispensable.... And if it is indispensable to the proper allocation of resources in a free enterprise system, it is also indispensable to the formation of intelligent opinions as to how that system ought to be regulated or altered. Therefore, even if the First Amendment were thought to be primarily an instrument to enlighten public decision making in a democracy, we could not say that the free flow of information does not serve that goal....

Nor is there any claim that prescription drug price advertisements are forbidden because they are false or misleading in any way. Untruthful speech, commercial or otherwise, has never been protected for its own sake.... Obviously, much commercial speech is not probably false, or even wholly false, but only deceptive or misleading. We foresee no obstacle to a State's dealing effectively with this problem. The First Amendment, as we construe it today, does not prohibit the State from insuring that the stream of commercial information flows cleanly as well as freely....

Also, there is no claim that the transactions proposed in the forbidden advertisements are themselves illegal in any way. Finally, the special problems of the electronic broadcast media are likewise not in this case....

What is at issue is whether a State may completely suppress the dissemination of concededly truthful information about entirely lawful activity, fearful of that information's effect upon its disseminators and its recipients. Reserving other questions, we conclude that the answer to this one is in the negative.

In an important footnote, the Court observed that

[t]here are commonsense differences between speech that does "no more than propose a commercial transaction," *Pittsburgh Press Co. v. Human Relations Comm'n*, 413 U.S., at 385, and other varieties. Even if the differences do not

justify the conclusion that commercial speech is valueless, and thus subject to complete suppression by the State, they nonetheless suggest that a different degree of protection is necessary to insure that the flow of truthful and legitimate commercial information is unimpaired. The truth of commercial speech, for example, may be more easily verifiable by its disseminator than, let us say, news reporting or political commentary, in that ordinarily the advertiser seeks to disseminate information about a specific product or service that he himself provides and presumably knows more about than anyone else. Also, commercial speech may be more durable than other kinds. Since advertising is the *sine qua non* of commercial profits, there is little likelihood of its being chilled by proper regulation and forgone entirely.

Attributes such as these, the greater objectivity and hardiness of commercial speech, may make it less necessary to tolerate inaccurate statements for fear of silencing the speaker.... They may also make it appropriate to require that a commercial message appear in such a form, or include such additional information, warnings, and disclaimers, as are necessary to prevent its being deceptive. ... They may also make inapplicable the prohibition against prior restraints.

Although the Court explicitly conferred constitutional status upon commercial speech, it stopped short of affording it unqualified protection. Rather, it sought to differentiate commercial from political expression and created a separate standard of review on grounds that the former was hardier and "more easily verifiable by its disseminator." Adverting to "commonsense differences" between commercial and other forms of speech, the Court concluded "that a different degree of protection is necessary to insure that the flow of truthful and legitimate commercial information is unimpaired." Given the nature and propensities attributed to commercial speech, the Court emphasized that government might legitimately require disclosure, disclaimers, or warnings. Furthermore, the Court noted that traditional presumptions against the validity of prior restraint would not operate.

Diminished constitutional status, at least to the extent that it is predicated upon notions of hardiness and verifiability, is problematic. The conclusion that commercial expression is uniquely durable underestimates, for instance, the resiliency of political speech. Although the profit motive may be a powerful force that enhances commercial expression's immunity against official chilling influences, durability is not a unique categorical feature. A politician's interest in being elected, for instance, constitutes a motivating force at least as significant as the impulse to make money. If resiliency were to be given its full logical impact, an important form of political expression would merit diminished protection. Hardiness thus may be less than adequate as a point for distinguishing commercial and other variants of speech satisfactorily. Any inherent resiliency possessed by commercial expression may be immaterial, moreover, given the consequences of regulation. The obvious effect of systems of prior restraint or compulsory disclosure is the forced weakening of any expression's propagating tendencies. The offer and sale of securities and the marketing of tobacco products, for instance, are governed by regulatory schemes that previously restrain and define the terms of expression. Speech that does not meet the demands of official criteria thus may be irretrievably lost.

The companion rationale that commercial speech is easier to verify also is troublesome. Deceptive commercial and political statements present potential problems that are essentially indistinguishable. Promotions of products, candidates, and ideas all can involve misrepresentation. To the extent that any expression shortchanges the truth, whether to obtain money or votes, the authentication problem is comparable.

Although the diminished constitutional status of commercial expression is not expressed in direct terms, it might be explicable as a matter of simple valuation that fits within a broader constitutional value system that affords less regard to economic rights and interests. Modern due process and equal protection analysis of regulation affecting commercial activity consists of a highly deferential standard of review, contrasted with the enhanced scrutiny for legislation touching various other individual rights. Even that value-based explication, however, is imperfect. If the generally lesser constitutional concern afforded commercial interests is carried to its logical extreme, it would swallow the particularized recognition that commercial speech may have value equal to or surpassing that of political expression.

The process of distinguishing commercial speech for constitutional purposes might consider or account for relativities in the nature or cause of identified harms. Injury from a misleading commercial advertisement affecting a purchasing decision, for instance, is likely to be more direct than false political promises affecting a person's vote. Although a false pledge not to raise taxes may translate into an identifiable harm if it is relied upon, the injury is a result of combined voting preferences rather than entirely individual influence. Because the collective action of voting also is susceptible to diverse influences, many of which may respond to concerns unconnected to the false statement, the linkage between cause and harm may be more attenuated.

False political expression also may have relatively higher value in effectuating informed decision making. In propounding his developmental theory of democracy, John Stuart Mill noted that competition among ideas, whether true or false, strengthened truth, compelled the continuous reevaluation of ideas, and promoted the evolution of principles based upon reason rather than prejudice. Although false political statements may have a connection to the broad philosophical underpinnings of a system of freedom of expression, the relationship for untrue commercial speech is less manifest.

Distinctions resting upon category would seem to assume that the type of speech at issue can be clearly identified. The Court has defined commercial speech as expression inviting a commercial transaction or relating to the economic interest of the speaker and the audience. The latter definition may subsume the former and afford an overarching delineation. It also presents overbreadth problems, as even the most manifestly political expression may have underlying economic motivation. Even the authoring, promotion, and dissemination of anticapitalist polemics may be associated with profit making. The Court has observed that the presence of a profit motive is not necessarily dispositive toward determining whether expression should be labeled as commercial. Evolving and increasingly fine labeling standards suggest that, like obscenity, commercial speech may lend itself better to being "known when seen" than to objective definition. Speech categorization is a treacherous process, moreover, insofar as singular classification may dismiss the multidimensional nature of expression and the chosen identification is determinative of First Amendment status.

The mixed nature of much speech and the consequent difficulties of drawing precise lines for the real world were evidenced in *Village of Schaumburg v. Citizens for a Better Environment*. The Court in that case invalidated a regulation prohibiting door-to-door solicitation by certain charitable organizations. In so doing, it attempted to distinguish such fund-raising from commercial speech on grounds that the former "does more than inform private economic decision and is not primarily concerned with providing information about the characteristics and costs of goods and services." Justice Rehnquist, in dissent, asserted that the activity was purely commercial in its nature and merited no special constitutional solicitude. Greater acuity and sophistication might have been evinced in either instance by forthright recognition of the mixed character of the speech. Such a denomination need not have altered the outcome but would have avoided the procrustean appearance, if not nature, of the analysis. Review nonetheless seems disposed to favor polar choices rather than finer distinctions and intermediary determinations accounting for degrees of political or commercial character.

The conferral of constitutional status upon commercial expression was not accompanied by a clear enunciation of standards for assessing the pertinence or influence of regulatory interests. Subsequently, the Court invalidated prohibition of the display of residential For Sale signs, promotion of contraceptives, and attorney advertising. In *Linmark Associates, Inc. v. Township of Willingboro*, the Court emphasized the importance of free-flowing information despite claims that the posting of For Sale signs encouraged white flight and undermined racial integration goals. Official justifications for precluding contraceptive advertisements on grounds that they were offensive were rejected as inadequate. Implicit was a balancing of First Amendment interests and the importance of regulatory concerns. The invalidation of restrictions upon attorney advertising further suggested a requirement that any official limitation upon commercial speech must be supported by a substantial state interest. The protective reach of the First Amendment was explicitly delineated, however, to exclude false advertising.

Critical to the invalidation of attorney advertising restraints was their operation against general publicity and not merely against face-to-face solicitations, which the Court considered more dangerous and subject to stricter control. Interests in protecting unsophisticated or distressed individuals from vexatious conduct thus were recognized as grounds for limiting the style of attorney solicitation. Solicitation for private gain was distinguished, however, from the activities of nonprofit organizations that litigate for political purposes. In-person solicitation may be proscribed when it is likely to result in deception or improper influence, but regulation may not "abridge unnecessarily the associational freedom of" politically oriented legal organizations.

Although the Court continued to recognize the value of commercial expression for constitutional purposes, actual standards of review were not well articulated or connected. Eventually, in *Central Hudson Gas & Electric Co. v. Public Service Commission of New York*, the Court formulated a comprehensive framework for analyzing commercial-speech problems. At issue was a regulation prohibiting power companies from promoting the use of electricity. The state had justified the ban on grounds that it advanced energy conservation. The Court invalidated the prohibition pursuant to a four-part test for determining the permissibility of official control.

In commercial speech cases, then, a four-part analysis has developed. At the outset, we must determine whether the expression is protected by the First Amendment. For commercial speech to come within that provision, it at least must concern lawful activity and not be misleading. Next, we ask whether the asserted governmental interest is substantial. If both inquiries yield positive answers, we must determine whether the regulation directly advances the governmental interest asserted, and whether it is not more extensive than is necessary to serve that interest.

In applying the four-part test, the Court determined that a constitutional interest was present because the expression was not deceptive and did not promote unlawful activity. It also recognized an important state interest in energy efficiency and acknowledged that the legislative methodology would effectuate that aim. The regulatory means failed, however, because it reached too far and because less burdensome alternatives existed for facilitating the state's objectives. The Court noted that advertisements for energy-efficient products were ensnared by the broad prohibition, and thus a more narrowly drawn restriction or review process must be employed.

Prior to *Central Hudson*, it was becoming evident that the Court might not hold firm to the *Virginia Board of Pharmacy* statement of principle disfavoring regulation unless expression is misleading or the underlying activity is illegal. In *Friedman v. Rogers*, the Court upheld regulation prohibiting optometrists from using trade names. The decision rested in part upon the predicate that trade names have "no intrinsic meaning," convey no real information, and may mislead the public. Justice Blackmun countered, however, that a trade name may denote product or service quality and "deceive only if it is used in a misleading context." In *Friedman*, the Court strained to justify the regulation within the contours of the falseness or deception allowance provided by *Virginia Board of Pharmacy*. More recently, the Court has expanded the focus on underlying illegality to include any activity that the state has authority to control even if the regulatory power is not exercised. In *Posadas de Puerto Rico Associates v. Tourism Co. of Puerto Rico*, it thus further relaxed the conditions that otherwise preclude official regulation of commercial speech.

The *Posadas de Puerto Rico Associates* decision is reminiscent, in a critical sense, of the devaluation of commercial speech in *Valentine v. Chrestensen* and its early progeny. For the first time since the shelving of *Chrestensen*, the Court in *Posadas* countenanced official restraint of truthful information regarding a lawful activity. The Court held that a legislature may ban expression concerning an activity it considers harmful, even if it is not made illegal, because "the greater power to completely ban casino gambling necessarily includes the lesser power to ban advertising of casino gambling."

By allowing restrictions on promotion of a lawful activity, the Court in *Posadas* distinguished its holding from earlier decisions invalidating bans on contraceptive and abortion advertisements on the ground that those matters were constitutionally protected but gambling was not. In making that distinction, however, it introduced the newly restrictive notion that the First Amendment precludes official abridgment of advertising when the underlying activity is not constitutionally protected. Few products, services, or activities are without potential for harm. Many are not constitutionally protected. Measuring First Amendment protection according to the constitutional status of the underlying activity, therefore, represents a check on legislative power that may prove illusory. In any event, the Court has significantly departed from jurisprudence regarding commercial speech differently only to the extent necessary to facilitate an unimpaired flow of truthful and legitimate information.

The Court in *Posadas* also effectively diluted the standard for judicial scrutiny of commercial speech. The Court purported to employ an elevated standard of review, as set forth in *Central Hudson*, requiring that the regulation directly advance a substantial state interest and restrict speech no more than necessary. Although the Court referenced its analysis to these criteria, it concluded that the legislature could decide the regulatory alternative that best serves its end. Such a determination translates in practice into a deferential model of review.

In addition to using a standard resembling a rational basis test, the Court appeared to discount, if not disregard, less restrictive means of effectuating regulatory aims. Justice Brennan suggested that if Puerto Rico was concerned with social harm from casino gambling, it could have monitored gambling operations to guard against infiltration by organized crime, aggressively enforced relevant criminal statutes, and promulgated competing speech calculated to discourage participation by residents. The availability of less restrictive alternatives led the Court just a few years earlier to conclude that government could not completely suppress commercial speech even if it was acting to further "an imperative national goal."

The deference to legislative judgment apparent in *Posadas* suggests a spirit more akin to *Chrestensen* than to later decisions that discredited it. During the *Chrestensen* era, commercial speech was not constitutionally protected. Absent a fundamental constitutional interest, the Court normally applied a rational basis test that deferred to legislative judgment. That approach contrasts with the elevated level of review used in later commercial-speech cases in which the Court demanded proof of a substantial state interest. In affirming the ban on casino gambling advertising, and particularly by concluding that Puerto Rico could have found the underlying activity harmful to the citizenry and thus prohibited it, the Court in *Posadas* seems to have retreated to a more deferential mode of review. Judicial speculation concerning what might constitute a proper and significant legislative purpose further denotes use of a rational basis test. Reversion toward a more deferential posture also seems evidenced by a determination that regulation, although required to be no more extensive than necessary, need not be the least restrictive option available to advance government's interest.

Commercial-speech analysis appears to be drifting away from traditional notions that the First Amendment is designed to prevent "highly paternalistic" intrusions by the state that would limit information available to the public. Until *Posadas*, modern revised analysis seemed less inclined to tolerate regulation reflecting government concern that the public might act irrationally on truthful information concerning a lawful activity. First Amendment jurisprudence traditionally holds the public responsible for evaluation of information and for making decisions by means of autonomous rather than authoritative selection. *Virginia Board of Pharmacy* integrated that principle to a considerable extent into commercial-speech doctrine. The Court later recognized that the First Amendment accepts the risk that the public might exercise poor judgment or even be deceived. More recent jurisprudence, however, allows states to regulate commercial speech on essentially paternalistic grounds.

The Court has observed that the distinction between commercial and other forms of expression is a commonsense one. It also acknowledged that the line "will not always be easy to draw." The latter confession has proved to be more accurate than the former expectation. Definitional problems and uncertainty about how standards will be applied continue to be the primary treacheries of commercial-speech analysis. At least for now, it is evident that traditional risk-assumption models, premised upon opportunity for response in a self-regulating marketplace of information, will not be relied upon exclusively to address concerns with the effects of commercial speech. Criteria settled in their articulation and application, however, await further development.

E. COPYRIGHT

First Amendment rights and First Amendment values collide in the area of copyright. The Constitution provides that "Congress shall have Power ... To Promote the Progress of Science and useful Arts, by securing for limited Times to Authors and Inventors the exclusive Right to their respective Writings and Discoveries." Copyright thus promotes First Amendment interests by "motivat[ing] the creative [process] by the provision of a special reward." The consequent privilege, however, creates First Amendment problems insofar as it denies access to or restricts use of materials. Congress's delicate task pursuant to its constitutional charge, therefore, is to balance creative interests that are the source of expression against social interests in a free flow of information and ideas. At the same time, copyright law must remain congruent with developing technology and advances in disseminating information.

Federal copyright law in its most basic form has been codified pursuant to congressional action that, since 1976, protects both published and unpublished works. The Copyright Act of 1976, responding to the emergence of new media that confounded its statutory antecedent, covers originally authored works "fixed in any tangible medium of expression, now known or later developed, from which they can be perceived, reproduced, or otherwise communicated either directly or with the aid of machine or device." Still, problems arise in determining ambits of coverage. In *Sony Corp. of America v. Universal City Studios, Inc.*, the Supreme Court refused without congressional direction to include home usage of videotape recorders as an act of infringement. Noting the fluidity of technology and concerns and the Constitution's specific assignment of responsibility to the legislative branch, the Court emphasized that "[s]ound policy, as well as history, supports our constant deference to Congress." Excluded from the Copyright Act's protective ambit is "any idea, procedure, process, system, method of operation, concept, principle, or discovery, regardless of the form in which it is described, explained, illustrated, or embodied in such work." The 1976 act preempts all state control, statutory or common-law, of the field.

The inherent tension with which copyright law struggles is protecting intellectual property but doing so in a fashion that does not impede the flow of information to the detriment of First Amendment values. Although the way in which news or history is packaged merits protection, therefore, raw information is not copyrighted. Copyright protection of ideas, facts, and theory is afforded as an economic incentive designed to enlarge general knowledge. It is not intended to confer exclusive rights to account for history or contemporary events, however, so actual protection only extends to the author's unique expression. Copyright interests seldom will have such public significance that the author's interest will be subordinated to unfettered usage.

As a general proposition, a copyright owner has the exclusive right to reproduce the subject work; prepare derivative works from it; market or distribute copies; and perform or display literary, musical, dramatic, pantomime, film, pictorial graphic, sculpture, or other audiovisual work in public. The right, which is segregable from the author in the event of a "work made for hire" or subsequent transfer, runs on one of two tracks. Pursuant to the present enactment, protection extends for fifty years beyond an author's death. Under preceding law, which is still relevant because many works were copyrighted under it, an initial period of protection was available for twenty-eight years followed by an opportunity to renew for a second period of equal duration. Procedures for obtaining a valid copyright include proper notice upon all copies and filing with the Register of Copyrights. Failure to do so may be curable, so long as the omission affected a small number of copies and reasonable efforts are made to correct the problem. Probably the grayest and thus most heavily litigated area of copyright law pertains to the doctrine of fair use. Federal statute provides that fair use is to be determined by

1. the purpose and character of the use, including whether such use is of a commercial nature or is for a nonprofit educational purpose;
2. the nature of the copyrighted work;

3. the amount and substantiality of the portion used in relation to the copyrighted work as a whole; and
4. the effect of the use upon the potential market for or value of the copyrighted work.

The law thus requires balancing of several competing interests to determine whether usage of a work constitutes infringement or fair use.

In *Harper & Row Publishers, Inc. v. Nation Enterprises*, the Court considered a fair-use argument by a magazine that excerpted segments concerning the pardon of Richard Nixon from President Ford's soon-to-be-published memoirs. Publication of the article occurred before another magazine, which had contracted to publish like excerpts, went to press. Although the information was newsworthy, the Court determined that the primary purpose of publication was commercial profit. Neither the fact that the work was factual in nature or that a small fraction was used proved dispositive. The Court emphasized that the fair-use defense had less pertinence to works that had not been published in their original form. Because a crucial part of the book had been excerpted, moreover, actual quantity was considered less pertinent. Finally, the actual loss of money suffered when the other magazine decided not to publish or pay convinced the Court that the unauthorized publication had hurt the book's marketability and diminished its value. Although publication of the excerpts easily might be characterized as news, the *Harper & Row* decision demonstrates that a strong public interest alone will not prevent a finding of infringement. It evinces, moreover, a sensitivity of the Court to proprietary interests even in expression that otherwise qualifies as the most highly protected form of speech.

Further illustrative of a restrictive fair-use doctrine is a Second Circuit decision, in *Salinger v. Random House, Inc.*, that enjoined publication of a biography because it included small excerpts from letters that the subject of the book had copyrighted but donated to libraries. In examining the factors relevant to determining fair use, the court first, despite recognizing a valid purpose for usage, found that the biographer's needs could have been satisfied without using the actual contents of the letters. Second, because the letters were unpublished, the scope of fair use was much narrower. Third, although only small excerpts from many letters had been used, the court found that in sum they permeated a substantial portion of the biography. Finally, because the letters constituted such a significant portion of the work, the court determined that the potential market for the copyrighted works would be impaired. Despite the significant impact upon editorial discretion, neither the *Harper & Row* nor the *Salinger* decision directly addressed First Amendment claims.

The Second Circuit revisited fair use in *New Era Publications Interna-*

tional, ApS v. Carol Publishing Group, in which numerous passages from an author's published works were included in an unflattering biography. Although the district court had enjoined publication pending elimination of what it considered to be infringing excerpts, the court of appeals found their incorporation to be fair use. Notwithstanding publication of the book for profit, the appeals court distinguished the circumstances from *Harper & Row* on grounds that they did not concern "underhanded" action calculated to realize "undeserved economic profit." It also emphasized the factual and published nature of the copyrighted works and that the book at issue did not draw too heavily upon them. Finally, the court determined that harm to the marketability of a forthcoming authorized biography resulting from a "devastating critique" was not a concern of copyright law.

Special copyright problems have arisen in the context of cable television. At a time when cable largely was a retransmission or siphoning medium, the Supreme Court held that its service was not a "performance for profit." Consequently, it was not subject to copyright liability and could retransmit broadcast signals without obtaining permission of copyright owners whose works might be implicated. Pursuant to the Copyright Act of 1976, Congress has required cable operators retransmitting copyrighted programming to pay a license fee. The amount of the fee is set by the Copyright Royalty Tribunal, which also distributes monies collected pursuant to a complex formula intended to account for the interests of broadcasters and the producers and syndicators of programs. Despite claims by broadcasters that the fee-distribution system grossly undervalues their interests, and by cablecasters that it makes signal carriage in some instances prohibitively expensive, the scheme has survived legal challenge.

REFERENCES

CASES

A Book Named "John Cleland's Memoirs of a Woman of Pleasure" v. Attorney General of Massachusetts, 383 U.S. 413 (1966).
American Booksellers Association, Inc. v. Hudnut, 771 F.2d 323 (7th Cir. 1985), cert. denied, 475 U.S. 1132 (1986).
Beauharnais v. Illinois, 343 U.S. 250 (1952).
Bigelow v. Virginia, 421 U.S. 809 (1975).
Branzburg v. Hayes, 408 U.S. 665 (1972).
Browning-Ferris Industries of Vermont, Inc. v. Kelso Disposal, Inc., 109 S. Ct. 2909 (1989).
Cantrell v. Forest City Publishing Co., 419 U.S. 245 (1974).
Capital Broadcasting Co. v. Mitchell, 333 F. Supp. 582 (D.D.C. 1971), aff'd., 415 U.S. 1000 (1972).

Central Hudson Gas & Electric Co. v. Public Service Commission of New York, 447 U.S. 557 (1980).

Chandler v. Florida, 449 U.S. 560 (1981).

Cox Broadcasting Corp. v. Cohn, 420 U.S. 469 (1975).

Curtis Publishing Co. v. Butts, 388 U.S. 130 (1967).

Dietemann v. Time, Inc., 449 F.2d 245 (9th Cir. 1971).

Dun & Bradstreet, Inc. v. Greenmoss Builders, Inc., 472 U.S. 749 (1985).

Estes v. Texas, 381 U.S. 532 (1965).

Farber, Matter of, 78 N.J. 259, 394 A.2d 330, *cert. denied*, 439 U.S. 997 (1978).

Federal Communications Commission v. Pacifica Foundation, 438 U.S. 726 (1978).

The Florida Star v. B.J.F., 109 S. Ct. 2603 (1989).

Friedman v. Rogers, 440 U.S. 1 (1979).

Gannett Co., Inc. v. DePasquale, 443 U.S. 368 (1979).

Gertz v. Robert Welch, Inc., 418 U.S. 323 (1974).

Ginsberg v. New York, 390 U.S. 629 (1968).

Ginzburg v. United States, 383 U.S. 463 (1966).

Globe Newspaper Co. v. Superior Court, 457 U.S. 596 (1982).

Harper & Row Publishers, Inc. v. Nation Enterprises, 471 U.S. 539 (1985).

Harte-Hanks Communications, Inc. v. Connaughton, 109 S. Ct. 2678 (1989).

Hustler Magazine v. Falwell, 108 S. Ct. 876 (1988).

Hutchinson v. Proxmire, 443 U.S. 111 (1979).

Jenkins v. Georgia, 418 U.S. 153 (1974).

Keeton v. Hustler Magazine, Inc., 465 U.S. 770 (1984).

Linmark Associates, Inc. v. Township of Willingboro, 431 U.S. 85 (1977).

Miller v. California, 413 U.S. 15 (1973).

Near v. Minnesota, 283 U.S. 697 (1931).

Nebraska Press Association v. Stuart, 427 U.S. 539 (1976).

New Era Publications International, ApS v. Carol Publishing Group, 904 F.2d 152 (2d Cir.), *cert. denied*, 111 S. Ct. 297 (1991).

New York Times Co. v. Sullivan, 376 U.S. 254 (1964).

Paris Adult Theater I v. Slaton, 413 U.S. 49 (1973).

Pittsburgh Press Co. v. Pittsburgh Commission on Human Relations, 413 U.S. 376 (1973).

Pope v. Illinois, 481 U.S. 497 (1987).

Posadas de Puerto Rico Associates v. Tourism Co. of Puerto Rico, 478 U.S. 328 (1986).

Press-Enterprise Co. v. Superior Court, 478 U.S. 1 (1986).

Richmond Newspapers, Inc. v. Virginia, 448 U.S. 555 (1980).

Rosenbloom v. Metromedia, Inc., 403 U.S. 29 (1971).

Roth v. United States, 354 U.S. 476 (1957).

Salinger v. Random House, Inc., 818 F.2d 90 (2d Cir.), *cert. denied*, 108 S. Ct. 218 (1987).

Sheppard v. Maxwell, 384 U.S. 333 (1966).

Sony Corp. of America v. Universal City Studios, Inc., 464 U.S. 417 (1984).

Stanley v. Georgia, 394 U.S. 557 (1969).

Time, Inc. v. Firestone, 424 U.S. 448 (1976).

Time, Inc. v. Hill, 385 U.S. 374 (1976).

Valentine v. Chrestensen, 316 U.S. 52 (1942).
Village of Schaumburg v. Citizens for a Better Environment, 444 U.S. 620 (1980).
Virgil v. Time, Inc., 527 F.2d 1122 (9th Cir. 1975), *cert. denied*, 425 U.S. 998 (1976).
Virginia State Board of Pharmacy v. Virginia Citizens Consumer Council, 425 U.S. 748 (1976).
Wolston v. Reader's Digest Association, 443 U.S. 157 (1979).
Young v. American Mini Theatres, Inc, 427 U.S. 50 (1976).
Zacchini v. Scripps Howard Broadcasting Co., 433 U.S. 562 (1977).
Zurcher v. Stanford Daily, 436 U.S. 547 (1978).

PUBLICATIONS

Ashdown, *Gertz and Firestone: A Study in Constitutional Policy Making*, 61 Minn. L. Rev. 645 (1977).
Barnett, *From New Technology to Moral Rights: Passive Carriers, Teletext, and Deletion as Copyright Infringement*, 31 J. Copyright Society 427 (1984).
Beard, *The Sale, Rental, and Reproduction of Motion Picture Videocassettes: Privacy or Privilege?*, 15 New Eng. L. Rev. 435 (1979–80).
Berney, *When Academic Freedom and Freedom of Speech Confront Holocaust Denial and Group Libel*, 8 Cardozo L. Rev. 559 (1987).
Brandeis & Warren, *The Right to Privacy*, 4 Harv. L. Rev. 193 (1980).
Cass, *Commercial Speech, Constitutionalism, Collective Choice*, 56 U. Cin. L. Rev. 1317 (1988).
Diamond, *Unanswered Defamation Questions*, 10 Comm/ent L.J. 125 (1987).
Francione, *Facing the Nation: The Standards for Copyright Infringement and Fair Use of Factual Works*, 134 U. Pa. L. Rev. 519 (1985).
Freedman, *Freedom of Information and the First Amendment in a Bureaucratic Age*, 49 Brooklyn L. Rev. 835 (1983).
Geyh, *The Regulation of Speech Incident to the Sale or Purchase of Goods and Services*, 52 U. Pitt. L. Rev. 1 (1990).
Halpern, *The Right of Publicity: Commercial Exploitation of the Associative Value of Personality*, 39 Vand. L. Rev. 1199 (1986).
Hill, *Solicitation By Lawyers: Piercing the First Amendment Veil*, 42 Maine L. Rev. 369 (1990).
Leaffer, Understanding Copyright Law (1989).
Lind, Jr. *Justice Rehnquist: First Amendment Speech in the Labor Context*, 8 Hastings Const. L.Q. 93 (1980).
Linder, *When Names Are Not News They're Negligence: Media Liability for Injuries Resulting from the Publication of Accurate Information*, 52 U.M.K.C. L. Rev. 421 (1984).
Lively, *The Sometimes Relevant First Amendment*, 60 Temple L.Q. 881 (1987).
Lively, *The Supreme Court and Commercial Speech: Old Words with a New Message*, 72 Minn. L. Rev. 289 (1987).
Lockhart & McClure, *Literature, the First Amendment, and the Law of Obscenity and the First Amendment*, 38 Minn. L. Rev. 295 (1954).
Logan, *Tort Law and the Central Meaning of the First Amendment*, 51 U. Pitt. L. Rev. 493 (1990).

Mackinnon, *Pornography, Civil Rights, and Speech,* 20 Harv. C.R.-C.L. L. Rev. 1 (1985).

Macpherson, The Life and Times of Liberal Democracy (1977).

Meiklejohn, *The First Amendment Is an Absolute,* 1961 Sup. Ct. Rev. 245.

Mill, On Liberty (1859).

Monk, *Evidentiary Privilege of the Journalist's Source: Theory and Statutory Protection,* 51 Mo. L. Rev. 1 (1986).

Nahmod, *Constitutional Damages and Correctional Justice,* 76 Va. L. Rev. 997 (1990).

Report of the Attorney General's Commission on Pornography (1986).

Report of the United States Commission on Obscenity and Pornography (1970).

Rosen & Babcock, *Of and Concerning Real People and Writers of Fiction,* 7 Comm/ent L.J. 221 (1985).

Shiffrin, *Defamatory, Non-Media Speech and First Amendment Methodology,* 25 U.C.L.A. L. Rev. 915 (1978).

Shiffrin, *The First Amendment and Economic Regulation: Away from a General Theory of the First Amendment,* 78 Nw. U. L. Rev. 1212 (1983).

Siegal, *Smart Shopping as Patriotism: Avoidance, Denial, and Advertising,* 7 Comm. L. 37 (1990).

Sims, *Right of Publicity: Commercial Exploitation of the Associative Value of Publicity,* 49 Fordham L. Rev. 453 (1981).

Sylvester, *How the States Govern the News Media—A Survey of Selected Jurisdictions,* 16 Sw. U. L. Rev. 723 (1986).

Watkins, *Gertz and the Common Law of Defamation,* 15 Tex. Tech. L. Rev. 823 (1984).

Chapter 4

Economic Regulation of the Media Industry

A free press stands as one of the great interpreters between the government and the people. To allow it to be fettered is to fetter ourselves.

Grosjean v. American Press Co., Inc.,
297 U.S. 233 (1936)

Regulation of the media, although it often implicates the First Amendment, routinely is predicated upon constitutional authorization. Media governance usually reflects an exercise of the commerce power at the federal level and the police power at the state level. Depending upon the subject of official attention, regulation also has been premised upon the taxing and spending clauses, the post–Civil War amendments, and the First Amendment itself. Much regulation, even if it may affect content, is economic in nature and responsive to what constitutes a significant industry. The most comprehensive regulatory scheme is the Communications Act of 1934, which originally covered governance of radio, television, and common carriers. By its terms the act applies to

all interstate and foreign transmission of energy by radio, which originates and/ or is received within the United States, and to all persons engaged within the United States in such communication or such transmission of energy by radio, and to the licensing and regulating of all radio stations.

The Communications Act in its present incarnation contains provisions applicable to cable television.

The general purpose of the act is to regulate "interstate and foreign commerce in communication by wire and radio so as to make available, so far as possible, to all the people of the United States a rapid, efficient, Nation-wide, and world-wide wire and radio communication service." More specifically, it is calculated "to maintain the control of the United States over all the channels of interstate and foreign radio transmission; and to provide for the use of such channels, but not the ownership thereof, by persons for limited periods of time, under licenses granted by Federal authority."

To effectuate the purposes of the act, the Federal Communications Commission (FCC) was established with the power, among other things, to classify radio stations; determine the nature of service to be provided by each class of station and by stations within each class; assign bands of frequencies to each class of station and specific frequencies to individual stations; determine the location of classes of and individual stations; set technical operational standards; encourage the larger and more effective use of radio in the public interest (a power that is the source of most content regulation); establish areas to be served by any station; make rules applicable to chain (or network) broadcasting; set licensee record-keeping requirements; suspend licenses of broadcasters for violating the law or transmitting obscene or profane language; adopt rules relating to international agreements concerning radio; and set standards for broadcast equipment used in broadcast reception.

I. FEDERAL PREEMPTION

Federal regulation of broadcasting is so pervasive that it raises immediately the question of whether such control occupies the entire field. The Constitution provides that federal law is "the Supreme Law of the Land" to the point of preempting any concurrent state law. To determine whether a federal enactment preempts state regulation, it is necessary first to ascertain whether a specific clause to that effect exists. Because the Communications Act of 1934 contains no such provision, a supremacy inquiry requires consideration of three factors. Congressional intent may be evidenced by the pervasiveness of the regulatory scheme, the dominance of the federal interest and the need for national uniformity, and the danger of conflict in the administration and enforcement of competing laws.

For most purposes, given the pervasive nature of federal regulation, strong federal interest and need for uniformity, and the dangers of conflicting governance, analysis leads to a determination of preemption. In *National Broadcasting Co. v. Board of Public Utility Commissioners of New Jersey*, a broadcaster challenged a state law requiring approval for construction of a transmitter even after its erection had been authorized by the FCC. Congress had empowered the FCC to grant such permits, but the state had a concurrent regulatory scheme requiring broadcasters to obtain "a certificate of public convenience" and enabling the pertinent board to set conditions that would avoid "unreasonable blanketing or interference with radio transmission and reception."

Because the broadcaster was operating in the field of interstate commerce, state law was preempted by the federal scheme. The district court refused to address the issue of whether purely intrastate transmissions might be concurrently regulated. Given the same set of facts, it is inconceivable that a modern court would not find that concerns of pervasiveness, dominance, uniformity, and potential for conflict all favor federal preemption.

Special circumstances may exist, however, that would militate against preemption. In *Ross v. Hatfield*, a federal district court rejected the argument that a restrictive covenant barring satellite dishes from a landowner's property was preempted by federal law. The claim was dismissed in part because of the absence of state action. Presumably, however, state action would exist and a constitutional question would arise if the covenant were judicially enforced. The issue also would be presented by a zoning ordinance or other state or local prohibition. As the district court noted, federal law would preempt zoning or other regulations differentiating "between satellite receiving antennae and other types of antennae." The possibility at least exists that a nondiscriminatory ordinance reflecting legitimate zoning or other concerns might survive supremacy-clause scrutiny.

By its terms, the Cable Communications Policy Act of 1984 confers upon state and local governments partial regulatory responsibility for cable. The general purposes of the Cable Act include establishment of a national policy concerning cable; provision of franchise procedures and standards that encourage industry growth and ensure responsiveness to local needs; facilitation of content diversity; creation of a fair and orderly process for franchise renewal; and promotion of industry competition and minimization of economically burdensome regulation. Although it is diminished in comparison to broadcasting, the federal interest in regulating cable nonetheless is strong. Federal dominance and pervasiveness are reduced by explicit assignments of power to state and local authority. As at least one court has noted, the Cable Act "establishes a national framework and standards for regulating the cable television industry. It authorizes local governments to regulate cable television through the franchise process, but at the same time it restricts that regulatory power."

The Supreme Court in *Capital Cities Cable, Inc. v. Crisp* considered a preemption question that arose prior to the Cable Act's passage but that undoubtedly would lead to the same result now. At issue was a state law requiring cable operators to eliminate all liquor advertisements from out-of-state signals retransmitted to cable subscribers. The Court determined that the FCC's power "plainly comprises authority to regulate the signals carried by cable television systems." Consequently, the advertising ban was found to have exceeded the authority reserved to local government by FCC rules and to have intruded upon an exclusive federal domain. The Court noted that the ruling did not alter or diminish local authority to regulate aspects of cable systems specifically assigned to it. Absent express investment of authority, therefore, local governance risks running afoul of the supremacy clause.

Preemption also was found, albeit by a slimmer margin, in *City of New York v. Federal Communications Commission*. The subject of the controversy was a commission rule predating the Cable Act of 1984 and barring local governments from imposing technical requirements on cable operators that were more stringent than federal standards. Although the stricter criteria were set as a condition of awarding a franchise, the FCC argued that they imposed divergent and sometimes unworkable demands and subverted its objective of promoting efficient and innovative service. The Court noted the Cable Act's division of responsibility between state and local franchising authorities and the FCC's interest in the operational aspects of cable service itself. It concluded that because legislation was enacted against the backdrop of the regulation, which was neither eliminated nor criticized in the process, Congress essentially had endorsed and affirmed the disputed provision.

II. ECONOMIC CONTROLS

Not all regulation of the press, at least as far as the Court is concerned, implicates First Amendment interests. Because the media are engaged in business, they are subject to most laws governing general economic activity. The diverse requirements of antitrust, securities, and tax law thus impinge upon the media. Although the media are subject to such demands, particular application of regulatory enactments may create problems of a constitutional order.

A. ANTITRUST LAW

The Court consistently has found that antitrust provisions apply with the same force to the media industry as they do to other lines of business. It has noted, moreover, that enforcement of antitrust laws may promote the same interests that underlie the First Amendment. In *Associated Press v. United States*, the Court determined that the Constitution provided no refuge from the prohibitions against combinations and conspiracies in restraint of trade. As a news service, the Associated Press collected, assembled, and distributed news solely for and to members of its organization. The Court found that such exclusivity was anticompetitive, monopolistic, and a legitimate regulatory concern. In concluding that the Sherman Antitrust Act applied unequivocally to such circumstances, the Court rejected arguments that its operation constituted an abridgment of freedom of the press. It thus observed that

[i]t would be strange indeed, . . . if the grave concern for freedom of the press which prompted the adoption of the First Amendment should be read as a command that the government was without power to protect that freedom. The First Amendment, far from providing an argument against application of the Sherman Act, here provides powerful reasons to the contrary. That Amendment rests on the assumption that the widest possible dissemination of information from diverse and antagonistic sources is essential to the welfare of the public, that a free press is a condition of a free society. Surely a command that the government itself shall not impede the free flow of ideas does not afford nongovernmental combinations a refuge if they impose restraints upon that constitutionally guaranteed freedom. Freedom to publish means freedom for all and not for some. Freedom to publish is guaranteed by the Constitution, but freedom to combine to keep others from publishing is not. Freedom of the press from governmental interference under the First Amendment does not sanction repression of that freedom by private interests. The First Amendment affords not the slightest support for the contention that a combination to restrain trade in news and views has any constitutional immunity.

Although the Court emphasized the harmony of antitrust and First Amendment objectives, its analysis may be subject to criticism that it mistook constitutional values for constitutional rights. The First Amendment operates against government rather than private action, but the *Associated Press* decision at times blurs the distinction between constitutional and statutory freedoms to publish. The constitutional liberty was defined in terms of "a command that the government itself shall not impede the free flow of ideas." Freedom of the press as provided by the First Amendment safeguards editorial discretion generally, which presumably includes autonomous judgment with respect to whether to publish at all and to whom information will be distributed. Statutory freedom, secured by antitrust laws, ensures opportunities to compete. Although multiplicity of competitors may promote diversity of information, restrictions on the use of information nonetheless implicate First Amendment interests of editorial discretion. The *Associated Press* decision might read better, therefore, if the actuality and pertinence of the constitutional concern had been clearly identified. First Amendment interests still might have been overridden by a determination that antitrust considerations presented a sufficiently compelling reason for displacing them.

The Court dismissed First Amendment concerns altogether in *Lorain*

Journal v. United States when it determined that an order restraining a publisher from engaging in anticompetitive practices did not constitute a prior restraint. A newspaper had responded to the licensing of a radio station in its market area by adopting a policy that denied advertising space to persons and entities buying time from the broadcaster. Contrary to the publisher's argument, the Court found that the injunction against its practice constituted no restriction upon freedom of the press but merely applied to him "what the law applies to others." Had the newspaper specifically or the media generally been singled out for special regulatory attention, as discussed later in this chapter, it then might have been possible to argue that the press was burdened in an unconstitutional fashion.

A publisher's requirement that advertisers pay for space in both a morning and afternoon newspaper has survived an antitrust challenge. Despite the government's contention that such a condition constituted an illegal tying arrangement, the Court in *Times-Picayune Publishing Co. v. United States* determined that the challenged policy did not force an unwanted service upon advertisers. In support of its conclusion, the Court found that the publishing company did not occupy a dominant position in the newspaper advertising market, as required by the Sherman Act. It further defined the relevant market as both morning and evening newspapers, described morning and evening readers as fungible, and found no discrimination against buyers of advertising in the third newspaper. The Court thus found "no leverage in one market exclud[ing] sellers in the second, because for present purposes the products are identical and the market the same."

A different result would have followed if the argument that morning and afternoon markets are different had been embraced. Under such circumstances, a unit pricing policy might be used to prop up a weak afternoon newspaper against its competition. The dissenters in the *Times-Picayune* case maintained that the publishing combine had used its monopoly on the morning newspapers to restrain unreasonably the competition between its evening newspaper and that of its rival. In regarding the morning and evening newspaper markets as distinct, the dissenters found advertising in the evening paper to be "an inescapable part of the price of access to the all-important columns of the single morning paper."

Commentary regarding the desirability of anticompetitive regulation and its ultimate consonance with First Amendment interests is not undivided. One observer has characterized government intervention to remedy structural or institutional constraints upon freedom of expression through the media as a logical extension of the First Amendment. The notion that private centers of power can be as much a threat to diversity of ideas and voices as the government comports with jurisprudential sentiments expressed in the *Associated Press* case. Agglomerations of power in the media marketplace even have been described as more worrisome than concentration in the general economic marketplace. A high degree of discretionary power enables the person exercising it to restrain ideas. Rational economic behavior, insofar as it is tied to profit maximization, does not necessarily parallel the exercise of editorial judgment. Because media operators have moneymaking motives mixed with ideological impulses, it is argued that a uniquely strong temptation exists to exclude ideas even at the cost of lost profits. The point is made, moreover, that if competition in the marketplace of ideas is the key to political freedom, it is only a small step from condemnation of government monopoly to intolerance of private monopoly. *See* B. Owen, Economics and Freedom of Expression (1975).

Responding to the interventionist model is the notion that information diversity is better advanced by relaxation of antitrust laws and their ilk. Underlying that premise is concern that competition can lead to negative results when resources are limited or scarce, so that the person or entity providing the cheapest and worst service survives. Modern broadcasting, for instance, pursues an economic strategy of maximizing profits by maximizing its audience—a formula that facilitates programming keyed to mainstream tastes or the lowest common denominator. When resources are limited or divided, coaction typified by commercial broadcasting's contributions of support to public broadcasting or antitrust immunity afforded failing newspapers is suggested as an alternative preferable to competition. Since antitrust laws work against cooperation, the argument is that a new plateau of enlightenment must be reached to strike a sensitive balance between "competitive and cooperative aspects of converging information services." *See* J. Inose and H. Pierce, Information Technology and Civilization (1984).

For now, the line of antitrust cases concerning the media evidences that the First Amendment affords no immunity from laws applicable to industry and business practices in general. Exemption from the reach of antitrust regulation requires a statutory provision to that effect. The Newspaper Preservation Act, discussed in Chapter 5, exemplifies precisely such an enactment. Short of such a congressionally conferred privilege, however, the courts have shown no inclination to limit the force of antitrust law.

B. SECURITIES REGULATION

The purpose of the federal securities laws is to protect investors and maintain the integrity of the investment marketplace. In pursuing these objectives, securities regulation can implicate the First Amendment in two basic ways. Controls upon the content of what issuers and promoters of securities can disseminate to the public affect expressive freedom and ultimately the collective pool of information for public consumption. Restrictions upon or accountability for what is published in any medium with respect to investment implicate even broader First Amendment concerns.

The Supreme Court, in *Paris Adult Theatre I v. Slaton*, characterized the purpose of the federal securities laws as protecting "the weak, the uninformed, the unsuspecting, and the gullible from the exercise of their own volition." In *Archer v. Securities and Exchange Commission*, the securities industry was singled out for regulation that must be constitutionally sensitive but enforceable against frauds that "take on more subtle and involved forms than those in which dishonesty manifests itself in cruder and less specialized activities." To the extent that regulation promotes disclosure of material information, it might appear harmonious with First Amendment values associated with expression from "a multitude of tongues." Insofar as content control makes government the head editor of information disseminated to investors, however, the model of governance is susceptible to depiction as "authoritative selection." The Securities and Exchange Commission (SEC) is empowered, among other things, to review and approve the content of offering materials before they may be disseminated to the public. As a condition to propagation, it may insist upon amplification, deletion, or alteration of content. The SEC may issue an order restraining dissemination of promotional materials to the public if this is necessary to enforce its content demands. The agency thus exercises censorship powers reminiscent of those associated with the long-abandoned English system of licensing.

Survival of a system of editorial oversight and prior restraint, with minimal constitutional scrutiny, is largely attributable to an analytical process that calibrates First Amendment protection according to how expression is classified. The promotion of investments and dissemination of investment advice would seem to qualify as commercial speech, which, until the mid–1970s, was unprotected. Even now, the conferral of First Amendment status upon commercial speech has been conditioned by the observation that the general prohibition against prior restraint may be inapplicable. Prior to its recognition that regulation of commercial expression implicated constitutional concerns, the Court observed that its control could be premised upon "unprovable assumptions." Given the constitutional standing of commercial speech now, even if it is limited, principled review would seem to require something more than the works of imagination or speculation as rationales.

Earlier cases deprecate any intimation of a First Amendment concern with respect to the promotion of securities. The SEC's position that editorial freedom of securities issues, promoters, and advisers is outweighed by the potential harm to investors has remained consistent despite commercial expression's evolution into a constitutionally protected speech form. In *Carl M. Loeb, Rhoades and Co.*, the commission rejected arguments that a statutory bar against dissemination of offering materials should not be construed to prohibit news releases and other publicity concerning a future offering. The SEC affirmed its intention to regard any publicity relevant to a marketing initiative as impermissible unless a registration statement was in effect. In so doing, it characterized the flow of normal corporate news unrelated to a selling effort as "natural, desirable and entirely consistent with the objective of disclosure to the public which underlies the federal securities laws." The commission expressed its special concern with sales-related publicity when an issue has "news value," since the potential for whipping up a "speculative frenzy" under such circumstances is enhanced. It distinguished the dissemination of information by reporters neither offering nor selling securities, however, and noted that its "interpretation . . . in no way restricts the freedom of news media to seek out and publish financial news."

The lines of distinction that determined regulatory interest were less easily drawn in another context. In *Lowe v. Securities and Exchange Commission*, the Court examined the commission's enforcement of the Investment Advisers Act of 1940, which provides for the licensing and regulation of persons who provide investment counseling. An investment adviser, for purposes of the act, is "any person who, for compensation, engages in the business of advising others, either directly or through publications or writings, as of the value of securities or as to the advisability of investing in [them] . . . or . . . as part of a regular business, issues or promulgates analyses or reports concerning securities." The definition at first blush could include many popular economic or financial publications or even daily general-interest newspapers and magazines that maintain business sections.

Such commonly recognized publications never felt the direct impact of the regulation, since the SEC assumed that they fit within an exclusion for "any bona fide newspaper, news magazine or business or financial publication of general and regular circulation." The *Lowe* case resulted from the commission's effort to suppress newsletters that also discussed the investment marketplace and offered insight and comment that was as much political, social, and economic as commercial. Its effort to restrain publication was not occasioned by proof of actual harm attributable to the newsletters' content, or that they were false and misleading, but on grounds that the publisher had been convicted of various fraud-related crimes. Publishing thus was regarded, at least by the SEC, as a further opportunity "for dishonesty and self-dealing."

Instead of confronting the First Amendment issue directly, the Court substituted its own definition of "bona fide publication" that disabled the SEC from suppressing the investment newsletters at issue. Specifically, it determined that a publication is "bona fide" and thereby excluded from the definition of an investment adviser if it provides impersonal or disinterested rather than individualized or promotional advice to the subscriber. It would appear, therefore, that the SEC retains broad powers to regulate the flow of investment information, including authority to restrain it entirely, when it is generated by a party having an interest in the offer, sale, or purchase of a security.

Even for a bona fide publication, the editorial process itself is not entirely immune from official oversight and control. In *United States v. Winans*, the government successfully prosecuted a *Wall Street Journal* columnist for a scheme to trade in securities based on information misappropriated from the newspaper. The plan, under which the defendant provided a broker advance notice of firms that would be discussed favorably in a widely read newspaper column, was characterized as a scheme to defraud and a breach of fiduciary duty between employer and employee. In convicting the defendant, the trial court rejected arguments that criminalization of that breach would create a threat to freedom of the press generally. The court concluded that the theory of liability created no new obligations but merely enforced preexisting ones. Nor did it find an unconstitutional imposition of duties upon editors with respect to how they must respond under such circumstances. Their freedom in deciding whether to seek criminal penalties, take disciplinary action, or do nothing was considered to be unaffected. It remained a matter of editorial discretion, moreover, whether to run the tainted article. The *Winans* case nonetheless evinces that the journalistic process itself can be adapted into a scheme to defraud and, to the extent that it is converted toward such ends, is a basis for civil and criminal liability.

C. TAXATION

The power to tax almost from the outset has been recognized as the power to destroy. The media generally have the same obligations to pay taxes as any other individual or entity. When taxation authority is used selectively or punitively, however, the power becomes destructive of First Amendment rights and interests. Such concern accounted for the decision in *Grosjean v. American Press Co., Inc.*, that a gross-receipts tax upon newspapers having a certain minimum circulation was unconstitutional. The effect of the tax was to impose a discriminatory burden upon major Louisiana newspapers that had become critical of the governor. The tax was defined by its own terms as a "license tax for the privilege of engaging in such business."

In determining the levy's unconstitutionality, the Supreme Court focused upon its operation as a prior restraint rather than its discriminatory design. The Court adverted to the history behind the First Amendment, with pointed references to the elimination of licensed publishing and the use of taxes to deter colonial protest. It characterized the American Revolution itself not as mere warfare against taxation but as a struggle to establish a right to full information regarding the operation of government. A few years before the First Amendment was drafted, Massachusetts had levied taxes on magazines, newspapers, and advertising that precipitated angry opposition and swift repeal. Based upon that history, the Court concluded that the First Amendment had been adopted "to preclude the states from adopting any form of previous restraint upon printed publications, or their circulation, including" restraint by means of taxation.

The Court noted that its decision did not exempt the media from ordinary forms of taxation that provide support for government. What it found constitutionally inimical was "a deliberate and calculated device in the guise of a tax to limit the circulation of information to which the public is entitled." Even so, the sweeping appearance of the decision prompted arguments that the Court had created a general immunity from taxation. The following year, the Court demonstrated that its interpretation was not so broad. In *Giragi v. Moore*, it dismissed for lack of a federal question an appeal claiming that a general sales and income tax was unconstitutional as applied to the media.

A year later, the Court rejected the argument that state and local taxes on gross receipts of advertising revenue imposed an unconstitutional burden on interstate commerce. In *Western Live Stock v. Bureau of Revenue*, the Court determined that levies did not unreasonably impair commerce. A critical determinant in assessing the constitutionality of any state tax for an entity doing interstate business, however, remains whether the levy is fairly apportioned.

Nearly half a century after *Grosjean*, the Court confronted again the issue of a special tax uniquely directed at a discrete segment of the press. In *Minneapolis Star and Tribune Co. v. Minnesota Commissioner of Revenue*, it declared unconstitutional a levy upon any publisher's annual paper and ink charges exceeding $100,000. Pursuant to the revenue enactment, 11 out of 388 newspapers incurred a tax liability, and one publisher's tax bill accounted for two-thirds of the total monies raised. Although the Court noted the applicability of general economic regulations, including tax provisions, to newspapers, it determined that a special or discriminatory tax could not stand unless it was supported by a compelling governmental interest. It found differential taxation problematic because the political constraints preventing passage of crippling taxes of general application diminish when one group is singled out. Especially when the special target is the press, the threat of regulation can check critical comment and thus neutralize a key function of the press. The interest asserted by the state in raising revenue was rejected as inadequate, since alternative taxes of general application could be used. The First Amendment thus was offended because the tax scheme singled out the press, targeted further a small group of newspapers, and was not adequately justified.

A similar result was reached in *Arkansas Writers' Project, Inc. v. Ragland,* when the Court considered a state law exempting all newspapers and religious, professional, trade, and sports journals. Discrimination among periodicals was found even more troublesome, insofar as it represented a content-based distinction. Because constitutional offense was established by discrimination within a particular class of media, the Court did not consider whether disparate taxation of different media would present a First Amendment problem.

It appears that taxes of general applicability, if they are challenged by the media, will be reviewed as mere economic regulations. Absent any cognizable First Amendment interest, judicial review will be executed pursuant to a deferential rational basis test. Selective taxation of the media, however, apparently will implicate First Amendment concerns automatically. In such an instance, the level of review will be elevated, and the state will thereby be required to justify the differential with a reason compelling enough to outweigh First Amendment interests.

REFERENCES

Cases

Archer v. Securities and Exchange Commission, 133 F.2d 795 (8th Cir. 1943).
Arkansas Writers' Project, Inc. v. Ragland, 481 U.S. 221 (1987).
Associated Press v. United States, 326 U.S. 1 (1945).
Capital Cities Cable, Inc. v. Crisp, 467 U.S. 691 (1984).
Carl M. Loeb, Rhoades and Co., 38 S.E.C. 843 (1959).
City of New York v. Federal Communications Commission, 108 S. Ct. 1637 (1988).
Giragi v. Moore, 301 U.S. 670 (1937).
Grosjean v. American Press Co., Inc., 297 U.S. 233 (1936).
Lorain Journal v. United States, 342 U.S. 143 (1951).
Lowe v. Securities and Exchange Commission, 472 U.S. 181 (1985).
Minneapolis Star and Tribune Co. v. Minnesota Commissioner of Revenue, 460 U.S. 575 (1983).
National Broadcasting Co. v. Board of Public Utility Commissioners of New Jersey, 25 F. Supp. 761 (C.D.N.J. 1938).
Paris Adult Theatre I v. Slaton, 413 U.S. 49 (1973).
Ross v. Hatfield, 640 F. Supp. 708 (D. Kan. 1986).
Times-Picayune Publishing Co. v. United States, 345 U.S. 594 (1953).
Tribune-United Cable of Montgomery County, Maryland v. Montgomery County, Maryland, 784 F.2d 1227 (4th Cir. 1986).

United States v. Winans, 612 F. Supp. 827 (S.D.N.Y. 1985).
Western Live Stock v. Bureau of Revenue, 303 U.S. 250 (1938).

PUBLICATIONS

Aman, Jr., *SEC v. Lowe: Professional Regulation and the First Amendment,* 1985 Sup.
    Ct. Rev. 93.
Inose & Pierce, Information Technology and Civilization (1984).
Owen, Economics and Freedom of Expression (1975).

Part Two

STRUCTURAL REGULATION OF THE MEDIA

Contemporary media regulation has reflected a special concern with industry trends toward concentrated ownership, diminishing sources of input, and the consequent impact upon diversity. The nature of the media industry has prompted official reaction on two levels. Content regulation, calculated to enhance diversity, is the primary concern of Part Three. Structural controls, which are the focus of Part Two, deal with the makeup and character of the various media. They too may be and have been used to promote diversity and First Amendment objectives. Invariably, therefore, they must be recognized as having content implications, albeit perhaps in a more indirect or less proximate fashion than the concepts discussed in Part Three.

Chapter 5

The Newspaper Industry

[The First] Amendment rests on the assumption that the widest possible dissemination of ideas from diverse and antagonistic sources is essential to the welfare of the public.

Associated Press v. United States, 326 U.S. 1 (1945)

I. CONCENTRATION AND RECONFIGURATION

The newspaper industry over the past several decades has been characterized not only by concentration but by a steadily declining number of metropolitan dailies in large cities. In 1910, a total of 2,600 daily metropolitan newspapers were being published. By 1988, the number had diminished to 1,745, and approximately two-thirds of the nation's daily newspapers were group owned. The Gannett chain, which is the largest, publishes daily newspapers and weekly or semiweekly newspapers in thirty-five communities. At the midpoint of this century, approximately 80 percent of the nation's cities with daily newspapers had but one publication, 10 percent had multiple newspapers controlled by a single publisher, and 10 percent had actual competition between or among publishers. A couple of decades later, in *Miami Herald Publishing Co. v. Tornillo*, the Supreme Court observed that one-newspaper towns "have become the rule, with effective competition operating in only four percent of our large cities." Declining competition has correlated with the phenomena of unprecedented personal mobility, freeways, modern mass transit systems, and other social and economic forces that collectively have contributed to migration from major cities to suburban communities. An economic reality of the late twentieth century is that investment and purchasing power has flowed out of traditional urban centers and into newer residential and business settings. The newspaper industry has not been immune to these demographic trends. Diminished readership and consequent disappearance of many metropolitan dailies, coupled with the emergence and flourishing of suburban publications serving discrete communities, are thus reflective of a broader societal phenomenon. Social change has not only altered the nature of competition among newspapers, it has transformed a medium that stood largely alone as the press at the turn of this century into one of several information sources available to the public. What is often loosely referred to as the demise of the newspaper industry, therefore, may be understood better as a process of reformation and evolution that has expanded media frontiers.

Although the Court has expressed concern about an increasingly concentrated mass medium that "places[s] in a few hands the power to inform the American people and shape public opinion," it has refused to countenance promotion of diversity by means that overtly would impair editorial discretion. Concentration is not an economic phenomenon unique to the media. Given concerns with diversity, however, the trend has prompted governmental initiatives that would ameliorate the impact on First Amendment values. Congress, with the assent of the judiciary so far, has fashioned statutory privileges designed to insulate major daily newspapers from the effects of an otherwise inclement economic environment. The policy it has chosen, instead of encouraging new competition, actually attempts to reconcile diversity needs with the realities of concentration.

Responding to the changing circumstances in which they functioned, newspapers half a century ago began merging noneditorial operations to save costs and maintain economic viability. The first joint operating agreement (JOA) was commenced in 1933, when three newspapers in Albuquerque combined their business and printing activities. In 1966, a total of twenty-two JOAs had been consummated. By then, the Justice Department had initiated an investigation of such arrangements to determine whether they breached antitrust law and soon brought suit against two newspapers in Tucson.

In *Citizen Publishing Co. v. United States*, the Supreme Court found that the JOA at issue constituted an antitrust violation. The newspapers had argued that the scheme was justified because one of them was in serious economic jeopardy and thereby qualified for antitrust immunity under the "failing-company" doctrine. The principle, derived from common law, permits otherwise prohibited mergers pursuant to the assumption that competition is nonexistent if the alternative is one company's failure and another's monopolization.

The Court, however, construed the failing-company doctrine so that it was unavailable unless three conditions were satisfied. Specifically, a purportedly failing company had to demonstrate that it was anticipating liquidation, so a JOA essentially would be its last alternative for survival. It also would have to show that the entity with which it merged was "the only available purchaser." Exemption finally would not be awarded unless the possibility for reorganization under federal bankruptcy law was "dim or nonexistent." The failure of the Tucson newspapers to satisfy the Court's stringent delineation of the failing-company defense resulted in the determination that their merger was at odds with antitrust law.

II. THE NEWSPAPER PRESERVATION ACT

Congressional response to the *Citizen Publishing Co.* decision was swift. One year after the judgment, Congress enacted the Newspaper Preservation Act (NPA). The legislation essentially codified the failing-company doctrine in terms that were friendlier to the effectuation of partial mergers of newspapers. Special regard for the newspaper industry, in the form of antitrust immunity, manifested a sense that "the economics of the newspaper industry make it more likely for newspapers to fail when faced with competition than other businesses." Experience has demonstrated that when a newspaper obtains even a relatively slight edge in circulation, a competing newspaper may plunge into a downward and irreversible spiral as advertisers opt for the publication reaching the larger audience. Unlike the strict test of *Citizen Publishing Co.* requiring contemplated liquidation and imminent bankruptcy, the NPA defines a newspaper as failing and thus eligible for a JOA when it is "in probable danger of financial failure." An even less demanding standard governs JOAs entered into prior to the NPA's enactment. These business combinations are legal if, when they were structured, only one of the publications was "likely to remain or become financially sound." A valid JOA enables newspapers to merge their business operations while maintaining independent editorial functions.

The Newspaper Preservation Act, 18 U.S.C. §§ 1801–04

§ 1801. Congressional declaration of policy

In the public interest of maintaining a newspaper press editorially and reportorially independent and competitive in all parts of the United States, it is hereby declared to be the public policy of the United States to preserve the publication of newspapers in any city, community, or metropolitan area where a joint operating arrangement has been heretofore entered into because of economic distress or is hereafter effected in accordance with the provisions of this Act [15 USCS §§ 1801 *et seq.*].

§ 1802. Definitions

As used in this Act [15 USCS §§ 1801 *et seq.*]

(1) The term "antitrust law" means the Federal Trade Commission Act [15 USCS §§ 41 *et seq.*] and each statute defined by section 4 thereof (15 U.S.C. 44) [15 USCS § 44] as "Antitrust Acts" and all amendments to such Act and such statutes and any other Acts in pari materia.

(2) The term "joint newspaper operating arrangement" means any contract, agreement, joint venture (whether or not incorporated), or other arrangement entered into by two or more newspaper owners for the publication of two or more newspaper publications, pursuant to which joint or common production facilities are established or operated and joint or unified action is taken or agreed to be taken with respect to any one or more of the following: printing; time, method, and field of publication; allocation of production facilities; distribution; advertising solicitation; circulation solicitation; business department; establishment of advertising rates; establishment of circulation rates and revenue distribution: Provided, That there is no merger, combination, or amalgamation of editorial or reportorial staffs, and that editorial policies be independently determined.

(3) The term "newspaper owner" means any person who owns or controls directly, or indirectly through separate or subsidiary corporations, one or more newspaper publications.

(4) The term "newspaper publication" means a publication produced on newsprint paper which is published in one or more issues weekly (including as one publication any daily newspaper and any Sunday newspaper published by the same owner in the same city, community, or metropolitan area), and in which a substantial portion of the content is devoted to the dissemination of news and editorial opinion.

(5) The term "failing newspaper" means a newspaper publication which, regardless of its ownership or affiliations, is in probable danger of financial failure.

(6) The term "person" means any individual, and any partnership, corporation, association, or other legal entity existing under or authorized by the law of the United States, any State or possession of the United States, the District of Columbia, the Commonwealth of Puerto Rico, or any foreign country.

§ 1803. Antitrust exemption

(a) **Joint operating arrangements entered into prior to July 24, 1970.** It shall not be unlawful under any antitrust law for any person to perform, enforce, renew, or amend any joint newspaper operating arrangement entered into prior to the effective date of this Act [enacted July 24, 1970], if at the time at which such arrangement was first entered into, regardless of ownership or affiliations, not more than one of the newspaper publications involved in the performance of such arrangement was likely to remain or become a financially sound publication: Provided, That the terms of a renewal or amendment to a joint operating arrangement must be filed with the Department of Justice and that the amendment does not add a newspaper publication or newspaper publications to such arrangement.

(b) **Written consent for future joint operating arrangements.** It shall be unlawful for any person to enter into, perform, or enforce a joint operating arrangement, not already in effect, except with the prior written consent of the Attorney General of the United States. Prior to granting such approval, the Attorney General shall determine that not more than one of the newspaper publications involved in the arrangement is a publication other than a failing newspaper, and that approval of such arrangement would effectuate the policy and purpose of this Act [15 USCS §§ 1801 *et seq.*].

(c) **Predatory practices not exempt.** Nothing contained in the Act [15 USCS §§ 1801 *et seq.*] shall be construed to exempt from any antitrust law any predatory pricing, any predatory practice, or any other conduct in the otherwise lawful operations of a joint newspaper operating arrangement which would be unlawful under any antitrust law if engaged in by a single entity. Except as provided in this Act [15 USCS §§ 1801 *et seq.*], no joint newspaper operating arrangement or any party thereto shall be exempt from any antitrust law.

§ 1804. Reinstatement of joint operating arrangements previously adjudged unlawful under antitrust laws

(a) Notwithstanding any final judgment rendered in any action brought by the United States under which a joint operating arrangement has been held to be unlawful under any antitrust law, any party to such final judgment may reinstitute said joint newspaper operating arrangement to the extent permissible under section 4 (a) hereof [15 USCS § 1803(a)].

(b) The provisions of section 4 [15 USCS § 1803] shall apply to the determination of any civil or criminal action pending in any district court of the United States on the date of enactment of this Act [enacted July 24, 1970] in which it is alleged that any such joint operating agreement is unlawful under any antitrust law.

The basic prerequisite for a JOA is a finding by the attorney general that a newspaper is in probable danger of economic failure and that the merger would serve the NPA's "policy and purpose." The overarching aim of the legislation, expressly identified by Congress, is to maintain "a newspaper press [that is] editorially and reportorially independent and competitive." The NPA assumes that such objectives, which tie into the general interest in a diversified information marketplace, are served best by combinations that cooperate at least as much as they compete. A possibility exists that although the NPA may preserve existing voices, the economic advantage acquired by the merged entity may deter future competition that would diversify the marketplace. A prospective publisher, for instance, might be unable to offer the favorable rate-to-circulation ratios available from newspapers publishing under a JOA. Experience demonstrates that both advertising display rates and the cost of purchasing a newspaper escalate immediately after a JOA is consummated. Advertising rates in Detroit newspapers increased up to 35 percent within a month of the most recently approved JOA. During the same time frame, the cost of purchasing the newspapers increased five cents. The earnings available under a partial merger, therefore, may be so attractive that newspapers not truly in danger of failing may consciously compound losses so that they qualify for a JOA. Such concerns have been responsible for legal challenges to JOAs and even for divisions within the Justice Department, which must consider any merger application. Since the NPA's enactment, five JOAs have been approved. Three have been contested, but no challenge has been successful.

The first post-NPA challenge to a JOA was couched largely in First Amendment terms. In *Bay Guardian Co. v. Chronicle Publishing Co.*, a monthly newspaper asserted that the merger of two daily San Francisco newspapers and elimination of a third destroyed or weakened any potential competition. The plaintiffs asserted that the cooperative features of the JOA, including profit sharing and joint advertising rates, created "a stranglehold on the San Francisco newspaper market." They thus argued that because the combine prevented or deterred publication of other newspapers, the NPA itself breached the guarantee of freedom of the press.

The district court refused to take the First Amendment argument seriously, noting that "[t]he simple answer to the plaintiffs' contention is that the Act does not authorize any conduct." It characterized the NPA as "a selective repeal of the antitrust laws" for the purpose of rescuing newspapers in danger of failing. Observing further that the legislation "was designed to preserve independent editorial voices," it concluded that the NPA, regardless of its underlying economic or social wisdom, was not at odds with the First Amendment.

Nor was the court willing to regard the consequences of a JOA as having imposed a restraint upon the publication of other newspapers. That disinclination was attributable to the court's conclusion that the NPA specifically prohibits merged publishers from engaging in predatory practices. It may be that the court skirted the issue of effect to some extent by characterizing the regulation at issue as essentially economic in nature. To the extent that legislation is so classified, judicial review becomes deferential and does not seriously evaluate the wisdom upon which an enactment is predicated.

Contentions that the NPA was inimical to competitive and constitutional interests surfaced again pursuant to the attorney general's approval of a JOA for two Seattle newspapers. In *Committee for an Independent P-I v. Hearst Corp.*, however, allegations also were considered that one of the newspapers was in danger of failing because of mismanagement rather than the economic realities of the industry. The administrative law judge who conducted the hearing had determined that the purportedly failing newspaper probably could have been sold to a third party who would have maintained its independence, but that inquiries concerning a possible sale had been rebuffed. Despite the Antitrust Division's objections, the attorney general rejected the hearing examiner's finding regarding probable marketability as unsupported by the evidence and approved the JOA.

First Amendment arguments that the antitrust exemption caused economic injury that would affect "the 'breadth' of one's freedom of press," as in the *Bay Guardian* case, were dismissed as "lack[ing] substantial merit." The court of appeals determined that the NPA did "not affect the content of speech of . . . smaller newspapers" claiming injury. Rather, it was a mere "economic regulation which has the intent of promoting and aiding the press." Although the court recognized that the regulatory scheme might affect negatively "the number of 'readers' a newspaper has," it refused characterization of that consequence as an abridgment. Consequently, it found an effect not unlike "any other economic regulation of the newspaper industry, . . . [no] First Amendment rights implicated," and grounds therefore for deferential rather than exacting review of legislative judgment. Insofar as the NPA might be unwise, the court noted that it was the responsibility of Congress to alter or repeal it.

The court also rejected the challenge that the JOA did not "effectuate the policy and purpose of the Act." The gist of the claim was that potential injury to other newspapers had been disregarded and that merger terms had not been limited to the least anticompetitive terms possible. In refusing to concern itself with the impact of a JOA upon other publications or to gloss the NPA with a least burdensome alternative requirement, the court concluded "that the Act itself is a policy determination that the preservation of editorial diversity through joint operating agreements outweighs any potentially anticompetitive effect this antitrust exemption might cause." Thus it found that Congress had performed all the balancing of competing interests required and had accepted any harm to other publishing voices. Such deference to legislative judgment again necessitated the assumption that no First Amendment interests were implicated.

Finally, the court determined that the failure to offer the newspaper for sale or to respond to inquiries about its availability did not merit disapproval of the JOA. Rather, it identified "[t]he critical question" as whether "it was shown that the . . . financial condition was such that new management might be successful in reversing the P-I's difficulties." Finding evidence of a downward spiral, management's competent and reasonable efforts to restore profitability, the unworkability of the challengers' proposal for profitable operations, and no proof that new management could turn the newspaper around, the court determined that "failure to consider purchase inquiries lost importance."

If a newspaper is not obligated to consider sale as an alternative to merger, concern exists that publishers will be motivated to lose money so they can attain effective market dominance and enhanced profitability afforded by a JOA. Such concern was central to objections to a JOA approved for Detroit's two daily newspapers. Unlike any prior circumstances leading to antitrust exemption, neither newspaper had entered into a "downward spiral." At the time of the JOA approval, the newspapers were owned respectively by Gannett and Knight-Ridder, the nation's two largest group owners. Both publications had competed fiercely for many years, with the dominant newspaper maintaining a consistent 51 percent to 49 percent circulation edge and a 60 percent share of advertising lineage. Critical to the operating losses of both newspapers was a circulation price war that had dropped the purchase price to twenty cents for the dominant publication and fifteen cents for its rival. An administrative law judge observed that unit costs more in line with the price of newspapers elsewhere would have resulted in profitability for both newspapers.

Testimony that the dominant newspaper would not raise its price was followed by its competition's promise to shut down operations if it was not allowed to enter into a JOA. Although neither newspaper had entered into a downward spiral or acquired dominance, the attorney general approved the merger on grounds that continuing pricing practices would enable one newspaper to outlast the other. The determination was upheld on appeal in *Michigan Citizens for an Independent Press v. Thornburgh.* The Supreme Court, divided four to four, affirmed the judgment without opinion.

The result has compounded concern that the availability of JOAs in an already-concentrated newspaper industry creates a dangerous combination. Critics maintain, as the dissent agreed, that partial mergers under circumstances as they existed in Detroit "allow deep pocket newspaper owners to obtain a JOA almost at will." Their concern is that large group owners, recognizing the economic advantage of a JOA, may be willing to purchase a newspaper, slash prices, absorb short-term losses, and then obtain a partial merger exempting them from antitrust law. Critics of the Detroit outcome note that the willingness of the dominant newspaper to divide profits evenly under the JOA suggests that the other newspaper was not about to exit the market and that the merger was a calculated corporate objective. The fundamental worry, therefore, is that the NPA, which was conceived to preserve editorial diversity where it otherwise could be lost, may operate as a means for "eliminating competitive newspapers even where both . . . would survive." In the *Michigan Citizens* case, the attorney general's determination that the record "did not present such a situation" was found "reasonable." Thus the court did "not consider the hypothetical situation where the initial and principal motivating factor behind a price was the prospect of a future JOA." The decision evoked a strong dissent on grounds that the attorney general might have misapplied the law with respect to "a large and attractive newspaper market, Detroit, one concededly capable of sustaining two profitable newspapers."

> It is accepted by the Attorney General that the *Free Press* and *News* have arrived at a "competitive stalemate," ... and that market dominanace is "no longer within the grasp of either paper." It is also a "given" that "the Detroit market could sustain two profitable newspapers if both circulation and advertising prices were increased." ... But "the unbroken pattern of annual operating losses" cannot be reversed by *Free Press* "unilateral actions," and that in the Attorney General's judgment, makes "probable" if not "imminent" the "danger of financial failure."
>
> Without the lure of a JOA, however, what reason is there to believe that the losses here "likely cannot be reversed"? Absent the Attorney General's promise of that large pot of gold, would the parties not have, as the Antitrust Division suggested, an effective "incentive to adopt strategies directed toward achieving profitability in a competitive marketplace"? ...
>
> Detroit, as the Attorney General said, "is a highly prized $300 million dollar market." ... That market could sustain two profitable newspapers. ... Market dominance is now beyond the grasp of the News as well as the Free Press. ... The Attorney General has not cogently explained why, on the facts thus far found, the proposed JOA has become "an available option." *Id.* Making the JOA an option now, in the situation artificially created and maintained by the *Free Press* and the *News*, moves boldly away from the "frame of reference [Congress] essentially embraced"—"the scenario of a strong newspaper poised to drive from the market a weaker competitor," a newspaper experiencing, "due to external market forces," a decline in revenues and circulation "that in all probability cannot be reversed." ... I therefore dissent from the majority's disposition approving instanter the giant stride the Attorney General has taken.

Any perversion of the NPA's utility and purpose, at least for now, is a matter that the courts continue to leave for congressional consideration. Such deference is manifested clearly by the court's reiteration of the attorney general's observation in the *Michigan Citizens* case that newspapers cannot be precluded from factoring a possible JOA into their business strategy or "faulted for considering and acting upon an alternative that Congress has created."

Concerns about the utility and ends of the NPA that transcend its susceptibility to abuse as a profit-maximizing device also endure. The need for this protective legislation has been questioned, for instance, on grounds that the measure is so narrowly focused that it loses sight of the broader realities of the modern media industry. Newspapers are not the only enterprises that have exited major cities in recent decades. Corporate investment has relocated into newer, mostly suburban communities rather than dried up altogether. Although the NPA is intended to save an endangered species, it actually operates not against a diminution but a redistribution of editorial outlets. Viewed from a macrocosmic perspective that includes new media forms, daily newspapers actually have more rivals now than ever. Competition as a whole thus may not have slipped as much as it has been reconfigured. The NPA in such a context nonetheless reflects a value judgment that a particular segment of the newspaper industry merits preservation in its existing form. Even if it confers a preferential advantage upon a class of publishers and impedes the emergence of competing voices, the NPA is destined to endure unless Congress revises its thinking or the judiciary becomes inclined to regard it as an abridgment of First Amendment interests rather than a mere economic regulation.

REFERENCES

CASES

Associated Press v. United States, 326 U.S. 1 (1945).
Bay Guardian Co. v. Chronicle Publishing Co., 344 F. Supp. 1155 (N.D. Cal. 1972).
Citizen Publishing Co. v. United States, 394 U.S. 131 (1969).
Committee for an Independent P-I v. Hearst Corp., 704 F.2d 467 (9th Cir. 1983).
Miami Herald Publishing Co. v. Tornillo, 418 U.S. 241 (1974).
Michigan Citizens for an Independent Press v. Thornburgh, 868 F.2d 1285 (D.C. Cir.), aff'd, 110 S. Ct. 229 (1989).

PUBLICATIONS

Bogart, Press and Public (1981).
Comment, *Local Monopoly in the Daily Newspaper Industry*, 61 Yale L.J. 948 (1952).
Lively, *Old Media, New Dogma*, 30 Ariz. L. Rev. 257 (1988).

Chapter 6

The Broadcasting Industry

Freedom of utterance is abridged to many who wish to use the limited facilities of radio. Because it cannot be used by all, some who wish to use it must be denied.

National Broadcasting Co. v. United States,
319 U.S. 190, 226 (1943)

For regulatory purposes, broadcasting has been historically distinguished from publishing on grounds that it uses a scarce public resource—the airwaves—for propagation. Insofar as publishers increasingly use satellites to distribute information from editorial centers to printing plants and traditionally have utilized public resources such as sidewalks and highways to disseminate their product, the distinction is less than perfect. The lines blur further because some broadcasters use satellites primarily to disseminate signals beyond their normal market and employ on-screen text to communicate.

I. THE NATURE OF BROADCASTING

Broadcasting over the course of this century has evolved from a virtually nonexistent state to being the most dominant and pervasive mass medium. In 1987, a total of 9,911 commercial radio and television stations were in operation. Radio was in more than 99 percent of the nation's homes, with an average of 5.6 receivers per household. Television was found in more than 98 percent of the nation's homes, with an average of 1.90 sets per household.

Prior to the twentieth century, radio was largely experimental and developmental. The first practical use of the medium in this country was for defense purposes, when the navy used it to broadcast orders to its fleet. After World War I, commercial development of radio commenced. Under license from the Department of Commerce, the first radio stations operated in Massachusetts and Pennsylvania. Network broadcasting, linking stations together and making simultaneous national programming possible, started in 1926. Radio broadcasting in 1940 expanded from the AM to the FM band. AM service continued to be dominant until relatively recently, when demand for FM licenses became so great that the FCC adopted rules permitting new stations to operate on the band provided that they do not interfere with existing service.

Experiments with electronic signals to carry impulses resulting in visual images as well as sound followed close behind those for radio. In 1927, an experimental television program was transmitted by wire between New York and Washington, D.C. The FCC began issuing licenses for commercial stations in 1941, and by midcentury, color programming was available. Television, which originally was consigned to VHF frequencies, proved so popular that its original channel allotment was expanded to include UHF assignments. Following a decade in which available channels were rapidly consumed, the FCC devised an allocation scheme calculated to provide nationwide television service and ensure that every community was served by at least one television station.

A. TECHNICAL ASPECTS OF BROADCASTING

The key characteristics of radio waves are frequency and wavelength, which vary inversely with one another. The former term refers to cycles per second, and the latter term relates to the distance between points in separate cycles. Mass-media services mostly are located on medium frequencies, denominated in terms of kilohertz (previously kilocycles) and very high and ultrahigh frequencies, classified in terms of megahertz. AM service operates between 530 kilohertz and 1605 kilohertz at 10-kilohertz intervals. FM broadcasting is assigned frequencies from 88 megahertz to 108 megahertz, allowing 100 channels at intervals of 200 kilohertz. Television requires wider channels to accommodate picture and sound. Thus VHF assignments are from 54 to 72 megahertz, 76 to 88 megahertz, and 174 to 216 megahertz—respectively, channels 2, 3, and 4; 5 and 6; and 7 through 13—at 6-megahertz intervals. UHF broadcasting occupies frequencies from 470 to 806 megahertz, which run from channels 14 to 69.

Broadcasting essentially entails the conversion of vibrations from voice or other inputs into electrical signals, which vary accordingly in strength and frequency and are amplified as they are transmitted onto a carrier wave. AM and FM are terms that denote the means by which audio or video details are impressed onto a carrier wave. Amplitude modulation (AM) refers to audio waves that vary in power and thus in length. With FM broadcasting, wave frequency varies, but amplitude is unchanged. Amplitude modulation is a methodology not only for radio service but for the video aspect of television in the United States and is employed worldwide for shortwave service. Frequency modulation provides FM radio service and the audio dimension of television.

Transmission of radio signals occurs at the speed of light along various routes, depending upon the nature of the signal. AM transmissions, for instance, proceed in waves that both follow the contour of the ground and move upward through the atmosphere. Skywaves are reflected back to the earth effectively at night, which can greatly enhance service range and the potential for interference with other signals. FM radiation, like other VHF emissions, travel by line of sight and are subject to distortion or absorption by obstacles between transmitting and receiving points.

AM stations are divided into four general channel classifications providing clear-channel (classes I and II), regional (class III), and local (class IV) service. Class I sets aside 47 clear channels that are allowed to provide service over a broad geographical area without significant interference with their primary and secondary service areas. Stations allowed to operate in class I may do so full time with 10 to 50 kilowatts of power. Class II stations may operate on clear channels insofar as they do not create objectionable interference with Class I stations and do not conflict with foreign service protected by international agreement. Such stations operate with 250 watts to 50 kilowatts of power but must alter or terminate their signal when it would conflict with class I service. Thus class II broadcasting may be subject not only to power restrictions but time restrictions to avoid interference with primary groundwave or secondary skywave service of class I stations.

A total of 41 regional channels are set aside for class III service. Stations operating in the class III category provide primary service to a major population center and surrounding areas. They operate at 500 watts to 5 kilowatts. Service hours and area vary according to the potential for interference with other stations.

Class IV stations, which serve suburban and rural communities, are assigned to the remaining 6 channels. The maximum power for such stations is 1 kilowatt.

Rules governing FM service divide the country into three geographical zones and provide six classes of commercial stations based upon power ratings. Because transmission correlates to line of sight, antenna height is a critical factor and is regulated as specifically as power. The FCC has composed a table that sets aside FM channels for the various states and communities. From that table, approximately 3,000 assignments have been made to nearly 2,000 communities on the mainland. Television channels are allotted in a similar fashion.

Educational broadcasting, which now has reserved space on the FM band, originally operated on the AM spectrum. By the time the FCC emerged in 1934, most AM educational broadcasting had been replaced by commercial service. Early congressional proposals to set aside a percentage of service for educational programming did not materialize. The opening up of the FM band to general broadcasting, however, led toward eventual dedication of 20 FM channels between 88 and 92 megahertz for noncommercial stations. Subsequently, television channel allotments were revised so that they also set aside space for educational use.

Upwards of 2,000 television channels, comprising 56 UHF positions and 12 VHF slots, have been assigned to 1,300 communities. Early use of the UHF band was impaired by the fact that most receivers were VHF only. Consequently, advertising revenue flowed primarily to VHF stations. Over the years, the problem has been ameliorated by FCC rules that require all televisions to receive both VHF and UHF signals and be fitted with compatible tuning mechanisms. Slow development of UHF, although it has accelerated in recent years due to the near universality of UHF-equipped receivers, improved tuning mechanisms and signal quality, and the growth of cable, nonetheless has resulted in reassignment of some frequencies for competing uses such as cellular telephones.

Broadcasting service over recent years has been augmented by technological developments that afford stereophonic service, multichannel sound in television, teletext service, closed-captioning FM subcarrier service, and subscription programming based on scrambling and decoding of signals. Awaiting final development and standardization is high-definition television, which is supposed to offer pictures of unprecedented quality and resolution. Further augmenting broadcast service are ground translators that amplify and retransmit FM radio and television signals to expand service areas, satellite relays for overseas and remote transmissions, direct broadcast satellite service, and low-power television, which was designed to enhance programming diversity choices by means of origination or retransmission. Such methodologies or enhancements, like the basis of broadcast service, are subject to FCC regulation and, where pertinent, to international agreement.

B. REGULATORY HISTORY

1. Early Regulation

Regulation of broadcasting commenced before the medium acquired its modern pervasive character. Federal regulation of radio commenced with the Wireless Ship Act in 1910, which reflected the medium's primary utility in its early incarnation as a facilitator of marine safety. Soon thereafter, Congress enacted legislation requiring radios and radio operators on board oceangoing passenger vessels and assigned enforcement responsibility to the Secretary of Commerce and Labor. Over the course of the next two decades, uses and usage of broadcasting multiplied at such a rate that service was unpredictable, chaotic, and largely beyond the ken of effective governance. In *National Broadcasting Co. v. United States*, the Supreme Court described how radio's early development, expansion, and conflict shaped a model of regulation that has endured over the past half century.

Federal regulation of radio begins with the Wireless Ship Act of June 24, 1910, 36 Stat. 629, which forbade any steamer carrying or licensed to carry fifty or more persons to leave any American port unless equipped with efficient apparatus for radio communication, in charge of a skilled operator. The enforcement of this legislation was entrusted to the Secretary of Commerce and Labor, who was in charge of the administration of the marine navigation laws. But it was not until 1912, when the United States ratified the first international radio treaty, 37 Stat. 1565, that the need for general regulation of radio communication became urgent. In order to fulfill our obligations under the treaty, Congress enacted the Radio Act of August 13, 1912, 37 Stat. 302. This statute forbade the operation of radio apparatus without a license from the Secretary of Commerce and Labor; it also allocated certain frequencies for the use of the Government, and imposed restrictions upon the character of wave emissions, the transmission of distress signals, and the like.

The enforcement of the Radio Act of 1912 presented no serious problems prior to the World War. Questions of interference arose only rarely because there were more than enough frequencies for all the stations then in existence. The war accelerated the development of the art, however, and in 1921 the first standard broadcast stations were established. They grew rapidly in number, and by 1923 there were several hundred such stations throughout the country. The Act of 1912 had not set aside any particular frequencies for the use of private broadcast stations; consequently, the Secretary of Commerce selected two frequencies, 750 and 833 kilocycles, and licensed all stations to operate upon one or the other of these channels. The number of stations increased so rapidly, however, and the situation became so chaotic, that the Secretary, upon the recommendation of the National Radio Conferences which met in Washington in 1923 and 1924, established a policy of assigning specified frequencies to particular stations. The entire radio spectrum was divided into numerous bands, each allocated to a particular kind of service. The frequencies ranging from 550 to 1500 kilocycles (96 channels in all, since the channels were separated from each other by 10 kilocycles) were assigned to the standard broadcast stations. But the problems created by the enormously rapid development of radio were far from solved. The increase in the number of channels was not enough to take care of the constantly growing number of stations. Since there were more stations than available frequencies, the Secretary of Commerce attempted to find room for everybody by limiting the power and hours of operation of stations in order that several stations might use the same channel. The number of stations multiplied so rapidly, however, that by November, 1925, there were almost 600 stations in the country, and there were 175 applications for new stations. Every channel in the standard broadcast band was, by that time, already occupied by at least one station, and many by several. The new stations could be accommodated only by extending the standard broadcast band, at the expense of the other types of services, or by imposing still greater limitations upon time and power. The National Radio Conference which met in November, 1925, opposed both of these methods and called upon Congress to remedy the situation through legislation.

The Secretary of Commerce was powerless to deal with the situation. It had been held that he could not deny a license to an otherwise legally qualified applicant on the ground that the proposed station would interfere with existing private or Government stations.... And on April 16, 1926, an Illinois district court held that the Secretary had no power to impose restrictions as to frequency, power, and hours of operation, and that a station's use of a frequency not assigned to it was not a violation of the Radio Act of 1912. This was followed on July 8, 1926, by an opinion of Acting Attorney General Donovan that the Secretary of Commerce had no power, under the Radio Act of 1912, to regulate the power, frequency or hours of operation of stations. 35 Ops. Atty. Gen. 126. The next day the Secretary of Commerce issued a statement abandoning all his efforts to regulate radio and urging that the stations undertake self-regulation.

But the plea of the Secretary went unheeded. From July, 1926, to February 23, 1927, when Congress enacted the Radio Act of 1927, 44 Stat. 1162, almost 200 new stations went on the air. These new stations used any frequencies they desired, regardless of the interference thereby caused to others. Existing stations changed to other frequencies and increased their power and hours of operation at will. The result was confusion and chaos. With everybody on the air, nobody could be heard. The situation became so intolerable that the President in his message of December 7, 1926, appealed to Congress to enact a comprehensive radio law:

> "Due to the decisions of the courts, the authority of the department [of Commerce] under the law of 1912 has broken down; many more stations have been operating than can be accommodated within the limited number of wave lengths available; further stations are in course of construction; many stations have departed from the scheme of allocations set down by the department, and the whole service of this most important public function has drifted into such chaos as seems likely, if not remedied, to destroy its great value. I most urgently recommend that this legislation should be speedily enacted." (H. Doc. 483, 69th Cong., 2d Sess., p.10.)

The plight into which radio fell prior to 1927 was attributable to certain basic facts about radio as a means of communication—its facilities are limited; they are not available to all who may wish to use them; the radio spectrum simply is not large enough to accommodate everybody. There is a fixed natural limitation upon the number of stations that can operate without interfering with one another. Regulation of radio was therefore as vital to its development as traffic control was to the development of the automobile. In enacting the Radio Act of

1927, the first comprehensive scheme of control over radio communication, Congress acted upon the knowledge that if the potentialities of radio were not to be wasted, regulation was essential.

The Radio Act of 1927 created the Federal Radio Commission, composed of five members, and endowed the Commission with wide licensing and regulatory powers. We do not pause here to enumerate the scope of the Radio Act of 1927 and of the authority entrusted to the Radio Commission, for the basic provisions of that Act are incorporated in the Communications Act of 1934, 48 Stat. 1064, 47 U.S.C. § 151 *et seq.*, the legislation immediately before us. As we noted in *Federal Communications Comm'n v. Pottsville Broadcasting Co.*, 309 U.S. 134, 137, "In its essentials the Communications Act of 1934 [so far as its provisions relating to radio are concerned] derives from the Federal Radio Act of 1927.... By this Act Congress, in order to protect the national interest involved in the new and far-reaching science of broadcasting, formulated a unified and comprehensive regulatory system for the industry. The common factors in the administration of the various statutes by which Congress had supervised the different modes of communication led to the creation, in the Act of 1934, of the Communications Commission. But the objectives of the legislation have remained substantially unaltered since 1927."

Section 1 of the Communications Act states its "purpose of regulating interstate and foreign commerce in communication by wire and radio so as to make available, so far as possible, to all the people of the United States a rapid, efficient, Nation-wide, and world-wide wire and radio communication service with adequate facilities at reasonable charges." Section 301 particularizes this general purpose with respect to radio: "It is the purpose of this Act, among other things, to maintain the control of the United States over all the channels of interstate and foreign radio transmission; and to provide for the use of such channels, but not the ownership thereof, by persons for limited periods of time, under licenses granted by Federal authority, and no such license shall be construed to create any right, beyond the terms, conditions, and periods of the license." To that end a Commission composed of seven members was created, with broad licensing and regulatory powers.

2. Modern Regulation

Contemporary regulation of broadcasting derives from the Communications Act of 1934. The 1934 act created the Federal Communications Commission, which was authorized to set and enforce standards for broadcasting. The FCC's general duties, as congressionally prescribed, include regulation that effectuates and facilitates efficient service. More specifically, the FCC is empowered to classify radio stations; prescribe the nature of service to be provided within each classification; assign bands of frequencies to classes of stations and frequency assignments, power usage, and operational times to individual stations; determine the location of stations; regulate and set standards for broadcasting equipment and signals; prevent interference between or among diverse transmissions; promote larger and more effective use of radio in the public interest; establish service areas for stations; regulate chain broadcasting; adopt and promulgate rules requiring licensees to keep records of programming and technical operations; suspend a license upon proof that the broadcaster violated a federal law that the FCC may administer or transmitted profanity or obscenity; and make such rules and regulations not inconsistent with law as are lawful and necessary to carry out the Act. In exercising its power and responsibility, the Commission is obligated to serve "the public interest, convenience or necessity."

The public interest standard has been described as the "touchstone" criterion for federal regulation of broadcasting. From the outset, its imprecision was recognized. An early critic characterized it as meaning "about as little as any phrase that the drafters of the Act could have used and still comply with the constitutional requirement that there be some standard to guide the administrative wisdom of the licensing authority." Nonetheless, the Supreme Court in *Federal Communications Commission v. Pottsville Broadcasting Co.* found it "as concrete as complicated factors for judgment in such a field of delegated authority permit." Delineation of the public interest in exact but comprehensive terms would be vain. In *National Broadcasting Co. v. United States*, the Court described it "as the interest of the listening public in the larger and more effective use of radio." Such a definition, although broad, hardly begins to afford guidance with respect to what constitutes "effective use" of the medium and in the end merely refers back in a circular fashion to indefinite statutory language. Because the FCC's powers range so broadly, the public interest governs rules and policy pertaining to industry structure and practices, licensing qualifications, and programming. Given the broad territory that it covers and the open-ended nature of the terminology, the public interest might be understood best as the function of values chosen to inspire it in these diverse settings.

FCC determinations of the public interest, within the scope of its authority, are subject to limited review. As the Court noted in *Federal Communications Commission v. RCA Communications, Inc.*:

Ours is not the duty of reviewing determinations of "fact," in the narrow, colloquial scope of that concept. Congress has charged the courts with the responsibility of saying whether the Commission has fairly exercised its discretion within the vaguish, penumbral bounds expressed by the standard of "public interest." It is our responsibility to say whether the Commission has been guided by proper considerations in bringing the deposit of its experience, the disciplined feel of the expert, to bear on applications for licenses in the public interest.

Judicial review may be more exacting when constitutional considerations are present. The Court has determined that the 1934 act itself represents a valid exercise of Congress's commerce power, and that the public interest standard by its mere existence does not contravene the First Amendment. Still, regulation that determines who is authorized to broadcast invariably implicates questions of editorial freedom and discretion. The licensing process and pertinent criteria affect both the content and structure of broadcasting. Given such consequences, differentiation between content and structural control may be somewhat illusory. For the sake of convenience, however, discussion of content regulation is reserved for Part Three.

II. LICENSING

Central to the Communications Act of 1934 is a scheme for licensing broadcasters. Licensing was the primary methodology chosen for addressing the chaos and confusion of an unregulated electronic marketplace. Although the 1934 act set some basic qualifications of citizenship, character, and financial and technical capability, it left the formulation of detailed licensing criteria to the FCC. Pursuant to its legislative charge, the Commission has fashioned and promulgated a panoply of governing rules and standards. Because the number of broadcasting frequencies generally has been less than the number of potential broadcasters, the FCC also has set qualitative standards to determine which applicant for a particular frequency would best serve the public interest.

The process is reminiscent in part of the English licensing system abandoned in the late seventeenth century. The Supreme Court, in its first freedom of the press case, observed that the fundamental purpose of the First Amendment is to safeguard against a system of prior restraint. Licensing of broadcasters in practice and effect is a form of prior restraint. Yet if it is measured against contemporary standards, it probably would survive. Although a prior restraint is presumptively invalid and imposes upon government a heavy burden of justification, the chaotic consequences of an unregulated marketplace are evidenced by history and provide a compelling reason for licensing. Methodologies exist that would remove government from content-related assessments in the course of licensing. Consistent with broadcasting's evolution as the medium with the least First Amendment status, however, analysis never has insisted upon licensing criteria and procedures that would have the least burdensome impact upon constitutional interests.

Considerations governing all license applications include whether basic citizenship, character, technical, and financial qualifications are satisfied and whether limits upon the number of broadcast holdings an individual or entity may own would be exceeded. When more than one application is received for the same frequency or a renewal is contested, comparative criteria operate. Standing to participate in the licensing process may extend to other stations demonstrating technical interference and to representatives of the public itself whose participation may be critical to determining whether a broadcaster has violated its fiduciary role. In *Office of Communications of United Church of Christ v. Federal Communications Commission*, therefore, citizen groups were allowed to challenge a renewal on the ground that the licensee consistently had underserved or disserved the interests of African-Americans. License terms are five years for television and seven years for radio, subject to revocation for certain violations of the law.

A. BASIC QUALIFICATIONS

Congress has provided that "the Commission by regulation may prescribe as to the citizenship, character, and financial, technical and other qualifications of a broadcast licensee." The Communications Act of 1934 by its own terms denies licenses to aliens or persons whose licenses have been revoked by a federal court as a consequence of antitrust violations. Beyond these two statutory proscriptions, it is the FCC's task to formulate basic qualification policies and other criteria for assessing license applications and renewals. Licensing standards by their nature narrow the class of potential broadcasters. Although they are basic in form, they are not entirely without controversy in substantive operation.

1. Citizenship

Alienage restrictions, which preclude noncitizens from obtaining a broadcasting license, may be regarded not only as a prior restraint but as an equal protection issue. For Fourteenth Amendment purposes, however, federal law that classifies on the basis of alienage tends to be less closely scrutinized than distinctions by state and local government. Thus it would seem that the 1934 Act's citizenship requirement is permissible so long as it is rationally related to a valid federal interest. Such deferential review recognizes the federal government's dominant interest in foreign affairs and immigration and naturalization. Even so, it might be asserted that unless it is evident that the restrictions advance a clear foreign-policy aim, they are essentially arbitrary.

2. Character

Consistent perhaps with the notion of broadcasters as public trustees, a licensee must satisfy official character requirements. The problem with such criteria, however, is identifying what, if any, concept of character is relevant and how it is to be measured. Over the years, character inquiries have been a source of regulatory inconsistency and problematic results.

Character qualifications until recently have factored in criminal convictions, anticompetitive practices, and general, albeit usually undefined, notions of morality. Such considerations would be entirely impermissible as a basis for determining whether a person may publish. In broadcasting, however, character is an independent ground for disqualification as well as a subsidiary factor in determining whether the public interest is served. In *Federal Communications Commission v. WOKO, Inc.*, the Court noted the potentially dispositive nature of a determination that a licensee's character was deficient.

We cannot say that the Commission is required as a matter of law to grant a license on a deliberately false application even if the falsity were not of this duration and character, nor can we say the refusal to renew the license is arbitrary and capricious under such circumstances. It may very well be that this Station has established such a standard of public service that the Commission would be justified in considering that its deception was not a matter that affected its qualifications to serve the public. But it is the Commission, not the courts, which must be satisfied that the public interest will be served by renewing the license. And the fact that we might not have made the same determination on the same facts does not warrant a substitution of judicial for administrative discretion since Congress has confided the problem to the latter. We agree that this is a hard case, but we cannot agree that it should be allowed to make bad law.

The problem with a character standard is defining it so that it has some relevance. A court once identified "character" as embracing "all of an individual's qualities and deficiencies regarding traits of personality, behavior, integrity, temperament, consideration, sportsmanship, altruism, etc, which distinguish him as a human being from his fellow men." Although such a standard would not necessarily predict quality service to the public, the FCC has not been reticent at times to assess character in similarly broad terms. Thus it has observed that character should be appraised on the basis of "past observance of moral, ethical, legal and professional rules of conduct."

Implicit in the standard's presence is the assumption that a nexus exists between good character and quality of service. Until recently, the FCC assumed that "[o]ne who has in the past led an exemplary life in and out of broadcasting has been presumed likely to serve the public interest as a broadcaster in the future." As it eventually realized, however, moral character does not guarantee competent broadcast service. Complications and inconsistency result, moreover, when the Commission is faced with similar conduct in different cases, draws distinctions based upon degree, and produces apparently conflicting results. License applicants who had violated federal regulations promulgated by other agencies, for instance, have been subject to favorable and negative determinations of character. Despite its refusal to consider a licensee's overall performance in circumstances leading to the aforementioned *WOKO, Inc.*, decision, the FCC determined that two other corporations found guilty of price fixing had provided consistent meritorious service. Taking into account a broader picture, therefore, the Commission renewed the licenses despite the criminal records.

Consideration of character in the context of a licensee's overall service may have afforded a fairer assessment of a licensee's record, but it also conferred an advantage upon incumbent broadcasters. A new applicant without any record of service in radio or television could offer only future promises to convince the FCC that past misconduct would not be repeated. Because there was no option of placing any character deficiency in perspective with actual broadcast service, established licensees had a preferential edge under the standard. Incumbent advantage in comparative proceedings, as discussed later, however, is not unique to the issue of character.

Problems also arose with respect to the effect of identified character defects upon licensees with multiple holdings. Insofar as moral character is portable, a logical implication is that a broadcaster's loss of one license for character shortcomings justifies denial or revocation of all licenses. Misrepresentation or deceit in a license application, for instance, is a character trait that transcends the particular proceeding. Adding to the confusion surrounding use of character, however, was the fact that loss of a license for dishonesty did not always affect the status of a broadcaster's other holdings.

Recognizing the potentially limitless reach of the character standard, its manipulability, and the inconsistency of results it had engendered, the FCC commenced an inquiry designed to yield "a more coherent licensing policy" on character. The commission itself acknowledged that

use of "character" as a license qualification is in our opinion, extremely troublesome. The term's definition is unclear and its measurement imprecise. Also, it may not be, in its strictest application, a sure indicator of future broadcast service. Its uniform application to existing licenses and new applicants yields disparate results; moreover, the Commission's attempts to apply the standard to multiple-owner licensees have resulted in decisions which contain confusing reasoning. The character requirement forces the Commission to perform the exceedingly difficult exercise of attempting to demonstrate why behavior in one case did not evidence bad "character" even though similar behavior in another case did. While the Commission has often asserted that an applicant lacking character must be denied, in practice the Commission has treated character as but one factor for predicting future service in the public interest. The Commission's inquiry into character qualifications is but an intermediate step in the licensing process. The ultimate licensing question to be answered under the Communications Act is whether an applicant can be expected to serve the public interest as a broadcaster. 47 U.S.C. §§ 308, 319. Any character inquiry supposedly is conducted to assist the Commission in reaching that public interest determination. To the extent that the character examination obfuscates rather than facilitates that determination, it is necessary to inquire whether the Commission has allowed the process to gain dominance over its goals.

Pursuant to its inquiry into the pertinence and utility of character, the FCC tightened its evaluative focus. Character assessment focuses especially upon honesty with the Commission, disregard of the law governing broadcasting, and fraudulent acts or performance that negatively affect the public. The FCC in its most recent character statement, however, has reenlarged the purview of official concern. It thus has announced its sense that all felonies and mass-media–related antitrust violations will be relevant to character assessment, subject to mitigating circumstances such as intent, extent, and magnitude of the wrong.

Despite the narrowed concern, consistency of results is not assured, as degrees of character deficiency are bound to exist even within discrete categories of interest. Nor does the continuing presence of character standards, even in a limited sense, render impertinent the overarching question of their pertinence and permissibility. It remains possible that a dishonest person, even one who has flouted FCC rules in a given instance, might serve the public's interest in receiving diverse and quality programming as well as or better than a "cleaner" individual. Notwithstanding recent FCC dicta to the effect that broadcasters and publishers should be on the same constitutional plane, a comparable requirement for the print media would be found contrary to the First Amendment. The continuing vitality of character requirements perhaps may be best understood as an extension or implication of the concept of broadcasters as public fiduciaries and the operation of a public interest standard that may override constitutional concerns.

3. Concentration

Concentrated ownership in the newspaper industry, as noted in Chapter 5, has evoked concern but no quantitative restrictions upon the total holdings of a particular individual or entity. Like a character requirement, limitations upon a publisher's entrepreneurial reach invariably would engender a constitutional challenge. Multiple-ownership rules have evolved, however, that limit the number of broadcast holdings a single individual or entity may possess. The rules speak in terms of ownership that subsequent glosses have defined in terms of a 5 percent interest, except for investment concerns, which may hold a 10 percent stake. Such regulation reflects a commitment to promoting information diversification in the electronic marketplace as a function of ownership diversification. The restrictions in general seek to effectuate their aim, subject to waiver upon a specific showing that the public interest would be advanced, by prohibiting multiple ownership in the same market, restricting the total number of licenses an individual or entity may hold, and forbidding cross-ownership of television stations and newspaper or cable service in the same community.

A. LOCAL CONCENTRATION

(1) Cross-ownership of like media. Multiple-ownership rules generally prohibit a single person or entity from owning more than one station providing the same type of service in the same community. If a party owns or controls an AM station, it may not have another AM station in the same service area. The same would be true respectively for FM and TV stations. Multiple ownership, to the extent that it involves different types of service, may be permissible depending upon the combination. AM and FM stations may be jointly owned pursuant to an early policy that recognized FM service as an underdeveloped resource and encouraged established AM station owners to acquire FM stations. Despite the dominance of FM radio in many markets, the allowance of joint ownership facilitates a reordered policy of cross-subsidization. Further restrictions prohibit mutual ownership in the same community of a VHF television station and an AM or FM radio station. Because of the slow development of UHF television, the FCC has chosen to evaluate applications resulting in multiple ownership on a case-by-case basis. Preexisting combinations were grandfathered in, subject to cross-ownership restrictions in the event of future sale. The rule may be waived in the event of ownership in a top twenty-five market that has at least thirty other licensees.

(2) Cross-ownership of different media. The FCC also has endeavored to promote local diversification by rules that prohibit acquisition of a broadcasting license by a person who owns a newspaper in the same service area. Like controls have been enacted by Congress forbidding cross-ownership of cable systems by television licensees and common carriers. Such regulations reflect concern that cross-ownership of mass media in a given community diminishes competition in both the economic and information marketplaces. Although most established newspaper-broadcasting combinations were grandfathered in, the commission ordered divestiture in sixteen instances. Given the scope and nature of the rules, they affect not only the broadcasting but the newspaper industry. Not surprisingly, they were challenged by both.

In *Federal Communications Commission v. National Citizens Committee for Broadcasting*, the Supreme Court held that the cross-ownership restrictions neither exceeded the commission's regulatory authority nor violated the constitutional rights of publishers. The Court cast its determination with past decisions recognizing "that the First Amendment and antitrust values underlying the Commission's diversification policy may properly be considered by the Commission in determining where the public interest lies." One objection to the rules was that they departed from factors that previously had been used to evaluate license applications by newspaper publishers. In fact, the FCC in the early years of television had encouraged newspaper owners to acquire co-located broadcast stations because of a shortage of qualified license applicants. Thereafter, the application pool had swelled, the number of available channels had diminished, and diversification had become more imperative and feasible. The Court thus found the policy change "a reasonable administrative response to changed circumstances in the broadcasting industry."

Constitutional arguments were rejected, despite the rules' inclusion of newspaper publishers within their purview. The Court acknowledged that policies intended to enhance the extent and quality of coverage of public issues may be permissible in broadcasting "where similar efforts to regulate the print media would not be." It resisted the invitation, however, to regard the cross-ownership rules as a regulation of newspapers. The Court concluded instead that "[r]equiring those who wish to obtain a broadcast license to demonstrate that such would serve the 'public interest' does not restrict the speech of those who are denied licensing, rather it preserves the interests of the 'people as a whole in free speech.' " Insofar as the public interest supported denial of a broadcast license, therefore, the Court determined that First Amendment interests were not compromised.

Equally unavailing as a constitutional argument was the claim that the regulations imposed a forfeiture upon publishers as a condition for receiving a license. The Court dismissed that characterization because, even if unable to procure a license in the same community, a publisher could acquire one elsewhere. The limited disqualification was distinguished from selection criteria that might operate on the basis of viewpoint. While such content-related considerations would be constitutionally problematic, the Court found that the cross-ownership rules' "purpose and effect is to promote free speech, not restrict it." Recognizing that the FCC must choose from multiple applicants, the Court observed that the policy had been "chosen on a 'sensible basis,' one designed to further, rather than contravene, 'the system of freedom of expression.' "

Because the FCC grandfathered in most existing combinations but ordered divestiture in what it depicted as sixteen "egregious cases," the prospective aspect of the regulation was challenged as arbitrary and capricious. The Court determined, however, that the FCC properly took into account the already-declining number of co-located combinations. Recognizing that widespread divestiture would disrupt the stability and continuity of meritorious service, cause economic dislocations that might impair program quality, and diminish local ownership, the Court noted that a more sweeping order might harm the public interest.

Finally, the Court endorsed the standards that the FCC had used to determine which publishers would be required to divest. The criteria assumed not that divestiture would be more harmful in the exempted markets but "that the need for diversification was especially great in cases of local monopoly." Thus the Court found it "hardly unreasonable for the Commission to confine divestiture to communities in which there is common ownership of the only daily newspaper and either the only television station or the only broadcast station of any kind encompassing the entire community with a clear signal." Nor was it considered unreasonable, given the dominance of broadcasting and newspapers as information sources, for the FCC to disregard the presence of other media.

Temporary waivers from the cross-ownership rules may be available so that a publisher-broadcaster, who otherwise would violate the rules upon award or transfer of a license, has time to sell the newspaper property. Two such waivers have been awarded, in each case to the same entity. Congress attempted to prohibit their extension in each instance. Because the action singled out only one individual, an appeals court invalidated it on equal protection and First Amendment grounds.

Paralleling the restrictions on newspaper-broadcaster combines are prohibitions of cross-owned television stations and cable systems in the same primary service area. Telephone companies also are barred from owning cable systems within their service areas, unless the cable operation is in a rural area. The exception is reminiscent of early encouragement of newspapers to acquire broadcast licenses in communities that otherwise would be slow in obtaining the benefits of radio or television service. The cross-ownership rules concerning cable, unlike those governing broadcasting, are mandated by statute. Future modification, if any, therefore, requires an act of Congress. The cable cross-ownership rules are discussed in the next chapter.

B. NATIONAL CONCENTRATION

Another aspect of regulatory policy slanted toward diversification is a ceiling upon the total number of broadcast holdings a person or entity may have nationwide. In their present incarnation, FCC rules set a limit of twelve AM, twelve FM, and twelve TV stations. The restriction on television station ownership is further qualified by a provision that limits total audience reach to 25 percent of the nation's population. Both the twelve-station and audience-reach limits may be relaxed if significant minority participation exists. In the event "that at least two of the stations in which they hold cognizable interests are minority controlled . . . , group owners of television and radio stations [may] utilize a maximum numerical cap of 14 stations." Moreover, a group owner may "reach a maximum of 30 percent of the national audience, provided that at least five percent of the aggregate reach of its audience is contributed by minority controlled stations."

The elevation of ceilings and expansion of audience reach are calculated to enhance minority ownership in broadcasting. Dissenting commissioners asserted that the evils of concentration are not diminished by the nature of an owner's race. The rules also may elicit claims that they undermine their aims if predominantly white group owners buy out minority businesses and effectively minimize minority presence and influence. The provisions exist in a constitutional context increasingly hostile to racial preferences. In *Metro Broadcasting, Inc. v. Federal Communications Commission,* however, the Court upheld preferential policies to the extent that they promote and are substantially related to achieving "the important government objective of broadcast diversity." It also has noted Congress's support for minority-ownership policies generally as a means of advancing program diversity and has announced a more deferential level of review insofar as such programs are legislatively approved or mandated.

Restrictions upon the total number of broadcast holdings have weathered judicial review. In *United States v. Storer Broadcasting Co.,* the Court determined that the multiple-ownership rules furthered Congress's regulatory aims. The restrictions had been challenged on grounds that they precluded a broadcaster from demonstrating in a hearing that the award of a license would further the public interest. Although the Court noted that a hearing might be required upon a sufficient showing that the public interest would benefit from a waiver, it observed that

[t]his commission, like other agencies, deals with the public interest.... Its authority covers new and rapidly developing fields. Congress sought to create regulation for public protection with careful provision to assure fair opportunity for open competition in the use of broadcasting facilities. Accordingly, we cannot interpret § 309(b) as barring rules that declare a present intent to limit the number of stations consistent with a permissible "concentration of control." It is but a rule that announces the Commission's attitude on public protection against such concentration. The Communications Act must be read as a whole and with appreciation of the responsibilities of the body charged with its fair and efficient operation. The growing complexity of our economy induced the Congress to place regulation of businesses like communication in specialized agencies with broad powers. Courts are slow to interfere with their conclusions when reconcilable with statutory directions. We think the Multiple Ownership Rules, as adopted, are reconcilable with the Communications Act as a whole. An applicant files his application with knowledge of the Commission's attitude toward concentration of control.

C. Network Influence and Control

Also pertinent to the issue of national concentration is the question of network influence. Like any other group owner, networks are subject to rules that quantitatively limit broadcast holdings. Networks provide significant amounts of broadcast programming, however, including most of what is watched during prime time. Their reach is magnified, therefore, by the distribution of their service through affiliated stations. Network practices, although exceeding the ken of ownership rules, are subject to antitrust law. Considerations of that nature may be factored into concepts of the public interest.

Pursuant to an inquiry into network activities, the FCC in 1941 promulgated regulations governing network and affiliate relationships. Among other things, the rules set limits on network programming time and ownership. Collectively the restrictions were designed to curtail control over programming decisions at the local level. Although the restrictions were challenged, the Court in *National Broadcasting Co. v. United States* found them within the purview of the public interest. In sum, the Court rejected arguments that the FCC's power to regulate chain broadcasting was limited to technical and engineering aspects. It noted too that "[t]he Commission's duty under the Communications Act of 1934 is not only to see that the public receives the advantages and benefits of chain broadcasting, but also, so far as its powers enable it, to see that practices which adversely affect the ability of licensees to operate in the public interest are eliminated."

Network regulation, as the aforementioned rules evince, is significantly effectuated by licensing policy. Directly responsive to concern with network influence is the Prime Time Access Rule. Specifically, it provides that television stations in the top fifty markets owned by or affiliated with a network may offer network programming during only three of the four hours of prime time. The central purpose of the rule was to encourage the development of independent programming. The policy translated not just into a structural reform but an overt content restriction. Nonetheless, it was upheld in *Mt. Mansfield Television, Inc. v. Federal Communications Commission* as a means for promoting First Amendment interests in diversity. Key to the outcome was the appeals court's determination that the unique scarcity of broadcasting defeated "an analogy between the . . . rule and an imaginary government edict prohibiting newspapers in the 50 largest cities from devoting more than a given portion of their news space to items taken from national news services." Like other results predicated upon the concept of scarcity, the Prime Time Access Rule would seem vulnerable to the Supreme Court's possible reservations about that purportedly peculiar attribute and the FCC's repudiation of it in the context of fairness regulation (*see* Chapter 10).

Nonetheless, the Prime Time Access Rule continues to operate, albeit in a version altered somewhat from its original form. In 1975, the FCC expanded the category of exemptions to include feature films and noted its expectation that licensees would use some of the time to address "needs or problems of [their] . . . communit[ies]." The modified rule was upheld in *National Association of Independent Television Producers and Distributors v. Federal Communications Commission.* In response to contentions that the rule was contrary to constitutional and statutory prohibitions against censorship, the court of appeals observed that

[t]he only way that broadcasters can operate in the "public interest" is by broadcasting programs that meet somebody's view of what is in the "public interest." That can scarcely be determined by the broadcaster himself, for he is in an obvious conflict of interest. "There is no sanctuary in the First Amendment for unlimited private censorship operating in a medium not open to all." *Red Lion, supra,* 395 U.S. at 392.... "It is the right of the viewers and listeners, not the right of the broadcasters, which is paramount." *Id.* at 390....

Since the public cannot through a million stifled yawns convey that their television fare, as a whole, is not in their interest, the Congress has made the F.C.C. the guardian of that public interest. All that the Commission can do about it is to encourage competitive fare. If a large segment of the public prefers game shows to documentaries, the Commission can hardly do more than admit paradoxically that taste *is* a matter for dispute [emphasis in original]. The Commission surely cannot do its job, however, without interesting itself in general program format and the kinds of programs broadcast by licensees.... Thus as we have seen, the F.C.C. was sustained when it abrogated by regulation the chain broadcasting clauses which forced network programs on affiliated stations.... It was also given a free hand to tell the subscription television people what types of programs they must not broadcast in order to qualify for a license....

The Commission by this amendment of the rule is not ordering any program or even any type of program to be broadcast in access time. It has simply lifted a restriction on network programs if the licensee chooses to avail himself of such network programs in specified categories of programming.

Results of the Prime Time Access Rule have been mixed at best and demonstrate certain practical realities to which the public interest is subject. With few exceptions, local programming has not increased significantly, and syndicated game shows and the like have filled time that previously would have been devoted to network programming. Any expectation that program quality would improve, however, probably was misplaced. As the appeals court observed in upholding the modified rule, the Commission may account for competition but not taste.

In an effort to account for enduring concerns with network influence and changing realities of competition in the communications industry, the FCC in 1991 adopted new financial interest and syndication rules for networks. The policy defines a network as any entity providing more than 15 hours of prime-time programming and relaxes previous rules prohibiting networks from acquiring and domestically syndicating their programs. The characterization is calculated to accommodate networks that are incipient or emerging. Networks are allowed to acquire full domestic and international rights in prime-time programs produced by others, although they may not syndicate such shows domestically. Negotiations for rights to such programs also must be conducted apart from and at least 30 days after agreeing to license the shows. Networks also are allowed to syndicate domestically and internationally in-house produced programs. Such productions, however, are subject to a ceiling of 40 percent of a network's prime-time entertainment schedule.

The rules have elicited criticism from independent producers, who claim they give networks too much leverage. The networks, however, maintain that new interest and syndication opportunities are undermined by detailed restrictions and conditions.

4. Programming

The FCC is barred from exercising "the power of censorship" or promulgating regulations that would "interfere with the right of free speech by means of radio communications." Despite that prohibition, the Commission has used its authority to influence programming in a variety of ways. Its capacity to do so in the licensing context was generally endorsed by the Supreme Court in *National Broadcasting Co. v. United States.* The Court observed then that a public interest determination may require qualitative assessment of proposed or actual service.

A certain amount of conflict exists between preclusion of official content control and the duty as it has evolved to regulate in the public interest. The FCC has avoided minimum programming requirements of any type on the ground that they are equivalent to censorship. Nonetheless, it has prohibited indecent or offensive expression that would be constitutionally protected if not broadcast. Although they are no longer employed, various programming guidelines of a general nature have operated in the past.

An early policy noted that the FCC would give particular consideration in a licensing proceeding to service factors that included unsponsored programming, locally originated programming, public affairs programming, and the amount of time devoted to advertising in any given hour. Later, it introduced a policy requiring applicants for a new commercial license or renewal to ascertain and report the programming needs of their communities. Among other things, it was necessary to determine the demographic composition of the service area and meet with leaders of relevant community groups and representatives of the public. License applications had to contain specific program proposals that would meet ascertained community needs. Failure to fulfill that obligation was grounds for denying a license even in an instance when a community was deprived of what would have been its only FM service.

Such formal guidelines largely have been eliminated pursuant to the FCC's recent philosophy that programming should be determined primarily by the marketplace. Ascertainment rules were lifted for radio in 1981 and for television in 1984. Pertinent to their abandonment is the notion that administrative costs were too high and that marketplace forces function toward effectuating the programming goals that originally prompted regulation.

5. Employment Practices

Broadcasters are prohibited not only by general federal law but by FCC rule from discriminating on the basis of race. License applicants, moreover, must file a form certifying that they do not discriminate against designated minorities and have an affirmative-action program in place. Evolving equal protection standards have proved increasingly hostile to remediation policies absent proven instances of past discrimination. Insofar as regulation might be congressionally mandated and "substantially related to the important governmental objective of broadcast diversity," however, it may survive constitutional scrutiny.

Absent a challenge to a licensee's employment figures or allegations of discrimination, the only question is "whether the aggregate picture presented by [a licensee's] employment policies and practices ma[k]e[s] a *prima facie* case for refusing to renew the station's license." Generally, a mere statistical disparity between the percentages of minorities employed and in the service area will be "[in]sufficient to require evidentiary exploration." The result may be different if the disparity is beyond a "zone of reasonableness." Although the perimeters of the zone are not defined in precise terms, they may vary depending upon considerations such as whether a broadcaster is just commencing operations or is well established. No license has ever been denied for failure to comply with employment standards.

B. COMPARATIVE REVIEW

Licensing is a relatively uncomplicated process when the FCC must consider only one application for a particular frequency. When competition exists for a new license or a renewal is subject to challenge, however, the Commission must make a choice. The Supreme Court has determined that a comparative hearing is required whenever mutually exclusive applications are filed. In an effort to maximize clarity of standards and consistency of results, the FCC has developed criteria that govern comparative proceedings in both an initial application and a renewal context.

1. New Applications

Evaluation of competing applications for a new license, under the governing regulatory scheme, does not work as a precise science. The

FCC has observed that relevant considerations "cannot be assigned absolute values, some factors may be present in some cases and not in others, and the differences between applicants with respect to each factor are almost infinitely variable." Like any other administrative decision, moreover, continuity is affected by turnover of personnel and individual perceptions of a pertinent factor's relative significance.

The FCC, in the interest of maximizing clarity and consistency, rendered a policy on comparative broadcast hearings that has generally informed the review process over the past quarter of a century. The policy statement identifies two overarching objectives: "first, the best practicable service to the public, and, second, a maximum diffusion of control of the mass media." Noting that "independence and individuality of approach are elements of rendering good program service," the FCC characterized "the primary goals of good service and diversification of control [as]...fully compatible." Primary factors identified as critical in a comparative proceeding include diversification of media ownership and control, participation by ownership in station operations, proposed program service, past broadcast record, and efficient use of frequency. The criteria are amplified in the FCC's *Policy Statement on Comparative Broadcast Hearings*.

1. *Diversification of control of the media of mass communications.*—Diversification is a factor of primary significance since, as set forth above, it constitutes a primary objective in the licensing scheme.

As in the past, we will consider both common control and less than controlling interests in other broadcast stations and other media of mass communications. The less the degree of interest in other stations or media, the less will be the significance of the factor. Other interests in the principal community proposed to be served will normally be of most significance, followed by other interests in the remainder of the proposed service area and, finally, generally in the United States. However, control of large interests elsewhere in the same State or region may well be more significant than control of a small medium of expression (such as a weekly newspaper) in the same community. The number of other mass communication outlets of the same type in the community proposed to be served will also affect to some extent the importance of this factor in the general comparative scale.

It is not possible, of course, to spell out in advance the relationships between any significant number of the various factual situations which may be presented in actual hearings. It is possible, however, to set forth the elements which we believe significant. Without indicating any order of priority, we will consider interests in existing media of mass communications to be more significant in the degree that they:

> (a) are larger, i.e., go towards complete ownership and control; and to the degree that the existing media:
> (b) are in, or close to, the community being applied for;

(c) are significant in terms of numbers and size, i.e., the area covered, circulation, size of audience, etc.;

(d) are significant in terms of regional or national coverage; and

(e) are significant with respect to other media in their respective localities.

2. Full-time participation in station operation by owners.—We consider this factor to be of substantial importance. It is inherently desirable that legal responsibility and day-to-day performance be closely associated. In addition, there is a likelihood of greater sensitivity to an area's changing needs, and of programming designed to serve these needs, to the extent that the station's proprietors actively participate in the day-to-day operation of the station. This factor is thus important in securing the best practicable service. It also frequently complements the objective of diversification, since concentrations of control are necessarily achieved at the expense of integrated ownership.

We are primarily interested in full-time participation. To the extent that the time spent moves away from full time, the credit given will drop sharply, and no credit will be given to the participation of any person who will not devote to the station substantial amounts of time on a daily basis. In assessing proposals, we will also look to the positions which the participating owners will occupy, in order to determine the extent of their policy functions and the likelihood of their playing important roles in management. We will accord particular weight to staff positions held by the owners, such as general manager, station manager, program director, business manager, director of news, sports, or public service broadcasting, and sales manager. Thus, although positions of less responsibility will be considered, especially if there will be full-time integration by those holding those positions, they cannot be given the decisional significance attributed to the integration of stockholders exercising policy functions. Merely consultative positions will be given no weight.

Attributes of participating owners, such as their experience and local residence, will also be considered in weighing integration of ownership and management. While, for the reasons given above, integration of ownership and management is important per se, its value is increased if the participating owners are local residents and if they have experience in the field. Participation in station affairs on the basis described above by a local resident indicates a likelihood of continuing knowledge of changing local interests and needs. Previous broadcast experience, while not so significant as local residence, also has some value when put to use through integration of ownership and management.

Past participation in civic affairs will be considered as a part of a participating owner's local residence background, as will any other local activities indicating a knowledge of and interest in the welfare of the Community. Mere diversity of business interests will not be considered. Generally speaking, residence in the principal community to be served will be of primary importance, closely followed by residence outside the community, but within the proposed service area. Proposed future local residence (which is expected to accompany meaningful participation) will also be accorded less weight than present residence of several years' duration.

Previous broadcasting experience includes activity which would not qualify as a past broadcast record, i.e., where there was not ownership responsibility for a station's performance. Since emphasis upon this element could discourage qualified newcomers to broadcasting, and since experience generally confers only an initial advantage, it will be deemed of minor significance. It may be examined qualitatively, upon an offer of proof of particularly poor or good previous accomplishment.

The discussion above has assumed full-time, or almost full-time, participation in station operation by those with ownership interests. We recognize that station ownership by those who are local residents and, to a markedly lesser degree, by those who have broadcasting experience, may still be of some value even where there is not the substantial participation to which we will accord weight under this heading. Thus, local residence complements the statutory scheme and Commission allocation policy of licensing a large number of stations throughout the country, in order to provide for attention to local interests, and local ownership also generally accords with the goal of diversifying control of broadcast stations. Therefore, a slight credit will be given for the local residence of those persons with ownership interests who cannot be considered as actively participating in station affairs on a substantially full-time basis but who will devote some time to station affairs, and a very slight credit will similarly be given for experience not accompanied by full-time participation. Both of these factors, it should be emphasized, are of minor significance. No credit will be given either the local residence or experience of any person who will not put his knowledge of the community (or area) or experience to any use in the operation of the station.

3. Proposed program service.—The U.S. Court of Appeals for the District of Columbia Circuit has stated that, "in a comparative consideration, it is well recognized that comparative service to the listening public is the vital element, and programs are the essence of that service." *Johnston Broadcasting Co. v. Federal Communications Commission*, 85 U.S. App. D.C. 40, 48, 175 F.2d 351, 359. The importance of program service is obvious. The feasibility of making a comparative evaluation is not so obvious. Hearings take considerable time and precisely formulated program plans may have to be changed not only in details but in substance, to take account of new conditions obtaining at the time a successful applicant commences operation. Thus, minor differences among applicants are apt to prove to be of no significance.

The basic elements of an adequate service have been set forth in our July 27, 1960 "Report and Statement of Policy Re: Commission en banc Programming Inquiry," 25 F.R. 7291, 20 Pike & Fischer, R.R. 1901, and need not be repeated here. And the applicant has the responsibility for a reasonable knowledge of the community and area, based on surveys or background, which will show that the program proposals are designed to meet the needs and interest of the public in that area. See *Henry v. Federal Communications Commission*, 112 U.S. App. D.C. 257, 302 F.2d 191, *cert. den.* 371 U.S. 821. Contacts with local civic and other groups and individuals are also an important means of formulating proposals to meet an area's needs and interests. Failure to make them will be considered a serious deficiency, whether or not the applicant is familiar with the area.

Decisional significance will be accorded only to material and substantial differences between applicants' proposed program plans. See *Johnston Broadcasting Co. v. Federal Communications Commission*, 85 U.S. App. D.C. 40, 175 F.2d 351. Minor differences in the proportions of the time allocated to different types of programs will not be considered. Substantial differences will be considered to the extent that they go beyond ordinary differences in judgment and show a superior devotion to public service. For example, an unusual attention to local community matters for which there is a demonstrated need, may still be urged. We will not assume, however, that an unusually high percentage of time to be devoted to local or other particular types of programs is necessarily to be preferred. Staffing plans and other elements of planning will not be compared in the hearing process except where an inability to carry out proposals is indicated.

In light of the considerations set forth above, and our experience with the similarity of the program plans of competing applicants, taken with the desirability of keeping hearing records free of immaterial clutter, no comparative issue will ordinarily be designated on program plans and policies, or on staffing plans or other program planning elements, and evidence on these matters will not be taken under the standard issues. The Commission will designate an issue where examination of the applications and other information before it makes such action appropriate, and applicants who believe they can demonstrate significant differences upon which the reception of evidence will be useful may petition to amend the issues.

No independent factor of likelihood of effectuation of proposals will be utilized. The Commission expects every licensee to carry out its proposals, subject to factors beyond its control and subject to reasonable judgment that the public's needs and interests require a departure from original plans. If there is a substantial indication that any party will not be able to carry out its proposal to a significant degree, the proposals themselves will be considered deficient.

4. Past broadcast record.—This factor includes past ownership interest and significant participation in a broadcast station by one with an ownership interest in the applicant. It is a factor of substantial importance upon the terms set forth below.

A past record within the bounds of average performance will be disregarded, since average future performance is expected. Thus, we are not interested in the fact of past ownership per se, and will not give a preference because one applicant has owned stations in the past and another has not.

We are interested in records which, because either unusually good or unusually poor, give some indication of unusual performance in the future. Thus, we shall consider past records to determine whether the record shows (i) unusual attention to the public's needs and interests, such as special sensitivity to an area's changing needs through flexibility of local programs designed to meet those needs, or (ii) either a failure to meet the public's needs and interests or a significant failure to carry out representations made to the Commission (the fact that such representations have been carried out, however, does not lead to an affirmative preference for the applicant, since it is expected, as a matter of course, that a licensee will carry out representations made to the Commission).

If a past record warrants consideration, the particular reasons, if any, which may have accounted for that record will be examined to determine whether they will be present in the proposed operation. For example, an extraordinary record compiled while the owner fully participated in operation of the station will not be accorded full credit where the party does not propose similar participation in the operation of the new station for which he is applying.

5. Efficient use of frequency.—In comparative cases where one of two or more competing applicants proposes an operation which, for one or more engineering reasons, would be more efficient, this fact can and should be considered in determining which of the applicants should be preferred. The nature of an efficient operation may depend upon the nature of the facilities applied for, i.e., whether they are in the television or FM bands where geographical allocations have been made, or in the standard broadcast (AM) band where there are no such fixed allocations. In addition, the possible variations of situations in comparative hearings are numerous. Therefore, it is not feasible here to delineate the outlines of this element, and we merely take this occasion to point out that the element will be considered where the facts warrant.

6. *Character*.—The Communications Act makes character a relevant consideration in the issuance of a license. See section 308(b), 47 U.S.C. 308(b). Significant character deficiencies may warrant disqualification, and an issue will be designated where appropriate. Since substantial demerits may be appropriate in some cases where disqualification is not warranted, petitions to add an issue on conduct relating to character will be entertained. In the absence of a designated issue, character evidence will not be taken.

7. *Other factors*.—As we stated at the outset, our interest in the consistency and clarity of decision and in expedition of the hearing process is not intended to preclude the full examination of any relevant and substantial factor. We will thus favorably consider petitions to add issues when, but only when, they demonstrate that significant evidence will be adduced.

As the FCC itself had observed, "a general statement cannot dispose of all problems or decide cases in advance." Qualitative evaluations still must be made, and, as experience has demonstrated, "[d]ifficult cases will remain difficult." Determination of which applicant will provide the best practicable service may involve more than determining who is superior in the most categories. An applicant's edge in a particular category may range from slight to substantial, so a qualitative and essentially subjective consideration would seem unavoidable.

Since the FCC announced its policy on comparative evaluations, it has flirted somewhat inconsistently with the use of race and gender as additional comparative factors. Its original position that race was irrelevant was rejected by the court of appeals, which found minority ownership and participation grounds for a comparative preference. A subsequent appeals court holding that the commission lacked statutory authority to award credit for female applicants was vacated and the case remanded so that the agency could reconsider its policy. Congress then passed and the president signed a law prohibiting the FCC from eliminating or modifying provisions for enhancing minority ownership. In *Metro Broadcasting, Inc. v. Federal Communications Commission*, the Supreme Court determined that comparative preferences on the basis of race were permissible because "they serve the important governmental objective of broadcast diversity ... [and] are substantially related to the achievement of that objective."

2. Renewal Proceedings

The task of choosing between an incumbent broadcaster and a challenger presents further perplexities to the comparative evaluation process. If performance is not rewarded, broadcasters may invest less in quality service, and the public interest may suffer as a consequence. Extensive turnover in licensees may have a disruptive effect not only upon the industry but, more importantly, upon the public interest. On the other hand, a system that favors incumbents may transform comparative review into an exercise that is more theoretical than real. To date, no television licensee has been denied a renewal on comparative grounds.

Standards governing comparative renewal proceedings have evolved from the FCC's determination in *Hearst Radio, Inc. (WBAL)* that meritorious service in the past was a dispositive factor. Both applicants were found equally qualified, and the challenger had proposed programming emphasizing extensive community input and local orientation. The Commission regarded the incumbent's programming proposal as superior, however, based on its past service and concern that the challenger might be overpromising on its actual ability to perform. The *Hearst* decision thus struck a balance in favor of a "high degree of probability of continuation of existing desirable performance [and] against paper proposals which ... we are not convinced can be fulfilled." Resultant policy was that "[e]xcellent performance as a licensee [would] be given favorable consideration where we find a reasonable likelihood that such performance will continue. ... [A] record of poor service ... will be given due weight in appraising the likelihood of effectuation of the licensee's proposals."

The FCC and the courts have wrestled with comparative renewal criteria since, and although actual standards have been refined, the practical advantage to incumbents has remained constant. In *Greater Boston Television Corp. v. Federal Communications Commission,* the court of appeals upheld the commission's decision to award a license to a challenger. The *Greater Boston* case, however, was the result of extraordinary circumstances. The original license had been tainted by ex parte contacts with the Commission initiated by what proved to be the successful applicant. Although the same entity was selected again, its wrongdoing was factored into an award of a short-term (four-month) license. While hearings proceeded, the incumbent was allowed to operate under a temporary license but eventually was displaced in what amounted to a new rather than a renewal proceeding. The court of appeals observed that absent the unusual conditions, a question would exist as to "whether the Commission had interfered with legitimate renewal expectancies implicit in the structure of the [Communications] Act."

Just before the *Greater Boston* decision, the FCC announced new comparative renewal standards that largely would have reduced such hearings to a single issue. Central to the criteria was a provision awarding a decisive preference for incumbents with a record of " 'substantial' past performance without serious deficiencies." In *Citizens Communications Center v. Federal Communications Commission*, the Court determined that the rule contravened requirements for a comparative hearing set forth by statute and precedent. As the court noted, "[u]nless the renewal applicant's past performance is found to be insubstantial or marred by serious deficiencies, the competing applications get no hearing at all. The proposition that the [policy] violates Section 309(e) . . . is so obvious it need not be labored." Surviving the decision nonetheless was the concept of a renewal expectancy fueled by the Court's observation that "*superior* performance should be a plus of major significance in renewal proceedings."

Subsequent litigation has been aimed at trying to ensure that the FCC does not as a practical matter give absolutely controlling preference to substantial past performance. In *Central Florida Enterprises, Inc. v. Federal Communications Commission*, the court of appeals reversed a license renewal on grounds that (1) the Commission had inadequately assessed factors weighing against the incumbent and (2) its "handling of the facts [had made] embarrassingly clear that [it had] practically erected a presumption of renewal that is inconsistent with the full hearing requirement." On remand, the FCC acknowledged that the challenger merited a clear preference on diversification grounds and a slight preference on integration grounds. It also discounted a license misconduct issue associated with illegally moving the station's main studio from one city to another in the same service area. Each of these factors nonetheless was outweighed, in the Commission's mind, by substantial past service. Diversification and integration factors in particular, the FCC observed, may have primary importance in a new license proceeding but should have lesser weight when performance has been tested and proved acceptable.

In upholding the renewal decision in *Central Florida Enterprises, Inc. v. Federal Communications Commission*, the court of appeals observed how in the past the Commission had "impermissibly raised renewal expectancy to an irrebuttable presumption in favor of the incumbent." Upon remand, the FCC employed criteria in the nature of a sliding scale. Thus,

the strength of the expectancy depends on the merit of the past record. Where, as in this case, the incumbent rendered substantial but not superior service, the expectancy takes the form of a comparative preference weighed against [the] other factors. . . . An incumbent performing in a superior manner would receive an even stronger preference. An incumbent rendering minimal service would receive no preference.

Or, as the Court described the formula in approving it, *"renewal expectancy is to be a factor weighed with all the other factors, and the better the past record, the greater the renewal expectancy weight* [emphasis in original]."

Despite its approval of the commission's findings, the court identified "an important caveat." As a reminder that review should serve the interest of the public rather than the convenience of the broadcasting industry, the court emphasized that "doctrine is a means to this end, and it should not become more. If in a given case . . . denial of a license renewal would not undermine renewal expectancy *in a way harmful to the public interest,* then renewal expectancy should not be invoked [emphasis in original]." Implicit is an expectancy that is not an automatic perquisite of incumbency or administrative shortcut but a facilitator of the public interest insofar as it weighs against overpromising by challengers, encourages investment in quality service, and avoids haphazard restructuring of the broadcast industry.

Somewhat ironically, as it turned out, the court observed that it was "reassured by a recent FCC decision granting for the first time since 1961, on *comparative* grounds the application of the challenger for a radio station license and denying the renewal application of the incumbent licensee [emphasis in original]." Despite the incumbent's advantages on diversity and integration grounds, the Commission in *Application of Simon Geller* was more impressed by the challenger's plans to increase greatly total programming time and service of community interests and needs. On review, the court of appeals vacated the decision on grounds that the FCC had deviated from and discounted the usual significance it attached to the factors favoring the incumbent.

The court previously had professed being "troubled . . . that the record remains that an incumbent *television* licensee has *never* been denied renewal in a comparative challenge [emphasis in original]." As it noted further:

American television viewers will be reassured, although a trifle baffled, to learn that even the worst television stations—those which are, presumably, the ones picked out as vulnerable to a challenge—are so good that they never need replacing. We suspect that somewhere, sometime, somehow, some television *licensee* should fail in a comparative renewal challenge, but the FCC has never discovered such a licensee yet.

A renewal has yet to be denied in the years since the court's observation.

A. SETTLEMENT

Comparative proceedings invite the possibility that a frivolous challenge will be mounted merely to extract a monetary payoff from the incumbent as the cost of voluntary dismissal. Recognizing the potential for abuse, Congress originally prohibited cash settlements that included payments beyond actual litigation costs. The policy, however, deterred serious challengers from considering settlement and thus magnified uncertainties that already existed. The bar eventually was relaxed, and settlements now are permissible provided (1) the FCC finds them in the public interest and (2) a competing application was not filed merely to extract a payoff.

B. FORMAT CHANGES

Although the public interest governs all licensing decisions, a community's general programming preferences must be dictated through the marketplace rather than by regulation. The issue of whether format changes are consonant with the public interest has arisen in both the renewal and transfer contexts. As a general rule, the FCC has attempted to distance itself from general programming as a licensing criterion. It has observed that significant programming differences are unusual and has expressed concern that applicants would overpromise and, once a license was obtained, underperform. Also implicated is the statutory prohibition against functioning as a censor or interfering with freedom of expression.

In 1976, the FCC adopted a policy to the effect "that the marketplace is the best way to allocate entertainment formats in radio, whether the hoped for result is expressed in First Amendment terms . . . or economic terms." The court of appeals rejected the FCC's position on grounds that "the Commission must sometimes consider the loss of diversity" in determining whether licenses "are used in the public interest." It also adverted to a previous ruling that "preservation of a format [that] would otherwise disappear, although economically and technically viable and preferred by a significant number of listeners, is generally in the public interest."

In *Federal Communications Commission v. WNCN Listeners Guild*, the Supreme Court reversed the appeals court's judgment and found the policy statement "not inconsistent with the [Communications] Act." Noting that the public interest is not self-defining, the Court found it reasonable for the Commission to conclude that "reliance on the market is the best method of promoting diversity in entertainment formation." The FCC had identified practical considerations that further supported its disinclination to regulate. Specifically, it complained about having to categorize past and subsequent formats to determine if a change had occurred, ascertain whether the prior programming was unique, and balance public harm from abandonment against public benefit from the change. It then "emphasized the difficulty of evaluating the strength of listener preferences, of comparing the desire for diversity within a particular type of programming to the desire for a broader range of formats and of assessing the financial feasibility of a unique format." Because a decision in that regard would be largely subjective and "only approximately serve the public interest," the Court agreed "that the market, although imperfect, would serve the public interest as well or better by responding quickly to changing preference and by inviting experiments with new types of programming."

Nor was the Court willing to regard format preservation as a logical extension of the public's paramount right in broadcasting "to receive suitable access to social, political, esthetic, moral, and other ideas and experiences." Emphasizing that the right did not confer upon individual listeners power to have the FCC "review the abandonment of their favorite entertainment programs," the Court found the Commission's reliance upon marketplace forces to promote diversity and satisfy entertainment preferences consonant with the First Amendment.

Justice Marshall dissented from the Court's decision on grounds that the FCC foreclosed entirely any consideration of whether a format change might be inconsistent with the public interest. He also criticized the selective exemption of entertainment programming from the Commission's scope of concern and suggested that it could assess the impact of a format change without enormous difficulty or subjectivity. A subsequent appeals court decision noted that the FCC is responsible for the consequences of its policy and must remain ready to alter its rule if the public interest requires this.

C. License Transfers

Licenses are transferable subject to the FCC's determination that "the public interest, convenience and necessity will be served thereby." A transfer proceeding operates under the same general standard, therefore, that governs new application or renewal proceedings. By law, however, the FCC may only consider whether the proposed purchaser rather than any other party would serve the public interest.

Because the broadcasting industry has proved to be so profitable, and the number of available frequencies is limited, transfers are a common occurrence. Noting that excessive licensee turnover may be inimical to the public interest, the FCC has imposed limits on how soon a broadcaster may transfer a license. Original rules that required a three-year waiting period absent a hardship waiver, however, have been modified to a one-year holding period for licenses obtained through a comparative hearing.

The transfer process has afforded the FCC an opportunity to promote minority-ownership aims. Broadcasters whose licenses have been designated for a revocation hearing or whose renewal applications have been subject to hearing on basic qualification grounds have been allowed "to transfer or assign licenses at a 'distress sale' price to applicants with a significant minority ownership interest, assuming the proposed assignee or transferee meets our other qualifications." The policy promotes minority ownership by encouraging broadcasters whose licenses are at risk on public interest grounds to sell their facilities with an effective license factored into the price. The preference has been limited to designated minorities, as the FCC explicitly has excluded women from its purview. In *Metro Broadcasting, Inc. v. Federal Communications Commission*, the Court rejected an equal protection challenge and upheld the policy on grounds that it promoted and was substantially related to effectuating "the important governmental objective of broadcast diversity."

In recent years, the FCC has had to consider transfers in the context of merging media conglomerates, friendly acquisitions, and even hostile takeovers. Issues have implicated not only questions of control, when corporate shareholders remain the same and a board of directors is changed, but diversification policies. To satisfy cross-ownership requirements, the Gannett Company in the late 1970s had to sell some of its broadcast properties when it merged with another major media company. Similarly, when Capital Cities Communications acquired the American Broadcasting Company, it had to sell off television properties to bring its total audience reach under the 25 percent ceiling. Transfer proceedings in such instances are a two-way proposition, requiring the FCC to make a public interest judgment on the acquisition of the merging or purchasing company and the necessary spin-off of previous holdings to another party.

D. LICENSE REVOCATION, DENIAL, AND SHORT-TERM RENEWAL

More common than denial of a renewal application in a comparative proceeding is a nonrenewal decision or other sanction because the licensee's actions have been found inconsistent with the public interest. Official action of this nature ordinarily reflects a determination that a licensee has defaulted either on character or some other basic qualification that factors into the public interest. Revocation or nonrenewal is the functional equivalent of the death penalty for a licensee's broadcast operation. Short-term renewal and forfeiture penalties enable the Commission to reach conduct that may not justify loss of a license but nonetheless merits sanction. Forfeitures may not exceed $25,000 per offense, although "[e]ach day of a continuing violation . . . constitute[s] a separate offense," provided the total amount does not exceed $250,000. A short-term renewal essentially amounts to a probation period that, if satisfactorily completed, precedes renewal for a regular license term.

From 1970 to 1978, the FCC revoked or denied renewal of sixty-eight licenses. Most of these decisions were based upon licensee conduct that intimated character shortcomings. Misrepresentations to the Commission constituted the most frequent basis for denial. Even when deceit was by an employee who may have made false entries into station records or otherwise misled the Commission, such wrongdoing has been imputed to a licensee who either knew or should have known of it or failed to exercise adequate control and supervision expected from a public trustee. Until recently, the FCC interested itself in nonbroadcast activities of a licensee, including fraudulent billing practices, false advertising, inflated audience ratings, and the like. In some instances, renewal was denied on such grounds. Activities covered by other federal laws or subject to state control since have been eliminated from the Commission's purview.

Loss of a license for content reasons creates tension with the statutory provision explicitly prohibiting censorship or "interfere[nce] with the right of free speech by means of radio communication." The Commission and the judiciary, when afforded multiple bases for revoking a license or denying renewal, generally have based decisions exclusively on non-speech grounds. The FCC, however, has emphasized that it will not shy away from imposing the most extreme sanctions available in some instances when content is the only concern. A broadcaster who violates rules against indecent or offensive expression, as discussed in Chapter 10, does so at the risk of its license. Failure to address the programming needs of a substantial part of the population in a licensee's service area also may result in the loss of a license. Findings that a state educational television system's programming policies discriminated on the basis of race and neglected the needs of African-American viewers led to a non-renewal decision. Content also was at the heart of a court of appeals decision vacating a renewal on grounds that a licensee had not served the public interest. Nearly half of the population in the television station's service area was African-American, but the licensee, among other things, had a policy of eliminating any programming that depicted blacks positively or focused on racial concerns.

Such results are the exception rather than the norm. Especially when controversy in the form of bigotry or prejudice has been the issue, the FCC and the judiciary have preferred to rely on less restrictive regulatory mechanisms such as the fairness doctrine. As evidenced by *Anti-Defamation League of B'nai B'rith v. Federal Communications Commission*, neither the agency nor the courts have evinced an inclination "to judge the merit, wisdom or accuracy of any broadcast discussion or commentary but has [sought] to insure that all viewpoints are given fair and equal opportunity for expression and that controverted allegations are balanced by the presentation of opposing viewpoints." Although the fairness doctrine has been discontinued, present regulatory philosophy probably would contemplate that the interests of balance and opportunity are fulfilled by a marketplace occupied by multiple and diverse media rather than by a licensing decision that constituted suppression.

E. Licensing Alternatives

Although well established, the licensing of broadcasters has evoked criticism both as a general concept and in the specific way it operates. Critical and legislative attention has focused in particular upon the marketplace concept. Professor Ronald Coase has advanced the notion that broadcasters should be subject to the same economic rules governing business in general.

There is no reason why users of radio frequencies should not be in the same position as other businessmen. There would not appear, for example, to be any need to regulate the relations between users of the same frequency. Once the rights of potential users have been determined initially, the rearrangement of rights could be left to the market. The simplest way of doing this would undoubtedly be to dispose of the use of a frequency to the highest bidder, thus leaving the subdivision of the use of the frequency to subsequent market transactions. Nor is it clear that the relations between users of adjacent frequencies will necessarily call for special regulation. It may well be that several people would normally be involved in a single transaction if conflicts of interests between users of adjacent frequencies are to be settled through the market. But, though an increase in the number of people involved increases the cost of carrying out a transaction, we know from experience that it is quite practicable to have market transactions which involve a multiplicity of parties. Whether the number of parties normally involved in transactions involving users of adjacent frequencies would be unduly large and call for special regulation, only experience could show. *Some* special regulation would certainly be required. For example, some types of medical equipment can apparently be operated in such a way as to cause interference on many frequencies and over long distances. In such a case, a regulation limiting the power of the equipment and requiring shielding would probably be desirable. It is also true that the need for wide bands of frequencies for certain purposes may require the exercise of the power of eminent domain; but this does not raise a problem different from that encountered in other fields. It is easy to embrace the idea that the interconnections between the ways in which frequencies are used raise special problems not found elsewhere or, at least, not to the same degree. But this view is not likely to survive the study of a book on the law of torts or on the law of property in which will be found set out the many (and often extraordinary) ways in which one person's actions can affect the use which others can make of their property.

Concern with the equities of a highest-bidder allocation system has evoked alternative marketplace approaches. In an article that he coauthored, former FCC Chairman Mark Fowler asserted that

Although a good way to have started in the 1920's, an auction would substantially disrupt current service and frustrate the expectations of those who have long held spectrum rights and of their customers. Another way to encourage optimum frequency use would be to allow licenses to be bought and sold freely after the initial grant, regardless of whether the initial grant is determined by auction, lottery, or under the old trusteeship approach. On resale, the seller, rather than the government, would capture the higher value of the frequency, but the allocation of resale profit would not prevent the frequency from reaching its highest use, thereby achieving the market objective.

To some, the major objection to free resale would be the windfall to incumbent licensees. The windfall, to the extent that it actually occurred, would consist of the increased value of a deregulated license created by its release from content and ownership restrictions and its new, freely transferable character. The problem presented by the windfall of free transferability is not entirely novel. Except for distressed properties or those that have never been transferred, the price paid to a transferor under existing assignment rules already reflects the steadily increasing value of the exclusivity. It is almost always greater than the value of the nonlicense assets being transferred. Restricted resales under section 310(d) of the 1934 Act have already occurred several times with respect to many licenses, so that the windfall has been captured.

More generally, the marketplace approach could be most expeditiously introduced to broadcasting by granting existing licensees "squatter's rights" to their frequencies. These rights embody the reasonable expectation of renewal that licensees presently enjoy for satisfactory past performance. The critical next step, from a market viewpoint, would be to deregulate fully the sale of licenses.

This approach to resale need not preclude the use of lotteries or auctions for new assignments to broadcasters or other spectrum users. Consider the Commission's handling of low-power television service. Announcement of this new service led to the submission of thousands of applications, many mutually exclusive, so that the Commission is faced with choosing among competing applicants. Although the Commission has approved a comparative process to license this new service, initial grants using either a lottery and resale or an auction could inject market incentives into the distribution of this service. Either technique would be likely to raise the frequency exclusivity to its highest use as a broadcast frequency.

Congress in recent years has authorized the FCC to use a lottery procedure that would randomly select licensees from a pool of applicants found to satisfy basic qualifications. If the FCC were to employ such a process in place of a comparative review procedure, it would be obligated, pending possible constitutional challenge, to extend a preference to applications of minority groups that would enhance overall diversification of the media. So far, however, the FCC has refrained from adopting random selection and persists with comparative review of broadcast license applicants.

REFERENCES

CASES

Anti-Defamation League of B'nai B'rith v. Federal Communications Commission, 403 F.2d 169 (D.C. Cir. 1968), cert. denied, 394 U.S. 930 (1969).
Central Florida Enterprises, Inc. v. Federal Communications Commission, 598 F.2d 37 (D.C. Cir. 1978).
Central Florida Enterprises, Inc. v. Federal Communications Commission, 683 F.2d 503 (D.C. Cir. 1982).
Citizens Communications Center v. Federal Communications Commission, 447 F.2d 1201 (D.C. Cir. 1971).
Federal Communications Commission v. National Citizens Committee for Broadcasting, 436 U.S. 775 (1978).
Federal Communications Commission v. RCA Communications, Inc., 346 U.S. 86 (1953).
Federal Communications Commission v. WNCN Listeners Guild, 450 U.S. 582 (1981).
Federal Communications Commission v. WOKO, Inc., 329 U.S. 223 (1946).
Federal Communications Commission v. Pottsville Broadcasting Co., 309 U.S. 134 (1940).
Geller, Simon, Application of, 102 F.C.C.2d 1443 (1985).
Greater Boston Television Corp. v. Federal Communications Commission, 444 F.2d 841 (D.C. Cir. 1970), cert. denied, 403 U.S. 923 (1971).
Hearst Radio, Inc. (WBAL), 15 F.C.C. 1149 (1951).
Metro Broadcasting, Inc. v. Federal Communications Commission, 110 S. Ct. 2997 (1990).
Mt. Mansfield Television, Inc. v. Federal Communications Commission, 442 F.2d 470 (2d Cir. 1970).
National Association of Independent Television Producers and Distributors v. Federal Communications Commission, 516 F.2d 526 (2d Cir. 1975).
National Broadcasting Co. v. United States, 319 U.S. 190 (1943).
Office of Communications of United Church of Christ v. Federal Communications Commission, 359 F.2d 994 (D.C. Cir. 1966).
Policy Regarding Character Qualifications in Broadcast Licensing, 87 F.C.C.2d 836 (1981).
Policy Statement on Comparative Broadcast Hearings, 1 F.C.C.2d 393 (1965).
United States v. Storer Broadcasting Co., 351 U.S. 192 (1956).

PUBLICATIONS

Caldwell, *The Standard of Public Interest, Convenience, or Necessity as Used in the Radio Act of 1927*, 1 Air L. Rev. 295 (1930).
Coase, *The Federal Communications Commission*, 2 J.L. & Econ. 1 (1959).

Collins, *The Local Service Concept in Broadcasting: An Evolution and Recommendation for Change*, 65 Iowa L. Rev. 553 (1980).

Fowler & Brenner, *A Marketplace Approach to Broadcast Regulation*, 60 Tex. L. Rev. 207 (1982).

Murchison, *Misrepresentation and the FCC*, 37 Fed. Com. L.J. 403 (1985).

Weiss, Ostroff & Clift, *Station License Revocations and Denials of Renewal, 1970–1978*, 24 J. Broadcasting 69 (1980).

Wirth, *The FCC's Multiple Ownership Rules and National Concentration in the Commercial Radio Industry*, 60 Den. L.J. 77 (1982).

Chapter 7

The Cable Industry

Regulation of emerging video technologies requires a delicate balancing of competing interests.

Quincy Cable TV, Inc. v. Federal Communications Commission,
768 F.2d 1434, 1462 (D.C. Cir. 1985),
cert. denied, 476 U.S. 1169 (1986)

Cable television originated essentially as an auxiliary of broadcasting but
has evolved into a medium of independent significance. Although broadcasting reaches more than 99 percent of the nation's citizens, cable pen-
etrates slightly more than half of the country's households. The FCC
describes cable as "[a] nonbroadcast facility consisting of a set of closed
transmission paths and associated signal generation, reception, and central equipment that is designed to provide cable service which includes
video programming and which is provided to multiple subscribers within
a community." Although both cable and broadcast services transmit electronic signals generating sound and pictures on a television screen, the
technology for propagation is different. Broadcast signals travel through
the air, while cable signals move along coaxial-cable or fiber-optic lines.

Problems with the effective transmission of broadcast signals originally
led to the development of cable service. Given the limited range of
broadcast emissions and their susceptibility to interference from any
obstacle between transmitting and receiving antennas, cable emerged as
a means for delivering television service of a high technical quality to
areas that otherwise would be unserved. The first cable systems thus

were constructed in areas that, because of remoteness or topographical impairment, essentially had no television. Cable service at the outset, therefore, consisted simply of a community antenna erected on high ground that picked up broadcast signals and retransmitted them by wire to subscribers.

I. INFERRED REGULATORY AUTHORITY

The Communications Act of 1934, as originally drawn, made no reference to cable. From cable television's emergence until Congress enacted legislation establishing a bifurcated scheme of federal and state regulation, considerable debate existed over whether the FCC had authority to regulate the new medium. Initially, the Commission itself declined jurisdiction on grounds that it was not specifically delegated responsibility and did not have adequate resources. Although it was empowered to regulate common carriers and television, the FCC decided against including cable within the purview of either. It further concluded that cable did not affect established television sufficiently to justify governance of the new medium concomitant with its duty to regulate broadcasting in the public interest.

After a decade of relative disinterest, the FCC began to take more seriously the impact of cable upon the broadcasting industry. It thus denied a common carrier's application to provide microwave service to a cable company because economic harm to a local broadcaster would adversely affect the public interest. Given the FCC's statutory mandate to maximize the benefits of broadcasting service to the public and guard the public interest, the court of appeals in *Carter Mountain Transmission Corp. v. Federal Communications Commission* concluded that the agency's concern for the economic viability of its licensees was appropriate. A predicate thus began to evolve (and continued to operate until FCC jurisdiction was codified) that enabled the Commission to regulate cable to the extent that it might impact broadcasting in a negative fashion. That concern soon became the underpinning for the Commission's formulation of a broad regulatory scheme. In 1966, the FCC assumed jurisdiction over all cable systems on grounds that regulation of the new medium was critical to effectuation of its obligation to ensure efficient broadcast service. Among other things, the Commission expressed concern that cable's ability to import distant signals fragmented the audience of local broadcasters, diminished their revenue base, and thus impaired their service and viability. Its particular worry was that UHF service, which was relatively underdeveloped and not on a sound economic footing, was especially vulnerable. Consequently, it adopted rules prohibiting the importation of distant signals into the one hundred largest television markets unless this would serve the public interest.

The Supreme Court delineated federal jurisdiction over cable, at least until Congress charted it by statute, when in *United States v. Southwestern Cable Co.* it upheld the FCC's prohibition against importation of distant signals. Finding "no need . . . to determine in detail the limits of the Commission's authority to regulate cable," the Court emphasized

that the authority which we recognize today under § 152(a) is restricted to that reasonably ancillary to the effective performance of the Commission's various responsibilities for the regulation of television broadcasting. The Commission may, for these purposes, issue "such rules and regulations and prescribe such restrictions and conditions, not inconsistent with law," as "public convenience, interest, or necessity requires." 47 U.S.C. § 303(r). We express no views as to the Commission's authority, if any, to regulate CATV under any other circumstances or for any other purposes.

The Court recognized that the consequences of an unregulated cable industry could not be accurately forecast. It found that the FCC's concerns with audience fragmentation and consequent revenue erosion in the broadcasting industry were legitimate and reasonable. Given the Commission's "broad responsibilities for the orderly development of an appropriate system of local television broadcasting," the Court considered it reasonable for the FCC to have concluded that "performance of these duties demands prompt and efficacious regulation of [cable] systems."

Following the *Southwestern Cable Co.* decision, the FCC embarked on a regulatory course that engendered a panoply of rules governing cable systems. Basing its action upon its recognized ancillary jurisdiction, the Commission promulgated regulations that affected both the industry's structure and programming content. Protection of the "system of local broadcasting" has been blamed for stunting cable's growth during the 1970s and into the early 1980s. The FCC's role attracted extensive criticism to the effect that it was "more concerned with protecting the economic interests of conventional broadcasters than with fully exploiting the resources of cable technology." Regulation, especially to the extent that it governed content, raised First Amendment questions. In reviewing the various rules, however, the courts generally refrained from constitutional evaluation. Such analysis in part reflected a preference for assessments of whether the FCC had exceeded the authority that was inferred from its statutory obligations. Equally if not more significant to the course of review was uncertainty over cable's nature and First Amendment status. The Supreme Court's references to community antenna television systems in its early opinions intimated that cable, at least then, was being conceptualized largely as an auxiliary broadcast methodology rather than an independent medium. Not until the mid-1980s did the Court declare in certain, albeit unexplicated, terms that cable was entitled to First Amendment protection. The extent to which cable regulation has been directly confronted on content-related grounds is discussed in Chapter 11.

As FCC control of the cable industry became more aggressive and sweeping, the Court soon warned that the Commission was pushing the limits of its jurisdiction. In *United States v. Midwest Video Corp.*, the Court upheld origination rules that obligated cable systems with at least 3,500 subscribers to establish facilities for local production and program presentation. The gist of the regulation was to make cablecasters originate their own programming if they wanted to retransmit broadcast signals. Without adverting to any constitutional issues concerning invasion of editorial discretion, the Court defined the critical question as "whether the Commission has reasonably determined that its origination rule will further the achievement of long-established regulatory goals in the field of television broadcasting by increasing the number of outlets for community self-expression and augmenting the public's choice of programs and types of services." In finding that the requirement advanced these aims, the Court broadened the predicate for the FCC's jurisdiction. It observed that "the Commission's legitimate concern in the regulation of [cable] is not limited to controlling the competitive impact [cable] may have on broadcast services." Rather,

Southwestern refers to the Commission's "various responsibilities for the regulation of television broadcasting." These are considerably more numerous than simply assuring that broadcast stations operating in the public interest do not go out of business. Moreover, we must agree with the Commission that its "concern with CATV carriage of broadcast signals is not just a matter of avoidance of adverse effects, but extends also to requiring CATV affirmatively to further statutory policies."...Since the avoidance of adverse effects is itself the furtherance of statutory policies, no sensible distinction even in theory can be drawn along those lines. More important, CATV systems, no less than broadcast stations, see, *e.g., Federal Radio Comm'n v. Nelson Bros. Co.*, 289 U.S. 266 (1933) (deletion of a station), may enhance as well as impair the appropriate provision of broadcast services. Consequently, to define the Commission's power in terms of the protection, as opposed to the advancement, of broadcasting objectives would artificially constrict the Commission in the achievement of its statutory purposes and be inconsistent with our recognition in *Southwestern* "that it was precisely because Congress wished 'to maintain, through appropriate administrative control, a grip on the dynamic aspects of radio transmission,'... that it conferred upon the Commission a 'unified jurisdiction' and 'broad authority.' "

The origination rule directly involved the FCC in regulation of the transmission of signals that did not primarily implicate the broadcast spectrum. Nonetheless, the Court concluded that

the regulation is not the less, for that reason, reasonably ancillary to the Commission's jurisdiction over broadcast services. The effect of the regulation, after all, is to assure that in the retransmission of broadcast signals viewers are provided suitably diversified programming—the same objective underlying regulations sustained in *National Broadcasting Co. v. United States*, . . . as well as the local-carriage rule reviewed in *Southwestern* and subsequently upheld. . . . In essence the regulation is no different from Commission rules governing the technological quality of CATV broadcast carriage. In the one case, of course, the concern is with strength of the picture and voice received by the subscriber, while in the other it is with the content of the programming offered. But in both cases the rules serve the policies of §§ 1 and 303(g) of the Communications Act on which the cablecasting regulation is specifically premised, . . . and also, in the Commission's words, "facilitate the more effective performance of [its] duty to provide a fair, efficient, and equitable distribution of television service to each of the several States and communities" under § 307(b). In sum, the regulation preserves and enhances the integrity of broadcast signals and therefore is "reasonably ancillary to the effective performance of the Commission's various responsibilities for the regulation of television broadcasting."

Chief Justice Burger, warning that the FCC had "strain[ed] the outer limits of . . . [its] jurisdiction," presaged an increasingly diminished role based upon ancillary authority. The FCC itself abandoned the cable origination rules in 1974. It adopted regulations, however, that obligated most cable systems to set aside four channels for public, educational, leased, and local-government access. A few years earlier it had rejected as a breach of the First Amendment a right of access in broadcasting, which it also has referred to as the least constitutionally protected medium. Avoiding any First Amendment issues, the Court in *Federal Communications Commission v. Midwest Video Corp.* determined that the access rules effectively had "relegated cable systems, *pro tanto*, to common-carrier status." Although it acknowledged the FCC's interest in maximizing opportunities for local expression and diversifying programming, the Court found that the Commission was precluded by statute from "treat[ing] persons engaged in broadcasting as common carriers." Oddly, it observed that the access rules more seriously abrogated editorial control over program composition than the origination rules. In another setting, the Court had depicted a mandatory publication rule as a patent invasion of editorial discretion. The outer limits of jurisdiction reasonably ancillary to effectuation of regulatory responsibilities in broadcasting, which were pushed in the first *Midwest Video* case, thereby were exceeded in the second *Midwest Video* case.

Shortly before invalidation of the access rules, the court of appeals in *Home Box Office, Inc. v. Federal Communications Commission* had struck down regulations prohibiting exhibition of certain feature films, major sporting events, and series programs on cable and subscription television. The rules also barred commercial advertising and limited the total amount of program time that could be devoted to sports and feature films. Such antisiphoning controls were designed to prevent the movement of popular fare from its established place on free television to pay services as a result of competitive bidding. The court of appeals criticized the FCC for mouthing rationales in support of its action that recited acknowledged regulatory grounds but established no nexus between means and ends. Noting that the rules prevented cable from competing for the subject programming, it could not see "[h]ow such an effect furthers any goal of the Communications Act." The court of appeals noted for future reference that "the Commission, in developing its cable television regulations, [must] demonstrate that the objectives to be achieved by regulating cable television are also objectives for which the Commission could legitimately regulate the broadcast media." As matters evolved, the FCC chose not to reintroduce the antisiphoning rules despite the court's observation that the Commission might, "after remand, be able to satisfy the jurisdictional prerequisites." Instead, the FCC moved in the direction of deregulation. In 1980, the Commission abandoned the distant-importation rules originally upheld in *Southwestern Cable*. It also eliminated exclusivity rules that authorized local television stations holding sole market rights to a syndicated program to require cable operators to delete such shows when they were carried in from another market. The court of appeals, in *Malrite T.V. of New York v. Federal Communications Commission,* characterized the Commission's action as "a major reversal of . . . regulatory policy." It nonetheless concluded that repeal of the rules "reflects the 'rational weighing of competing policies' Congress intended to be exercised by the agency and to be sustained by a reviewing court."

The FCC's sense after approximately a decade of detailed regulation of the cable industry was that the public interest would be promoted and served more effectively by increasing the exposure of both the broadcasting and cable industries to marketplace forces. Surviving until recently from the initial outpouring of regulation governing the cable industry were must-carry rules, which obligated cable systems to carry the signals of local stations. Even these controls have been invalidated pursuant to the court of appeals' decision in *Century Communications Corp. v. Federal Communications Commission*. Reflecting cable's evolution from an auxiliary into an independent medium, the decision confronted constitutional questions and struck down the rules on First

Amendment grounds. Details of the issue are reserved for Chapter 11. Further indicative of cable's significance, however, was congressional enactment of a comprehensive scheme for regulating cable.

II. THE CABLE COMMUNICATIONS POLICY ACT OF 1984

Exactly half a century after Congress enacted a comprehensive regulatory scheme for broadcasting, it did likewise for cable. Unlike other provisions of the Communications Act of 1934, the Cable Communications Policy Act of 1984 divides regulatory authority between federal and state governments. The Cable Act is the product of competing and converging interests of federal, state, and local authorities and the cable industry itself. Prior to the Cable Act's enactment, regulation largely was an extension of federal power asserted ancillary to governance of broadcasting in the public interest. To the distress of state and local governments, the FCC had adopted a stance to the effect that its rules and regulations largely preempted their role. In *Capital Cities Cable, Inc. v. Crisp,* the Supreme Court appeared to endorse the FCC's position that it had exclusive jurisdiction over the operational aspects of cable. The cable industry itself tended to favor a minimum role for state and local governments, which made competing and, in the opinion of operators, unrealistic demands upon potential franchisees. A special point of concern for cable operators was that even if they received a franchise and invested the substantial amount of capital necessary to commence service, no assurance existed that the grant would be renewed.

The Cable Act thus emerged from negotiations among federal, state, and local governments and the industry for the purpose of "establish[ing] a national policy concerning cable communications." Among its other aims are to

(2) establish franchise procedures and standards which encourage the growth and development of cable systems and which assure that cable systems are responsive to the needs and interests of the local community;

(3) establish guidelines for the exercise of Federal, State, and local authority with respect to the regulation of cable systems;

(4) assure and encourage that cable communications provide and are encouraged to provide the widest possible diversity of information sources and services to the public;

(5) establish an orderly process for franchise renewal which protects cable operators against unfair denials of renewal where the operator's past performance and proposal for future performance meet the standards established by this title; and

(6) promote competition in cable communications and minimize unnecessary regulation that would impose an undue economic burden on cable systems.

Lower courts have identified

two predominant objectives of the Cable Act: 1) to make the local franchising process the primary means of cable television regulation, and 2) to insure that the public receives the widest possible diversity of information services, in a manner which is responsive to the needs and interests of the local communities.

Jurisdiction over cable thus is partially vested in the FCC, which sets policy concerning pole attachments, access, cross-ownership, rates, technical standards, and employment policy. Primary franchising authority is conferred upon state and local governments.

The Cable Act specifies that "[n]othing in this title shall be construed to affect any authority of any State, political subdivision, or agency thereof, or franchising authority, regarding matters of public health, safety and welfare consistent with the express provision of this title." Such language, while it expressly acknowledges the pertinence of state and local police powers, makes it clear that they may not be used contrary to the terms or implications of the Cable Act. Litigation already has demonstrated that the lines between federal and state or local responsibility are less than clear. Although express statutory commands make it certain that states may not adopt conflicting cross-ownership rules, regulate rates, or treat cable operators as common carriers, disputes seem likely to arise or already have emerged in other areas where lines of authority are less clear. Such questions, which almost invariably center upon whether states can impose higher standards than the federal government, have arisen with respect to technical rules. In *City of New York v. Federal Communications Commission*, the Supreme Court sided with federal regulators in determining that Commission standards governing technical quality preempted stricter local criteria. Since the FCC explicitly had stated its intent to preempt state and local regulation, the outcome turned upon whether it was acting within the purview of its authority. Although franchising authorities under the Cable Act "could regulate 'services, facilities, and equipment' in certain respects," the Court found dispositive a specific charge for the FCC to govern technical standards. That legislative command, the Court determined, preserved the regulatory state of affairs preceding the Cable Act. Nothing in the act itself or history, moreover, "indicate[d] that Congress explicitly had disapproved of the Commission's preemption of local technical standards."

Although the Court narrowly construed the state's power to regulate service, facilities, and equipment in the *City of New York* case and has consistently endorsed a preemptive federal role in the controversies presented to it so far, the potential for a mixed federal and state role with varying standards remains in other areas. Federal law governing cable employment practices, for instance, might not preempt state equal employment opportunity laws that set higher standards or impose redundant or stiffer reporting requirements. Such variances between federal and state law exist and are countenanced in the general marketplace.

Arguments that a state may not prohibit a cable company from collecting monetary contributions from certain residents to finance construction in sparsely populated parts of a franchise area have been couched in terms of preemption. Characterizing the construction contributions as rates, one cable company asserted that they were the exclusive concern of the FCC. The district court in *Housatonic Cable Vision Co. v. Department of Public Utility Control*, however, determined that such contributions were not rates for purposes of the Cable Act. It further concluded that provisions prohibiting "discrimination among customers of basic cable service" and ensuring service to all potential groups of subscribers regardless of income supported the state's regulatory action. The short history of the Cable Act thus demonstrates that lines of regulatory authority are to be influenced as much by litigation as by legislation.

A. FRANCHISING

A franchise for a cable operator in many ways is the functional equivalent of a license for a broadcaster. Both enable the grantee to provide service for a fixed period of time. Unlike a broadcast license, which is awarded by the FCC, franchises are the responsibility of state and local governments. The Cable Act provides that a franchising authority, bounded by the terms of the statute, "may award . . . one or more franchises within its jurisdiction." The terms of empowerment include a provision obligating the franchising authority to "assure that access to cable service is not denied to any group of potential cable subscribers because of the income of the residents of the local area in which such group resides." A district court has cited that statutory charge in precluding a cable operator from effectively imposing higher charges on residents in a less profitable part of its franchise area as the condition for extending service to them. The Cable Act also provides for modification and renewal of a franchise.

1. Initial Franchise Decision

Award of an exclusive cable franchise by a city may constitute an antitrust violation. In *Community Communications Co., Inc. v. City of Boulder, Colorado*, the Supreme Court determined that a home-rule municipality did not qualify for state action immunity from federal antitrust laws unless it was effectuating a clear and overt state policy. Although cable television franchises as a consequence tend to be nonexclusive in their terms, in reality they amount to a de facto monopoly. That consequence is a function of investment considerations. Because front-end costs of wiring a community are so substantial, it generally is assumed that divided subscriptions would destroy profitability.

Given the practical status of cable in most instances as a monopoly, the franchising process has witnessed enormous competition and abuse. Local government has an interest in receiving the best possible service, which may induce unrealistic promises and bids by cable operators or unreasonable demands by officials. Often, overpromises that led to a franchise have been followed by efforts to renegotiate terms when it became clear that profitability would be dubious. Under such circumstances, franchising authorities have a choice of either acceding to scaled-down service or pursuing costly litigation that will delay the advent of cable in the community. A seamy appearance to the whole process was compounded by the tactics of applicants who, for instance, would award shares in the local cable company to prominent citizens. Since it was obvious that the value of the stock would soar if their company received the franchise, it was assumed that the individuals would exert whatever influence they might possess upon the selection process.

The assumption that cable is a natural monopoly is not universally accepted. A court of appeals observed that one city's cable television market was then a natural monopoly that, under present technology, offered room for only one operator at a time. Another court, however, found award of an exclusive franchise inimical to First Amendment interests. In so doing, it demanded proof of a substantial government interest beyond mere recitation of the notion that a service area will economically support only one cable operator. Critics of the natural monopoly concept assert that competition facilitates better service and lower rates.

Barnes, "The Cable Conspiracy," *The Washington Monthly*, June 1989, at 12.*

Cynics may suspect that the politicians who concocted the current system had more than the public interest in mind. The benefits to the politicians? They could shake down potential cable operators for hefty campaign contributions. Their stretched city budgets could be replenished with "franchise fees." Community groups could demand that franchises build elaborate "public access" studios for local programing, often starring—surprise!—the groups and the politicians themselves. . . .

After much lobbying, the franchise contract first went to the United Tribune Cable Co. in 1982. Though the company had seemed eager to promise the world in exchange for the franchise, subsequently it balked at some of its extravagant pledges, such as planting 20,000 trees in the area. United Tribune dropped out. The bidding was reopened.

One of the bidders was River City Cable Company, formed by a group of 73 local investors— whom the press later dubbed the "Gang of 73"— each making $2,000 investments. None of the people involved with River City had the least experience is running a cable television company, and $146,000 in working capital isn't much for starting one. But they had something more important: clout. The Gang of 73 was a Who's Who of Sacramento's politically powerful and well-connected, including Michael Deaver and a sitting federal district judge. Each investor was told by the organizers of the venture that they stood to realize a profit of as much as $120,000 or more by the mid–1990s, according to subsequent trial testimony. To actually run the system, the shell that called itself River City Cable teamed up with Scripps-Howard Broadcasting to form Sacramento Cable Television; the Gang of 73 owned 5 percent of this corporation. The combination of clout and capability worked. In 1983, Sacramento Cable was selected over four other bidders by the Sacramento Metropolitan Cable Commission to run the local system. All seemed smooth sailing.

One man who wasn't satisfied, however, was Rod Hansen, president of Pacific West Cable and one of the unsuccessful bidders. All he had was a cable company—no Gang of 73. He decided to apply to operate a second cable system in the city. "(The cable commission) told me that I was wasting my time," Hansen says. "When I persisted, they said I would have to put up a $40,000 nonrefundable deposit and all this other stuff. And even if I did that, they still told me my chances were nonexistent."

Had Hansen accepted that answer, that's where things would have ended. Instead, he got in touch with Harold Farrow, a noted First Amendment lawyer in Oakland. Hansen filed suit in 1983 charging that the city and county of Sacramento had violated his First Amendment rights of free speech by awarding what amounted to a monopoly to one company. Farrow argued that the process of granting cable franchises was akin to "the business of licensing the press that we thought we were done with a couple of hundred years ago."

It took four years for the case to come to trial in federal district court, but when the jury ruled, the whole cable television industry sat up and took notice. The judge asked the jury for certain findings of fact. The answers shocked the defendants.

Question: "Was the 'natural monopoly' argument a sham by defendants (city and council) to obtain increased campaign contributions for local elected officials?"

Answer: "Yes."

Question: "Were defendants motivated to provide such benefits (public access channels and other community grants) by either a desire to obtain increased political influence for elected or appointed local officials or a desire to favor local officials' political supporters?"

Answer: "Yes."

Jurors later told local press that it was the "influence peddling" by the Gang of 73 that had obtained the franchise for Sacramento Cable. "We felt the way the whole thing was written up was to exclude competition and it had to do with this Gang of 73," juror Judith Mosier told the *Sacramento Bee*.

This unexpected defeat was so total that the city and county did not even bother to appeal the jury verdict. Instead, the cable commission immediately rewrote its ordinance to allow free competition, requiring applicants only to obtain a license and bond from the government before tearing up the streets. Subsequently *two* other companies entered the fray—Hansen's Pacific West and Cable AmeriCal, which Sacramento Cable eventually bought out for $11 million.

One of the most frequently repeated arguments in favor of franchising is that without the guaranteed profits that come with a monopoly, no cable company would provide service to the poorest neighborhoods. Fewer poor people would buy the service, and they would default more often than their more prosperous neighbors—or so the theory went. Sacramento Cable set out to make this a self-fulfilling prophecy when, upon losing its monopoly status, it announced it was dropping plans to wire the low-income neighborhood of Oak Park. But a storm of public protest caused Sacramento Cable to reverse its decision. At the same time, Pacific West applied for a license to wire Oak Park, too. So it is supremely ironic that one of the city's lowest-income sections is likely to be one of the first in the area with competing cable systems.

The poor-will-suffer theory of cable monopoly was flawed anyway—poor people tend to watch television more avidly than others, making poor neighborhoods ripe markets. And the bunching of homes close together makes them cheaper to wire. In fact it's the poor who often subsidize service to affluent suburbs, which pay the same rates even though the distance between homes makes them more expensive to reach.

Competition brought another boon to Sacramento consumers: cheaper prices. As part of the settlement of a lawsuit by the city against Sacramento Cable for various non-payments, the company won the right to charge different rates in different neighborhoods, something the franchise agreement had prohibited. A few months after raising its rates to $16.50 for basic service, Sacramento Cable turned around and waived installation fees, offered several months of free viewing, and matched Pacific West's price of $13.50—but only, of course, in those areas where Pacific West had begun stringing cable. None of this solicitous behavior was on display in neighborhoods where Sacramento Cable still had its monopoly....

Where cable operators have managed to keep their monopolistic grip, consumers have paid the price. Thomas Hazlett, a professor of economics at the University of California at Davis who has testified as an expert witness in numerous anti-franchising lawsuits, estimates that all the "bells and whistles" promised in order to win the franchise probably add 20 to 30 percent to the average customer's bill. "If a typical cable consumer pays $25 a month for basic service and a premium channel," he says, "at least $5 to $7 of that results from politically imposed costs, most of which is pure waste ... (a) dollar so the mayor and his friends can have their own talk shows that nobody watches, and on and on."

Promise-the-moon is the m.o. only until the ink dries. The next step is equally predictable: once the franchise is awarded, the lucky winner shuffles sheepishly back to the city and admits that many of the promises were, financially speaking, quite unrealistic. The "giveback" negotiations then get under way. In a study of the 30 largest markets in the country, Hazlett found that 21 of them had acceded to givebacks. In eight of those instances, the givebacks occurred before a single home was wired.

Speedy hookups, anyone? Washington, D.C. began its franchising process in 1982, and the city is still less than half wired. Meanwhile, suburbs of San Diego, Phoenix, and parts of Fairfax, Va.—some of the few areas of the country that did not bother with franchising—got their MTV faster than their neighbors who enjoyed the "protection" of the monopoly system....

Decades of Cable Monopoly have put franchise holders on Park Place, sent local officials directly to jail, and left hapless consumers with Virginia Avenue service.

Competing cable franchises at least until recently have been relatively rare phenomena. Especially in communities where service or rates have prompted extensive customer dissatisfaction, competition has become an increasingly attractive and selected policy option.

2. Franchise Modification

The Cable Act sets forth conditions under which a cable operator may have its franchise modified. By its terms, it does not necessarily operate as a deterrent to overpromising as a means of obtaining a franchise. A not uncommon demand upon applicants as the condition of receiving a franchise has been the setting aside of access channels along with the construction of facilities and provisions of equipment for access programming. Federal law provides, however, that

[d]uring the period a franchise is in effect, the cable operator may obtain from the franchising authority modifications of the requirements...for facilities or equipment, including public, educational, or governmental access facilities, or equipment, if the cable operator demonstrates that (i) it is commercially impracticable for the operator to comply with the requirement, and (ii) the proposal by the cable operator for modification of such requirement is appropriate because of commercial impracticability.

Since the touchstone for modifying terms and conditions of access is "commercial impracticability," authorities have to assume responsibility that promises made are realistic or assume the risk that the cable operator is entitled to relief after the franchise is awarded. Not surprisingly, many of the extravagant promises that preceded a franchise decision have been reduced or abandoned pursuant to a showing that they were commercially impracticable. Service requirements also are subject to modification "if the cable operator demonstrates that the mix, quality and level of services required by the franchise at the time it was granted will be maintained after such modification." Among other things, the latter provision takes into account problems that may arise with product design and supplies. Once a request for modification is filed, the franchising authority must render a decision within 120 days unless time is extended by mutual consent. In the event of denial, the cable operator may obtain review in a federal court, which may grant relief if it finds commercial impracticability. The statutory provision for modification has been depicted as reflecting congressional "recogni[tion] that cable operators compete in a changing marketplace. . . . [Congress] was sufficiently concerned with the plight of some cable operators, particularly urban franchisees committed to state-of-the-art systems, to create a federally protected right to modification of commercially impractical agreements."

The court of appeals in *Tribune-United Cable of Montgomery County v. Montgomery County, Maryland* thus precluded local authorities from commencing franchise revocation proceedings or enforcing penalty provisions of the franchise agreement until it acted upon a modification request. The cable company had encountered problems of construction and equipment delays, operational failures, and softer-than-anticipated consumer demand. It thus sought modification of terms including access and origination, equipment type, and construction schedule. Emphasizing Congress's protective aim, the appeals court concluded that the right to modify "would mean very little if local franchising authorities were able to burden it by enforcing massive penalties during the pendency of the modification proceedings." It thus concluded that "[s]hort of a bad faith or frivolous application for modification, . . . such application automatically stays any action on the part of the franchising authority to enforce the penalty provisions of the franchise agreement."

3. Franchise Renewal

The Cable Act addresses perhaps the cable industry's paramount interest in uniform regulation of a national order by identifying the criteria for renewal. Prior to congressional action, cable operators were subject to state and local standards that at best were vague and at worst nonexistent. Having invested substantial capital for purposes of establishing a system, cable operators were concerned that they would lose their franchises at the whim of public officials or be subject to constant pressure for expensive alterations and improvements.

The FCC has responded to similar concerns of broadcasters by creating a renewal expectancy for licensees that provide a certain quality of service. The Cable Act accomplishes a similar aim by requiring a franchise renewal proceeding, at the request of the cable operator or upon the regulating authority's own initiative, to assess past performance and the community's future needs. A renewal decision must be tied to consideration of whether the franchisee has (1) substantially complied with material terms of the franchise and relevant law; (2) provided quality of service in a technical and business sense that is reasonable in light of community needs; (3) demonstrated sufficient financial, legal, and technical ability to provide proposed future service; and (4) offered a proposal that is reasonable to meet future cable-related community needs and interests. Denial of a franchise renewal must be based upon an identified deficiency in one of these four categories.

4. Franchise Fees

Congress has expressly provided that an annual franchise fee may not exceed 5 percent of a cable operator's gross revenues. For purposes of the Cable Act, a franchise fee is "any tax, fee, or assessment of any kind imposed by a franchising authority or other government entity on a cable operator or cable subscriber, or both, solely because of their status as such." Taxes or assessments of general applicability are not considered franchise fees unless they are "unduly discriminatory." In *Group W Cable, Inc. v. City of Santa Cruz*, a federal district court cited the federal fee controls in determining that a municipality's easement and right-of-way charges were subject to limitation.

The best available approximation of the fair market value of the use of the easements to provide cable service is the value to a cable operator of access to the Santa Cruz market. Cable operators will presumably pay a fee for use of the easements and rights of way that will enable them to serve the Santa Cruz market while earning a reasonable return on their investment. The First Amendment does not necessarily preclude allowing the market place to control the allocation of communication resources. . . . In theory, this leaves Santa Cruz free to fix a fee higher than Group W is willing to pay, but, in reality, Santa Cruz is restrained in two ways: (1) California Government Code § 53066 and the Cable Communications Policy Act, 47 U.S.C. § 542(b), limit any fee to not more than five percent of the gross revenue derived from cable operations in Santa Cruz, and, (2) Santa Cruz's interest in gaining cable service for its residents will also limit the fee it charges Group W, since it is not free to charge any other operator either less or more. Within the range from zero to five percent, Santa Cruz must set a content-neutral, nondiscriminatory fee; it cannot use the fee as a vehicle for selecting a preferred operator. Any fee set must be the same for any cable operator regardless of the nature of the service offered or any other consideration or distinction.

Following enactment of the Cable Act, the FCC abandoned its preexisting regulations on franchise fees and "its past practice of adjudicating disputes over . . . what constituted a franchise fee." Respectively, the Commission's rationales were that Congress had eliminated the need for the previous fee ceiling and that all fee controversies were best resolved in court. Following a challenge to its policy against adjudicating disputes, the FCC modified its position to the effect that it no longer had an interest in most franchise fee controversies. Disclaiming any expertise in local taxation matters it considered best left to local courts, the Commission limited exercise of its jurisdiction to concerns directly affecting national cable communications policy and implicating its special area of knowledge. Absent a specific contrary directive from Congress, the court of appeals in *American Civil Liberties Union v. Federal Communications Commission* concluded that the FCC's forbearance policy was neither irrational nor contrary to statute. It noted, however, that its affirmance was "based on our assessment that the Commission has *not totally abdicated its ultimate responsibility* for enforcing the franchise fee provision [emphasis in original]." The decision thus remains that the franchise fee section, like other parts of the Cable Act, must be viewed in context with Congress's broader purpose of "establish[ing] a 'national policy' concerning cable communications."

B. RATES

Disputes over the regulation of rates predate the Cable Act. Several years before its enactment, the state of New York attempted to check rising rates for cable service. Upon review, the court of appeals determined that rate governance was within the FCC's ancillary jurisdiction and thus had been preempted. Soon thereafter, the Commission verified its policy to the effect that its intent was to preempt any local and state regulation in the field.

The Cable Act generally prohibits federal or state authorities from regulating rates for cable service. The only exception is (1) with respect to basic service, but (2) only if the cable system is not subject to effective competition. In determining whether "effective competition" exists, the FCC has ruled that the proper reference point is not a natural monopoly but cable's presence within a larger media universe. If a service area receives at least three broadcast signals, therefore, the Commission has determined that effective competition exists.

The policy, although contested, largely has been upheld. In *American Civil Liberties Union v. Federal Communications Commission*, the rules were challenged as arbitrary and irrational insofar as they used the single criterion of available broadcast signals to define effective competition and depicted availability in terms of theoretical accessibility. The appeals court found the Commission's determination reasonable, given the broad latitude it had for defining effective competition, but also identified provisions that could not stand. First, the court determined that Congress had defined "basic cable service" and that the FCC could not substitute its own meaning. Second, the court found that the FCC had exceeded its authority by allowing cable systems automatically to pass through any readily identifiable cost increase or decrease attributable to provision of basic service. Examples of what would have qualified for automatic pass-through included price changes in programming or altered copyright fees. The court determined that Congress's provision for annual automatic 5 percent increases at the cable operator's discretion accounted for the gap that the FCC unnecessarily had filled. It thus concluded that the augmentative rule "simply removed the five-percent cap that Congress placed on automatic increases." Finally, the appeals court required the Commission in determining "effective competition" to figure signal availability upon a more meaningful basis than its counting of every signal that covers "*any* portion of the cable community [emphasis in original]." Thus "it was incumbent upon the FCC to craft the standard more carefully, to ensure that a signal is at least theoretically available over the entire cable community or at least some significant portion of it."

The Commission on remand redefined "effective competition" to include a minimum of three broadcast signals, although not necessarily the same ones, throughout the cable service area. Availability now is presumed when minimum criteria for signal coverage are satisfied or a signal is "significantly viewed" in the service area.

Cable systems functioning under a franchise awarded prior to the Cable Act were subject to rate regulation by state and local authorities for two years after its effective date. Since rates have been largely deregulated, considerable consternation has been evidenced over rising cable rates. During the two years immediately after decontrol, rates for basic service jumped from an average of $11.23 to $14.48—a 29 percent increase. Although the upward price movement was four times the rate of inflation, the cable industry claims that the increases are justified because service is improving and earlier regulated prices were artificially low. The FCC has proposed standards that would fortify the concept of "effective competition" and expand local power to regulate cable rates. Pursuant to those criteria, cable would be subject to effective competition and exempt from rate regulation if a franchise area were served by at least six broadcast signals or by a multichannel provider available to at least half of the homes in the market and serving at least 10 percent of them. A cable industry study asserts that the effective competition standard would expose more than half of the nation's cable systems to local rate regulation. Notwithstanding the FCC proposal, some state and local governments and consumer groups have pushed Congress for legislation further liberalizing the conditions for rate control. A bill, permitting rate regulation in communities where no competing cable service or other multichannel provider exists, passed the House in 1990 but died in the Senate. Similar legislation has been reintroduced.

C. CONCENTRATION

The Cable Act incorporates diversification policies akin to those that restrict ownership of broadcast stations. Unlike the rules that bar cross-ownership of co-located broadcasting stations and newspapers, cross-ownership of cable systems and television stations in the same community is proscribed by statute rather than by agency rule. The provision further authorizes the FCC to "prescribe rules with respect to the ownership or control of cable systems by persons who own or control other media of mass communications which serve the same community served by a cable system." Although the FCC is seemingly authorized to reach media other than television, FCC rules go no further than the statute except to proscribe altogether cable ownership by broadcasting networks.

Prior to the Cable Act, the FCC had adopted a cross-ownership rule that exempted cable systems owned in 1970. The rule was challenged on grounds that (1) the Commission did not have authority to promulgate it prior to receiving jurisdiction under the act and (2) a right of first refusal obtained in 1968 constituted an ownership interest. In *Marsh Media, Ltd. v. Federal Communications Commission*, the court of appeals noted the Commission's well-established authority under the reasonably ancillary jurisdiction test. It also noted that a right of first refusal did not qualify as an ownership interest under the agency rules. Finally, it determined that any First Amendment claim was "foreclosed by the Supreme Court's decision in *Federal Communications Commission v. National Citizens Committee for Broadcasting* upholding . . . [the] rule . . . restricting cross-ownership of co-located daily newspapers and television stations." The *Marsh Media* case is a useful reminder that despite enactment of the Cable Act, its freshness means that some issues still may arise that require assessment under preexisting standards.

D. EXCLUSIVITY

In 1988, the FCC reinstated syndicated exclusivity rules that had been abandoned several years earlier. In repealing such regulation in 1980, the Commission had determined that viewer interest in seeing programs when desired outweighed local-broadcaster exclusivity interests. Following an inquiry into the consequences of such deregulation, the FCC reintroduced syndicated exclusivity rules pursuant to its sense that broadcasters otherwise were at a competitive disadvantage "with other media for product from which the programming producers can receive full value." As a consequence, local broadcasters with exclusive rights to syndicated programming may prohibit cable operators from importing it from a distant station.

In *United Video, Inc. v. Federal Communications Commission*, the court of appeals upheld the rules. It found substantial evidence that regulation was necessary to prevent diversion of "a substantial portion of the broadcast audience to cable" and consequent diminution of "the value of the programming [from] lowe[red] advertising revenues." The court also found the FCC's discernment of a "link between lack of program diversity and lowered broadcast revenues due to lack of exclusivity... sufficiently in accord with accepted economic theory." Although the court acknowledged that the exclusivity requirement would "affect the content of cable programming," the court concluded that "it is content neutral." It thus found the rules unaffected by a provision of the Cable Communications Policy Act of 1984 forbidding imposition of any content requirement. Finally, the court rejected a constitutional challenge to the rules as a "desire to make commercial use of the copyrighted works of others [for which] [t]here is no First Amendment right."

REFERENCES

CASES

American Civil Liberties Union v. Federal Communications Commission, 823 F.2d 1554 (D.C. Cir. 1987).

Capital Cities Cable, Inc. v. Crisp, 467 U.S. 691 (1984).

Carter Mountain Transmission Corp. v. Federal Communications Commission, 321 F.2d 359 (D.C. Cir. 1963).

Century Communications Corp. v. Federal Communications Commission, 835 F.2d 292 (D.C. Cir. 1987), cert. denied, 108 S. Ct. 2015 (1988).

City of New York v. Federal Communications Commission, 108 S. Ct. 1637 (1988).

Community Communications Co., Inc. v. City of Boulder, Colorado, 445 U.S. 40 (1982).

Federal Communications Commission v. Midwest Video Corp., 440 U.S. 689 (1979).

Federal Communications Commission v. National Citizens Committee for Broadcasting, 436 U.S. 775 (1978).

Group W Cable, Inc. v. City of Santa Cruz, 679 F. Supp. 977 (N.D. Cal. 1984).

Home Box Office, Inc. v. Federal Communications Commission, 567 F.2d 9 (8th Cir.), cert. denied, 434 U.S. 839 (1977).

Housatonic Cable Vision Co. v. Department of Public Utility Control, 622 F. Supp. 798 (D. Conn. 1985).

Malrite T.V. of New York v. Federal Communications Commission, 652 F.2d 1140 (2d Cir. 1981), cert. denied, 454 U.S. 1143 (1982).

Marsh Media, Ltd. v. Federal Communications Commission, 798 F.2d 772 (5th Cir. 1986).

Quincy Cable TV, Inc. v. Federal Communications Commission, 768 F.2d 1434 (D.C. Cir. 1985), cert. denied, 476 U.S. 1169 (1986).

Rollins Cablevue, Inc. v. Saienni Enterprises, 633 F. Supp. 1315 (D. Del. 1986).

Tribune-United Cable of Montgomery County v. Montgomery County, Maryland, 784 F.2d 1227 (4th Cir. 1986).

United States v. Midwest Video Corp., 406 U.S. 649 (1972).

United States v. Southwestern Cable Co., 392 U.S. 157 (1968).

United Video, Inc. v. Federal Communications Commission, 890 F.2d 1173 (D.C. Cir. 1989).

PUBLICATIONS

Barnes, *The Cable Conspiracy,* Washington Monthly, June 1989, at 12–15.

Bollinger, *Freedom of the Press and Public Access: Toward a Theory of Partial Regulation of the Mass Media,* 75 Mich. L. Rev. 1 (1976).

Brotman, *Time to Pull the Cable?* Nat'l. L. J., December 18, 1989, at 13.

Mallamud, *Courts, Statutes, and Administrative Agency Jurisdiction: A Consideration of Limits on Judicial Creativity,* 35 S.C. L. Rev. 191 (1984).

Chapter 8

The Common Carrier Industry

> If we will not endure a king as a political power we should not endure
> a king over the ... sale of any other necessities of life.
>
> *United States v. American Telephone & Telegraph Co.*,
> 552 F. Supp. 131 (D.D.C. 1982), *aff'd*, 460 U.S. 1001 (1983),
> *quoting* 21 Cong. Rec. 2457 (1890)(Sen. Sherman)

I. THE NATURE AND REGULATION OF COMMON CARRIERS

Common carriers are like other media insofar as they provide a system
for disseminating information. Unlike print, broadcasting, and cable,
common carriers generally do not make editorial decisions regarding
content. Telephone lines or transmissions actually may be the passageway
for signals that ultimately are converted into a print, broadcast, cable,
or other format. They are easily accessible and extensively accessed by
individuals and serve as a linkage medium for computers, telefacsimile,
and other technologies. The key distinguishing characteristic of a common carrier thus is a duty "by wire or radio to furnish ... communication
service upon reasonable request therefore." Given the special role performed by common carriers, regulation of their traditional function has
raised few real First Amendment questions.

The Communications Act of 1934 defines a common carrier in terms
of being "engaged ... for hire, in interstate or foreign radio transmission

of energy." Even before enactment of the Communications Act, the basic duties of common carriers were well established. Telegraph operators thus had "the duty of fairness and equality in the treatment of [their] customers and [were obligated to] serve them at reasonable rates and without unjust discrimination." Requirements of equal access and non-discrimination govern "like communication service." The meaning of like service is left for the FCC to determine on a case-by-case basis.

What a common carrier is in some ways may be clarified by under-standing what it is not. When cable was in its infancy, the FCC specifically considered whether it was a common carrier. Because subscribers had no control over the particular information they received, the Commission determined that cable did not so qualify. The Supreme Court, in *United States v. Southwestern Cable Co.*, essentially embraced the FCC's view in noting that cable for purposes of the Communications Act was not a common carrier. In the mid–1970s, however, the FCC adopted access rules that effectively imposed upon cable operators the common-carrier obligations of equal access and nondiscrimination. The Supreme Court, in *Federal Communications Commission v. Midwest Video Corp.*, invalidated the access rules and identified the differing natures and statuses of cable and common carriers.

With its access rules, . . . the Commission has transferred control of the content of access cable channels from cable operators to members of the public who wish to communicate by the cable medium. Effectively, the Commission has relegated cable systems, *pro tanto*, to common-carrier status.[a] A common-carrier service in the communications context[b] is one that "makes a public offering to provide [communications facilities] whereby all members of the public who choose to employ such facilities may communicate or transmit intelligence of their own design and choosing. . . ." . . . A common carrier does not "make individualized decisions, in particular cases, whether and on what terms to deal."

The access rules plainly impose common-carrier obligations on cable opera-tors.[c] Under the rules, cable systems are required to hold out dedicated channels on a first-come, nondiscriminatory basis. 47 CFR §§ 76.254 (a), 76.256 (d) (1977). Operators are prohibited from determining or influencing the content of access programming. § 76.256 (b). And the rules delimit what operators may charge for access and use of equipment. § 76.256 (c).

[a] A cable system may operate as a common carrier with respect to a portion of its service only. See *National Association of Regulatory Utility Comm'rs v. FCC*, 174 U.S. App. D. C. 374, 381, 533 F.2d 601, 608 (1976) (opinion of Wilkey, J.) ("Since it is clearly possible for a given entity to carry on many types of activities, it is at least logical to conclude that one can be a common carrier with regard to some activities but not others"); *First Report and Order in Docket No. 18397*, 20 F. C. C. 2d 201, 207 (1969).

[b] Section 3 (h) defines "common carrier" as "any person engaged as a common carrier for hire, in interstate or foreign communication by wire or radio or interstate or foreign radio transmission of energy. . . ." Due to the circularity of the definition, resort must be had to court and agency pronouncements to ascertain the term's meaning. See

National Association of Regulatory Utility Comm'rs v. *FCC*, 173 U.S. App. D. C. 413, 423, 525 F. 2d 630, 640, cert. denied, 425 U.S. 992 (1976); *Frontier Broadcasting Co.* v. *Collier*, 24 F. C. C. 251, 254 (1958); H. R. Conf. Rep. No. 1918, 73d Cong., 2d Sess., 46 (1934).
    ᶜ As we have noted, and as the Commission has held, cable systems otherwise "are not common carriers within the meaning of the Act." *United States* v. *Southwestern Cable Co.*, 392 U. S., at 169 n. 29; see *Frontier Broadcasting Co.* v. *Collier, supra*.

II. THE RESTRUCTURING OF THE TELEPHONE INDUSTRY

Defined most broadly, common carrier include air and ground carriers, telegraph companies, and other systems for movement of goods or data. The most prominent contemporary issue concerning the field of common carriage, given the importance of the industry and the attention it has received, is that of telephone service. The dominance and influence of the American Telephone and Telegraph Company (AT&T), which through its subsidiaries effectively monopolized local and long-distance telephone communications until recently, have been enduring concerns of federal regulation.

In 1956, the Department of Justice and AT&T negotiated an antitrust settlement incorporated into a final judgment that for the next quarter of a century defined the Bell System's scope of operations. Terms of the decree required AT&T's manufacturing subsidiary, Western Electric Company, to refrain from producing any common-carrier equipment of a type not sold or leased to Bell System companies. AT&T itself largely was barred from engaging in any business other than the furnishing of common-carrier services. Such structural controls reflected a sense that AT&T's resources, technological expertise, and leverage, if unrestrained, would be a threat rather than an advantage to national economic interests. In entering the final judgment, the district court retained jurisdiction "for the purpose of enabling any of the parties for this Final Judgment to apply to this Court at any time for such further orders and directions as may be necessary or appropriate."

"[A]ny time" arrived more than two decades later when AT&T and the federal government filed a stipulation in *United States v. American Telephone & Telegraph Co.* consenting to the entry of a "Modification of Final Judgment." The modified final judgment was the result of a Justice Department action alleging antitrust violations and originally seeking divestiture from AT&T of its Bell operating companies and the dissolution of Western Electric. The modified final judgment reflected a settlement between the parties that essentially required AT&T to divest itself of the operating companies and thereby abandon its role as a supplier of local telephone service. Geographic service zones, denominated as "exchange areas," defined the new service regions of the spin-off companies. Such areas were conceived "to comprehend contiguous areas having common social and economic characteristics but not so large as to defeat the intent of the decree to separate the provision of intercity service from the provision of local exchange service." Central to the new order, therefore, was that the new companies (sometimes referred to as Baby Bells) would "provide telephone service from one point in an exchange area to other points in the same exchange area—'exchange telecommunications'—and they would originate and terminate calls from one exchange area to another exchange area—'exchange access'. The interexchange portion of calls would . . . , however, be carried by AT&T" or its new competitors in the long-distance business. The relationships between AT&T and its manufacturing arm, Western Electric, and research arm, Bell Laboratories, were preserved. All were obligated, however, to provide various types of support for the operating companies to ensure their viability and compliance with the decree.

A prerequisite for divestiture, which proved to be the heart of the modified final judgment, was a determination that it served "the public interest." The district court found the standard satisfied, despite AT&T's claim that its depressed local rates were a function of FCC policy that required national rate averaging and thus were reasonable under federal law. The court noted that FCC policy had changed in recent years, but that AT&T's anticompetitive practice of using long-distance service to subsidize local rates had not. In addition, it was found that AT&T, again contrary to the public interest, had prohibited attachment of competitors' equipment to its network and had forced its operating companies to purchase equipment from Western Electric even when superior products were available from other sources.

Apart from such specific identified acts, the court concluded that antitrust relief was justified by "AT&T's substantial domination of the telecommunications industry in general." It referred to general antitrust policy that favors decentralization rather than aggregations or concentrations of industrial power. These concerns were magnified, in the court's view, by the crucial role of the telecommunications industry and the reality that "[t]he only pervasive two-way communication system is the telephone network." While noting that Bell System officials mostly "have been careful not to take advantage of [their] central position in American economic life," the court nonetheless observed that "[t]here is no guarantee . . . that future managers will be equally careful." It thus regarded the decree as a means not only of halting objectionable practices but of ensuring that others did not occur.

A. The American telecommunications industry is presently dominated by one company—AT&T. It provides local and long-distance telephone service; it manufactures and markets the equipment used by telephone subscribers as well as that used in the telecommunications network; and it controls one of the leading communications research and development facilities in the world. According to credible evidence, this integrated structure has enabled AT&T for many years to undermine the efforts of competitors seeking to enter the telecommunications market.

The key to the Bell System's power to impede competition has been its control of local telephone service. The local telephone network functions as the gateway to individual telephone subscribers. It must be used by long-distance carriers seeking to connect one caller to another. Customers will only purchase equipment which can readily be connected to the local network through the telephone outlets in their homes and offices. The enormous cost of the wires, cables, switches, and other transmission facilities which comprise that network has completely insulated it from competition. Thus, access to AT&T's local network is crucial if long distance carriers and equipment manufacturers are to be viable competitors.

AT&T has allegedly used its control of this local monopoly to disadvantage these competitors in two principal ways. First, it has attempted to prevent competing long distance carriers and competing equipment manufacturers from gaining access to the local network, or to delay that access, thus placing them in an inferior position vis-a-vis AT&T's own services. Second, it has supposedly used profits earned from the monopoly local telephone operations to subsidize its long distance and equipment businesses in which it was competing with others.

For a great many years, the Federal Communications Commission has struggled, largely without success, to stop practices of this type through the regulatory tools at its command. A lawsuit the Department of Justice brought in 1949 to curb similar practices ended in an ineffectual consent decree. Some other remedy is plainly required; hence the divestiture of the local Operating Companies from the Bell System. This divestiture will sever the relationship between this local monopoly and the other, competitive segments of AT&T, and it will thus ensure—certainly better than could any other type of relief—that the practices which allegedly have lain heavy on the telecommunications industry will not recur.

Terms of the consent decree, although requiring AT&T to divest itself of its operating companies, lifted all restrictions imposed by the 1956 decree and left it "free to compete in all facets of the marketplace." AT&T was allowed to enter the computer and information services market, but a significant exception barred it from entering into electronic publishing. The restriction raises First Amendment questions and thus is considered in Chapter 12. Constraints upon the divested operating companies preclude them from furnishing interexchange and information services and manufacturing telecommunications equipment. Such restrictions reflect concern with marketplace competition, but restraints upon marketing customer-premises equipment or publishing directories were rejected as contrary to the public interest. Finally, because "a substantial AT&T bias has been designed into the integrated telecommunications network," the decree obligated the operating companies to provide all long-distance carriers with equal access to "interexchange and information services." The terms of existence and operation for AT&T and its former operating companies were set forth in *United States v. American Telephone & Telegraph Co.*

The 1956 Decree and Line of Business Restrictions

The basic agreement embodied in the 1956 consent decree in the *Western Electric* case was that AT&T would not be required to divest itself of Western Electric, provided that AT&T would restrict its operations to the provision of common carrier communications services and that Western Electric would manufacture only the types of equipment used by the Bell System.

The decree which has now been submitted by the parties would eliminate all of the restrictions of the 1956 consent judgment. If that decree is entered by the Court, AT&T would be free to enter the computer market as well as to provide the full range of so-called information services.

There has been no serious opposition to the entry of AT&T into manufacturing and marketing of computers and other electronic equipment, and there is no question that this development would be in the public interest. It will accordingly be approved. By contrast, others who have submitted comments object to AT&T's entry into the information services market.

"Information services" are defined in the proposed decree at Section IV(J) as:

> the offering of a capability for generating, acquiring, storing, transforming, processing, retrieving, utilizing or making available information which may be conveyed via telecommunications. . . .

Two distinctly different types of information services fall within this general category: services which would involve no control by AT&T over the content of the information other than for transmission purposes (such as the traditional data processing services), and services in which AT&T would control both the transmission of the information and its content (such as news or entertainment). Because these two types of services raise different concerns, they will be addressed separately.

> A. *Data Processing and Other Computer-Related Services*
>
> As technology has advanced, the line between communications and data processing has become blurred. Advances in communications technology, for example, now allow otherwise incompatible computers to converse with each other. New sophisticated telephone equipment located on a customer's premises not only performs switching and call routing functions but it also retrieves information much as does a traditional computer. Even ordinary telephones may be capable of performing functions that formerly required the support of a separate computer.
>
> Providers of data processing services—like others who have commented on the decree in other contexts—contend that AT&T should be prohibited from entering these fields because of its market power in the area of interexchange services. Shaping the argument to support their particular interests, these persons contend that AT&T will use the monopoly profits from its interexchange services to subsidize its computer-related services, and that it will use its control over the interexchange network to discriminate against other data processing competitors in providing access to that network.

As explained in Part V *supra*, there is little possibility that AT&T will be able to use its revenues from the interexchange market to subsidize its prices for computer services. That being true, AT&T would not possess any anticompetitive advantages over competitors on this basis, and the possibility of cross subsidization as a basis for rejecting this portion of the proposed decree may therefore be completely discounted.

The discrimination argument is slightly more serious. Since AT&T will be offering its own computer-related services, it may well have an incentive to discriminate in transmitting competitors' services. But what defeats the objections is that AT&T's actual ability to discriminate is quite remote. This segment of the information services industry is already well established, comprised of some of the nation's leading corporate giants, as well as of many smaller concerns. The FCC has found that "[t]here are literally thousands of unregulated computer service vendors offering competing services connected to the interstate telecommunications network."... These strongly competitive conditions will limit AT&T's ability to practice discrimination in two ways. First, AT&T's competitors will have the economic resources necessary to combat any attempt at discrimination. Second, the growing demand for information services will necessarily increase the demand for transmission facilities for these services. Such an increase in demand is likely to stimulate AT&T's interexchange competitors to offer satisfactory alternatives to the AT&T network, and any attempt by AT&T to discriminate would only further enhance this eventuality.

This fairly limited possibility of discrimination clearly does not outweigh the substantial advantages to the public that would be gained by allowing AT&T to develop this new technology. AT&T's entry into these technologically sophisticated fields will stimulate competition, and it is therefore likely to produce further technological advances, new products, and better services—all of which are likely to benefit the American consumer, American foreign trade, and national defense.

Since AT&T's participation in these areas will foster the traditional objectives of the Sherman Act and is not likely to lead to anticompetitive practices, the Court will not sustain the objections to this aspect of the proposed decree.

• • •
Restrictions on the Divested Operating Companies

The proposed decree limits the Operating Companies, upon their divestiture, to the business of supplying local telephone service. In addition to a general prohibition against the provision of "any product or service that is not a natural monopoly service actually regulated by tariff," there are more specific restrictions in Section II(D) which deny the Operating Companies the opportunity to engage in the following activities: (1) the provision of interexchange services; (2) the provision of information services; (3) the manufacture of telecommunications products and customer premises equipment; (4) the marketing of such equipment and (5) directory advertising, including the production of the "Yellow Pages" directories.

The restrictions are based upon the assumption that the Operating Companies, were they allowed to enter the forbidden markets, would use their monopoly power in an anticompetitive manner. It is accordingly necessary for the Court first to determine whether these companies will actually have the incentive and opportunity to act anticompetitively. Second, the restrictions are, at least in one sense, directly anticompetitive because they prevent a potential competitor from entering the market. The Court must accordingly also consider the extent to which the participation of the Operating Companies would contribute to the creation of a competitive market.

A. Interexchange Services

The proposed decree prohibits the divested Operating Companies from providing interexchange services. This restriction is clearly necessary to preserve free competition in the interexchange market....

B. Information Services

The proposed decree prohibits the Operating Companies from providing information services, an umbrella description of a variety of services including electronic publishing and other enhanced uses of telecommunications. This prohibition is necessary for reasons similar to those justifying the restriction on interexchange services, as well as for additional reasons not relevant to the interexchange problem....

C. Manufacture of Equipment

The provision in the proposed decree which prohibits the Operating Companies from manufacturing telecommunications equipment and customer premises equipment (CPE) is also an outgrowth of the government's case in the *AT&T* action. The basic rationale of the procurement portion of that case was that

> a combination of vertical integration and rate-of-return regulation ... tended to generate decisions by the Operating Companies to purchase equipment produced by Western [Electric] that is more expensive or of less quality than that manufactured by the general trade....
>
> The government presented evidence to support this theory, which tended to show that AT&T headquarters and the service components of the Bell System—the Bell Operating Companies and the Long Lines Department—engaged in systematic efforts to disadvantage outside suppliers.... That theory and that evidence directly support the proposed prohibition on the manufacture of equipment by the Operating Companies....

D. Marketing of Customer Premises Equipment

The proposed decree would also prohibit the Operating Companies from selling or leasing customer premises equipment. While the Department of Justice's comments and briefs tend to blur the distinction between manufacturing and marketing, in fact the restrictions on the two activities present wholly different considerations. Based upon a realistic assessment, marketing of CPE presents little potential for anticompetitive behavior by the Operating Companies. While the Operating Companies would have the theoretical ability to engage in the types of anticompetitive activities which support the prohibition on manufacturing of CPE, their incentives and their practical ability to do so would be minimal....

E. Directory Advertising

Each Bell Operating Company presently publishes Yellow Pages directories for its service area. The proposed decree would bar the divested Operating

Companies from all activities related to directory advertising, including the production of the so-called Yellow Pages. This restriction lacks an appropriate basis and is not in the public interest.

Neither of the reasons underlying the other restrictions on the Operating Companies—the need to prevent cross subsidization and the importance of preventing competitor discrimination—has any relevance to the printed directory market.

All parties concede that the Yellow Pages currently earn supra-competitive profits.... There is no warrant therefore for proceeding on the premise that the advertising prices charged by the Operating Companies are artificially low as the result of a subsidy from local exchange service. Similarly, there is no possibility of improper discrimination by the Operating Companies against competing directory manufacturers since access to the local exchange network is not required for production of a printed directory. In short, the Operating Companies would have little or no ability to discriminate against competitors in the printed directory market, and this restriction thus has no procompetitive justification whatever.

To the contrary, the prohibition on directory production by the Operating Companies is distinctly anticompetitive in its effects, for at least two reasons. In the first place, the production of the Yellow Pages will be transferred from a number of smaller entities to one nationwide company—AT&T. This type of concentration is itself anathema to the antitrust laws. Furthermore, possession of the franchise for the printed directories will give AT&T a substantial advantage over its competitors in providing electronic directory advertising—a market in which the Operating Companies will not be engaged.

In addition to these factors directly related to competition, there are other reasons why the prohibition on publication of the Yellow Pages by the Operating Companies is not in the public interest. All those who have commented on or have studied the issue agree that the Yellow Pages provide a significant subsidy to local telephone rates. This subsidy would most likely continue if the Operating Companies were permitted to continue to publish the Yellow Pages.

The loss of this large subsidy would have important consequences for the rates for local telephone service. For example, the State of California claims that a two dollar increase in the rates for monthly telephone service would be necessary to offset the loss of revenues from directory advertising. Other states assert that increases of a similar magnitude would be required. Evidence submitted during the *AT&T* trial indicates that large rate increases of this type will reduce the number of households with telephones and increase the disparity, in terms of the availability of telephone service, between low income and well-off citizens. This result is clearly contrary to the goal of providing affordable telephone service to all Americans.

The district court has retained jurisdiction enabling the parties and operating companies to apply for further orders, direction, or modification. The Department of Justice has undertaken to report to the court every three years on the continuing need for line-of-business restrictions. Divested companies interested in expanding their entrepreneurial horizons soon filed for waivers of the line-of-business restrictions. Expressing concern that the companies would divert resources away from furnishing effective telephone service or engage in anticompetitive practices, the court in *United States v. Western Electric Co., Inc.* determined that waivers would not be considered until the operating entities had lost their monopoly status and substantial competition existed at the local level.

The Court embraced diversification as it applies to AT&T, reasoning that, should that company squander its resources on unprofitable non-telecommunications ventures, raise its rates, or fail to render quality service, its customers could easily take their business to one of its long distance or equipment competitors. That is not so, however, with respect to the customers of the Operating Companies. These companies are at present the only entities with the license and the capacity to provide local telephone service to the general public. Thus, if they neglect their responsibilities in that regard in order to pursue what they may consider more interesting ventures, or if they are diverted from those responsibilities by unrelated or speculative business objectives, the public, unable to go elsewhere, will suffer in higher rates, deteriorating service, or both. Such a result would be entirely inconsistent with the basic purposes of the decree, and the Court will not approve requests which would help to bring it about.

Beyond these considerations, there is the overriding principle that the Court is obligated under the decree to make certain that the Regional Holding Companies do not impede competition in the non-telecommunications markets they seek to enter. Here again, wide diversification presents a serious threat in terms of cross subsidization and other anticompetitive practices.

The decree assumes, as does the Court, that the Regional Holding Companies may diversify on a significant scale only as they demonstrate the centrality to their corporate life of the responsibilities imposed upon them by the decree, their firm commitment to low-cost, high-quality telephone service, and the improbability of their involvement in anticompetitive conduct based upon their monopoly status. The rules established herein are designed to achieve these objectives while also permitting the Regional Holding Companies to enter into new business ventures to the extent that this will not be a threat to the fundamental purposes of the decree.

Following the Justice Department's first triennial review, the district court lifted restrictions that had barred the divested companies from participating in nontelecommunications business, modified the prohibition against entering the information services market, and left intact interexchange and manufacturing restrictions. Upon review, the court of appeals remanded the case for purposes of determining whether the information services restriction should be lifted entirely. The appeals court instructed that the decision on whether "generation of information" would be anticompetitive should be made according to "*present* market conditions [emphasis in original]." Reference points for reconsidering the information services waiver were whether a company had the ability to raise prices or restrict output in the relevant market, which was defined as "the market to be entered." In 1991, the district court lifted the information services restriction but stayed its order pending appellate review.

The court of appeals also noted that waivers should be granted so long as they were not inconsistent with the public interest, which, it advised, should be construed flexibly not in terms of what "will *best* serve society" but of what "is within the *reaches* of the public interest [emphasis in original]." Finally, the appeals court asserted that construction of the consent decree was subject to "*de novo* appellate review." Waivers from line-of-business restrictions have been granted also with respect to equipment leasing, computer sales, foreign operations, cellular telephone systems, office equipment, and real-estate investment.

III. CONCENTRATION

Concern with aggregated power in the economic marketplace and its influence upon the information marketplace has led to cross-ownership restrictions upon telephone companies akin to those governing broadcasters and cablecasters. The Cable Communications Policy Act of 1984 essentially codified a preexisting FCC rule barring cross-ownership of cable and telephone systems in the same service area. Exceptions are provided for service of rural regions or when "a cable system [otherwise] demonstrably could not exist." Pursuant to any waiver it secures from the FCC, a telephone company also must obtain a franchise from the pertinent state or local authority. Operating companies created pursuant to the reorganization of AT&T also are barred by terms of the modified final judgment from "providing information services . . . including electronic publishing and other enhanced uses of telecommunications."

The cross-ownership restraints in recent years have been subject to outside challenge and internal review. In *Northwestern Indiana Telephone Co. v. Federal Communications Commission*, the restraints were contested at first on somewhat technical grounds concerning the specific type of business relationships prohibited. After remand, the court of appeals deferred to the Commission's interpretation of its rules as applied to cover an array of relationships including loan and financial guarantees, consulting fees, leased office and pole space, subleased property, and signal facility construction and maintenance. Intervening parties, in the meantime, asserted that the cross-ownership rules had been rendered inoperable by the Cable Act and in any event were unconstitutional. Because these issues had not been raised in the initial proceeding, however, the court refused to address them.

While continuing to enforce the cross-ownership rules, the FCC itself actually has concluded that they perform a disservice. A 1981 report favored retention of the rules until cable operators could compete more effectively against telephone companies or the restrictions began to hinder development of new technologies. In 1987, the Commission commenced an inquiry to determine whether the restraints still were justified. Its conclusion was that the cable industry, which itself is now dominated by major corporations, no longer is a fledgling industry requiring protection. Furthermore, it found that the rules were not promoting the desired competition among cable operators, so new services were not evolving as anticipated. The FCC thus concluded that the restrictions should be lifted and that telephone companies should be allowed to compete with cable operators. Despite its findings and deregulatory stance, the controls remain in place, as congressional action ultimately is required to alter terms of competition.

Modern peculiarities aside, dispute over the cross-ownership rules in some ways is reminiscent of the rivalry between broadcasters and cablecasters during the 1960s and 1970s. Cable as a new technology offered benefits in terms of signal clarity and program choice that presented a threat to broadcasters and contributed to regulation that slowed the new industry's growth. The benefits of coaxial cable now in place may be surpassed by the offerings of fiber-optic lines. The transmission of light impulses along channels of glass or plastic presents advantages over traditional cables because the lines are smaller, lighter, easier to store and transport, more efficient, and better able to transmit over long distances. Most significantly, they have enormous signal carriage capacity that creates a potential for a single-line home or office hookup providing telephone, cable, computer, and information services.

The basic position of the telephone companies is that the public interest is served by such service consolidation and efficiencies. Cross-ownership rules thus are regarded as a means for impeding progress and protecting an industry that has outgrown the need for nurturing. The telephone companies further assert that their presence in the marketplace would provide a competitive prod that would help cable maximize its diversification potential and lower rates in the process.

The cable industry has maintained that the telephone companies have wrapped themselves in the cloth of the public interest, which hides their real self-interest. It alleges that the telephone companies regard entry into the cable television business as a way of updating their depreciated facilities with fiber-optic technology. Given high conversion costs and the speculative nature of the investment, the argument is that the public interest may be disserved by the loss of inexpensive telephone service. Because fiber-optic networks already can be constructed, and cross-ownership rules essentially prohibit program retailing, the cable industry's position seems to be that decontrol would benefit only the telephone companies at considerable risk to the public. The competing arguments seem destined to influence the saga of common-carrier and cable cross-ownership restrictions as maintained or revised by Congress or the judiciary.

REFERENCES

CASES

Federal Communications Commission v. Midwest Video Corp., 440 U.S. 689 (1979).
Northwestern Indiana Telephone Co. v. Federal Communications Commission, 872 F.2d 465 (D.C. Cir. 1987).
Northwestern Indiana Telephone Co. v. Federal Communications Commission, 824 F.2d 1205 (D.C. Cir. 1987).
United States v. American Telephone & Telegraph Co., 552 F. Supp. 131 (D.D.C. 1982), aff'd, 460 U.S. 1001 (1983).
United States v. Southwestern Cable Co., 392 U.S. 157 (1968).
United States v. Western Electric Co., Inc., 900 F.2d 283 (D.C. Cir. 1990).
United States v. Western Electric Co., Inc., 673 F. Supp. 525 (D.D.C. 1987).
United States v. Western Electric Co., Inc., 592 F. Supp. 846 (D.D.C. 1984).
United States v. Western Electric Co., Inc., 1956 Trade Cases, § 68, 246, at 71,134 (D.N.J.).

PUBLICATIONS

Botein & Pearce, *The Competitiveness of the United States Telecommunications Industry: A New York Case Study*, 6 Cardozo Arts & Ent. L.J. 233 (1988).
Lavey & Carlton, *Economic Goals and Remedies of the AT&T Modified Final Judgment*, 71 Geo. L.J. 1497 (1983).
McKenna & Slyter, *MFJ: Judicial Overkill—Further Perspective and Response*, 9 Comm/ent L.J. 565 (1987).
Mooney, *Cross-Ownership Restrictions: The Cable View*, 7 Comm. & L. 20 (1989).
Sodolski, *Elimination of the Cross-Ownership Rules Would Serve the Public Interest and Benefit the Consumer*, 7 Comm. & L. 1 (1989).
Worthington, *If It Ain't Broke, Don't Fix it*, 9 Comm/ent L.J. 583 (1987).

Part Three

CONTENT REGULATION OF THE MEDIA

The text of the First Amendment has remained fixed since its constitutional enshrinement in 1791. The universe that it governs and societal attitudes toward the media, however, have mutated significantly. Two centuries ago, the press essentially comprised an assortment of partisan publications pushing competing political agendas. Given technology of the time, information disseminated by the press traveled in weeks and months rather than immediately. In a manner consistent with a singular service of commencing and maintaining political debate, discrete audiences identified with particular publishers and tended to be forgiving of distortion and imbalance. The freedom of the press clause did not enter into constitutional jurisprudence for another 130 years after its ratification. By that time, new media never contemplated by the constitution's framers had emerged and acquired a presence that almost certainly would have exceeded their imagination.

The traditional concern of the free press clause is with editorial freedom. Modern concepts, which have attempted to account for the consequences of an expanded and concentrated media industry, are more complex. Contemporary First Amendment protection has become a function of both the nature of the medium and the variant of expression being propagated. The Supreme Court essentially has created dual hierarchies within which media and speech types are ranked for First Amendment purposes. The print media, as the prevalent system of communication at the time of the Constitution's framing and political expression, as the most prominent concern, thus are afforded maximum First Amendment status. Nonpolitical expression, regardless of the medium in which it appears, may be less safeguarded or entirely unprotected. The parallel construction of a media hierarchy might seem paradoxical. When the First Amendment was drafted, the print media represented the dominant, indeed the only, facet of the press. Although broadcasting is the most pervasive medium of modern times, it is afforded the least constitutional protection. Even if terms of security for the print media have remained constant, therefore, it may be argued that the ambit of freedom for the press in a practical sense has been narrowed.

Contemporary regulation largely has responded to economic and social forces that have altered the information marketplace and prompted concern for consequences of, rather than just freedom of, the press. Given movement away from a soapbox society and toward a concentrated media industry, a particular concern over the course of this century has been ensuring diversity and balance. Since meaningful individual input into the information marketplace has been confounded by evolution toward a concentrated and centralized media industry, concepts have emerged that would compensate by means of official mandate. A prominent debate thus continues with respect to whether insistence upon a fair and responsible press is reconcilable with the notion of a free press.

A second but equally significant concern is with the actual influence of modern media upon society. As the media have become an omnipresent force concerned with matters not confined to raw politics, worries over the press's reach and effect have worked their way into regulatory initiatives. Louis Brandeis, as noted in Chapter 2, expressed alarm a century ago over the power, direction, and photojournalistic capacity of the print media. Brandeis's distress with a medium that catered to "prurient taste," "occup[ied] the indolent," and concerned itself not with matters of "real interest" but with "idle gossip" is essentially indistinguishable from contemporary reaction to television as "a vast wasteland." A sense that the press should focus upon "matters of real interest to the community" epitomizes some of the concerns that have helped shape a public interest standard and fairness responsibilities in broadcasting.

Radio and television in particular have engendered anxiety tied to perceptions reminiscent of reactions that delayed First Amendment recognition of motion pictures on grounds that they were a dangerous influence. The constitutional status of broadcasting has been encumbered not only by concern with its allegedly negative influences but because it is an entrepreneurial and editorial opportunity available only to a relative few. The consequence for all media as they have evolved, but especially for newer electronic technologies, has been persistent controversy over the practical meaning of the First Amendment, the glossing of the Constitution to afford the public a right to receive diverse information in some contexts, and freedom of the press analysis that has moved beyond singular concern with editorial autonomy to factor in the consequences of press freedom.

Chapter 9

The Print Media

It has yet to be demonstrated how regulation of this crucial [editorial]
process can be exercised consistent with First Amendment guarantees of a free press as they have evolved to this time.

Miami Herald Publishing Co. v. Tornillo,
418 U.S. 241, 258 (1974)

Freedom of the press, as it has evolved, affords maximum protection to
the print media. The ordering of constituent elements of the press, apart
from constitutional concerns associated with it, is a source of increasing
and significant practical difficulty. It also is subject to criticism and official
reappraisal. As discussed in Chapter 10, the Federal Communications
Commission's abandonment of the fairness doctrine was premised upon
the notion that the First Amendment standards for broadcasters and
publishers should be identical. Medium-specific analysis and resultant
variances in First Amendment status and security nonetheless originate
from the premise that "[e]ach [medium] tends to present its own peculiar
problems" and thus requires "a law unto itself."

Because modern media possess palpably distinct structural characteristics, the identification of unique attributes is not a daunting task. Print
traditionally has enabled the reader to be exposed to information at an
individualized rate and may lend itself to more depth and detail. Electronic media project visual and aural imagery that may etch indelible
impressions or escape perception because it is fleeting or bypasses an

unfocused mind. Research has yielded mixed results with respect to the influence of broadcasting upon behavior.

Even within the electronic media, significant differences exist beyond those that are structurally obvious. Broadcasting and cablecasting, for instance, offer different programming menus attributable to divergent economic realities. Television profits are maximized by appealing to and maximizing a single mass audience. Given its multichannel capacity, cable serves a variety of audiences. While television as a consequence tends to invest in programming calculated to attract the most viewers and offend the fewest, it is more sensible as a matter of economics for cable to diversify service in a way that compounds multiple discrete audiences. Radio, television, cable, and motion pictures, unlike traditional print media, do not have a strict literacy prerequisite.

Despite discernible differences among media, advertence to them for purposes of constitutional standing may be problematic insofar as characterizations fail to accommodate further evolution or discount universal rather than distinctive features. Scarcity as a characteristic justifying special regulation of the broadcast media has proved at least as discernible with respect to newspapers. The point has been made, however, that all resources, including media, are scarce, and barriers to entry ultimately are a function more of capital requirements than any medium-peculiar constraint. The process of fashioning constitutional distinctions has become further confounded by increasingly merging capabilities of modern media that, whether denominated as publishing, broadcasting, or cable, to some extent may utilize the atmosphere, transmit electronically, and generate imagery upon a television screen. Even if a medium may be structured better for purposes of maximizing diversity, moreover, potential may outreach actual performance. Risks of medium-specific analysis, therefore, may include generalizing too little and too much.

Even if it is easy to identify differences among media, jurisprudence has demonstrated how difficult it may be to explain the reason for such an exercise. The vexing nature of the exercise was evidenced by two decisions in which the Court respectively upheld and invalidated regulations that imposed fairness obligations respectively upon broadcasters and publishers. Despite a scarcity argument in the latter and later instance, the Court's decision avoided any reference whatsoever to its previous holding acceding to such concern.

I. PROMOTION OF CONTENT DIVERSITY AND BALANCE

The central issue in *Miami Herald Publishing Co. v. Tornillo* was "whether a state statute granting a political candidate a right to equal space to reply to criticism and attacks on his record by a newspaper violates the guarantees of a free press." In assessing the constitutionality of the law, which presented an undeniable challenge to editorial autonomy, the Court recounted how the newspaper industry increasingly had become characterized by diminished intramural competition and how ownership and control had become ever more concentrated. The consequence of these trends, as the Court observed, has been "to place in a few hands the power to inform the American people and shape public opinion." Because much editorial product is the work of centralized and "homogen[ized] . . . editorial opinion, commentary, and analysis," the claim was advanced that "the public has lost any ability to respond to or contribute in a meaningful way to the debate on issues." Further triggering official concern was a sense that reportorial bias and manipulation were functions "of the vast accumulations of unreviewable power in the modern media empires."

The Court at least implicitly acknowledged that "[t]he right of free public expression . . . has lost its earlier reality." Citing economic factors that have made entry into the modern publishing business "almost impossible," it noted that the solution of increased competition that was "available . . . when entry into publishing was relatively inexpensive" no longer was feasible. Despite the altered circumstances in which the First Amendment operates, the Court refused to brook any premise or implication that official action was appropriate to ensure "fairness and accuracy [or] to provide for some accountability" by publishers. Notwithstanding earlier references to the effect that the First Amendment does not immunize the press from certain responsibilities and betokens "a profound national commitment to the principle that debate on public issues should be uninhibited, robust, and wide-open," it dismissed their pertinence as a possible predicate for a legislated right of access. Rather, the Court emphasized that it consistently had been alert to and intolerant of any official, as opposed to private, inhibition upon editorial autonomy. Even if the notion of "a responsible press" might be a "desirable goal," it could not be "mandated by the Constitution and like many other virtues . . . cannot be legislated."

The Court, in sum, found the core issue to be whether government may compel "editors or publishers to publish that which 'reason tells them should not be published.'" The access provision thereby was denominated as a functional prior restraint insofar as it required dedication of "space that could be devoted to other material the newspaper may have preferred to print." Apart from violating editorial freedom, the measure was derogated for undermining First Amendment values. The Court observed that publishers, confronted with the possibility of penalties, might steer a safe course that avoided controversy to the detriment of the information marketplace and public. Even without such consequences, the statute was found fatally defective "because of its intrusion into the function of editors." The Court thus was unable to reconcile the right-of-reply law with traditional notions of a free press.

Appellee's argument that the Florida statute does not amount to a restriction of appellant's right to speak because "the statute in question here has not prevented the *Miami Herald* from saying anything it wished" begs the core question. Compelling editors or publishers to publish that which " 'reason' tells them should not be published" is what is at issue in this case. The Florida statute operates as a command in the same sense as a statute or regulation forbidding appellant to publish specified matter. Governmental restraint on publishing need not fall into familiar or traditional patterns to be subject to constitutional limitations on governmental powers.... The Florida statute exacts a penalty on the basis of the content of a newspaper. The first phase of the penalty resulting from the compelled printing of a reply is exacted in terms of the cost in printing and composing time and materials and in taking up space that could be devoted to other material the newspaper may have preferred to print. It is correct, as appellee contends, that a newspaper is not subject to the finite technological limitations of time that confront a broadcaster but it is not correct to say that, as an economic reality, a newspaper can proceed to infinite expansion of its column space to accommodate the replies that a government agency determines or a statute commands the readers should have available.

Faced with the penalties that would accrue to any newspaper that published news or commentary arguably within the reach of the right-of-access statute, editors might well conclude that the safe course is to avoid controversy. Therefore, under the operation of the Florida statute, political and electoral coverage would be blunted or reduced. Government-enforced right of access inescapably "dampens the vigor and limits the variety of public debate," *New York Times Co.* v. *Sullivan*, 376 U.S., at 279. The Court, in *Mills* v. *Alabama*, 384 U.S. 214, 218 (1966), stated:

> "[T]here is practically universal agreement that a major purpose of [the First] Amendment was to protect the free discussion of governmental affairs. This of course includes discussions of candidates...."

Even if a newspaper would face no additional costs to comply with a compulsory access law and would not be forced to forgo publication of news or opinion by the inclusion of a reply, the Florida statute fails to clear the barriers of the First Amendment because of its intrusion into the function of editors. A newspaper is more than a passive receptacle or conduit for news, comment, and advertising. The choice of material to go into a newspaper, and the decisions made as to limitations on the size and content of the paper, and treatment of public issues and public officials—whether fair or unfair—constitute the exercise of editorial control and judgment. It has yet to be demonstrated how governmental regulation of this crucial process can be exercised consistent with First Amendment guarantees of a free press as they have evolved to this time. Accordingly, the judgment of the Supreme Court of Florida is reversed.

II. CONTENT RESTRICTION

Although the print media generally have been afforded maximum First Amendment protection, even that security is relative rather than absolute. Editorial autonomy, like any other cognizable constitutional interest, may be eclipsed by what is perceived as a compelling or substantial regulatory concern. Reflective of the consequent balancing process that at times may favor official concerns over constitutional interests was the Court's validation of an ordinance that prohibited employment discrimination on the basis of gender and reached classified advertising of job opportunities designated in terms of sex. In *Pittsburgh Press Co. v. Pittsburgh Commission on Human Relations*, the Court concluded that the provision did not violate freedom of the press. It acknowledged that the regulation impaired editorial discretion. The infringement nonetheless was justified and First Amendment interests discounted because of the illegal nature of the underlying activity. Justice Stewart was unmoved by the Court's reasoning and dissented on grounds that the regulation was an obvious prior restraint.

That question, to put it simply, is whether any government agency—local, state, or federal—can tell a newspaper in advance what it can print and what it cannot. Under the First and Fourteenth Amendments I think no government agency in this Nation has any such power.[1] . . .

So far as I know, this is the first case in this or any other American court that permits a government agency to enter a composing room of a newspaper and dictate to the publisher the layout and makeup of the newspaper's pages. This is the first such case, but I fear it may not be the last. The camel's nose is in the tent. "It may be that it is the obnoxious thing in its mildest and least repulsive form; but illegitimate and unconstitutional practices get their first footing in that way. . . . "

So long as Members of this Court view the First Amendment as no more than a set of "values" to be balanced against other "values," that Amendment will remain in grave jeopardy. . . .

It is said that the goal of the Pittsburgh ordinance is a laudable one, and so indeed it is. But, in the words of Mr. Justice Brandeis, "Experience should teach us to be most on our guard to protect liberty when the Government's purposes are beneficent. Men born to freedom are naturally alert to repel invasion of their liberty by evil-minded rulers. The greatest dangers to liberty lurk in insidious encroachment by men of zeal, well-meaning but without understanding." . . . And, as Mr. Justice Black once pointed out, "The motives behind the state law may have been to do good. But . . . [h]istory indicates that urges to do good have led to the burning of books and even to the burning of 'witches.' "

The Court today holds that a government agency can force a newspaper publisher to print his classified advertising pages in a certain way in order to carry out governmental policy. After this decision, I see no reason why government cannot force a newspaper publisher to conform in the same way in order to achieve other goals thought socially desirable. And if government can dictate the layout of a newspaper's classified advertising pages today, what is there to prevent it from dictating the layout of the news pages tomorrow?

Those who think the First Amendment can and should be subordinated to other socially desirable interests will hail today's decision. But I find it frightening. For I believe the constitutional guarantee of a free press is more than precatory. I believe it is a clear command that government must never be allowed to lay its heavy editorial hand on any newspaper in this country.

The *Pittsburgh Press* decision adverted in part to the then constitutionally unprotected status of commercial speech. Notwithstanding jurisprudential recontouring of the First Amendment to shelter such expression, subsequent doctrine still allows government to prohibit advertisement of illegal activities. Although the decision was influenced by the presence of commercial speech, the result thus would be identical pursuant to modern analysis. The episode demonstrates nicely how First Amendment protection may be influenced not only by the nature of the medium but by the type of expression at issue. It reveals also a fundamental truth concerning constitutional rights and liberties, including editorial freedom. The First Amendment by its terms and as explicated in the *Tornillo* decision may appear to be cast in unequivocal terms. The *Pittsburgh Press* decision exemplifies how broad statements of principle are seldom absolute but subject to qualification and exception.

REFERENCES

CASES

Miami Herald Publishing Co. v. Tornillo, 418 U.S. 241 (1974).
Pittsburgh Press Co. v. Pittsburgh Commission on Human Relations, 413 U.S. 376 (1973).

PUBLICATIONS

Bazelon, *FCC Regulation of the Telecommunications Press,* 1975 Duke L.J. 213.
Bollinger, *Freedom of the Press and Public Access: Toward a Theory of Partial Regulation of the Mass Media,* 75 Mich. L. Rev. 1 (1976).
Canby, *The First Amendment and the State as Editor: Implications for Public Broadcasting,* 52 Tex. L. Rev. 1123 (1974).
Chatzky & Robinson, *A Constitutional Right of Access to Newspapers: Is There Life After Tornillo?* 16 Santa Clara L. Rev. 453 (1976).

Chapter 10

Broadcasting

[I]t is axiomatic that broadcasting may be regulated in light of the rights of the viewing and listening audience.

Metro Broadcasting, Inc. v. Federal Communications Commission,
110 S. Ct. 2997, 3410 (1990)

I. PROMOTION OF CONTENT DIVERSITY AND BALANCE

Traditional constitutional norms that suffer no official interference with the editorial process, even to promote First Amendment interests of diversity, have not operated fully with respect to broadcasting. As the Supreme Court observed in *Federal Communications Commission v. Pacifica Foundation,* radio and television "of all forms of communication . . . ha[ve] received the most limited First Amendment protection." The sense that broadcasting might be subject to editorial oversight predates the Communications Act of 1934 and has evolved further over the course of time. The FCC's regulatory predecessor, the Federal Radio Commission, thus observed in *Great Lakes Broadcasting Co.* that if broadcasters do not afford an opportunity "for every school of thought, religious, political, social, and economic, . . . a well-founded complaint will receive the careful consideration of the Commission in its future action with reference to the station complained of." The Federal Radio Commission, despite being prohibited from engaging in censorship, was not reluctant to factor content into licensing decisions. In *Trinity Methodist Church, South v. Fed-*

eral Communications Commission, the court of appeals considered the commission's denial of license renewal for a religious broadcaster whose verbal assaults upon Jews, Catholics, organized labor, government, and the legal profession dominated his programming. Nonrenewal was upheld pursuant to a determination that no prior restraint operated and the public interest was disserved by the licensee's defamatory and one-sided commentary.

However inspired Dr. Shuler may have been by what he regarded as patriotic zeal, however sincere in denouncing conditions he did not approve, it is manifest, we think, that it is not narrowing the ordinary conception of "public interest" in declaring his broadcasts—without facts to sustain or to justify them—not within that term, and, since that is the test the Commission is required to apply, we think it was its duty in considering the application for renewal to take notice of appellant's conduct in his previous use of the permit, and, in the circumstances, the refusal, we *think*, was neither arbitrary nor capricious.

If it be considered that one in possession of a permit to broadcast in interstate commerce may, without let or hindrance from any source, use these facilities, reaching out, as they do, from one corner of the country to the other, to obstruct the administration of justice, offend the religious susceptibilities of thousands, inspire political distrust and civic discord, or offend youth and innocence by the free use of words suggestive of sexual immorality, and be answerable for slander only at the instance of the one offended, then this great science, instead of a boon, will become a scourge, and the nation a theater for the display of individual passions and the collision of personal interests. This is neither censorship nor previous restraint, nor is it a whittling away of the rights guaranteed by the First Amendment, or an impairment of their free exercise. Appellant may continue to indulge his strictures upon the characters of men in public office. He may just as freely as ever criticize religious practices of which he does not approve. He may even indulge private malice or personal slander—subject, of course, to be required to answer for the abuse thereof—but he may not, as we think, demand, of right, the continued use of an instrumentality of commerce for such purposes, or any other, except in subordination to all reasonable rules and regulations Congress, acting through the Commission, may prescribe.

Official intervention into broadcast content received an early constitutional boost when the Supreme Court, in *National Broadcasting Co. v. United States*, determined that the FCC was more than a "traffic officer, policing the engineering and technical aspects of broadcasting." Another quarter of a century would pass before the Court directly considered the First Amendment issues raised by fairness regulation and concluded, pursuant to the notion of spectrum scarcity, that "Government is permitted to put restraints on licensees in favor of others whose views should be expressed on this unique medium." In the interim, Congress and the FCC respectively had codified and promulgated requirements intended to facilitate comprehensive and balanced coverage of public issues.

Fairness regulation in its broadcast sense breaks down into statutory and administrative mandates that provide access for viewpoints and in some instances for individuals. The fairness doctrine exemplifies facilitation of viewpoint access in the sense that the licensee retains discretion to present competing perspectives or to decide who will do so. Such a concept is distinguishable from access in the event of a personal attack and access or equal opportunity provisions for political candidates, which afford designated individuals the opportunity to present ideas or information under certain circumstances.

A. VIEWPOINT ACCESS

The fairness doctrine itself began to take formal shape in 1949 when the FCC authored the *Report on Editorializing by Broadcast Licensees* that delineated a two-part responsibility for broadcasters. Essentially, licensees were obligated to "[1] devote a reasonable percentage of their broadcast time to the ... consideration and discussion of public issues ... [and] [2] make sufficient time available for full discussion thereof." Balance of a presentation implicating fairness responsibilities was the responsibility of the licensee, who had the option to designate another person to offer a competing view, and was to be effectuated at the licensee's expense if no sponsorship was available. In 1959, Congress amended Section 315 of the Communications Act of 1934 in a way that later was construed as approving the fairness doctrine. The inference was drawn from modification of the equal time provision for political candidates to make clear that it exempted licensees "from the obligation imposed upon them under this Chapter to operate in the public interest and to afford reasonable opportunity for their discussion of conflicting views on issues of public importance." In 1967, the FCC promulgated rules affording access rights to individuals whose honesty, character, integrity, or other personal qualities were attacked in the course of a broadcast and to candidates whose opponents had been endorsed in a licensee's political editorial. The basic fairness doctrine and related personal attack and political editorial rules soon were contested on grounds that they abrogated freedom of the press.

The challenge arose after a licensee had refused to provide free reply time to an individual claiming that a religious broadcast that portrayed him as sympathetic to communism and antipatriotic had constituted a personal attack upon him. In *Red Lion Broadcasting Co. v. Federal Communications Commission*, the Court upheld the Commission's finding that the broadcast constituted a personal attack and that the licensee must provide free reply time. It also provided a lengthy discourse in support of fairness regulation and held that such control did not exceed the Commission's authority and "enhance[d] rather then abridge[d] the freedoms of speech and press protected by the First Amendment." Adverting to the chaotic circumstances that preceded government control of what it characterized as a "scarce resource," the Court emphasized how experience had demonstrated that use of "broadcast frequencies... could be regulated and rationalized only by the Government." Minus such control, it observed, "the medium would be of little use because of the cacophony of competing voices, none of which could be clearly and predictably heard."

The FCC's authority to promulgate the regulations at issue derived from its general obligation to regulate in the public interest. Apart from finding that the fairness doctrine paralleled statutory provisions relating to political candidates and was supported by legislative history, the Court observed that "the 'public interest' in broadcasting clearly encompasses the presentation of controversial issues of importance and concern to the public." Responding to the contention that the Constitution safeguarded the exercise of editorial discretion by broadcasters to use and exclude from their frequencies whomever they chose, the Court acknowledged that broadcasting was "a medium affected by a First Amendment interest." Consistent with freedom of the press analysis for newer media, however, it emphasized that "differences in the characteristics of new media justify differences in the First Amendment standards applied to them." From the Court's perspective, the crucial characteristic of broadcasting was spectrum scarcity. As the Court put it, "[w]here there are substantially more individuals who want to broadcast than there are frequencies to allocate, it is idle to posit an unabridgeable First Amendment right to broadcast comparable to the right of every individual to speak, write, or publish."

The broadcasters challenge the fairness doctrine and its specific manifestations in the personal attack and political editorial rules on conventional First Amendment grounds, alleging that the rules abridge their freedom of speech and press. Their contention is that the First Amendment protects their desire to use their allotted frequencies continuously to broadcast whatever they choose, and to exclude whomever they choose from ever using that frequency. No man may be prevented from saying or publishing what he thinks, or from refusing in his speech or other utterances to give equal weight to the views of his opponents. This right, they say, applies equally to broadcasters....

Although broadcasting is clearly a medium affected by a First Amendment interest, *United States* v. *Paramount Pictures, Inc.*, 334 U. S. 131, 166 (1948), differences in the characteristics of new media justify differences in the First Amendment standards applied to them. *Joseph Burstyn, Inc. v. Wilson*, 343 U. S. 495, 502 (1952). For example, the ability of new technology to produce sounds more raucous than those of the human voice justifies restrictions on the sound level, and on the hours and places of use, of sound trucks so long as the restrictions are reasonable and applied without discrimination....

Just as the Government may limit the use of sound-amplifying equipment potentially so noisy that it drowns out civilized private speech, so may the Government limit the use of broadcast equipment. The right of free speech of a broadcaster, the user of a sound truck, or any other individual does not embrace a right to snuff out the free speech of others.

When two people converse face to face, both should not speak at once if either is to be clearly understood. But the range of the human voice is so limited that there could be meaningful communications if half the people in the United States were talking and the other half listening. Just as clearly, half the people might publish and the other half read. But the reach of radio signals is incomparably greater than the range of the human voice and the problem of interference is a massive reality. The lack of know-how and equipment may keep many from the air, but only a tiny fraction of those with resources and intelligence can hope to communicate by radio at the same time if intelligible communication is to be had, even if the entire radio spectrum is utilized in the present state of commercially acceptable technology.

It was this fact, and the chaos which ensued from permitting anyone to use any frequency at whatever power level he wished, which made necessary the enactment of the Radio Act of 1927 and the Communications Act of 1934, as the Court has noted at length before. *National Broadcasting Co.* v. *United States*, 319 U.S. 190, 210–214 (1943). It was this reality which at the very least necessitated first the division of the radio spectrum into portions reserved respectively for public broadcasting and for other important radio uses such as amateur operation, aircraft, police, defense, and navigation; and then the subdivision of each portion, and assignment of specific frequencies to individual users or groups of users. Beyond this, however, because the frequencies reserved for public broadcasting were limited in number, it was essential for the Government to tell some applicants that they could not broadcast at all because there was room for only a few.

Where there are substantially more individuals who want to broadcast than there are frequencies to allocate, it is idle to posit an unabridgeable First Amendment right to broadcast comparable to the right of every individual to speak, write, or publish. If 100 persons want broadcast licenses but there are only 10 frequencies to allocate, all of them may have the same "right" to a license; but if there is to be any effective communication by radio, only a few can be licensed and the rest must be barred from the airwaves. It would be strange if the First Amendment, aimed at protecting and furthering communications, prevented the Government from making radio communication possible by requiring licenses to broadcast and by limiting the number of licenses so as not to overcrowd the spectrum.

This has been the consistent view of the Court. Congress unquestionably has the power to grant and deny licenses and to eliminate existing stations. *FRC* v. *Nelson Bros. Bond & Mortgage Co.*, 289 U. S. 266 (1933). No one has a First Amendment right to a license or to monopolize a radio frequency; to deny a station license because "the public interest" requires it "is not a denial of free speech." *National Broadcasting Co.* v. *United States*, 319 U. S. 190, 227 (1943).

By the same token, as far as the First Amendment is concerned those who are licensed stand no better than those to whom licenses are refused. A license permits broadcasting, but the licensee has no constitutional right to be the one who holds the license or to monopolize a radio frequency to the exclusion of his fellow citizens. There is nothing in the First Amendment which prevents the Government from requiring a licensee to share his frequency with others and to conduct himself as a proxy or fiduciary with obligations to present those views and voices which are representative of his community and which would otherwise, by necessity, be barred from the airwaves.

This is not to say that the First Amendment is irrelevant to public broadcasting. On the contrary, it has a major role to play as the Congress itself recognized in § 326, which forbids FCC interference with "the right of free speech by means of radio communication." Because of the scarcity of radio frequencies, the Government is permitted to put restraints on licensees in favor of others whose views should be expressed on this unique medium. But the people as a whole retain their interest in free speech by radio and their collective right to have the medium function consistently with the ends and purposes of the First Amendment. It is the right of the viewers and listeners, not the right of the broadcasters, which is paramount. *See FCC v. Sanders Bros. Radio Station*, 309 U.S. 470, 475 (1940); *FCC v. Allentown Broadcasting Corp.*, 349 U.S. 358, 361–362 (1955); 2 Z. Chafee, Government and Mass Communications 546 (1947). It is the purpose of the First Amendment to preserve an uninhibited marketplace of ideas in which truth will ultimately prevail, rather than to countenance monopolization of that market, whether it be by the Government itself or a private licensee. . . . It is the right of the public to receive suitable access to social, political, esthetic, moral, and other ideas and experiences which is crucial here. That right may not constitutionally be abridged either by Congress or by the FCC. . . .

It would be better if the FCC's encouragement were never necessary to induce the broadcasters to meet their responsibility. And if experience with the administration of these doctrines indicates that they have the net effect of reducing rather than enhancing the volume and quality of coverage, there will be time enough to reconsider the constitutional implications. The fairness doctrine in the past has had no such overall effect.

That this will occur now seems unlikely, however, since if present licensees should suddenly prove timorous, the Commission is not powerless to insist that they give adequate and fair attention to public issues. It does not violate the First Amendment to treat licensees given the privilege of using scarce radio frequencies as proxies for the entire community, obligated to give suitable time and attention to matters of great public concern. To condition the granting or renewal of licenses on a willingness to present representative community views on controversial issues is consistent with the ends and purposes of those constitutional provisions forbidding the abridgment of freedom of speech and freedom of the press. Congress need not stand idly by and permit those with licenses to ignore the problems which beset the people or to exclude from the airways anything but their own views of fundamental questions. The statute, long administrative practice, and cases are to this effect.

The First Amendment status of broadcasters thus was set consciously and explicitly at a different level than that of publishers. The variance was premised upon circumstances that required licensing of broadcasters but did not thereby confer a "right . . . to monopolize a radio frequency." Given the unique nature of broadcasting, the Court found "nothing in the First Amendment which prevents the Government from requiring a licensee to share his frequency with others and to conduct himself as a proxy or fiduciary with obligations to present those views and voices which are representative of his community and which would otherwise, by necessity, be barred from the airwaves." Scarcity thus was the premise for recognizing a right of the public "to have the medium function consistently with the ends and purposes of the First Amendment" and elevating it above the constitutional rights of broadcasters. What would become referred to as an "unusual ordering" of constitutional interests essentially prioritized First Amendment values over traditional concepts of editorial freedom. As the Court noted, "[i]t is the right of the public to receive suitable access to social, political, esthetic, moral, and other ideas and experiences which is crucial here."

Arguments that fairness demands would deter rather than enhance coverage of controversial issues because broadcasters would avoid pre-sentations that would obligate them to provide free air time proved unavailing. The Court observed that such a possibility was unlikely in view of the industry's past performance and lack of evidence that broad-casters intended to avoid controversy. It pointed out, however, that "if present licensees should prove timorous, the Commission is not pow-erless to insist that they give adequate and fair attention to public issues." The Court thus spoke approvingly of conditioning the award or reten-tion of a license upon compliance with fairness duties.

Also rejected were arguments that technological progress was increas-ingly diminishing the significance of spectrum scarcity. Because com-petition for frequencies persisted, VHF spectrum space was mostly occupied, UHF operation only recently had showed possibilities of com-mercial viability, and radio had become so crowded that new applications at times had been suspended, the Court determined that "[s]carcity is not entirely a thing of the past." It concluded that because of spectrum scarcity, government's role in allocating frequencies, and diminished viewpoint diversity absent official control, fairness regulation was "au-thorized by statute and constitutional."

The fairness doctrine in the years since *Red Lion* has been a prominent subject of controversy and criticism. In 1974, the FCC issued a report that detailed extensively the reasons for the fairness doctrine and es-sentially reaffirmed the dual responsibilities of licensees: (1) an affirm-ative obligation to provide reasonable amounts of time for coverage of public issues and (2) a companion duty to ensure opportunities for con-trasting views. The report, in terms largely similar to those of the *Red Lion* decision, also recited the fairness doctrine's compatibility with First

Amendment interests and values. Despite the FCC's eventual abandonment of the fairness doctrine in 1987, Congress has attempted to reinstitute it. A bill to codify the fairness doctrine passed the House and Senate in the same year that the Commission liquidated it, but the president vetoed the enactment.

Most litigation concerning the fairness doctrine has centered upon the duty to present balancing viewpoints. A West Virginia radio station's failure to air a tape furnished by a congresswoman responding to a program favoring strip mining led to a rare violation of the fairness doctrine's issue-raising component. The FCC, in *Rep. Patsy Mink*, noted that strip mining was an issue of central importance to residents of the state and concluded that the broadcaster's decision was "unreasonable." It emphasized, however, that the circumstances were "exceptional . . . and would not counter our intention to stay out of decisions concerning the selection of specific programming matter." For fairness responsibilities to be triggered, the issue in a given instance must be discernible in terms that are neither too narrow nor too broad. A matter of interest only to a discrete few may fail to qualify as an issue of "public importance." The concept of "national security," in contrast, may be too wide-ranging to afford an effective reference point for assessing balance. A fairness claim tied to a study alleging imbalance in a network's coverage of affairs concerning national security thus failed because the issue was too amorphous. A detailed analysis of news accounts over a year's time concerning "[1] United States military and foreign affairs; [2] Soviet Union military and foreign affairs; [3] China military and foreign affairs; [4] Vietnam affairs" argued that national security threats had been reportorially discounted more than half of the time. In *American Security Council Foundation v. Federal Communications Commission,* the court of appeals upheld the commission's rejection of the fairness claim. In so doing, it observed that "the indirect relationships among the issues aggregated . . . under the umbrella of 'national security' do not provide a basis for determining whether the public received a reasonable balance of conflicting views."

Review of licensee responses to fairness requests largely has been deferential. In opposing the continuing operation of the fairness doctrine, one commissioner noted that in 1973 and 1974 only 19 out of 4,280 fairness complaints led to findings against the licensee. A prominent exception, in which the FCC found a network documentary on private pension plans to be biased and subject to fairness requirements, was reversed by an appeals court. The reviewing court in *National Broadcasting Co. v. Federal Communications Commission* emphasized that it was the network's responsibility to determine program content and that the commission was limited to determining whether a licensee's judgment was reasonable and in good faith. Although the decision was dismissed as moot, pending reconsideration, deference to licensee discretion has proved to be the norm in fairness analysis.

Implementation of the fairness doctrine in connection with commercial advertising was curtailed after some experimentation. The FCC in 1967 required licensees to balance cigarette advertisements with programming identifying the hazards of smoking. Soon thereafter, in 1971, it rejected a fairness claim by environmentalists who sought to balance commercials implicating ecological concerns. In *Friends of the Earth v. Federal Communications Commission* the court of appeals determined that the cigarette and environmental issues were alike for fairness purposes and that the Commission must apply a consistent rule. Subsequently, the FCC determined that only advertisements "which obviously address, and advocate a point of view on, a controversial issue of public importance" would be subject to fairness requirements. Although the change was challenged, an appeals court determined that the Commission was free to alter policy absent constitutional or statutory impediment.

B. PERSONAL ACCESS

Although the fairness doctrine is framed in terms of viewpoint access, construction of a paramount First Amendment right on the part of the viewers and listeners has engendered concepts of personal access rights. Jurisprudence has evolved in a direction that has precluded any notion of a general right of access but has acknowledged and upheld access rights of a discrete nature.

1. General Access

Although the FCC rejected the notion of a general right of access, an appeals court found it to be a logical extension of the public's paramount rights recognized in *Red Lion*. In *Columbia Broadcasting System, Inc. v. Democratic National Committee*, the Supreme Court rejected the idea of an unqualified right of public access. At the same time, it reiterated the status of licensees as public trustees and their duty to comply with fairness standards.

The case arose out of a failed effort by an antiwar group to obtain time to air its views on a Washington, D.C., radio station. Although the Court recited the same history of broadcasting that prompted it to endorse the fairness doctrine, the Court found it "clear that Congress intended to permit private broadcasting to develop with the widest journalistic freedom consistent with its public obligation." It regarded access as a right that would enlarge government's role contrary to the First Amendment and statute. Unlike the fairness doctrine, access would require the FCC "to oversee far more of the day-to-day operations of broadcasters' conduct deciding such questions as whether a particular individual or group has had sufficient opportunity to present its viewpoint and whether a particular viewpoint has been sufficiently aired." Apart from the need for what it considered excessively detailed oversight, the Court found access objectionable on grounds that the information marketplace would be "heavily weighted in favor of the financially affluent, or those with access to wealth." A further concern was "that the time allotted for editorial advertising could be monopolized by those of one political persuasion."

The Court disparaged the notion of access on grounds that it not only eroded journalistic discretion but subordinated the public's paramount constitutional interests to private whim. Dismissing the court of appeals' view that individual speakers are " 'the best judge' of what the listening public ought to hear," it found that journalistic experience had proved the contrary. Adding that "[f]or better or worse, editing is what editors are for," the Court concluded that even abuse of editorial power did not justify cramping or undercutting editorial discretion. Although the Court acknowledged the First Amendment value of "robust and wide-open" debate on public issues, it determined that this did not justify trading " 'public trustee' broadcasting, with all its limitations, for a system of self-appointed editorial commentators." The Court recognized that the fairness doctrine was imperfect but that any "remedy does not lie in diluting licensee responsibility." In closing, it observed that "some kind of limited right of access that is both practicable and desirable" might be devised in the future and that other media, such as cable, might enhance opportunities for discussion of public issues.

Justice Douglas concurred in the judgment but would have predicated it on grounds that broadcasting should have the same First Amendment status as publishing. He furthermore asserted that fairness controls were a major mistake and an encroachment upon the First Amendment. Noting that scarcity is a characteristic of the print media too, Douglas found it inadequate as a reason for revamping the First Amendment's basic nature. Even a scheme designed to promote First Amendment values, from his perspective, cut "against the grain of the First Amendment" insofar as it entailed "censorship or editing or screening by Government."

In a dissenting opinion, Justice Brennan expressed sympathy for a right of access as a means for remedying circumstances that had blunted the original meaning of press freedom. Brennan's support of access was based in large part upon his sense that the fairness doctrine underserved First Amendment interests. He thus observed that, given profit-maximization aims of broadcasters, it was naive to expect them to offer meaningful controversy and thereby risk alienating sponsors and audience. Instead of journalistic discretion as the exclusive determinant for apprising the public of competing views, Brennan considered it "imperative that citizens be permitted at least *some* opportunity to speak for themselves as genuine advocates on issues that concern them [emphasis in original]." For Brennan, therefore, access was attractive as a methodology accounting not just for public viewing and listening interests but for input opportunities largely foreclosed by the evolution of mass media. Further appealing to him was a means for facilitating presentation of views and voices that were truly "novel, unorthodox or unrepresentative of mainstream opinion" rather than merely representative of established or mainstream controversy.

The Court's observation that a "limited right of access might be devised in the future" prompted two proposals that were rejected by the Commission. One suggestion would have afforded licensees the option of operating under the fairness doctrine or being deemed in compliance with it if they set aside one hour per week for a minimum number of access spots of varying length. The proposal responded to concern expressed in the *Democratic National Committee* decision that unconditional access would favor the wealthy or be monopolized by a single viewpoint by allocating time on a first-demand and representative spokesperson basis. Another suggestion would have obligated a licensee to identify annually the ten controversial issues it had covered most heavily in the prior year, the offers it had made for responses, and the respective programming presented on each issue.

In *National Citizens Committee for Broadcasting v. Federal Communications Commission*, the court of appeals determined that the FCC had failed "to consider carefully" the suggestions and thus remanded them for further examination. In subsequently detailing its reasons for rejecting the "access as fairness" proposal, the FCC asserted that the "emphasis upon speakers rather than ideas is at cross-purposes to that of the Fairness Doctrine." Because the presentation of balanced viewpoints is designed "to inform the public," the Commission noted that any substitute principle must do likewise, and the access proposal failed on that count. With respect to the listing and reporting suggestion, the Commission found it redundant with then existing ascertainment obligations and at odds with review of fairness complaints on a particularized basis rather than at renewal time. To date, the FCC has not found a general-access proposal consistent with its essential requirements

that [1] licensee discretion be preserved...[2] no right of access accrue[s] to particular persons or groups...[3] the access system would not...allow important issues to escape timely discussion...[and] [4] the system [would] not draw the government into the role of deciding who should be allowed on the air and when.

Although the final criterion was denominated the "most important," a continuing implication of the fairness doctrine was the power of government to decide what "should be allowed on the air."

2. Limited Access

Notwithstanding rejection of broadly conceived access rights, Congress and the Commission have devised access rights of a limited nature. Other than a right of reasonable access for political candidates, the opportunities are contingent upon triggering events rather than affirmative in nature.

A. Personal Attack Rule

The personal attack rule has been regarded as a component of fairness regulation even though it creates a conditional right of access. In essence, the rule provides that an individual whose honesty, character, integrity, or like personal quality is attacked in the course of coverage of a controversial issue of public importance has a right to respond in person. Upon the occurrence of such an attack, the licensee has affirmative duties to notify the victim of the time, date, and nature of the broadcast, provide a script or tape of the incident, and offer a reasonable opportunity to respond. The rule does not operate with respect to personal attacks on foreign groups or foreign public figures, attacks by legally qualified candidates for public office or their proxies, or in the event of bona fide news reporting.

The right of access in the event of a personal attack is subject to significant constraints and deference to licensee judgment. If the attack does not occur in the course of discussion of a controversial issue of public importance, the rule does not operate, and a claimant must seek more traditional relief in the nature of a defamation or privacy action. A Commission determination that a personal attack related back to an earlier discussion and thus activated the rule was vacated in *Straus Communications, Inc. v. Federal Communications Commission*. The reviewing court determined that instead of substituting its own judgment regarding the continuity of the controversy, the FCC must assess "the objective reasonableness" of the licensee's judgment that it had ended. Appraisal of a broadcaster's decision, consistent with general fairness standards, has been subject to standards of unreasonableness or bad faith.

B. Political Editorials

In the event that a licensee endorses or opposes a legally qualified candidate for public office, an opportunity exists for other candidates or their spokespersons or the opposed candidate or a spokesperson to respond. As with the personal attack rule, affirmative obligations exist for the licensee to furnish within twenty-four hours the date and time of the editorial, a script or tape, and a reasonable opportunity to respond. If the editorial is broadcast within seventy-two hours of the election, the licensee must ensure that notice and opportunity are afforded in a way that ensures a reasonable chance to reply. Editorializing on ballot issues rather than candidates does not trigger operation of the political editorial rule.

C. Equal Opportunity for Political Candidates

Section 315 of the Communications Act provides in general terms that "[i]f any licensee shall permit any person who is a legally qualified candidate for any public office to use a broadcasting station, he shall afford equal opportunities to all other such candidates for that office in the use of such broadcasting station." A "legally qualified candidate" has been defined as a person who has (1) publicly announced an intention to run for office, (2) is qualified by pertinent law to hold the office being sought, or (3) has made a substantial showing of being a bona fide candidate by having participated in campaign activities such as speech making, distribution of literature or press releases, operating a campaign committee, or establishing a campaign headquarters.

(1) *Use*. The concept of "use" for purposes of Section 315 is defined in terms of an appearance by the actual candidate. When a representative or spokesperson makes an appearance to promote a candidate, however, the fairness doctrine may apply. When "one side of a controversial issue of public importance was presented," the FCC in *Letter to Nicholas Zapple* determined that "barring unusual circumstances" it would not be reasonable for a licensee to refuse time to rival supporters or representatives. The licensee, however, is not obligated to provide such response time for free. Even if an appearance includes criticism of an opposing candidate, fairness principles operate in the sense that "mere criticism [does] not constitute a personal attack within the meaning of [agency] rules."

"Use [of] a broadcasting station" has to be significant enough to activate the equal opportunity obligation. Appearances of a few seconds have been dismissed as inconsequential and not implicating the terms of the statute. Use has been construed to include a comedian's satirical campaign for public office, despite claims that the interpretation deprived him of his livelihood. The broadcast of old movies starring Ronald Reagan during his 1976 presidential campaign, challenged in *Adrian Weiss*, proved to be a use for purposes of Section 315.

Identifiable on-air talent, even if it appears in a routine role, such as a newscaster, that is unrelated to candidacy, also is subject to equal opportunity obligations. Because equal opportunity obligations arise in connection with each appearance by a candidate, broadcast personnel may be compelled to leave their employment in the event that they choose to run for public office. A challenge to Section 315 because it allegedly (1) deprived a journalist of the right to seek public office and (2) invaded First Amendment guarantees was rejected on both grounds. In *Branch v. Federal Communications Commission*, the court of appeals held that the law did not extinguish or unreasonably burden the claimant's right to run for public office. Given the diminished First Amendment status of broadcasters, the appeals court concluded that a licensee's editorial discretion was not wrongfully diluted. It thereby declined an invitation to find the scarcity rationale obsolete and that Section 315 no longer was constitutionally congruent.

(2) *Exemptions*. Even if its basic prerequisites are met, the contingent right of equal opportunity is not available in the event that a candidate's appearance is in the course of bona fide news coverage or a documentary. Section 315 imposes no affirmative duty to provide time, and a candidate's appearance in a

> (1) bona fide newscast,
> (2) bona fide news interview,
> (3) bona fide news documentary (if the appearance of the candidate is incidental to the presentation of the subject or subjects covered by the news documentary), or
> (4) on-the-spot coverage of bona fide news events (included but not limited to political conventions and activities incidental thereto),

shall not be deemed to be use of a broadcasting station within the meaning of this subsection. Nothing in the foregoing sentence shall be construed as relieving broadcasters, in connection with the presentation of newscasts, news interviews, news documentaries, and on-the-spot coverage of news events, from the obligation imposed upon them under this chapter to operate in the public interest and to afford reasonable opportunity for the discussion of conflicting views on issues of public importance.

The exemptions reflect congressional response to FCC rulings in the 1950s requiring equal opportunity for rivals of incumbents whose activities had been the subject of routine news reporting. Section 315, as amended, attempts to strike a balance between general interests in an informed public and more particularized concern with the accrual of special advantage or influence in the course of a political campaign.

The question of what constitutes exempt programming has proved to be perhaps the thorniest issue under Section 315. Congress itself suspended the equal opportunity provision in 1960 to enable Democratic and Republican presidential candidates to debate without creating an obligation to provide time to other contestants. During the course of the 1964 campaign, the FCC rendered a decision that proved problematic to coverage of news in the course of a political campaign. In *Columbia Broadcasting System*, it determined that news conferences by an incumbent and primary rival were not exempt as "bona fide news events." The ruling contrasted with a nearly simultaneous finding in *Republican National Committee (Dean Burch)* that the provision of network time to President Johnson for discussion of two major foreign policy events a couple of weeks before the election qualified as "on-the-spot coverage of a bona fide news event." Both rulings essentially reflected the Commission's determination that the subjective judgment of the licensee alone should not determine the availability of the exemption. Later, in 1972, the FCC in *Hon. Shirley Chisholm* determined that a regularly scheduled Sunday interview program that was expanded from its normal length to feature a joint appearance by two main candidates for the Democratic nomination constituted a "bona fide news interview." Upon review, the Commission's ruling was reversed on grounds that the departure from normal format transformed the interview into a debate. As a consequence, the FCC was compelled to order the award of free time to a candidate excluded from the program.

The operation of Section 315 thus proved troublesome insofar as free-time obligations deterred coverage of news events and confounded any organized debates. Regulation designed to facilitate informed self-government was operating at cross-purposes with that goal. Since the mid–1970s, the Commission has steered a course of review that is more deferential to a licensee's subjective judgment regarding the availability of an exemption. The FCC, moreover, initiated affirmative steps to ensure that political news reporting would not be chilled and that debates would not be impaired. News conferences or debates thus could be covered without incurring equal time obligations pursuant to a licensee's good-faith determination that they were newsworthy. The ruling reflected the Commission's growing sense that the risk of political favoritism was less than the danger of inadequate coverage of issues central to self-government.

The substantial deference now accorded licensee judgment was evinced in 1980 when President Carter held a news conference that was carried by all networks in prime time and contained several comments critical of his main rival for the Democratic nomination. Despite any advantage that incumbency affords to a candidate, the FCC refused to second-guess licensee determinations in the particular instance and asserted that it would not do so "absent strong evidence" that bona fide news judgment was not being exercised. The Commission's ruling was upheld in *Kennedy for President Committee v. Federal Communications Commission*.

(3) *Lowest unit charges.* Congress has structured Section 315 in a way that prevents broadcasters from reaping windfall profits from the imperative of political campaigning. Rates for political candidates generally are not to exceed "charges made for comparable use of such stations by

other users thereof." That provision subjects candidates to general marketplace forces. During the forty-five-day period preceding a primary election or the sixty-day period preceding a federal election, however, rates for candidates may not exceed "the lowest unit charge of the station for the same class and amount of time for the same period." The provision essentially obligates licensees to provide bulk discounts that would be afforded to their heaviest advertisers even if the candidate purchases time but once. Broadcasters are not required to eliminate rate classes based on time of day or extend the lowest unit rate to representatives of a candidate.

(4) *Censorship and liability.* A licensee is expressly prohibited from censoring any "material broadcast under the provisions of" Section 315. Absent special protection, a liability problem would arise in the event that a candidate beyond a licensee's control uttered actionable statements. In *Farmers Educational & Cooperative Union of America v. WDAY, Inc.*, the Supreme Court thus conferred upon broadcasters immunity from liability for any defamatory comments made by a candidate in the course of a Section 315 appearance. In so doing, it also exempted such remarks altogether from actionability in the form of a traditional defamation action. Such a determination was considered essential to full effectuation of the legislation's underlying purpose.

D. REASONABLE ACCESS FOR POLITICAL CANDIDATES

Unlike rules governing political editorials, personal attacks, and equal opportunity, Section 312(a)(7) of the Communications Act affords political candidates a right of reasonable access that is affirmative rather than contingent in nature. Without such a right, it is conceivable that a licensee could avoid equal opportunity obligations altogether by denying time to any candidate. By its terms, Section 312(a)(7) authorizes the FCC to revoke a license "for willful or repeated failure to allow reasonable access to or to permit purchase of reasonable amounts of time for the use of a broadcasting station by a legally qualified candidate for Federal elective office on behalf of his candidacy." In operation, the law has been read as "creat[ing] an affirmative, promptly enforceable right of reasonable access to the use of broadcast stations for individual candidates seeking federal elective office."

The access right was formally recognized in *CBS, Inc. v. Federal Communications Commission* after three networks responded negatively to requests by President Carter's reelection committee to purchase half an hour of air time. The Court found generally "that the statutory right of access ... properly balances the First Amendment rights of federal candidates, the public, and broadcasters." It distinguished the limited access right from the general right of access, rejected several years earlier, and found the former permissible because it did not significantly cramp editorial discretion. Moreover, the Court found the right of reasonable access promotive of the First Amendment interests not only of candidates in presenting but of the public in receiving "information necessary for the operation of the democratic process."

Just prior to the *CBS, Inc.*, decision, an appeals court determined that "broadcasters may fulfill their obligation [under Section 312(a)(7)] either by allotting free time to a candidate *or* by selling the candidate time at the rates prescribed by Section 315(b) [emphasis in original]." In *Kennedy for President Committee v. Federal Communications Commission*, the court denied a candidate's request for free time under Section 312(a)(7) to respond to a rival's critical remarks. It concluded that the provision did not create a right to use a licensee's "facilities without charge." The court further observed that a contingent right to reply for free would undercut the exemptions for bona fide news reporting and documentaries created by Section 315(a). A legitimate claim under Section 312(a)(7) would have been presented, therefore, only if the candidate had been denied an opportunity to purchase time.

C. Fairness Regulation Reconsidered

The existence of fairness regulation and operation of the fairness doctrine in particular have provoked extensive controversy, especially after the Supreme Court constitutionalized the concept in 1969. Criticism has been couched in both practical and First Amendment terms. Although arguments against the fairness doctrine were consistently dismissed by the FCC for more than a decade, these arguments ultimately were subscribed to by the FCC itself in abandoning it.

In respectively formulating and validating the fairness doctrine, the FCC and the Court originally assumed that it would ensure comprehensive and balanced coverage of controversial public issues. Detractors maintained that instead of facilitating robust debate, the fairness doctrine miscomprehended marketplace forces and thus deterred it. Because profit optimization is a function of audience maximization, television programming strategies cater to mainstream tastes. Such commentary echoed Justice Brennan's sense that orthodox rather than provocative controversy was the result of licensee concerns with potential alienation of audience and sponsors who might be offended by radical or unpopular views.

By imposing fairness responsibilities upon broadcasters, the FCC reserved for itself significant content-related and editorial responsibility. In deference to traditional notions of freedom of the press, however, the Commission in reviewing fairness complaints almost invariably presumed and deferred to good-faith licensee judgment. An actual fairness violation proved to be the rare exception in a system affording licensees broad leeway "in selecting the manner of coverage, the appropriate spokesmen, and the technique of production and presentation." Such deference to constitutional imperatives, however, fueled objections that the fairness doctrine offered little utility in exchange for potentially profound First Amendment treachery.

The fairness doctrine thus became subject to comprehensive reproach for deviating from traditional First Amendment norms that protected editorial autonomy, actually disserving the public's paramount right to receive program diversity, and endangering First Amendment values generally. By the mid-1980s, concerns and distress that previously had been confined to dissenting opinion or critical commentary began surfacing in mainstream jurisprudence and the FCC's own reassessments. In *Federal Communications Commission v. League of Women Voters*, the Supreme Court invited Congress or the FCC to notify it if the time had come to discard the fairness doctrine's scarcity rationale as an obsolete notion. The Court clarified general grounds and constitutional perimeters for broadcast regulation, acknowledged the possibility that the scarcity premise might be less viable than previously assumed, and noted that the commission was welcome to demonstrate that the fairness doctrine undermined rather than advanced First Amendment interests.

The fundamental principles that guide our evaluation of broadcast regulation are by now well established. First, we have long recognized that Congress, acting pursuant to the Commerce Clause, has power to regulate the use of this scarce and valuable national resource. The distinctive feature of Congress' efforts in this area has been to ensure through the regulatory oversight of the FCC that only those who satisfy the "public interest, convenience, and necessity" are granted a license to use radio and television broadcast frequencies. 47 U. S. C. § 309(a).[a]

Second, Congress may, in the exercise of this power, seek to assure that the public receives through this medium a balanced presentation of information on issues of public importance that otherwise might not be addressed if control of the medium were left entirely in the hands of those who own and operate broadcasting stations. Although such governmental regulation has never been allowed with respect to the print media, *Miami Herald Publishing Co. v. Tornillo*, 418 U. S. 241 (1974), we have recognized that "differences in the characteristics of new media justify differences in the First Amendment standards applied to them." *Red Lion Broadcasting Co. v. FCC*, 395 U. S. 367, 386 (1969). The fundamental distinguishing characteristic of the new medium of broadcasting that, in our view, has required some adjustment in First Amendment analysis is that "[b]roadcast frequencies are a scarce resource [that] must be portioned out among applicants." *Columbia Broadcasting System, Inc. v. Democratic National Committee*, 412 U. S. 94, 101 (1973). Thus, our cases have taught that, given spectrum scarcity, those who are granted a license to broadcast must serve in a sense as fiduciaries for the public by presenting "those views and voices which are representative of [their] community and which would otherwise, by necessity, be barred from the airwaves." *Red Lion, supra*, at 389. As we observed in that case, because "[i]t is the purpose of the First Amendment to preserve an uninhibited marketplace of ideas in which truth will ultimately prevail,...the right of the public to receive suitable access to social, political, esthetic, moral, and other ideas and experiences [through the medium of broadcasting] is crucial here [and it] may not constitutionally be abridged either by Congress or by the FCC." 395 U. S., at 390.

Finally, although the Government's interest in ensuring balanced coverage of public issues is plainly both important and substantial, we have, at the same time, made clear that broadcasters are engaged in a vital and independent form of communicative activity. As a result, the First Amendment must inform and give shape to the manner in which Congress exercises its regulatory power in this area. Unlike common carriers, broadcasters are "entitled under the First Amendment to exercise 'the widest journalistic freedom consistent with their public [duties].' " *CBS, Inc.* v. *FCC*, 453 U. S. 367, 395 (1981) (quoting *Columbia Broadcasting System, Inc.* v. *Democratic National Committee, supra*, at 110). See also *FCC* v. *Midwest Video Corp.*, 440 U. S. 689, 703 (1979). Indeed, if the public's interest in receiving a balanced presentation of views is to be fully served, we must necessarily rely in large part upon the editorial initiative and judgment of the broadcasters who bear the public trust. See *Columbia Broadcasting System, Inc.* v. *Democratic National Committee, supra*, at 124–127.

Our prior cases illustrate these principles. In *Red Lion*, for example, we upheld the FCC's "fairness doctrine"—which requires broadcasters to provide adequate coverage of public issues and to ensure that this coverage fairly and accurately reflects the opposing views—because the doctrine advanced the substantial governmental interest in ensuring balanced presentations of views in this limited medium and yet posed no threat that a "broadcaster [would be denied permission] to carry a particular program or to publish his own views." 395 U. S., at 396.[b] Similarly, in *CBS, Inc.* v. *FCC, supra*, the Court upheld the right of access for federal candidates imposed by § 312(a)(7) of the Communications Act both because that provision "makes a significant contribution to freedom of expression by enhancing the ability of candidates to present, and the public to receive, information necessary for the effective operation of the democratic process," *id.*, at 396, and because it defined a sufficiently "*limited* right of 'reasonable' access" so that "the discretion of broadcasters to present their views on any issue or to carry any particular type of programming" was not impaired. *Id.*, at 396–397 (emphasis in original). Finally, in *Columbia Broadcasting System, Inc.* v. *Democratic National Committee, supra*, the Court affirmed the FCC's refusal to require broadcast licensees to accept all paid political advertisements. Although it was argued that such a requirement would serve the public's First Amendment interest in receiving additional views on public issues, the Court rejected this approach, finding that such a requirement would tend to transform broadcasters into common carriers and would intrude unnecessarily upon the editorial discretion of broadcasters. *Id.*, at 123–125. The FCC's ruling, therefore, helped to advance the important purposes of the Communications Act, grounded in the First Amendment, of preserving the right of broadcasters to exercise "the widest journalistic freedom consistent with [their] public obligations," and of guarding against "the risk of an enlargement of Government control over the content of broadcast discussion of public issues." *Id.*, at 110, 126.

Thus, although the broadcasting industry plainly operates under restraints not imposed upon other media, the thrust of these restrictions has generally been to secure the public's First Amendment interest in receiving a balanced presentation of views on diverse matters of public concern. As a result of these restrictions, of course, the absolute freedom to advocate one's own positions without also presenting opposing viewpoints—a freedom enjoyed, for example, by newspaper publishers and soapbox orators—is denied to broadcasters. But, as our cases attest, these restrictions have been upheld only when we were satisfied that the restriction is narrowly tailored to further a substantial governmental interest, such as ensuring adequate and balanced coverage of public issues, *e. g., Red Lion*, 395 U. S., at 377. See also *CBS, Inc.* v. *FCC, supra*, at 396–397; *Columbia Broadcasting System, Inc.* v. *Democratic National Committee*, 412 U. S., at 110–111; *Red Lion, supra*, at 396. Making that judgment requires a critical examination of the interests of the public and broadcasters in light of the particular circumstances of each case. *E. g., FCC* v. *Pacifica Foundation*, 438 U. S. 726 (1978).

The FCC's refusal to extend the fairness doctrine to another medium led to the rule's further destabilization. In *Telecommunications Research and Action Center v. Federal Communications Commission*, the court of appeals upheld the Commission's determination that teletext resembled

---

[a]See *FCC* v. *National Citizens Committee for Broadcasting*, 436 U. S. 775, 799–800 (1978); *Columbia Broadcasting System, Inc.* v. *Democratic National Committee*, 412 U. S. 94, 101–102 (1973); *Red Lion Broadcasting Co.* v. *FCC*, 395 U. S. 367, 387–390 (1969); *National Broadcasting Co.* v. *United States*, 319 U. S. 190, 216 (1943); *Federal Radio Comm'n* v. *Nelson Bros. Bond & Mortgage Co.*, 289 U.S. 266, 282 (1933).

The prevailing rationale for broadcast regulation based on spectrum scarcity has come under increasing criticism in recent years. Critics, including the incumbent Chairman of the FCC, charge that with the advent of cable and satellite television technology, communities now have access to such a wide variety of stations that the scarcity doctrine is obsolete. See, *e.g.*, Fowler & Brenner, A Marketplace Approach to Broadcast Regulation, 60 Texas L. Rev. 207, 221–226 (1982). We are not prepared, however, to reconsider our longstanding approach without some signal from Congress or the FCC that technological developments have advanced so far that some revision of the system of broadcast regulation may be required.

[b]We note that the FCC, observing that "[i]f any substantial possibility exists that the [fairness doctrine] rules have impeded, rather than furthered, First Amendment objectives, repeal may be warranted on that ground alone," has tentatively concluded that the rules, by effectively chilling speech, do not serve the public interest, and has therefore proposed to repeal them. Notice of Proposed Rulemaking In re Repeal or Modification of the Personal Attack and Political Editorial Rules, 48 Fed. Reg. 28298, 28301 (1983). Of course, the Commission may, in the exercise of its discretion, decide to modify or abandon these rules, and we express no view on the legality of either course. As we recognized in *Red Lion*, however, were it to be shown by the Commission that the fairness doctrine "[has] the net effect of reducing rather than enhancing" speech, we would then be forced to reconsider the constitutional basis of our decision in that case. 395 U. S., at 393.

the print media more than broadcasting and thus should not be governed by the implications of scarcity, including fairness obligations. In so doing, the appeals court sharply attacked the scarcity rationale as a selective concept creating an indefensible constitutional dichotomy for print and other media. It expressed the hope, moreover, that "the Supreme Court will one day revisit this area of the law and either eliminate the distinction . . . , or announce a constitutional distinction that is more usable than the present one."

The Commission believes that the regulation of teletext falls not within the permissive approach of *Red Lion*, but rather within the strict first amendment rule applied to content regulation of the print media. In *Miami Herald Publishing Co. v. Tornillo*, 418 U.S. 241, 94 S.Ct. 2831, 41 L.Ed.2d 730 (1974), the Court struck down an editorial right-of-reply statute that applied to newspapers. The content regulation in *Tornillo* bore a strong resemblance to that upheld in *Red Lion*. In *Tornillo* the Court held that such regulation impermissibly interfered with the newspapers' "editorial control and judgment." *Id.* at 258, 94 S.Ct. at 2840. The Court made the broad assertion that "[i]t has yet to be demonstrated how governmental regulation of this crucial [editorial] process can be exercised consistent with the First Amendment guarantees of a free press." *Id.* If the Commission's view is correct, and *Tornillo* rather than *Red Lion* applies to teletext, that service is entitled to greater first amendment protections than ordinary broadcasting and it would be proper, at a minimum, to construe political broadcasting provisions narrowly to avoid constitutionally suspect results.

The Commission has offered two grounds for its view that *Tornillo* rather than *Red Lion* is pertinent. Both reasons relate to the textual nature of teletext services. First the Commission read an "immediacy" component into the scarcity doctrine:

> Implicit in the "scarcity" rationale . . . is an assumption that broadcasters, through their access to the radio spectrum, possess a power to communicate ideas through sound and visual images in a manner that is significantly different from traditional avenues of communication because of the immediacy of the medium.

53 Rad.Reg.2d (P&F) at 1324. Second, the Commission held that the print nature of teletext "more closely resembles, and will largely compete with, other print communication media such as newspapers and magazines." *Id.* Under this analysis, scarcity of alternative first amendment resources does not exist with respect to teletext. We address these points in turn.

With respect to the first argument, the deficiencies of the scarcity rationale as a basis for depriving broadcasting of full first amendment protection, have led some to think that it is the immediacy and the power of broadcasting that causes its differential treatment. Whether or not that is true, we are unwilling to endorse an argument that makes the very effectiveness of speech the justification for according it less first amendment protection. More important, the Supreme Court's articulation of the scarcity doctrine contains no hint of any immediacy rationale. The Court based its reasoning entirely on the physical scarcity of broadcasting frequencies, which, it thought, permitted attaching fiduciary duties to the receipt of a license to use a frequency. This "immediacy" distinction cannot, therefore, be employed to affect the ability of the Commission to regulate public affairs broadcasting on teletext to ensure "the right of the public to receive suitable access to social, political, esthetic, moral, and other ideas and experiences." *Red Lion*, 395 U.S. at 390.

The Commission's second distinction—that a textual medium is not scarce insofar as it competes with other "print media"—also fails to dislodge the hold of *Red Lion*. The dispositive fact is that teletext is transmitted over broadcast frequencies that the Supreme Court has ruled scarce and this makes teletext's content regulable. We can understand, however, why the Commission thought it could reason in this fashion. The basic difficulty in this entire area is that the line drawn between the print media and the broadcast media, resting as it does on the physical scarcity of the latter, is a distinction without a difference. Employing the scarcity concept as an analytic tool, particularly with respect to new and unforeseen technologies, inevitably leads to strained reasoning and artificial results.

It is certainly true that broadcast frequencies are scarce but it is unclear why that fact justifies content regulation of broadcasting in a way that would be intolerable if applied to the editorial process of the print media. All economic goods are scarce, not least the newsprint, ink, delivery trucks, computers, and other resources that go into the production and dissemination of print journalism. Not everyone who wishes to publish a newspaper, or even a pamphlet, may do so. Since scarcity is a universal fact, it can hardly explain regulation in one context and not another. The attempt to use a universal fact as a distinguishing principle necessarily leads to analytical confusion.

Neither is content regulation explained by the fact that broadcasters face the problem of interference, so that the government must define usable frequencies and protect those frequencies from encroachment. This governmental definition of frequencies is another instance of a universal fact that does not offer an explanatory principle for differing treatment. A publisher can deliver his newspapers only because government provides streets and regulates traffic on the streets by allocating rights of way. Yet no one would contend that the necessity for these governmental functions, which are certainly analogous to the government's function in allocating broadcast frequencies, could justify regulation of the content of a newspaper to ensure that it serves the needs of the citizens.

There may be ways to reconcile *Red Lion* and *Tornillo* but the "scarcity" of broadcast frequencies does not appear capable of doing so. Perhaps the Supreme Court will one day revisit this area of the law and either eliminate the distinction between print and broadcast media, surely by pronouncing *Tornillo* applicable to both, or announce a constitutional distinction that is more usable than the present one.

The influence of critical ferment also had become evident in the FCC's own review of the fairness doctrine. In 1985, it asserted that "the multiplicity of voices in the marketplace today" had erased the problem of spectrum scarcity, so the regulation no longer was a "necessary ... or appropriate means by which to effectuate this interest." Despite evidence it cited in support of the fairness doctrine's deficiencies, and articulated judicial misgivings about the principle, the FCC deferred steps that would negate the principle pending legislative action. Although Congress voted to incorporate the fairness doctrine into statute, the president vetoed it. In the meantime, the FCC was under increasing pressure to correlate policies and actions with its new sense that the fairness doctrine subverted First Amendment interests. A direct challenge to the doctrine's constitutionality was dismissed on jurisdictional grounds, although a companion claim regarding the Commission's failure to commence a rulemaking to eliminate or modify the fairness doctrine was found reviewable. The order subsequently was vacated following resolution of *Meredith Corp. v. Federal Communications Commission.* The court of appeals ordered the FCC, which had found a fairness violation, to consider the licensee's contention that the fairness doctrine was unconstitutional. Consistent with an approving cue from the *Telecommunications Research and Action Center* decision to the effect that the fairness doctrine had not been implicitly codified by congressional action, the Commission abandoned the fairness doctrine for virtually all of the reasons sounded over the years by critics.

Without reaching the constitutional issues, the court of appeals upheld the FCC's decision in *Syracuse Peace Council v. Federal Communications Commission* as a legitimate rendition under the "public interest" standard. Finding that the fairness doctrine was not absolutely compelled by the Constitution or by statute, the appeals court deferred to the FCC's determination that it chilled coverage of important issues, subjected the editorial process to official second-guessing and potential abuse, and no longer was necessary owing to the expanded availability of broadcasting outlets. The commission's ruling in *Syracuse Peace Council* provides a comprehensive examination of the history, purpose, deficiencies, and demise of fairness regulation. The FCC thus invested in the notion that the doctrine chilled rather than promoted expressive diversity.

In sum, the fairness doctrine in operation disserves both the public's right to diverse sources of information and the broadcaster's interest in free expression. Its chilling effect thwarts its intended purpose, and it results in excessive and unnecessary government intervention into the editorial processes of broadcast journalists. We hold, therefore, that under the constitutional standard established by *Red Lion* and its progeny, the fairness doctrine contravenes the First Amendment and its enforcement is no longer in the public interest.

The Commission then determined that the scarcity rationale, upon which the fairness doctrine was premised, no longer was compelling.

75. Because there is no longer a scarcity in the number of broadcast outlets, proponents of a scarcity rationale for the justification of diminished First Amendment rights applicable to the broadcast medium must rely on the concept of

spectrum (or allocational) scarcity. This concept is based upon the physical limitations of the electromagnetic spectrum. Because only a limited number of persons can utilize broadcast frequencies at any particular point in time, spectrum scarcity is said to be present when the number of persons desiring to disseminate information on broadcast frequencies exceeds the number of available frequencies. Consequently, these frequencies, like all scarce resources, must be allocated among those who wish to use them.

76. In fact, spectrum scarcity was one of the bases articulated by the Court in *Red Lion* for the disparate treatment of the broadcast and the print media. Reliance on spectrum scarcity, however, "has come under increasing criticism in recent years." For example, the Court of Appeals has recently questioned the rationality of spectrum scarcity as the basis for differentiating between the print and broadcast media. In *TRAC v. FCC*, the Court asserted that:

> [T]he line drawn between the print media and the broadcast media, resting as it does on the physical scarcity of the latter, is a distinction without a difference. Employing the scarcity concept as an analytic[al] tool...inevitably leads to strained reasoning and artificial results.

> It is certainly true that broadcast frequencies are scarce but it is unclear why that fact justifies content regulation of broadcasting in a way that would be intolerable if applied to the editorial process of the print media. All economic goods are scarce, not least the newsprint, ink, delivery trucks, computers, and other resources that go into the production and dissemination of print journalism.... Since scarcity is a universal fact, it can hardly explain regulation in one context and not another. The attempt to use a universal fact as a distinguishing principle necessarily leads to analytical confusion.

We agree with the court's analysis of the spectrum scarcity rationale, and we believe that it would be desirable for the Supreme Court to reconsider its use of a constitutional standard based upon spectrum scarcity in evaluating the intrusive type of content-based regulation at issue in this proceeding.

77. At the outset, we note that the limits on the number of persons who can use frequencies at any given time is not absolute, but is, in part, economic: greater expenditures on equipment and/or advances in technology could make it possible to utilize the spectrum more efficiently in order to permit a greater number of licensees. So the number of outlets in a market is potentially expandable, like the quantities of most other resources.

78. Nevertheless, we recognize that technological advancements and the transformation of the telecommunications market described above have not eliminated spectrum scarcity. All goods, however, are ultimately scarce, and there must be a system through which to allocate their use. Although a free enterprise system relies heavily on a system of property rights and voluntary exchange to allocate most of these goods, other methods of allocation, including first-come-first-served, administrative hearings, lotteries, and auctions, are or have been relied on for certain other goods. Whatever the method of allocation, there is not any logical connection between the method of allocation for a particular good and the level of constitutional protection afforded to the uses of that good.

79. In the allocation of broadcast frequencies, the government has relied, for the most part, on a licensing scheme based on administrative hearings to promote

the most effective use of this resource. Congress has also authorized the allocation of frequencies through the use of lotteries. Moreover, although the government allocates broadcast frequencies to particular broadcast speakers in the initial licensing stage, approximately 71% of today's radio stations and 54% of today's television stations have been acquired by the current licensees on the open market. Hence, in the vast majority of cases, broadcast frequencies are "allocated"—as are the resources necessary to disseminate printed speech—through a functioning economic market. Therefore, after initial licensing, the only relevant barrier to acquiring a broadcast station is not governmental, but—like the acquisition of a newspaper—is economic.

80. Additionally, there is nothing inherent in the utilization of the licensing method of allocation that justifies the government acting in a manner that would be proscribed under a traditional First Amendment analysis. In contexts other than broadcasting, for example, the courts have indicated that, where licensing is permissible, the First Amendment proscribes the government from regulating the content of fully protected speech. There are those who argue that the acceptance by broadcasters of government's ability to regulate the content of their speech is simply a fair exchange for their ability to use the airwaves free of charge. To the extent, however, that such an exchange allows the government to engage in activity that would be proscribed by a traditional First Amendment analysis, we reject that argument. It is well-established that government may not condition the receipt of a public benefit on the relinquishment of a constitutional right. The evil of government intervention into the editorial process of the press (whether print or electronic) and the right of individuals to receive political viewpoints unfettered by government interference are not changed because the electromagnetic spectrum (or any other resource necessary to convey expression) is scarce or because the government (in conjunction with the marketplace) allocates that scarce resource. Indeed, the fact that government is involved in licensing is all the more reason why the First Amendment protects against government control of content.

Finally, the FCC determined that the First Amendment rights of broadcasters should be at parity with those of publishers.

3. Divergence of *Red Lion* from Traditional First Amendment Precepts

83. We believe that the articulation of lesser First Amendment rights for broadcasters on the basis of the existence of scarcity, the licensing of broadcasters, and the paramount rights of listeners departs from traditional First Amendment jurisprudence in a number of respects. Specifically, the Court's decision that the listeners' rights justifies government intrusion appears to conflict with several fundamental principles underlying the constitutional guarantee of free speech.

84. First, this line of decisions diverges from Supreme Court pronouncements that "the First Amendment 'was fashioned to assure *unfettered* interchange of ideas for the bringing about of political and social changes desired by the people.' " The framers of that Amendment determined that the best means by

which to protect the free exchange of ideas is to prohibit any governmental regulation which "abridg[es] the freedom of speech or of the press." They believed that the marketplace of ideas is too delicate and too fragile to be entrusted to governmental authorities.

85. In this regard, Justice Potter Stewart once stated that "[t]hose who wrote our First Amendment put their faith in the proposition that a free press is indispensable to a free society. They believed that 'fairness' was far too fragile to be left for a government bureaucracy to accomplish." In the same vein, Justice Byron White has stated that:

> Of course, the press is not always accurate, or even responsible, and may not present full and fair debate on important public issues. But the balance struck by the First Amendment with respect to the press is that society must take the risk that occasionally debate on vital matters will not be comprehensive and that all viewpoints may not be expressed.... Any other accommodation—any other system that would supplant private control of the press with the heavy hand of government intrusion—would make the government the censor of what the people may read and know.

Indeed, the Supreme Court has often emphasized that:

> The freedom of speech and of the press guaranteed by the Constitution embraces at the least the liberty to discuss publicly and truthfully all matters of public concern without previous restraint *or fear of subsequent punishment.*

Consequently, a cardinal tenet of the First Amendment is that governmental intervention in the marketplace of ideas of the sort involved in the enforcement of the fairness doctrine is not acceptable and should not be tolerated.

86. The fairness doctrine is at odds with this fundamental constitutional precept. While the objective underlying the fairness doctrine is that of the First Amendment itself—the promotion of debate on important controversial issues—the means employed to achieve this objective, government coercion, is the very one which the First Amendment is designed to prevent. As the Supreme Court has noted, "By protecting those who wish to enter the marketplace of ideas from governmental attack, the First Amendment protects the public's interest in receiving information." Yet the fairness doctrine *uses* government intervention in order to foster diversity of viewpoints, while the scheme established by the framers of our Constitution *forbids* government intervention for fear that it will stifle robust debate. In this sense, the underlying rationale of the fairness doctrine turns the First Amendment on its head....

....

94. Finally, we believe that under the First Amendment, the right of viewers and listeners to receive diverse viewpoints is achieved by guaranteeing them the right to receive speech unencumbered by government intervention. The *Red Lion* decision, however, apparently views the notion that broadcasters should come within the free press and free speech protections of the First Amendment as antagonistic to the interest of the public in obtaining access to the marketplace of ideas. As a result, it is squarely at odds with the general philosophy underlying the First Amendment, *i.e.,* that the individual's interest in free expression and the societal interest in access to viewpoint diversity are both furthered by proscribing governmental regulation of speech. The special broadcast standard ap-

plied by the Court in *Red Lion*, which sanctions restrictions on speakers in order to promote the interest of the viewers and listeners, contradicts this fundamental constitutional principle.

95. Under a traditional First Amendment analysis, the type of governmental intrusion inherent in the fairness doctrine would not be tolerated if it were applied to the print media. Indeed, in *Miami Herald Publishing Co. v. Tornillo*, the Supreme Court struck down, on First Amendment grounds, a Florida statute that compelled a newspaper to print the response of a political candidate that it had criticized. Invoking a purpose strikingly similar to the fairness doctrine, the state had attempted to justify the statute on the grounds that the "government has an obligation to ensure that a wide variety of views reach the public." The Court reasoned that the mechanism employed by the state in implementing this objective, however, was "governmental coercion," and thus contravened "the express provisions of the First Amendment and the judicial gloss on that Amendment developed over the years." The Court also found that a governmentally imposed right of reply impermissibly "intrud[ed] into the function of editors." In addition, the Court stated that the inevitable result of compelling the press "to print that which it would not otherwise print" would be to reduce the amount of debate on governmental affairs:

> Faced with the penalties that would accrue to any newspaper that published news or commentary arguably within the reach of the right-of-access statute, editors might well conclude that the safe course is to avoid controversy. Therefore, under the operation of the Florida statute, political and electoral coverage would be blunted or reduced. Government-enforced right of access inescapably " 'dampens the vigor and limits the variety of public debate.' "

Also, the fact that a newspaper could simply add to its length did not dissuade the Court from concluding that the access requirement would improperly intrude into the editorial discretion of the newspaper.

96. Relying on *Tornillo*, the Court . . . recently determined that a state administrative order requiring a utility to place the newsletter of its opponents in its billing envelopes contravened the First Amendment. "[B]ecause access was awarded only to those who disagreed with [the utility's] views and who are hostile to [the utility's] interests," Justice Lewis Powell, in the plurality opinion expressed concern that "whenever [the utility] speaks out on a given issue, it may be forced . . . to help disseminate hostile views." As a consequence, the regulation had the effect of reducing the free flow of information and ideas that the First Amendment seeks to promote. In evaluating the utility's First Amendment rights to be free from governmentally-coerced speech, the plurality expressly stated that it was irrelevant that the ratepayers, rather than the utility, owned the extra space in the billing envelopes. It asserted that the "forced association with potentially hostile views burdens the expression of views . . . and risks forcing [the utility] to speak where it would prefer to remain silent" irrespective of who is deemed to own this extra space.

97. We believe that the role of the electronic press in our society is the same as that of the printed press. Both are sources of information and viewpoint. Accordingly, the reasons for proscribing government intrusion into the editorial discretion of print journalists provide the same basis for proscribing such in-

terference into the editorial discretion of broadcast journalists. The First Amendment was adopted to protect the people *not from journalists, but from government.* It gives the people the right to receive ideas that are unfettered by government interference. We fail to see how that right changes when individuals choose to receive ideas from the electronic media instead of the print media. There is no doubt that the electronic media is powerful and that broadcasters can abuse their freedom of speech. But the framers of the Constitution believed that the potential for abuse of private freedoms posed far less a threat to democracy than the potential for abuse by a government given the power to control the press. We concur. We therefore believe that full First Amendment protections against content regulation should apply equally to the electronic and the printed press....

. . . .

99. We further believe, as the Supreme Court indicated in *FCC v. League of Women Voters of California,* that the dramatic transformation in the telecommunications marketplace provides a basis for the Court to reconsider its application of diminished First Amendment protection to the electronic media. Despite the physical differences between the electronic and print media, their roles in our society are identical, and we believe that the same First Amendment principles should be equally applicable to both. This is the method set forth in our Constitution for maximizing the public interest; and furthering the public interest is likewise our mandate under the Communications Act. It is, therefore, to advance the public interest that we advocate these rights for broadcasters.

The FCC's abandonment of the fairness doctrine suggests the logical possibility that related concepts, such as the personal attack rule, must fall to the extent that they are premised upon scarcity. The ultimate destiny of fairness regulation, however, remains in doubt. Although its legislative resurrection was defeated by presidential veto, congressional interest in its reintroduction persists. Fairness advocates continue to regard the principle as a critical methodology for ensuring coverage of pluralistic views, especially minority sentiments. They also emphasize notable accomplishments of fairness regulation, including the effectiveness of antismoking messages, which, as discussed later in this chapter, effectively enhanced public awareness of health risks associated with tobacco use.

Although the Supreme Court invited reconsideration of the premise for fairness regulation, it has yet to rule on its abandonment. The possibility that the scarcity rationale may retain some vitality is evidenced, however, by the Court's decision in *Metro Broadcasting, Inc. v. Federal Communications Commission.* Although the Court considered Congress's power to promote program diversity by means of preferential minority-ownership policies, discussed in Chapter 6, it stated:

We have long recognized that "[b]ecause of the scarcity of [electromagnetic] frequencies, the Government is permitted to put restraints on licensees in favor of others whose views should be expressed on this unique medium." *Red Lion*. The Government's role in distributing the limited number of broadcast licenses is not merely that of a "traffic officer;" rather, it is axiomatic that broadcasting may be regulated in light of the rights of the viewing and listening audience and that "the widest possible dissemination of information from diverse and antagonistic sources is essential to the welfare of the public." Safeguarding the public's right to receive a diversity of views and information over the airwaves is [consistent] with "the ends and purposes of the First Amendment"....

The benefits of such diversity are not limited to the members of minority groups who gain access to the broadcasting industry by virtue of the ownership policies; rather, the benefits redound to all members of the viewing and listening audience. [W]e conclude that the interest in enhancing broadcast diversity is, at the very least, an important governmental objective and is therefore a sufficient basis for the Commission's minority ownership policies. Just as a "diverse student body" contributing to a "robust exchange of ideas" is a "constitutionally permissible goal" on which a race-conscious university admissions program may be predicated, *Bakke* (opinion of Powell, J.), the diversity of views and information on the airwaves serves important First Amendment values.

Although she dissented from the Court's holding affirming the minority-ownership policies at issue, Justice O'Connor, joined by Chief Justice Rehnquist and Justices Scalia and Kennedy, observed that broadcasting is subject to special constitutional rules.

The Court has recognized an interest in obtaining diverse broadcasting viewpoints as a legitimate basis for the FCC, acting pursuant to its "public interest" statutory mandate, to adopt limited measures to increase the number of competing licensees and to encourage licensees to present varied views on issues of public concern. See, e.g., *Red Lion*. We have also concluded that [such] measures do not run afoul of the First Amendment's usual prohibition of Government regulation of the marketplace of ideas, in part because first amendment concerns support limited but inevitable Government regulation of the peculiarly constrained broadcasting spectrum. See, e.g., *Red Lion*. But the conclusion that measures adopted to further the interest in diversity of broadcasting viewpoints are neither beyond the FCC's statutory authority nor contrary to the First Amendment hardly establishes the interest as important for equal protection purposes.

The FCC's extension of the asserted interest in diversity of views in this case presents, at the very least, an unsettled First Amendment issue. The FCC has concluded that the American broadcasting public receives the incorrect mix of ideas and claims to have adopted the challenged policies to supplement programming content with a particular set of views. Although we have approved limited measures designed to increase information and views generally, the Court has never upheld a broadcasting measure designed to amplify a distinct set of views or the views of a particular class of speakers. [Even] if an interest is determined to be legitimate in one context, it does not suddenly become important enough to justify distinctions based on race.

II. CONTENT RESTRICTION

A. INDECENCY

Notwithstanding the FCC's determination that broadcasters should be accorded constitutional parity with publishers, distinctions continue to be made resulting in identifiable variances in status. Regardless of media context, obscenity is constitutionally unprotected expression and may be entirely proscribed. Sexually explicit material falling short of an obscenity definition and depicted in terms of indecency may be subject to constraint even though it is constitutionally protected. The distribution of adult literature or exhibition of adult motion pictures, for instance, is subject to a reasonable time, place, and manner requirement. As a consequence, zoning ordinances mandating the concentration or dispersal of adult bookstores or movie houses have been upheld. Similarly, time restrictions have been imposed upon the airing of what is officially classified as indecent programming. Unlike quality-of-life interests that have justified regulation limiting the availability of published indecency, control of sexually explicit broadcasting is referenced to purportedly unique characteristics of radio and television. Restrictions thus are a function of merged concern with broadcasting's pervasive nature, interference with privacy, and accessibility to children. Although time channeling and zoning restrictions have been presented as comparable concepts, in practice the scope of broadcast material subject to the former requirement appears to be more sweeping than expression governed by zoning.

The regulation of indecent broadcasting results from tension between two statutes. The Communications Act specifically prohibits the FCC from exercising "the power of censorship." A general criminal statute, however, subjects "[w]hoever utters any obscene, indecent, or profane language by means of radio communication [to being] fined not more than $10,000 or imprisoned not more than two years, or both." Not until the late 1970s, in *Federal Communications Commission v. Pacifica Foundation*, did the Supreme Court speak authoritatively on the subject. Even before then, extensive programming that was "on its face ... coarse, vulgar, suggestive and indecent [and] ... by any standards ... flagrantly and patently offensive in the context of the broadcast field" contributed to an FCC determination that the public interest had been disserved and that license renewal should be denied. Since *Pacifica*, the Commission has adopted a sterner demeanor and has formulated criteria for purposes of defining and curtailing indecent programming. Although the FCC has long warned of the potential for serious penalties, only recently has it begun to impose significant sanctions on a widespread basis.

1. Pre-*Pacifica* Regulation

The Commission's first major statement concerning indecent programming arose in the course of reviewing license renewal applications of stations owned by the Pacifica Foundation. The frequent implication of Pacifica in the context of indecency controversies illustrates the conflict that exists between diversity goals and concerns with offensive programming. Pacifica stations tend to provide precisely the heterodox programming that critics have found lacking in a broadcasting industry catering to mainstream tastes. Its capacity for unsettling majoritarian conventions or dominant tastes, however, has regularly pitted it and diversity values against content concerns.

The first complaint against a Pacifica station in 1964 related to readings of poems and a novel by their respective authors and a discussion among several homosexuals regarding their concerns and attitudes. With the exception of one poetry reading, all of the programs were presented late at night. Distinguishing the content from programs that were "patently offensive," the Commission in *Pacifica Foundation* upheld the licensee's judgment that it served "the needs and interests of its listening public." Seemingly influential was the perception of the dramatic works as serious and their authorship by "eminent" or "notable" writers and playwrights. The licensee, moreover, demonstrated that passages not meeting its "broadcast standards of good taste" were edited out. Although the FCC recognized that provocative programming, "as shown by the complaints here, . . . may offend some listeners," it concluded that "those offended [did not] have the right, through the Commission's licensing power, to rule such programming off the airwaves." A contrary result would allow "only the wholly inoffensive, the bland, [to] gain access to the radio microphone or TV camera." In sum, the FCC expressed reluctance to take action unless "the facts of the particular case, established in a hearing record, flagrantly call for" it.

Although the Commission had intimated that undue official concern with indecency might undermine "diversity of programming" aims, a subsequent decision presaged a trend toward increased content concern. In *Eastern Educational Radio (WUHY-FM)*, the FCC considered a counterculture musician's use of various "patently offensive" words in the course of a taped interview. Although routine use of expletives is a common aspect of many persons' conversations and in particular cultural settings, the Commission found an indecency violation and imposed a $100 forfeiture.

The conflict between diversity and indecency concerns became more palpable when the FCC determined that a radio call-in program concerning sexual topics was not merely indecent but obscene. Acknowledging a licensee's right to present provocative programming that might offend some, and asserting that it did not intend to prohibit all discussion of sex, the FCC nonetheless determined that "we are not dealing with works of dramatic or literary art."

The Commission's action prompted a challenge by citizens groups alleging that they "were being deprived of listening alternatives in violation of their First Amendment rights." Typifying the programming at issue was the following exchange between a talk-show host and listener:

Female Listener: . . . of course I had a few hangups at first about—in regard to this, but you know what we did—I have a craving for peanut butter all that [sic] time so I used to spread this on my husband's privates and after a while, I mean, I didn't even need the peanut butter anymore.

Announcer: (Laughs) Peanut butter, huh?

Listener: Right. Oh, we can try anything—you know—any, any of these women that have called and they have, you know hangups about this. I mean they should try their favorite—you know like—uh. . . .

Announcer: Whipped cream, marshmallow, . . .

In reaffirming its order, the FCC maintained that its decision was predicated upon the presence of children in the audience and more importantly upon "the pervasive, intrusive nature of radio." In *Illinois Citizens Committee for Broadcasting v. Federal Communications Commission,* the court of appeals agreed that the subject matter constituted "commercial exploitation of interests in titillation [as] the broadcaster's sole end." Consequently, it was denominated under standards of obscenity governing expression that, even if inoffensive in part, panders to prurient interests.

2. The *Pacifica* Decision

The premise of the *Illinois Citizens Committee* decision, combined with the purportedly special characteristics of the medium adverted to by the Commission, suggested the possibility of an obscenity standard that would vary by medium. Eventually, the Supreme Court was drawn into the controversy of reconciling interests of diversity and taste. At issue for the Court was the broadcast of a satirist's twelve-minute monologue, recorded in a live performance, containing repeated references to "words you couldn't say on the public . . . airwaves." The presentation included detailed renditions of the terms' meanings and implications and use of them in a variety of contexts that evoked consistent laughter from the audience. The entire monologue was reproduced in the appendix to the Court's opinion.

When the monologue was aired by a New York Pacifica station in the middle of a weekday afternoon, it was preceded by warnings that it might offend some listeners. It elicited a single complaint, however, from a man who did not hear the warning while driving with his young son. Despite Pacifica's argument that the humorist, George Carlin, was a "significant social satirist who 'like Twain and Sahl before him' examines the language of ordinary people," the Commission found the broadcast subject to administrative sanction. Choosing not to impose a formal penalty, it filed the order for reference in the event of future complaints. The FCC asserted as grounds for special regulatory consideration for broadcasting (1) the medium's accessibility by unsupervised children; (2) special privacy interests of the home; (3) the possibility of unconsenting adults being exposed to offensive language without warning; and (4) spectrum scarcity requiring government to license in the public interest.

Although the court of appeals reversed the Commission's determination, the Supreme Court in *Federal Communications Commission v. Pacifica Foundation* held that the Commission had not breached statutory curbs upon censorship, had properly found the broadcast indecent, and had crossed no First Amendment interest. With respect to an alleged violation of the statutory prohibition of censorship, the Court determined that Section 326 essentially translated into a bar against advance meddling or excision. It then found that the provision "has never been construed to deny the Commission the power to review the content of completed broadcasts in the performance of its regulatory duties." Responding to the other statutory question, that the material did not appeal to prurient interests, the Court found that the concept of indecency was not coextensive with but more encompassing than that of obscenity. Dismissing as unrealistic the contention "that Congress intended to impose precisely the same limitations on the dissemination of patently offensive matter by different" media, it found the absence of prurient appeal nondeterminative of whether a broadcast might be considered as indecent.

Pursuant to the notion "that each medium presents special First Amendment problems," the Court identified two of the four rationales advanced by the FCC as having "relevance to the present case." It thus observed that "[f]irst, the broadcast media have established a uniquely pervasive presence in the lives of all Americans." Because an individual's privacy interests were implicated by exposure to unwanted expression in public and at home, and warnings might not be effective in all cases, the Court concluded that private remediation in the form of tuning out was insufficient. "Second, [the Court found that] broadcasting is uniquely accessible to children, even those too young to read." Easy availability and "government's interest in the 'well being of its youth' and in supporting" parental authority, "amply justify special treatment of indecent broadcasting."

In noting the perimeters of its holding, the Court emphasized that the case did "not involve a two-way radio conversation between a cab driver and a dispatcher, or a telecast of an Elizabethan comedy." Nor had it subjected to sanction "an occasional expletive in either setting" or determined that a criminal prosecution in the case at hand was appropriate. Given an analysis analogous to nuisance theory, the Court noted that "context is all-important." Relevant variables included time of day, program content, and audience composition. Adverting to the adage that a "nuisance may be merely a right thing in the wrong place—like a pig in the parlor instead of the barnyard," the Court closed by noting "that when the Commission finds that a pig has entered the parlor, the exercise of its regulatory power does not depend on proof that the pig is obscene."

Having granted the Commission's petition for certiorari, 434 U. S. 1008, we must decide: (1) whether the scope of judicial review encompasses more than the Commission's determination that the monologue was indecent "as broadcast"; (2) whether the Commission's order was a form of censorship forbidden by § 326; (3) whether the broadcast was indecent within the meaning of § 1464; and (4) whether the order violates the First Amendment of the United States Constitution....

The prohibition against censorship unequivocally denies the Commission any power to edit proposed broadcasts in advance and to excise material considered inappropriate for the airwaves. The prohibition, however, has never been construed to deny the Commission the power to review the content of completed broadcasts in the performance of its regulatory duties....

We conclude, therefore, that § 326 does not limit the Commission's authority to impose sanctions on licensees who engage in obscene, indecent, or profane broadcasting....

Pacifica makes two constitutional attacks on the Commission's order. First, it argues that the Commission's construction of the statutory language broadly encompasses so much constitutionally protected speech that reversal is required even if Pacifica's broadcast of the "Filthy Words" monologue is not itself protected by the First Amendment. Second, Pacifica argues that inasmuch as the recording is not obscene, the Constitution forbids any abridgment of the right to broadcast it on the radio....

When the issue is narrowed to the facts of this case, the question is whether the First Amendment denies government any power to restrict the public broadcast of indecent language in any circumstances. For if the government has any such power, this was an appropriate occasion for its exercise.

The words of the Carlin monologue are unquestionably "speech" within the meaning of the First Amendment. It is equally clear that the Commission's objections to the broadcast were based in part on its content. The order must therefore fall if, as Pacifica argues, the First Amendment prohibits all governmental regulation that depends on the content of speech. Our past cases demonstrate, however, that no such absolute rule is mandated by the Constitution....

The question in this case is whether a broadcast of patently offensive words dealing with sex and excretion may be regulated because of its content. Obscene materials have been denied the protection of the First Amendment because their content is so offensive to contemporary moral standards. *Roth* v. *United States*, 354 U.S. 476. But the fact that society may find speech offensive is not a sufficient reason for suppressing it. Indeed, if it is the speaker's opinion that gives offense, that consequence is a reason for according it constitutional protection. For it is a central tenet of the First Amendment that the government must remain neutral in the marketplace of ideas. If there were any reason to believe that the Commission's characterization of the Carlin monologue as offensive could be traced to its political content—or even to the fact that it satirized contemporary attitudes about four-letter words—First Amendment protection might be required. But that is simply not this case. These words offend for the same reasons that obscenity offends. Their place in the hierarchy of First Amendment values was aptly sketched by Mr. Justice Murphy when he said: "[S]uch utterances are no essential part of any exposition of ideas, and are of such slight social value as a step to truth that any benefit that may be derived from them is clearly outweighed by the social interest in order and morality." *Chaplinsky* v. *New Hampshire*, 315 U.S., at 572.

Although these words ordinarily lack literary, political, or scientific value, they are not entirely outside the protection of the First Amendment. Some uses of even the most offensive words are unquestionably protected. See, *e.g.*, *Hess* v. *Indiana*, 414 U.S. 105. Indeed, we may assume, *arguendo*, that this monologue would be protected in other contexts. Nonetheless, the constitutional protection accorded to a communication containing such patently offensive sexual and excretory language need not be the same in every context. It is a characteristic of speech such as this that both its capacity to offend and its "social value," to use Mr. Justice Murphy's term, vary with the circumstances. Words that are commonplace in one setting are shocking in another. To paraphrase Mr. Justice Harlan, one occasion's lyric is another's vulgarity....

In this case it is undisputed that the content of Pacifica's broadcast was "vulgar," "offensive," and "shocking." Because content of that character is not entitled to absolute constitutional protection under all circumstances, we must consider its context in order to determine whether the Commission's action was constitutionally permissible....

We have long recognized that each medium of expression presents special First Amendment problems. *Joseph Burstyn, Inc.* v. *Wilson*, 343 U.S. 495, 502–503. And of all forms of communication, it is broadcasting that has received the most limited First Amendment protection. Thus, although other speakers cannot be licensed except under laws that carefully define and narrow official discretion, a broadcaster may be deprived of his license and his forum if the Commission decides that such an action would serve "the public interest, convenience, and necessity." Similarly, although the First Amendment protects newspaper publishers from being required to print the replies of those whom they criticize, *Miami Herald Publishing Co.* v. *Tornillo*, 418 U.S. 241, it affords no such protection to broadcasters; on the contrary, they must give free time to the victims of their criticism. *Red Lion Broadcasting Co.* v. *FCC*, 395 U.S. 367.

The reasons for these distinctions are complex, but two have relevance to the present case. First, the broadcast media have established a uniquely pervasive presence in the lives of all Americans. Patently offensive, indecent material presented over the airwaves confronts the citizen, not only in public, but also in the privacy of the home, where the individual's right to be left alone plainly outweighs the First Amendment rights of an intruder. *Rowan* v. *Post Office Dept.*, 397 U.S. 728. Because the broadcast audience is constantly tuning in and out, prior warnings cannot completely protect the listener or viewer from unexpected program content. To say that one may avoid further offense by turning off the radio when he hears indecent language is like saying that the remedy for an assault is to run away after the first blow. One may hang up on an indecent phone call, but that option does not give the caller a constitutional immunity or avoid a harm that has already taken place.

Second, broadcasting is uniquely accessible to children, even those too young to read. Although Cohen's written message might have been incomprehensible to a first grader, Pacifica's broadcast could have enlarged a child's vocabulary in an instant. Other forms of offensive expression may be withheld from the young without restricting the expression at its source. Bookstores and motion picture theaters, for example, may be prohibited from making indecent material available to children. We held in *Ginsberg* v. *New York*, 390 U.S. 629, that the government's interest in the "well-being of its youth" and in supporting "parents' claim to authority in their own household" justified the regulation of otherwise protected expression. *Id.*, at 640 and 639. The case with which children may obtain access to broadcast material, coupled with the concerns recognized in *Ginsberg*, amply justify special treatment of indecent broadcasting.

It is appropriate, in conclusion, to emphasize the narrowness of our holding. This case does not involve a two-way radio conversation between a cab driver and a dispatcher, or a telecast of an Elizabethan comedy. We have not decided that an occasional expletive in either setting would justify any sanction or, indeed, that this broadcast would justify a criminal prosecution. The Commission's decision rested entirely on a nuisance rationale under which context is all-important. The concept requires consideration of a host of variables. The time of day was emphasized by the Commission. The content of the program in which the language is used will also affect the composition of the audience, and differences between radio, television, and perhaps closed-circuit transmissions, may also be relevant. As Mr. Justice Sutherland wrote, a "nuisance may be merely a right thing in the wrong place,—like a pig in the parlor instead of the barnyard." *Euclid* v. *Ambler Realty Co.*, 272 U.S. 365, 388. We simply hold that when the Commission finds that a pig has entered the parlor, the exercise of its regulatory power does not depend on proof that the pig is obscene.

The judgment of the Court of Appeals is reversed.

Justice Stevens, who authored the Court's opinion, included a section commanding the support of Chief Justice Burger and Justice Rehnquist. Although the plurality did not represent the views of a majority, it maintained that indecent expression, even if it was constitutionally protected, "surely lies at the periphery of First Amendment concern." A majority of the Court has yet to coalesce formally in support of the notion that protected, albeit indecent, expression should be afforded less constitutional regard. Justice Powell, in a concurring opinion, disagreed with the notion that the Court could decide on the basis of content what "speech protected by the First Amendment is most 'valuable' and hence deserving of the most protection." He joined in upholding the FCC's action, however, based upon interests in protecting children and unconsenting adults from the expression at issue. Powell also expressed doubt whether the decision would prevent any adult wanting "to receive Carlin's message in Carlin's words from doing so."

Justice Brennan, in a lengthy dissent, maintained that the Court had misconceived the privacy interests of persons who voluntarily had allowed radio into their presence and wrongly derogated the concerns of those who would be willing participants in discourse offensive to some. He criticized the Court for denying minors "access to materials that are not obscene, and are therefore protected" and undercutting parental autonomy to decide the subjects to which children are exposed. Unlike zoning ordinances governing the location of adult expression, Brennan found no purpose in the FCC's action but to control content.

It is quite evident that I find the Court's attempt to unstitch the warp and woof of First Amendment law in an effort to reshape its fabric to cover the patently wrong result the Court reaches in this case dangerous as well as lamentable. Yet there runs throughout the opinions of my Brothers POWELL and STEVENS another vein I find equally disturbing: a depressing inability to appreciate that in our land of cultural pluralism, there are many who think, act, and talk differently from the Members of this Court, and who do not share their fragile sensibilities. It is only an acute ethnocentric myopia that enables the Court to approve the censorship of communications solely because of the words they contain.

"A word is not a crystal, transparent and unchanged, it is the skin of a living thought and may vary greatly in color and content according to the circumstances and the time in which it is used." *Towne* v. *Eisner*, 245 U.S. 418, 425 (1918) (Holmes, J.). The words that the Court and the Commission find so unpalatable may be the stuff of everyday conversations in some, if not many, of the innumerable subcultures that compose this Nation. Academic research indicates that this is indeed the case. See B. Jackson, "Get Your Ass in the Water and Swim Like Me" (1974); J. Dillard, Black English (1972); W. Labov, Language in the Inner City: Studies in the Black English Vernacular (1972). As one researcher concluded, "[w]ords generally considered obscene like 'bullshit' and 'fuck' are considered neither obscene nor derogatory in the [black] vernacular except in particular contextual situations and when used with certain intonations." C. Bins, "Toward an Ethnography of Contemporary African American Oral Poetry," Language and Linguistics Working Papers No. 5, p. 82 (Georgetown Univ. Press 1972). Cf. *Keefe* v. *Geanakos*, 418 F.2d 359, 361 (CA1 1969) (finding the use of the word "motherfucker" commonplace among young radicals and protesters).

Today's decision will thus have its greatest impact on broadcasters desiring to reach, and listening audiences composed of, persons who do not share the Court's view as to which words or expressions are acceptable and who, for a variety of reasons, including a conscious desire to flout majoritarian conventions, express themselves using words that may be regarded as offensive by those from different socio-economic backgrounds. In this context, the Court's decision may be seen for what, in the broader perspective, it really is: another of the dominant culture's inevitable efforts to force those groups who do not share its mores to conform to its way of thinking, acting, and speaking.

The *Pacifica* opinion thus evinces the collision of diversification ideals and dominant tastes.

3. Post-*Pacifica* Regulation

Twice emphasizing an "inten[t] strictly to observe the narrowness of the *Pacifica* holding," the Commission (1) renewed a license despite a morality organization's objection that a public television station's broadcast of "Masterpiece Theater," "Monty Python's Flying Circus," and other programs "consistently [propagated] offensive, vulgar . . . material" and (2) denied a request to prohibit use of the word "nigger," which had been uttered on the air by a political candidate. In the latter instance, the agency further noted that its concern with indecency was limited to references of a sexual or excretory nature. Even prior to the Court's decision in *Pacifica*, the Commission had issued a clarification to the effect that it was not concerned with offensive speech arising in the course of news coverage, at least when no opportunity existed for editing. The limiting principles, however, did not deter critical evaluation of the FCC's regulatory pitch and of the *Pacifica* decision itself.

The rationales for regulating indecent expression are both new and old. Concern with the medium's pervasive or intrusive nature and its accessibility to children represented fresh grounds for content control of the least protected component of the press. The regulatory predicates, however, borrow from rationales constructed near the turn of the century in response to the development and emergence of other mass media. Unlike the scarcity premise, which has operated as a platform from which diversity aims were pursued, even if unsatisfactorily, the predicate of *Pacifica* is candidly conceived to inhibit expression and define permissible bounds of diversity.

The unique characteristics attributed to broadcasting and its consequently diminished First Amendment status help explain why the Court employed what appeared to be a less exacting standard of review than it would in another setting. A city ordinance that barred exhibition of nudity on drive-in theater screens, for instance, was invalidated. Despite arguments in support of the need to protect children, the Court in *Erznoznik v. Jacksonville* found the measure overbroad to the extent that it reached nonobscene expression. With respect to privacy interests, it noted that offended persons could "avoid further bombardment of [their] sensibilities by averting [their] eyes."

Also "pitting the First Amendment rights of speakers against the privacy rights of those who may be unwilling viewers or auditors," and raising questions relating to the presence of children, was the case of an individual wearing a jacket with the words "fuck the draft" on it. Although it may be no less difficult to avert one's gaze under such circumstances than to switch channels, and it is conceivable that a child might focus for a prolonged time upon the message, the Court found such expression comfortably within a First Amendment ambit that presumed official inability to make principled distinctions based upon taste. In *Cohen v. California*, it thus lectured that

[s]urely the State has no right to cleanse public discourse to the point where it is grammatically palatable to the most squeamish of us. Yet no readily ascertainable general principle exists for stopping short of that result were we to affirm the [conviction for offensive conduct]. For, while the four-letter word being litigated here is perhaps more distasteful than most others of its genre, it is nevertheless often true that one man's vulgarity is another's lyric. Indeed, we think it is largely because governmental officials cannot make principled decisions in this area that the Constitution leaves matters of taste and style so largely to the individual.

Upon examination, the rationales enabling the Court to "avert its eyes" from the instruction of *Cohen* seem to raise as many questions as they answer. Concern that children have ready access to, or are peculiarly vulnerable to the influence of, radio and television has yet to translate into conclusive findings of profoundly adverse effects. If access and exposure are relative realities and lend themselves to variable context-based standards, it is unclear why equally if not more stringent controls do not operate against adult-oriented publications and offensive street or playground epithets. Finally, the Court has long recognized parental autonomy as a constitutionally protected interest and adverted to it in facilitating other First Amendment guarantees and even curtailing a competing fundamental right. Despite the availability of inexpensive technology enabling parents to control television viewing of a child even when they are not present and thereby to exercise more effective control than exists against chance encounters in public, its pertinence has yet to be extensively factored into the context of broadcasting.

Privacy concerns, although adverted to in support of content regulation, arguably cut in the opposite direction. Constitutional concepts of privacy pertain not only to intrusion into a protected sphere but to personal autonomy. Insofar as a constitutional violation requires state action, it is the latter notion of privacy that would seem to be implicated in a constitutional sense by indecent or offensive broadcasting. Traditional First Amendment notions favoring autonomous over authoritative selection also might favor further an emphasis upon personal rather than official control. Pursuant to a focus upon personal autonomy rather than official protection of sensitivity, self-help remedies akin to asking an unwanted house guest to leave might figure more prominently. Such questions were avoided, however, given a diminished standard of review for a less protected medium.

In *Telecommunications Research and Action Center v. Federal Communications Commission*, the court of appeals suggested that the real worry about broadcasting, especially its pervasiveness, is the sense that "it is the immediacy and power of broadcasting that [warrant] different treatment." If so, the premise would deviate from constitutional norms that disfavor official control tied to degree of influence. The *Pacifica* decision, in sum, has elicited criticism for departing from the concept of the First Amendment as guaranteeing diverse expressive opportunities and individualizing responsibility for selection.

The first amendment, in theory, trusts the public to make sound decisions and assumes the risk that it will not. A system of official control designed to curb expression that may offend or affront has the potential for reaching views that merely are unpopular or unorthodox. The transfer of responsibility for content evaluation thus has more profoundly subversive potential than any harmful tendencies of indecent or offensive expression.

In a constitutional value system that supposedly favors pluralism and autonomous over authoritative selection, adverse consequences of expression may be addressed or remedied by preemptive or reactive personal action. Official catering to the tastes of some to dictate what information is available to others represents inverted thinking. Individuals wanting to see or hear what may not be broadcast, it is true, have alternative means of obtaining access to such material. The burden and cost of practical private regulation that would effectively screen out unwanted expression, however, would be incurred only once and consequently be less imposing than the tariff on multiple diversity-motivated purchases. Despite the disparity of costs, which seem to favor first amendment concerns, the Court essentially has favored the taxing of pluralism rather than intolerance.

Competing against criticism that the FCC had reached too deeply into a constitutionally protected sphere was the claim that it had not gone far enough. A decade after *Pacifica*, the Commission revisited the question of indecency in response to complaints concerning sexually explicit programming. In a series of orders against three broadcast stations and an amateur radio operator, and in an accompanying announcement of new enforcement standards, the FCC attempted "to clarify when it will exercise its enforcement authority...in the future." In so doing, the commission expressly observed that instead of concerning itself merely with the seven words at issue in *Pacifica*, it would "apply the generic definition of broadcast indecency advanced in *Pacifica*, which is: 'language or material that depicts or describes, in terms patently offensive as measured by contemporary community standards for the broadcast medium, sexual or excretory activities or organs.' "

Unlike previous indecency actions that had concerned programming directed toward small, discrete audiences, one of the complaints concerned a "shock radio" format that drew a large audience in a major market. Rejecting characterizations of the speech at issue as "incidental use of sexually-oriented language, sexual innuendo and double entendre," the FCC in *Infinity Broadcasting Corp. of Pennsylvania* found "explicit references to masturbation, ejaculation, breast size, penis size, sexual intercourse, nudity, urination, oral-genital contact, erections, sodomy, bestiality, menstruation, and testicles." Although finding none of the subjects "*per se* beyond the realm of acceptable broadcast discussion," the Commission determined that particular references were "patently offensive, and their sexual and excretory import...clear." It noted that presentation consisted not of an "occasional off-color reference or expletive but a dwelling on matters sexual and excretory, in a pandering and titillating fashion." Context thus "aggravate[d] rather then dilute[d] or ameliorate[d] the patent offensiveness of what [was] said."

Citing again the notion of indecency as "largely a function of context," and noting that indecency is actionable when "a reasonable risk [exists] that children may be in the audience," the FCC in *The Regents of the University of California* found sexually explicit lyrics in recorded music played on a university radio station to be indecent. Specifically, it identified "several clearly discernible references to sexual organs and activities...[that were] patently offensive by contemporary community standards for the broadcast medium." The observation suggested the possibility that standards for discerning indecency, unlike the determination of obscenity pursuant to local or state community criteria, are national. Later, the FCC would confirm that the standard was of "an average broadcast viewer," based not "on a local standard, but...on a broader standard for broadcasting generally." The *Regents of the University of California* case also introduced a significant modification with respect to the timing of indecent programming. Although the FCC had previously "indicat[ed] that it might be permissible to air programs containing indecent material after 10 p.m. when accompanied by a warning," it asserted that "no such arbitrary time of day will govern hereafter." Instead, it would examine "[d]ata concerning audience composition... to assess the risk that children may be present." Pursuant to such an assessment, the Commission found that "a significant number of children remain in the...area radio audience during the time here in question."

In the third broadcasting case, *Pacifica Foundation, Inc.*, the FCC found that the presentation of excerpts from a play appearing in Los Angeles and an interview with its directors and actors constituted actionable indecency. The director had characterized the play, which concerned two homosexuals dying of AIDS, as "blazingly erotic." The FCC, however, focused upon extensive use of "patently offensive" language referring to sexual and excretory organs or functions. Rejecting claims that the presentation should be considered in light of the play's broader message, the Commission concluded that its patently offensive nature was aggravated rather than diminished by context. It also dismissed arguments that the station's audience rarely consisted of children and "point[ed] out that the test of indecency focuses on the *risk* of the presence of children in the audience [emphasis in original]."

Because prior actions had suggested the possibility that the Commission might be concerned with indecency to the extent that it implicated the specific words at issue in *Pacifica* and broadcasts after 10 P.M., the FCC imposed no actual sanctions. Rather, it issued warnings in the individual cases and to all broadcasters that the material at issue would be actionable under newly clarified indecency standards. From its rulings in the three broadcast cases and another case concerning an amateur radio licensee, the Commission extracted and abstracted a general statement of principle encased in *New Indecency Enforcement Standards to be Applied to All Broadcast and Amateur Radio Licenses.*

The Commission, by this public notice, puts all broadcast and amateur radio licensees on notice as to new standards that the Commission will apply in enforcing the prohibition against obscene and indecent transmissions.

Reaffirming its authority to regulate the broadcast and amateur radio transmission of indecent or obscene material, the Commission took action on April 16, 1987, against four licensees and articulated standards to clarify when it will exercise its enforcement authority over such situations in the future. The actions reflect the Commission's intent to apply the definition of indecent transmissions set forth in the *Pacifica* case, which was affirmed by the Supreme Court in 1978. *Pacifica Foundation*, 56 FCC 2d 94 (1975). *aff'd. FCC v. Pacifica Foundation*, 438 U.S. 726 (1978). Prior to the Commission's April 16 actions, the Commission had limited its enforcement efforts to the specific material involved in *Pacifica*, that is, to seven particular words that were broadcast in a George Carlin monologue.

On April 16, however, the Commission determined that it is more appropriate to apply the *generic* definition of broadcast indecency advanced in *Pacifica*, which is:

"language or material that depicts or describes, in terms patently offensive as measured by contemporary community standards for the broadcast medium, sexual or excretory activities or organs."

The Commission specifically ruled that such indecency will be actionable if broadcast or transmitted at a time of day when there is a "reasonable risk that children may be in the audience," a standard also upheld by the Supreme Court in the *Pacifica* case. Section 1464 of the Criminal Code, 18 U.S.C. Section 1464, prohibits the broadcast of obscene or indecent material; and the Communications Act of 1934 empowers the Commission to impose a range of civil sanctions when a violation of Section 1464 occurs, including the issuance of warnings, the imposition of fines and, in severe cases, the revocation of licenses. *See* 47 U.S.C. Sections 312(a)(6), 503(b)(1)(D).

With respect to indecent speech, the Commission stated that repetitive use of specific sexual or excretory words or phrases is not the only material that can constitute indecency. It further stated, however, that if a broadcast consists solely of the use of expletives, then deliberate and repetitive use of such expletives in a patently offensive manner would be a requisite to a finding of indecency. If a broadcast goes beyond the use of expletives, the Commission noted, then the context in which the allegedly indecent language is broadcast will serve as an important factor in determining whether it is, in fact, indecent.

The Commission reaffirmed the *Pacifica* test that indecency will be actionable when there is a reasonable risk that children may be in the audience, but found that this benchmark is not susceptible to a uniform standard. The Commission addressed the risk of children in the audience during the time frame and with regard to the market before it in each case.

The Commission found that, despite prior assumptions that children were not in the broadcasting audience at 10:00 p.m., recent evidence for the markets involved indicates that there is still a reasonable risk that children may be in the listening audience at the hours during which the relevant broadcasts were made. The Commission further stated that indecent broadcasts could be made at times when there is not a reasonable risk that children may be in the audience and that, when such broadcasts were made, advance warnings would continue to be required.

In reaffirming its authority to regulate indecent broadcasts and amateur transmissions, the Commission specifically rejected the rationale that scarcity of the airwaves gives it the requisite authority to regulate indecency. The Commission also explained that it was not diminishing the First Amendment rights of broadcasters. Rather, the Commission pointed out that the regulation of indecency by channeling it to hours when there is not a reasonable risk that children may be in the audience is consistent with the First Amendment rights afforded newspapers and magazines.

The Commission relied on the nuisance rationale propounded in *Pacifica*, which generally speaks to channeling behavior rather than prohibiting it. Furthermore, the Commission found its action consistent with the principle established by the Supreme Court in *Young v. American Mini-Theatres*, 427 U.S. 50 (1976), and reaffirmed in *Renton v. Playtime Theatres, Inc.*, 106 S. Ct. 925 (1986), that reasonable time, place and manner restrictions may be imposed on the dissemination of indecent material consistent with the First Amendment. The Commission concluded that, in order to limit children's access to such material on radio and television, time channeling is a reasonable time, place and manner restriction. The Commission noted that the owner of a movie theater is able to separate adults from children and can be forced to refuse children admission to certain films, and, likewise, the owner of a book store is able to separate adults from children and can be required not to sell certain publications to children. For the broadcast medium, however, the Commission reasoned that the only practicable means for separating adults from children in the broadcast audience is to impose time restrictions.

In applying the newly articulated standards to the three broadcast cases and the amateur radio case before it, the Commission determined that each of the licensees in question had broadcast or transmitted material that would constitute actionable indecency. The Commission also acknowledged, however, that prior rulings may have indicated to licensees that only repetitive use of the specific words at issue in the 1978 *Pacifica* case would be actionable if broadcast prior to 10:00 p.m. Accordingly, the FCC limited its sanctions in the broadcast cases to issuing a warning to each licensee. The Commission stated however, that violations by these licensees occurring after their receipt of their respective warnings would render them liable to more severe sanctions. The Commission hereby notifies all other broadcasters and amateur radio licensees that violations of the Commission's new standards occurring after the publication of this Public Notice will subject them to the full range of sanctions available to the Commission.

The broadcast of obscene material, by contrast, is prohibited at all times. To be obscene, material must meet a three-prong test: (1) an average person, applying contemporary community standards, must find that the material, as a whole, appeals to the prurient interest; (2) the material must depict or describe, in a patently offensive way, sexual conduct specifically defined by the applicable state law; and (3) the material, taken as a whole, must lack serious literary, artistic, political, or scientific value. *See Miller v. California*, 413 U.S. 15 (1973).

In each of the cases before it, the Commission noted that, although it was addressing the particular facts therein, the decisions will have a precedential effect on all broadcast and amateur licensees. The Commission also noted that there have been questions as to the Commission's enforcement policy in this complicated area of the law and, through its authority to issue declaratory rulings in order to remove uncertainty, *see* 5 U.S.C. Section 554(e), it has sought to resolve those questions in these proceedings.

The new standards were particularly significant to the extent that they broadened the concept of indecency and assigned to licensees responsibility for determining whether children might be in the audience and figuring out what, if any, time was appropriate for programming that might offend some persons. Concern with identifying proper perimeters was particularly acute insofar as the Supreme Court's decision in *Pacifica* related back to a single complaint over a program aired at a time when it might have been reasonable to assume that children were in school. Responding to requests for further clarification, the FCC constructed a safe harbor for indecent programs and reaffirmed its rulings and rationales in a reconsideration order. It thus determined that indecent material could be broadcast from midnight to 6 A.M. The court of appeals, in *Action for Children's Television v. Federal Communications Commission*, determined that the time restriction had not been adequately justified. In remanding the orders in *Regents of the University of California* and *Pacifica Foundation* pertaining to material aired after 10 P.M. but before midnight, it directed the FCC to provide clear notice of reasonably determined times when indecent programming could be safely broadcast.

Soon thereafter, Congress directed the Commission to enforce its indecency standards comprehensively rather than by time channeling. The FCC promulgated a rule prohibiting indecent broadcasting at all hours, but the court of appeals stayed implementation pending judicial review. Before the merits of the ban were argued, the Supreme Court, in *Sable Communications of California, Inc. v. Federal Communications Commission,* invalidated a congressional enactment insofar as it prohibited indecent telephone communications. The *Sable* decision, discussed in Chapter 12, noted that "government may . . . regulate the content of constitutionally protected speech in order to promote a compelling interest if it chooses the least restrictive means to further the articulated interest."

Following the Supreme Court's determination that the congressional ban on telephone dial-a-porn services was unconstitutional to the extent that it proscribed nonobscene expression, discussed in Chapter 12, the FCC readjusted its regulatory bearing. After the case concerning the congressionally directed twenty-four-hour-a-day ban was remanded to it, the FCC in 1990 abandoned time-channeling notions in favor of comprehensive proscription. Critical to the Commission's revised policy was its sense that, unlike the situation in the dial-a-porn context, technology did not afford a less restrictive regulatory alternative. Because children are part of the audience at all hours, the FCC in *Enforcement of Prohibitions Against Broadcast Indecency in 18 U.S.C. § 1464,* concluded that a total ban was the least restrictive means of accounting for a compelling regulatory interest.

Based on the record in this proceeding and the Court's decision in *Sable,* we believe that the Commission's enforcement of a 24-hour prohibition on indecent broadcast programming comports with the First Amendment. Using the "compelling interest/narrowly tailored" standard set forth in *Sable,* we conclude that a 24-hour prohibition is the most narrowly tailored means of effectively promoting the government's compelling interest in protecting children from broadcast indecency because there is a reasonable risk that a significant number of children are in the broadcast audience at all times of day and night. . . . In order to tailor our enforcement of the 24-hour prohibition on indecent broadcasting as narrowly as possible, however, in actual cases of alleged indecent broadcasting stations will be permitted to demonstrate that children were not in fact present in the broadcast audience for the market at the time the programming at issue aired.

In *Action for Children's Television v. Federal Communications Commission,* consistent with its earlier decision, the court of appeals determined that "curtailment of 'safe harbor' broadcast periods impermissibly intruded on constitutionally protected expression interests." The court emphasized that speech characterized as indecent but not obscene is constitutionally protected and may be regulated "only with due respect for the high value our Constitution places on freedom and choice in what the people say and hear." It asserted that content restriction is allowable only when "the regulation is a precisely drawn means of serving a compelling governmental interest in the physical and psychological well-being of minors." Although acknowledging a compelling interest, the court concluded that the precision necessary to accommodate first amendment interests could not be satisfied without a reasonable safe harbor rule. Accordingly, it directed the FCC to identify when indecent expression may be broadcast, specifically define "children" and "reasonable risk" for time channeling purposes, and amplify the scope of the government's interest in regulating indecent broadcasts. The decision, as the court of appeals noted, left the Commission in the same position it occupied after the previous *Action for Children's Television* decision and before Congress's directive.

Regulation of broadcast indecency suggests at least the possibility of doctrinal incongruity. Insofar as the Commission emphasizes the opportunity to obtain indecent expression from nonbroadcasting sources, it appears to abandon media-specific standards and factor in the existence of a broader media universe. By singling out broadcasting for special indecency controls, however, the Commission has qualified the notion of First Amendment parity articulated in the fairness context. Paradoxically, by referring to other media and refusing to examine broadcasting in an isolated sense, the FCC has reinforced the medium's unique status as the least constitutionally protected element of the press.

B. CHILDREN'S PROGRAMMING

Concern with the presence of youth in the audience and with their well-being also has engendered proposals for officially influencing the general nature and availability of children's programming. The FCC's response to such initiatives, however, has been more consonant with the deference to licensee discretion characterizing fairness regulation than its more assertive posture with respect to indecency. Interest in promoting the number and variety of programs directed at children implicates issues of editorial discretion. Concern with actual content on grounds that it might have an adverse impact on children must compete against constitutional principles that militate against "reducing the adult population . . . to [receiving] only what is fit for children."

1. Quantitative Concerns

The FCC at times has flirted with, but nonetheless has refrained from, adopting quantitative standards for children's programming. In 1974, it issued a policy statement that essentially requested licensees to make reasonable efforts to increase programming on weekdays and weekends that would educate and inform rather than just entertain children. The proposal had no appreciable effect upon the amount of such programming provided by broadcasters. The commission concluded that the size of the particular audience and the limited interest of advertisers in it combined to create a disincentive for commercial programming aimed at children. In 1979, therefore, the FCC initiated a rulemaking to consider various options ranging from establishing mandatory programming requirements to considering programming from sources other than commercial broadcasting.

Four years later, the FCC determined that licensees had an obligation to consider the needs and interests of all segments of the communities they serviced. The Commission rejected, however, the concept of mandatory quotas on grounds that they would invade constitutionally protected editorial interests and discourage innovation and experimentation. Critical to its decision was a broadened focus upon sources other than commercial broadcasting that led to the conclusion, contrary to previous intimation, that an extensive and diverse menu of children's programming existed. In *Action for Children's Television v. Federal Communications Commission*, the court of appeals upheld the Commission's consideration of the media universe rather than the specific medium. Although the court noted that alternatives such as public broadcasting and cable did not relieve commercial broadcasters of their obligation to serve the public interest, it allowed that the FCC need not disregard the presence and effect of other media.

While the FCC's decision not to impose quantitative standards was under review, a challenge arose in the course of a license renewal proceeding based upon a broadcaster's failure to provide any regularly scheduled weekday children's programming. The petitioning group in *Washington Association for Television and Children v. Federal Communications Commission* claimed that such neglect violated the Commission's policy on children's programming. The court of appeals, however, found no requirement for regularly scheduled programming explicit or implicit in the policy. It noted the anomaly that would result, moreover, if a broadcaster providing regularly scheduled cartoons was found in compliance and a licensee offering educational specials was found in violation.

2. Qualitative Concerns

Concern with the actual content of broadcasting has engendered official response not only with respect to indecency but in regard to violence and advertising. Although the FCC has been generally deferential in its posture, it has acted at least unofficially to respond to concerns with excessive violence.

A. VIOLENCE

The FCC has refrained from taking action to control directly programming of a violent nature. Following a request that the Commission respond to televised violence in the same way it did to cigarette advertisements, the FCC explicated its reasons for exercising restraint. Despite determinations by the surgeon general that violent programs, like cigarettes, might have undesirable individual and societal results, the FCC concluded in *George D. Corey* that programming of a general nature did not present a controversial issue of public importance. It thus refused to invoke the fairness doctrine or require broadcast warnings that subject matter might be hazardous to a child's "mental health and well being." A dissenting commissioner found the presence of violence in general programming an even stronger reason for intervention.

In a subsequent *Report on Violent, Indecent, and Obscene Material*, the FCC observed that with respect to "sexually-oriented or violent material which might be inappropriate for [children], industry self-regulation [was] preferable to the adoption of rigid governmental standards." Its preference for private control was premised upon grounds that government regulation would intrude "too deeply in[to] programming content, raising serious constitutional questions," and necessitate judgments that were too subjective. The report also documented the Commission's efforts to encourage broadcasters to police themselves. What resulted was the family viewing hour, which, as a function of licensee practice rather than official mandate, was designed to eliminate violent or sexually oriented programming from early prime-time viewing hours.

Regulatory action to limit violent and sexually-oriented programming which is neither obscene nor indecent is less desirable than effective self-regulation, since government-imposed limitations raise sensitive First Amendment problems. In addition, any rule making in these areas would require finding an appropriate balance between the need to protect children from harmful material and the adult audience's interest in diverse programming. Government rules could create the risk of improper governmental interference in sensitive, subjective decisions about programming, could tend to freeze present standards and could also discourage creative developments in the medium.

With these considerations in mind, Chairman Wiley initiated the first of a series of discussions with the executives of the three major television networks on November 22, 1974. In suggesting such meetings, the Chairman sought to serve as a catalyst for the achievement of meaningful self-regulatory reform. He suggested the following specific proposals for the networks to consider:

> (1) *New Commitment*—There should be a new commitment to reduce the level and intensity of violent and sexually-oriented material.
> (2) *Scheduling*—Programs which are considered to be inappropriate for viewing by young children should not be broadcast prior to 9 p.m. local time.
> (3) *Warnings*—At times when such programs are broadcast, they should include

audio and video warning at the outset of the program (and at the first "break"), in addition, similar to the practice in France, a small white dot might be placed in the corner of the screen during the course of a program to warn those viewers who tune in while the program is in progress that it may not be appropriate for viewing by young children.

(4) *Advance Notice*—Affiliates should be provided warnings in advance to be included in local TV Guide and newspaper program listings and promotional materials.

In addition, the Chairman raised the possibility of adoption of a rating system similar to that used in the motion picture industry. In making these suggestions, it was understood that the decision as to which programs are so excessively violent or explicitly sexually-oriented as to be inappropriate for young children would remain in the broadcaster's sound discretion. Also, it was recognized that non-entertainment programming, such as news, public affairs, documentaries and instructional programs would be exempt from the scheduling rule....

Not all of the proposals advanced by the Commission were found to be acceptable by the networks. However, each of the networks developed a set of guidelines which it believed should govern its programming, and policy statements incorporating these guidelines were released to the public. A common element of the three statements is that they provide that the first hour of network entertainment programming in prime time will be suitable for viewing by the entire family....

Taken together, the three network statements and the NAB proposed policy would establish the following guidelines for the Fall 1975 television season:

(1) *Scheduling*—"The first hour of network entertainment programming in prime time" and "the immediately preceding hour," is to be designated as a "Family Viewing" period. In effect, this would include the period between 7 p.m. and 9 p.m. Eastern Time during the first six days of the week. On Sunday, network programming typically begins at a different time; the guidelines would therefore provide that the "Family Viewing" period will begin and end a half-hour earlier.

(2) *Warnings*—"Viewer advisories" will be broadcast in audio and video form "in the occasional case when an entertainment program" broadcast during the "Family Viewing" period contains material which may be unsuitable for viewing by younger family members. In addition, "viewer advisories" will be used in later evening hours for programs which contain material that might be disturbing to significant portions of the viewing audience.

(3) *Advance Notice*—Broadcasters will attempt to notify publishers of television program listings as to programs which will contain "advisories." Responsible use of "advisories" in promotional material is also advised.

Thus, the network and NAB proposals are designed to give parents general notice that after the evening news, and for the duration of the designated period, the broadcaster will make every effort to assure that programming presented (including series and movies) will be appropriate for the entire family. After that time, parents themselves will have to exercise greater caution to be confident that particular programs are suitable for their children. Warnings would continue to be broadcast in later hours to notify viewers of those programs that might be disturbing to significant portions of the audiences.

The Commission believes that the recent actions taken by the three networks and the National Association of Broadcasters Television Code Review Board are commendable and go a long way toward establishing appropriate protections for children from violent and sexually-oriented material. This new commitment suggests that the broadcast industry is prepared to regulate itself in a fashion that will obviate any need for governmental regulation in this sensitive area.

It is inevitable that there will be some disagreements over particular programs and the question of their suitability for children. Interpretation of which programs are appropriate for family viewing remains, as it should, the responsibility of the broadcaster. The success of this program will depend upon whether that responsibility is exercised both with good faith and common sense judgment. Thus, meaningful evaluation by Congress and the public of the efficacy of these self-regulatory measures must await observation of how they are interpreted and applied by the broadcasters.

The industry proposal represents an effort to strike a balance between two conflicting objectives. On the one hand, it is imperative that licensees act to assist parents in protecting their children from objectionable programming. On the other hand, broadcasters believe that if the medium is to achieve its full maturity, it must continue to present sensitive and controversial themes which are appropriate, and of interest, to adult audiences.

Parents, in our view, have—and should retain—the primary responsibility for their children's well-being. This traditional and revered principle, like other examples which could be cited has been adversely affected by the corrosive processes of technological and social change in twentieth-century American life. Nevertheless, we believe that it deserves continuing affirmation.

Television, as a guest in the American home, also has some responsibilities in this area. In providing a forum for the discussion of excessive violence and sexual material on television, the Commission has sought to remind broadcasters of their responsibility to provide some measure of support to concerned parents.

The family viewing hour accurately may be depicted as an example of regulation by raised eyebrow. In fact, the action was challenged as a product of official coercion. Although the court of appeals in *Writers Guild of America West, Inc. v. American Broadcasting Co., Inc.* remanded various claims to the Commission, the issues were never formally resolved in court. Nor is the family viewing hour an enforced policy.

B. ADVERTISING

Consistent with its general deregulatory posture and consequent disinclination to set quantitative standards for children's programming, the FCC in 1986 refused to ban or limit advertising on children's programs. Its determination "that the general deregulation of television commercialization extends to children's television" was found to be without a "reasoned basis," in *Action for Children's Television v. Federal Communications Commission,* especially given the commission's long-standing premise that "the television marketplace *does not* function adequately when children make up the audience [emphasis in the original]." The FCC has implemented qualitative standards requiring a clear distinction between programming and advertising on children's programs. The Commission has determined that programs based upon products marketed for children did not constitute a commercial. Key to its findings was a lack of "interweaving of commercials and program content," given actual dedication of advertising time to products other than those featured in the program. Congress, however, has directed the agency to pursue an inquiry into commercial guidelines for children's television that would focus upon programs developed around such products.

In 1988, Congress enacted legislation directing the FCC to set standards for children-oriented advertising and prescribing quantitative standards, but the president vetoed it. Two years later, the Children's Television Act of 1990 was passed. The law limits advertising aimed at children to 12 minutes per hour on weekdays and 10.5 minutes per hour on weekends.

C. DRUGS

Prompted in part by concern with children is the FCC's response to programming that may cast illegal drug use in a favorable light. The FCC placed broadcasters on notice that they were required "to have knowledge of the content of their programming and on the basis of this knowledge to evaluate the desirability of broadcasting music dealing with drug use." Licensees may fulfill their obligation to obtain specific knowledge by prescreening by a responsible station employee, monitoring selections as they are played, or evaluating public complaints.

A First Amendment challenge in *Yale Broadcasting Co. v. Federal Communications Commission* claimed an analogy to the principle that a bookseller cannot be required to examine every book in the store to ensure that none is obscene. The court of appeals distinguished the circumstances of broadcasting from bookselling, however, on grounds that fewer works had to be evaluated and that knowledge could be obtained without prescreening. It also minimized the possibility of any serious sanctions in the event that a licensee misinterpreted or failed to identify what are often incoherent or obscure lyrics. In a manner reminiscent of the *Pacifica* decision, the court observed that "[a]t some point along the scale of human intelligibility the sounds produced may slide over from characteristics of free speech, which should be protected, to those of noise pollution, which the Commission has ample authority to debate."

Chief Judge Bazelon, in dissent, maintained that the "responsibility" requirement in practice could translate into "prohibition." Even though he conceded the significance of the regulatory interest, he suggested that the court had neglected pertinent constitutional considerations, including whether the expression was protected or was actually harmful and, if so, whether alternative remedies would have been more appropriate. Serious First Amendment concerns also were expressed in Justice Douglas's dissent from the Supreme Court's refusal to review the case.

MR. JUSTICE DOUGLAS, dissenting

In March 1971, the FCC issued a public notice, Licensee Responsibility to Review Records Before Their Broadcast, 28 F. C. C. 2d 409, which was interpreted in many quarters as a prohibition on the playing of "drug related" songs by licensees. That belief was strengthened five weeks later when the Commission's Bureau of Complaints and Compliance provided broadcasters with the names of 22 songs labeled "drug oriented" on the basis of their lyrics. The industry widely viewed this as a list of banned songs, and many licensees quickly acted to remove other songs from the air as well. Some announcers were fired for playing suspect songs.

In April the Commission denied a petition for reconsideration, but attempted to "clarify" its previous order. 31 F. C. C. 2d 377. But although it repudiated the list of banned songs, it reiterated the basic threat by noting that "the broadcaster could jeopardize his license by failing to exercise licensee responsibility in this area." The nature of that responsibility was unclear. The new statement indicated reaffirmation of the prior decision, yet two concurring commissioners indicated that it restored the status quo to the March notice. It seems clear, however, that the Commission majority intended to coerce broadcasters into refusing to play songs that in the Commission's judgment were somehow "drug related." The April order suggested the prescreening of songs as one method of compliance. And in subsequent testimony before Congress, the Chairman of the Commission stated that if a licensee was playing songs that in the Commission's judgment "promote the use of hard drugs," "I know what I would do, I would probably vote to take the license away."

Still unsure of its responsibilities, but desiring to avoid distorting its artistic judgments by superimposing the Commission's vague sociological ones, petitioner Yale Broadcasting Company drafted its own station policy and submitted it to the Commission, asking for a declaratory ruling on whether it complied with the Commission's orders. The station proposed to fulfill its duties in this area by public service and news programming rather than by censoring its music. It elaborated its policy in a six-page statement. The Commission, finding the proposed policy too "abstract," declined to issue any declaratory ruling. The petitioners then brought this action, challenging the Commission's actions on First Amendment grounds, and arguing that the regulations were impermissibly vague. Petitioners also argued that they should have been the subject of formal rule-making procedures.

In *Columbia Broadcasting System, Inc.* v. *Democratic National Committee*, 412 U.S. 94, 148 (1973) (concurring in judgment), I indicated my view that TV and radio stand in the same protected position under the First Amendment as do newspapers and magazines. I had not participated in the earlier opinion in *Red Lion Broadcasting Co.* v. *FCC*, 395 U.S. 367 (1969), which placed broadcasters under a different regime, authorizing governmental regulation to ensure "fairness" of presentation. I explained in *Columbia Broadcasting, supra*, the inevitable danger resulting from placing such powers in governmental hands—a danger appreciated by the Framers of the First Amendment. "The Fairness Doctrine has no place in our First Amendment regime. It puts the head of the camel inside the tent and enables administration after administration to toy with TV or radio in order to serve its sordid or its benevolent ends." 412 U.S., at 154. The instant case well illustrates those dangers.

I doubt that anyone would seriously entertain the notion that consistent with the First Amendment the Government could force a newspaper out of business if its news stories betrayed too much sympathy with those arrested on marihuana charges, or because it published articles by drug advocates such as Timothy Leary. The proposition is so clear that rarely has the Government ever tried such a thing. . . . If the Government set up a new bureau with the job of reviewing newspaper stories for such "dangerous" tendencies, and with the power to put out of business those publications which failed to conform to the bureau's standards, the publisher would not have to wait until his newspaper had been destroyed to challenge the bureau's authority. The threat of governmental action alone would impose a prohibited restraint upon the press. "[I]nhibition as well as prohibition against the exercise of precious First Amendment rights is a power denied to government." . . .

Yet this is precisely the course taken here by the FCC. The Commission imposes on the licensees a responsibility to analyze the meaning of each song's lyrics and make a judgment as to the social value of the message. The message may be clear or obscure, and careful scrutiny would seem required. This task is to be carried out under the Commission's watchful eye and with the knowledge that repeated errors will be punished by revocation of the license. For now the regulation is applied to song lyrics; next year it may apply to comedy programs, and the following year to news broadcasts.

In *New York Times Co.* v. *Sullivan*, 376 U.S. 254, 279 (1964), we said that the State could not impose on newspapers the burden, under penalty of civil liability, of checking out every controversial statement for "truth." "Under such a rule, would-be critics of official conduct may be deterred from voicing their criticism, even though it is believed to be true and even though it is in fact true, because of doubt whether it can be proved in court or fear of the expense of having to do so. They tend to make only statements which 'steer far wider of the unlawful zone.' . . . The rule thus dampens the vigor and limits the variety of public debate. It is inconsistent with the First and Fourteenth Amendments." *Ibid.* Songs play no less a role in public debate, whether they eulogize the John Brown of the abolitionist movement, or the Joe Hill of the union movement, provide a rallying cry such as "We Shall Overcome," or express in music the values of the youthful "counterculture." The Government cannot, consistent with the First Amendment, require a broadcaster to censor its music any more than it can require a newspaper to censor the stories of its reporters. Under our system the Government is not to decide what messages, spoken or in music, are of the proper "social value" to reach the people.

I dissent.

Apart from its content concerns with drug-related lyrics, the FCC has adopted policies for licensees who themselves have participated in the drug trade. Broadcasters convicted of drug trafficking face sanctions, including the possibility of license revocation.

D. COMMERCIALS

Advertising is a form of commercial expression that, as discussed previously, until recently was entirely beyond the First Amendment's pale and even now has diminished constitutional status. Consistent with its inclination during the 1980s to rely upon marketplace forces, the FCC eliminated all quantitative commercial guidelines for television. Notwithstanding policy trends, First Amendment principles remain subject to dilution, given broadcasting's bottom rank in the constitutional hierarchy of the media. Broadcast advertising, in sum, is subject to all conditions governing commercial speech generally plus other constraints that are medium specific.

Typifying the unique status of and standards for radio and television advertising is the prohibition of commercials promoting use of tobacco. An FCC determination that "radio and television stations which carry cigarette advertising [must] devote a significant amount of broadcast time to presenting the case against cigarette smoking" was upheld in *Banzhaf v. Federal Communications Commission*. Soon afterward, as noted previously, the commission aborted use of the fairness doctrine as a means for promoting balanced coverage of issues raised by commercials. A couple of years after *Banzhaf*, however, fairness obligations prompted by cigarette advertisements were displaced by a total ban of such commercials "on any medium of electronic communication subject to the jurisdiction of the FCC." Although the law was challenged by broadcasters as an invasion of their First Amendment freedom, a district court in *Capital Broadcasting Co. v. Mitchell* upheld the prohibition. The court premised its decision both upon the unprotected status of commercial speech at the time and the diminished constitutional status of broadcasting. A dissenting opinion by Judge Wright suggested that both regulatory and constitutional goals were served better by reliance on the fairness doctrine rather than proscription. He noted that antismoking commercials had such "a devastating effect on cigarette consumption" that tobacco companies actually considered the ban preferable to public debate. Wright thus asserted that the congressional act constituted misguided paternalism insofar as it cut off controversial speech and thereby deprecated First Amendment interests and undermined public health aims.

The history of cigarette advertising since *Banzhaf* has been a sad tale of well meaning but misguided paternalism, cynical bargaining and lost opportunity. In the immediate wake of *Banzhaf*, the broadcast media were flooded with exceedingly effective anti-smoking commercials. For the first time in years, the statistics began to show a sustained trend toward lesser cigarette consumption. The *Banzhaf* advertising not only cost the cigarette companies customers, present and potential; it also put the industry in a delicate, paradoxical position. While cigarette advertising is apparently quite effective in inducing brand loyalty, it seems to have little impact on whether people in fact smoke. And after *Banzhaf*, these advertisements triggered the anti-smoking messages which were having a devastating effect on cigarette consumption. Thus the individual tobacco companies could not stop advertising for fear of losing their competitive position; yet for every dollar they spent to advance their product, they forced the airing of more anti-smoking advertisements and hence lost more customers.

It was against this backdrop that the Consumer Subcommittee of the Senate Committee on Commerce met to consider new cigarette legislation. The legislative prohibition against requiring health warnings in cigarette advertisements had just expired, and the Federal Trade Commission had indicated that it might soon require such warnings if not again stopped by Congress. In addition, the FCC was moving toward rule making which would have removed cigarette advertising from the electronic media. Thus Congress had to decide whether to extend the ban on FTC action and institute a similar restraint against the FCC or, alternatively, to allow the regulatory agencies to move forcefully against cigarette advertisements.

The context in which this decision had to be made shifted dramatically when a representative of the cigarette industry suggested that the Subcommittee draft legislation permitting the companies to remove their advertisements from the air. In retrospect, it is hard to see why this announcement was thought surprising. The *Banzhaf* ruling had clearly made electronic media advertising a losing proposition for the industry, and a voluntary withdrawal would have saved the companies approximately $250,000,000 in advertising costs, relieved political pressure for FTC action, and removed most anti-smoking messages from the air.

At the time, however, the suggestion of voluntary withdrawal was taken by some as a long delayed demonstration of industry altruism. Congress quickly complied with the industry's suggestion by banning the airing of television and radio cigarette commercials. Moreover, the new legislation provided additional rewards for the industry's "altruism" including a delay in pending FTC action against cigarette advertising and a prohibition against stricter state regulation of cigarette advertising and packaging. The result of the legislation was that as both the cigarette advertisements and most anti-smoking messages left the air, the tobacco companies transferred their advertising budgets to other forms of advertising such as newspapers and magazines where there was no fairness doctrine to require a response.

The passage of the Public Health Cigarette Smoking Act of 1969 marked a dramatic legislative *coup* for the tobacco industry. With the cigarette smoking controversy removed from the air, the decline in cigarette smoking was abruptly halted and cigarette consumption almost immediately turned upward again. Thus whereas the *Banzhaf* ruling, which required that both sides of the controversy be aired, significantly depressed cigarette sales, the 1969 legislation which effectively banned the controversy from the air, had the reverse effect. Whereas the *Banzhaf* decision had increased the flow of information by air so that the American people could make an informed judgment on the hazards of cigarette smoking, the 1969 Act cut off the flow of information altogether.

Of course, the fact that the legislation in question may be a product of skillful lobbying or of pressures brought by narrow private interests, or may have been passed by Congress to favor a particular industry, does not necessarily affect its constitutionality.... But when the "inevitable effect" of the legislation is the production of an unconstitutional result, the statute cannot be allowed to stand. *See* Gomillion v. Lightfoot, 364 U.S. 339, 342, 81 S.Ct. 125, 5 L.Ed.2d 110 (1960). The legislative history related above shows that the effect of this legislation was to cut off debate on the value of cigarettes just when *Banzhaf* had made such a debate a real possibility. The theory of free speech is grounded on the belief that people will make the right choice if presented with all points of view on a controversial issue. *See* Emerson, Toward a General Theory of the First Amendment, 72 Yale L.J. 877, 881 (1963); A. Meiklejohn, Political Freedom 26–28 (1960). When *Banzhaf* opened the electronic media to different points of view on the desirability of cigarette smoking, this theory was dramatically vindicated. Once viewers saw both sides of the story, they began to stop or cut down on smoking in ever increasing numbers. Indeed, it was presumably the very success of the *Banzhaf* doctrine in allowing people to make an informed choice that frightened the cigarette industry into calling on Congress to silence the debate....

This opinion is not intended as a Magna Carta for Madison Avenue. In my view, Congress retains broad power to deal with the evils of cigarette advertising. It can force the removal of deceptive claims, require manufacturers to couple their advertisements with a clear statement of the hazardous nature of their product, and provide for reply time to be awarded to anti-cigarette groups. But the one thing which Congress may not do is cut off debate altogether.

Although the *Capital Broadcasting* decision was rendered prior to the emergence of commercial expression as a constitutionally protected form of speech, the twists of modern commercial-speech doctrine suggest that it retains not only vitality but possible potential for expansion. The Court's more recent determination in *Posadas de Puerto Rico Associates v. Tourism Co. of Puerto Rico* (discussed in Chapter 3), that government may ban expression concerning an activity it has the power to make illegal even if the authority is not actually exercised, suggests that a ban on cigarette advertising irrespective of medium might be permissible. A like implication may follow for any product or service that, even if it is not unlawful, could be declared illegal.

REFERENCES

CASES

Action for Children's Television v. Federal Communications Commission, 756 F.2d 899 (D.C. Cir. 1985).

Action for Children's Television v. Federal Communications Commission, 821 F.2d 741 (D.C. Cir. 1987).

Action for Children's Television v. Federal Communications Commission, 852 F.2d 1332 (D.C. Cir. 1988).

Action for Children's Television v. Federal Communications Commission,___ F. 2d___ (D.C. Cir. 1991).

American Security Council Foundation v. Federal Communications Commission, 607 F.2d 438 (D.C. Cir. 1979).

Banzhaf v. Federal Communications Commission, 405 F.2d 1082 (D.C. Cir. 1968), *cert. denied*, 396 U.S. 842 (1969).

Branch v. Federal Communications Commission, 824 F.2d 37 (D.C. Cir. 1987), *cert. denied*, 108 S. Ct. 1220 (1988).

Capital Broadcasting Co. v. Mitchell, 333 F. Supp. 52 (D.D.C. 1971), aff'd, 415 U.S. 1000 (1972).

CBS, Inc. v. Federal Communications Commission, 453 U.S. 367 (1981).

Chisholm, Hon. Shirley, 35 F.C.C.2d 579 (1972).

Cohen v. California, 403 U.S. 15 (1971).

Columbia Broadcasting System, 3 R.R.2d 623 (1964).

Columbia Broadcasting System, Inc. v. Democratic National Committee, 412 U.S. 94 (1973).

Corey, George D., 37 F.C.C.2d 641 (1972).

Eastern Educational Radio (WUHY-FM), 24 F.C.C.2d 498 (1970).

Enforcement of Prohibitions Against Broadcast Indecency in 18 U.S.C. § 1464, 5 F.C.C. Rcd. 5297 (1990).

Erznoznik v. Jacksonville, 422 U.S. 205 (1975).

Farmers Educational & Cooperative Union of America v. WDAY, Inc., 360 U.S. 525 (1959).

Federal Communications Commission v. League of Women Voters, 468 U.S. 364 (1984).

Federal Communications Commission v. Pacifica Foundation, 438 U.S. 726 (1978).

Friends of the Earth v. Federal Communications Commission, 449 F.2d 1164 (D.C. Cir. 1971).

Great Lakes Broadcasting Co., 3 F.R.C. Ann. Rep. 32 (1929), aff'd in part, rev'd in part, 37 F.2d 993 (D.C. Cir.), *cert. denied*, 281 U.S. 706 (1930).

Illinois Citizens Committee for Broadcasting v. Federal Communications Commission, 515 F.2d 397 (D.C. Cir. 1974).

Infinity Broadcasting Corp. of Pennsylvania, 3 F.C.C. Rcd. 930 (1987).

Kennedy for President Committee v. Federal Communications Commission, 636 F.2d 417 (D.C. Cir. 1980).

Kennedy for President Committee v. Federal Communications Commission, 636 F.2d 433 (D.C. Cir. 1980).

Meredith Corp. v. Federal Communications Commission, 809 F.2d 863 (D.C. Cir. 1987).

Metro Broadcasting, Inc. v. Federal Communications Commission, 110 S. Ct. 2997 (1990).

National Broadcasting Co. v. Federal Communications Commission, 516 F.2d

1101 (D.C. Cir. 1974), *dismissed as moot* (1975), *cert. denied*, 424 U.S. 910 (1976).

National Broadcasting Co. v. United States, 319 U.S. 190 (1943).

National Citizens Committee for Broadcasting v. Federal Communications Commission, 567 F.2d 1095 (D.C. Cir. 1977).

New Indecency Enforcement Standards to Be Applied to All Broadcast and Amateur Radio Licenses, 2 F.C.C. Rcd. 2726 (1987).

Pacifica Foundation, 36 F.C.C. 147 (1964).

Pacifica Foundation, Inc., 2 F.C.C. Rcd. 2698 (1987).

Posadas de Puerto Rico Associates v. Tourism Co. of Puerto Rico, 478 U.S. 328 (1986).

Red Lion Broadcasting Co. v. Federal Communications Commission, 395 U.S. 367 (1969).

The Regents of the University of California, 2 F.C.C. Rcd. 2703 (1987).

Report on Editorializing by Broadcast Licensees, 13 F.C.C. 1246 (1949).

Report on Violent, Indecent, and Obscene Material, 51 F.C.C.2d 418 (1975).

Rep. Patsy Mink, 59 F.C.C.2d 987 (1976).

Republican National Committee (Dean Burch), 3 R.R.2d 647 (1964).

Sable Communications of California, Inc. v. Federal Communications Commission, 109 S. Ct. 2829 (1989).

Straus Communications, Inc. v. Federal Communications Commission, 530 F.2d 1001 (D.C. Cir. 1976).

Syracuse Peace Council, 2 F.C.C. Rcd. 5043 (1987).

Syracuse Peace Council v. Federal Communications Commission, 867 F.2d 654 (D.C. Cir. 1989).

Telecommunications Research and Action Center v. Federal Communications Commission, 801 F.2d 501 (D.C. Cir. 1986), *cert. denied*, 482 U.S. 919 (1987).

Trinity Methodist Church, South v. Federal Communications Commission, 62 F.2d 850 (D.C. Cir. 1932), *cert. denied*, 288 U.S. 599 (1933).

Washington Association for Television and Children v. Federal Communications Commission, 712 F.2d 677 (D.C. Cir. 1983).

Weiss, Adrian, 58 F.C.C.2d 342 (1976).

Writers Guild of America West, Inc. v. American Broadcasting Co., Inc., 609 F.2d 355 (9th Cir. 1979), cert. denied, 449 U.S. 824 (1980).

Yale Broadcasting Co. v. Federal Communications Commission, 478 F.2d 594 (D.C. Cir.), cert. denied, 414 U.S. 914 (1973).

Zapple, Nicholas, Letter to, 23 F.C.C.2d 707 (1970).

PUBLICATIONS

Albert, *Constitutional Regulation of Televised Violence*, 64 Va. L. Rev. 1299 (1978).

Bazelon, *F.C.C. Regulation of the Telecommunications Press*, 1975 Duke L.J. 213.

Bickel, The Morality of Consent (1975).

Bollinger, *Freedom of the Press and Public Access: Toward a Theory of Partial Regulation of the Mass Media*, 75 Mich. L. Rev. 1 (1976).

Cox, The Role of the Supreme Court in American Government (1976).

Fowler & Brenner, *A Marketplace Approach to Broadcast Regulation*, 60 Tex. L. Rev. 207 (1982).

Krattenmaker & Powe, *Televised Violence: First Amendment Principles and Social Science Theory*, 64 Va. L. Rev. 1123 (1978).

Lacey, *The Electric Church: An FCC "Established" Institution?*, 31 Fed. Com. L.J. 235 (1979).

Lively, *Deregulatory Illusions and Broadcasting: The First Amendment's Enduring Forked Tongue*, 66 N.C. L. Rev. 963 (1988).

Powe, *American Voodoo: If Television Doesn't Show It Maybe It Won't Exist*, 59 Tex. L. Rev. 879 (1981).

Price, *Taming Red Lion: The First Amendment and Structural Approaches to Media Regulation*, 31 Fed. Com. L.J. 215 (1979).

Robinson, *The FCC and the First Amendment: Observations on Forty Years of Radio and Television Programming*, 52 Minn. L. Rev. 119 (1967).

Simmons, The Fairness Doctrine and the Media (1978).

Van Alstyne, *The Mobius Strip of the First Amendment: Perspectives on Red Lion*, 29 S.C. L. Rev. 539 (1978).

Weinberg, *Questioning Broadcast Regulation*, 86 Mich. L. Rev. 1296 (1988).

Chapter 11

Cable

Cable television is a powerful form of communication. Used properly, it can edify and inspire as well as entertain. Used improperly, it can seriously damage the quality of life that we have and reduce public tastes to their lowest common denominator.

Community Television of Utah, Inc. v. Wilkinson,
611 F. Supp. 1099 (D. Utah 1985), *aff'd*, 800 F.2d 989
(10th Cir. 1986), *aff'd*, 107 S. Ct. 1559 (1987)

Cable television's constitutional status is even less resolved than broadcasting's. Although cable may be indistinguishable from traditional over-the-air television service from the perspective of many viewers, many courts have analogized it to the print media for constitutional purposes. Because cable is an even newer medium than broadcasting, it is conceivable that many of the lessons learned from the constitutional appraisal of broadcasting could lead to a more efficient appraisal of cable. Insofar as official sense may focus upon functional similarities rather than structural differences of media, as the FCC did in abandoning the fairness doctrine, cable's First Amendment standing might be quickened.

I. EVOLVING CONSTITUTIONAL STANDARDS

During cable's early developmental period, the industry was subjected to an array of controls that would have seemed to implicate obvious First Amendment questions. Distant-importation, origination, access, and antisiphoning rules directly impinged on editorial discretion. The FCC's access requirements in particular imposed upon cablecasters a demand that the commission and the Supreme Court had concluded was constitutionally impermissible when applied in broadcasting—the least protected of all media. Eventually, in *Federal Communications Commission v. Midwest Video Corp.*, access rules were invalidated on grounds that they effectively converted cable into a common carrier. Avoidance of the constitutional question reflected uncertainty with respect to what, if any, First Amendment status cable should have. Implicit in the determination that cable could not be equated with a common carrier, however, was the sense that cablecasters possessed some degree of editorial discretion of a constitutional order. Not until 1984 did the Supreme Court speak directly to the First Amendment interests of cable. Even then, references were general and glancing. In *City of Los Angeles v. Preferred Communications, Inc.*, the Court considered a lower-court ruling dismissing a cable company's complaints contesting franchising regulations that prevented it from competing against another operator. The company had been unsuccessful in obtaining a franchise from the city and subsequently was turned down by a local utility when, in seeking to bypass the municipality's denial, it sought pole space anyway. Although the city did not deny that excess physical capacity existed to accommodate additional cable service, it justified its action in terms of physical scarcity of pole space, limited economic demand for cable, "and the practical and esthetic disruptive effect that installing and maintaining a cable system has on the public right-of-way."

We do think that the activities in which respondent allegedly seeks to engage plainly implicate First Amendment interests. Respondent alleges:

> "The business of cable television, like that of newspapers and magazines, is to provide its subscribers with a mixture of news, information and entertainment. As do newspapers, cable television companies use a portion of their available space to reprint (or retransmit) the communications of others, while at the same time providing some original content." ...

Thus, through original programming or by exercising editorial discretion over which stations or programs to include in its repertoire, respondent seeks to communicate messages on a wide variety of topics and in a wide variety of formats. We recently noted that cable operators exercise "a significant amount of editorial discretion regarding what their programming will include." *FCC* v. *Midwest Video Corp.*, 440 U.S. 689, 707 (1979). Cable television partakes of some of the aspects of speech and the communication of ideas as do the traditional enterprises of newspaper and book publishers, public speakers, and pamphleteers. Respondent's proposed activities would seem to implicate First Amendment interests as do the activities of wireless broadcasters, which were found to fall within the ambit of the First Amendment in *Red Lion Broadcasting Co.* v. *FCC*, *supra*, at 386, even though the free speech aspects of the wireless broadcasters' claim were found to be outweighed by the Government interests in regulating by reason of the scarcity of available frequencies.

Although the Court acknowledged a First Amendment presence, left largely unamplified, it noted that identification of such an interest did "not end the inquiry." It observed that even protected speech is subject to reasonable time and place restrictions. Furthermore, "where speech and conduct are joined in a single course of action, the First Amendment values must be balanced against competing societal interests." Such a limiting principle, speaking in terms of speech and conduct, intimates a legitimate regulatory interest in consequences unrelated to content. Never directly addressed, therefore, was the precise status of cable as an element of the press. Given the undeveloped nature of the litigation, the Court chose not to pursue further its constitutional inquiry other than to observe that when speech and conduct merge, "First Amendment values must be balanced against competing societal interests."

In a concurring opinion, Justice Blackmun spoke in terms of the medium's First Amendment status. He thus adverted to the traditional and fundamental notion that "[d]ifferent communications media are treated differently for First Amendment purposes." To be discerned from that premise, according to Blackmun, was "whether the characteristics of cable television make it sufficiently analogous to another medium to warrant application of an already existing standard or whether those characteristics require a new analysis."

Lower courts have taken signals from both the majority and concurring opinions in the *Preferred* decision. In *Quincy Cable TV, Inc. v. Federal Communications Commission*, the court of appeals considered whether must-carry rules, obligating cable operators to carry the signals of local broadcasters, were "fundamentally at odds with the First Amendment." Determining whether rules purportedly aimed at activity unrelated to speech have an acceptable secondary impact upon expression depends upon the presence of a substantial state interest and the breadth of the regulatory sweep. The court of appeals invalidated the must-carry rules on grounds that their justification, to prevent "the destruction of free, local television," was fanciful rather than substantial. It also found them fatally overbroad insofar as they "indiscriminately protected every local broadcaster, regardless of whether it was in fact threatened, and regardless of the quantity of local service in the community and the degree to which the cable operator in question already carried local outlets."

The *Quincy* court also examined the nature of cable to determine what medium it was most akin to and thus what status it should possess within the constitutional hierarchy of media. It noted that even if "cable and broadcast television appear virtually indistinguishable" to viewers, they differ in at least one critical respect. Key to the appeals court's conclusion that cable was more akin to publishing than to broadcasting, therefore, was its perception that cable was not affected by the scarcity problems associated with radio and television. The court also could not "discern other attributes of cable television that would justify a standard of review analogous to the more forgiving First Amendment analysis applied to the broadcast media." It rejected the notion that "use of a public right of way" supported less exacting constitutional review. Although recognizing the community disruption and inconvenience inherent in the process of constructing a cable system, the court of appeals found no connection between that reality and an interest in controlling program content. Nor did it find any natural monopoly characteristic of cable comparable "to the physical constraints imposed by the limited size of the electromagnetic spectrum." To the contrary, it noted that any economic constraint was analogous to those characteristics of the print media previously dismissed as a basis for content control. Finally, the appeals court was sufficiently impressed with "cable's virtually unlimited channel capacity" to dispense entirely with suggestions that broadcasting was the appropriate reference point for assessing cable.

Prior to the *Preferred* and *Quincy* decisions, a competing judicial view had equated cable with broadcasting for First Amendment purposes. In *Berkshire Cablevision of Rhode Island, Inc., v. Burke*, a district court examined the constitutionality of public access requirements and concluded that cable and newspapers "*are* constitutionally distinguishable [emphasis in original]." The court noted that newspapers traditionally have operated free from any form of official content control—a point subject to criticism on grounds that it merely identifies a tradition instead of examining the validity of it. It further observed that wholesale comparisons to economic scarcity were misplaced insofar as the franchising process accounts for scarcity akin to that in broadcasting. The court determined that inexpensive print alternatives to newspapers, such as pamphlets or leaflets, were more available than electronic options to cable. Observing that "scarcity is scarcity [regardless of] its particular source," it concluded that economic scarcity had special relevance and that broadcasting represented the proper First Amendment model for cable.

A subsequent district court decision, affirmed without opinion by the Supreme Court, sided with the analysis expounded by the *Quincy* court to the extent that it rejected analogies to broadcasting. In *Community Television of Utah, Inc. v. Wilkinson*, the district court concluded that scarcity concepts had no relevance to cable.

The physical scarcity of broadcast spectrum space justifies governmental regulation of the use of that space. "There is a fixed natural limitation upon the number of stations that can operate without interfering with one another."

National Broadcasting Co., Inc. v. United States, 319 U.S. 190, 213, 63 S.Ct. 997, 1008, 87 L.Ed. 1344 (1943). The regulation of the broadcast medium is vital as a "traffic control" device. Licensing is required to avoid interference between stations; without governmental rationing of broadcast frequencies, chaos would result. *See id.* . . .

Seizing on scarcity as the justification for broadcast regulation, *amicus* tries to prove that cable is a scarce medium. Because each locality generally only has one cable franchise, it is argued that cable television is "economically" scarce. *Amicus* claims that this "economic" scarcity, like the "physical" scarcity characteristic of the broadcast medium, justifies content regulation.

It is not clear from the record before the court whether the cable medium truly is scarce in the "economic" sense discussed above. Under the new Policy Act, states may allow as many or as few cable franchises as they choose. Policy Act § 621(a)(1). Yet even if the cable medium is "economically" scarce, this scarcity does not justify content regulation like that in the broadcast medium. *See, e.g., Home Box Office, Inc. v. FCC,* 567 F.2d 9, 44–45 (D.C.Cir.1977). This is true because cable is not limited to a finite number of channels the way broadcasting is. The demand for cable services determines the number of cable channels. The number of additional channels, in a technical sense, is subject to extensive expansion. *See, e.g., Home Box Office, Inc. v. Wilkinson,* 531 F.Supp. 987, 1002 (D.Utah 1982). As a result, there is no danger of interference between channels. The government therefore need not "control traffic" by rationing channels. As long as the material carried on cable channels is protected by the Constitution, licensing authorities need not police the content of those channels in the public interest, because no physically scarce public resource is involved. The supply and demand of the market place will determine the type of programming that will be successful.

The sense that broadcasting is not an apt model for setting standards governing cable does not ensure status on a par with the print media. Although it affirmed the result in *Wilkinson,* the Supreme Court is free at a later date to introduce a superseding rationale. Equally important, the district court's seemingly approving reference to the Cable Act's access rules suggest countenance of a regulation that is constitutionally intolerable for both print and broadcasting. The possibility remains, therefore, that cable will be governed by an entirely new rather than an existing set of criteria and be a "law unto itself."

II. PROMOTION OF CONTENT DIVERSITY
AND BALANCE

Concerns with First Amendment values of diversity and a balanced marketplace of ideas have been as profoundly sounded in connection with cable as with other mass media. Federal access requirements were invalidated in *Federal Communications Commission v. Midwest Video Corp.,* as discussed in Chapter 7, by avoiding any First Amendment issues.

Although the Court expressed no view on the constitutional question, it "acknowledge[d] that it [was] not frivolous." The FCC has subjected cable operators to the entire panoply of fairness regulation, including the fairness doctrine, personal attack and political editorial rules, and equal opportunity provisions, that governs broadcasting. The pertinence of the Court's observation and future operation of these rules may depend not only upon the eventual constitutional status afforded cable but upon the future vitality, if any, of the fairness doctrine for broadcasting.

The Cable Communications Policy Act of 1984 introduced the possibility of access as a permissible franchise condition rather than a constitutional right. Specifically, it provides that "[a] franchising authority may establish requirements in a franchise with respect to the designated use of channel capacity for public, educational, or governmental use." The Cable Act also authorizes franchising authorities to set terms for other use if access channels are not being utilized for their designated purpose. A separate provision requires cable systems with at least thirty-six channels to set aside capacity for commercial access and subjects smaller operators to a like requirement if they are obligated by franchise terms. Cable operators are prohibited from "exercis[ing] any editorial control over any" access channels. However, they are free to set rates.

First Amendment challenges to content requirements as a franchise condition so far have experienced mixed results. A constitutional claim in response to a franchise requirement obligating a cable company to originate four and one-half hours per week of local programming, moreover, proved entirely unavailing. In *Chicago Cable Communications v. Chicago Cable Commission,* the court of appeals determined that the differences between cable and other media justified its stricter regulation. It found that the origination requirement was supported by the "important or substantial interest" of "localism." The court also determined that the "minimal requirements [did] not divest [cable operators] of discretion" over what to transmit, and that the provision's incidental impact upon First Amendment interests was no greater than necessary to effectuate a substantial governmental interest in local, diversified, and participatory programming.

First Amendment considerations aside, the question exists whether access ever will be a meaningful concept in a practical sense. Experience even in service areas with large audiences and significant funding so far has demonstrated underuse as the norm rather than the exception. To the extent that this reality continues to hold true, access may be a theory well linked to First Amendment theory but a methodology that is marginally relevant to both the speaking and viewing or listening interests of the public.

III. CONTENT RESTRICTION

Official restrictions upon the content of cable programming present in a different context many of the same problems examined in connection with other media. Must-carry rules requiring cablecasters to retransmit local broadcast signals impose upon cable operators the functional equivalent of requiring a publisher to print "that which 'reason' tells them should not be published." Restrictions upon indecent programming raise questions that, in the context of broadcasting, were answered by allowing such constraints to operate. Past analytical experience with respect to other media has proved relevant in assessing modern problems of cable content regulation.

A. Must-Carry Rules

The requirement that cable operators must carry the signals of local broadcasters relates back to the array of rules that emerged in the 1960s, when the FCC regulated cable under jurisdiction that was "reasonably ancillary" to its governance of broadcasting. Must carriage reflects the sense that exclusion of local signals from a cable system would subject local broadcasting to audience erosion and diminished advertising revenue and thus undermine its viability. Although the rules were invalidated in *Quincy Cable TV, Inc. v. Federal Communications Commission*, the court of appeals left open the possibility that a more narrowly tailored variant of must carriage might be permissible. The Commission subsequently adopted new must-carry rules that would operate for a fixed period ending after five years. Its rationale for the narrower requirement was that viewers needed time to become familiar with devices enabling them to switch between cable and broadcast service that it was requiring cable systems to provide. The number of must-carry signals also varied in accordance with a cable system's channel capacity.

In *Century Communications Corp. v. Federal Communications Commission*, the court of appeals found the revised must-carry rules incompatible with the First Amendment. Review consisted of a four-part inquiry into whether the regulation was "within the constitutional power of the Government; . . . further[ed] an important or substantial governmental interest; . . . [was] unrelated to the suppression of free expression; and if the incidental restriction on First Amendment freedoms [was] no greater than . . . [was] essential to the furtherance of that interest." As in *Quincy Cable TV, Inc.*, the appeals court determined that the government interest was not substantial enough to justify the must-carry rules. It determined that the commission's assertion that consumers were ignorant of the differences between broadcast and cable technology and needed five years to become educated was based upon conjecture rather than evidence. The court found, based upon actual experience pursuant to the *Quincy Cable TV, Inc.*, decision and other government studies, "that the absence of must carry would not harm local broadcasting." Missing from its perspective, therefore, was evidence of "a substantial governmental interest...outweigh[ing] the incidental burden on first amendment interests conceded by all parties here."

The court of appeals further determined that even the scaled-down must-carry rules were not tailored narrowly enough. That conclusion too was premised upon a failure of proof. Thus the court noted that "[i]t is wholly unclear to us why it should take five years to inform consumers that with the installation of [the] switch and a television antenna they can view more local channels." In sum, the reincarnated must-carry rules fell because the FCC had "failed 'to put itself in a position to know' whether the problem that its regulations seek to solve 'is a real or fanciful threat.' " Even so, the court of appeals pointed out that it did "not suggest that must carry rules are *per se* unconstitutional [or] mean to intimate that the FCC may not regulate the cable industry so as to advance substantial governmental interests."

Pursuant to a statutorily prescribed inquiry into the cable industry, the FCC has recommended congressional enactment of a must-carry requirement. Must carriage has been proposed, absent elimination of compulsory copyright licensing for local programming, to ensure that the competitive relationship between the cable industries and broadcasting is not "drastically changed [so as] to upset the balance of the market."

B. SYNDICATION EXCLUSIVITY

The retransmission by cable of broadcast signals has been a source of distress to broadcasters who purchase exclusive television rights. In 1968, the Supreme Court in *Fortnightly Corp. v. United Artists Television, Inc.,* equated cable retransmissions from a hilltop antenna with the pickup of broadcast signals by an individual homeowner who ran a cable from the rooftop to a television. Several years later, in *Teleprompter Corp. v. CBS, Inc.,* the Court determined that cable retransmissions did not qualify as a "performance" and thereby run afoul of copyright laws. As a consequence, cable companies that retransmitted broadcast signals were effectively exempted from copyright laws that applied to other broadcasters. Exclusivity rules, originating in 1965, represented the FCC's effort to protect local broadcasters from the importation of distant signals violating exclusive rights to network and syndicated programs. In 1976, as discussed in Chapter 3, Congress included in the new copyright law a scheme requiring cable companies to pay a fee for carriage. Thereafter, in 1980, the FCC concluded that syndicated exclusivity rules no longer were necessary.

After an unsuccessful petition for reconsideration in 1984, broadcasters in 1987 succeeded in having the FCC review the elimination of syndicated exclusivity rules. Alluding to cable's expansive growth, the Commission concluded that broadcasting was being harmed by the absence of syndicated exclusivity rules and that the supply of syndicated programming itself might be adversely impacted. In 1988, the Commission, thus reinstated the rules. Noting among other things that the FCC reasonably had inferred that audience diversion diminished the value of programming by reducing its advertising value, the court of appeals in *United Video, Inc. v. Federal Communications Commission* upheld the rules as within the Commission's authority and neither arbitrary nor capricious.

C. INDECENCY

The Cable Act compounds the general criminal statute against obscenity by providing that anyone transmitting "over any cable system any matter which is obscene or otherwise unprotected by the Constitution of the United States shall be fined not more than $10,000 or imprisoned not more than two years." Indecency, although more vulnerable to regulation in medium-specific contexts, remains constitutionally protected speech and thus should be unaffected by the statute.

The power of states to regulate cable indecency was the central issue of *Community Television of Utah, Inc. v. Wilkinson*. The Cable Act provides for "the criminal or civil liability of cable programmers or cable operators pursuant to the Federal, State, or local law of libel, slander, obscenity, incitement, invasions of privacy, false or misleading advertising, or other similar laws." The state law at issue in the *Wilkinson* case subjected indecent programming as defined by statute to fines up to $10,000. Because the prohibited expression was not obscene and thus was constitutionally protected, the district court found that the state law was fatally overbroad. It refused to find persuasive, moreover, the contention that the Supreme Court's approval of broadcast indecency controls justified validation of the state's enactment. The district court noted a significant factual difference between the state's chilling monetary penalty and the "very mild" sanction in *Federal Communications Commission v. Pacifica Foundation*, discussed in Chapter 10. The court, adverting to a brief filed by the FCC, distinguished cable from broadcasting for purposes of indecency regulation. Dismissing or discounting concerns with pervasiveness, privacy, and accessibility by children, it noted that (1) cable service requires the affirmative act of subscribing and payment of fees on a regular basis, (2) viewers receive guides providing notice of the nature and content of programs, and (3) lockboxes are available to prevent exposure to unwanted programming.

Defendants attempt to show that *Pacifica*'s rationale applies to cable television. The Court's reasoning in *Pacifica* was twofold. First, broadcasting has a pervasive presence which might intrude into the home and violate an individual's right to be left alone. Second, children may easily obtain access to indecent broadcast material, undermining both the "government's interest in the 'well-being of its youth' " and parents' authority over their children. . . .

a. *Interference with the Right of Privacy.*—Defendants argue that cable television is more pervasive than the FM radio broadcasting at issue in *Pacifica*. Therefore, defendants claim, indecency on cable television can be regulated through civil sanctions. This analysis oversimplifies the *Pacifica* Court's decision. The Court did not say that pervasiveness by itself establishes a right to regulate protected expression. According to the Court, pervasiveness which *results* in an unwarranted intrusion upon one's right to be left alone justifies regulation of FM broadcasts. That is, the right to be left alone in one's own home outweighs the first amendment rights of those who wish to intrude into that home. *Id.* at 748.

The practical and critical distinction between *Pacifica* and the present case is apparent: cable television is not an uninvited intruder. As the FCC observed in its *amicus curiae* brief submitted to this court:

> First, cable is a subscriber medium, generally only available if the person who views it has affirmatively contacted the cable system and asked that a wire be brought into his home and attached to his television set. Without that voluntary act, there is no cable programming. Second, as to certain interstate-transmitted services, particularly as to entertainment channels such as HBO, Showtime, and the Movie Channel, a subscriber must usually pay a premium in addition to its subscriber fee in order to receive service. Otherwise, the signal is scrambled both aurally and visually, precluding reception in the home. Third, a subscriber may, if it so chooses, acquire a "lock box" which prevents reception of any particular cable programming without his authorization. [Fourth], television guides, providing advance notice of the nature of upcoming program offerings, are almost always available. . . .

The distinction that the FCC and plaintiffs urge is that cable TV is not an intruder but an invitee whose invitation can be carefully circumscribed. *See Pacifica* at 748–49. . . . Because a subscriber must initiate the service, there is no uninvited intrusion into the privacy interest that the Court articulated in *Pacifica*. The individual who complained about Carlin's monologue never subscribed to radio programs. In addition, the complainant did not pay an additional fee to be able to listen to Carlin's monologue, as a subscriber to HBO, Showtime or the Movie Channel must. No lock box device even existed. In addition, it does not appear that a radio program guide provided any information in advance to warn potential listeners of the content of Carlin's monologue.

b. *The Interests of Children.*—Defendants argue alternatively that the state's interest in protecting children justifies regulation of indecency. In *Pacifica* the Court wrote that the "ease with which children may obtain access to broadcast material, coupled with the concerns recognized in *Ginsberg*, amply justify special treatment of indecent broadcasting." *Id.* at 750, . . . In *Ginsberg v. New York*, 390 U.S. 629 . . . (1968), the Court upheld a New York law that prohibited the sale of "harmful" indecent material, not legally obscene, to persons under 17 years of age. The concerns emphasized in *Ginsberg v. New York* consisted of two separate interests that justified a different constitutional standard for minors. First, the state has an interest in the well-being of its youth. Second, parents have an interest in exercising authority over their children.

(1) *The State's Interest in the Well-Being of its Youth.* In *Ginsberg* the governmental and parental interests listed above both gave support to the same conclusion that the law was valid. In contrast, defendants set parental and governmental interests at odds with each other. Defendants allege that "not all parents will exercise [the] necessary degree of control. Many parents may be indifferent to this material or ignorant of its harmful effect."...In so arguing, defendants make a fundamental departure from *Pacifica.* According to the defendants, since not all parents will do their job in limiting their children's access to indecent material, the state must step in....

Although protecting children is a very desirable and legitimate goal, the Act itself does not mention children anywhere. It does not provide any systematic procedure for protecting children. Section –1702(4) provides no limiting principle consistent with applicable constitutional standards. Even assuming *arguendo* that *Pacifica* validates a prohibition limited to the daytime, the statutory language does not channel indecency to specific viewing hours. The legal infirmities of the statute are so great that this court could not so limit the statute even through purposive construction without engaging in improper judicial legislation. Thus, the scope of the language is so uncertain as to chill legitimate expression in a way that the overbreadth doctrine forbids....

A further fact that must be taken into account is that the Act does not consider the rights of consenting adults under *Miller* to view nonobscene material. In *Pacifica* Justice Powell's concurrence emphasized the importance of protecting the rights of adults while at the same time insulating children from indecency. Justice Powell feared that the *Pacifica* ruling might "have the effect of 'reduc(ing) the adult population . . . to (hearing) only what is fit for children.' [citation omitted] This argument is not without force." *Pacifica,* 438 U.S. at 760....Justice Powell concluded that the holding of the Court "does not prevent respondent Pacifica Foundation from broadcasting the monologue during late evening hours when fewer children are likely to be in the audience." *Id.* at 760....Thus, *Pacifica* seems to preserve the right of adults to listen to Carlin's monologue on the radio. Utah's cable television law would prevent adults from exercising their rights in a manner consistent with the rationale of *Pacifica.*

(2) *The Parental Interest in Supervising Children.*—Restrictions in the Utah Act may well be inconsistent with the right of parental control articulated in *Pacifica* and *Ginsberg.* The enforcement of the Act could result in a ban of certain defined materials that may have serious literary, artistic, political or scientific value and that some parents want to show their children. Under Utah's law they could not do so, even though rulings of the Supreme Court allow parents to provide materials for their children that the children themselves cannot purchase: "the prohibition against sales to minors does not bar parents who so desire from purchasing the magazines for their children." *Ginsberg v. New York,* 390 U.S. at 630....

Thus, the distinctions between *Pacifica* and the present case are manifest. *Pacifica* does not authorize the regulation attempted by the Utah Legislature. At best *Pacifica* stands for the proposition that a federal regulatory agency can monitor consumer complaints directed at broadcasters who operate in the public domain. The differences between radio and cable make *Pacifica* easily distinguishable and contradict defendants' argument....

Cable television is a powerful form of communication. Used properly, it can edify and inspire as well as entertain. Used improperly, it can seriously damage the quality of life that we have and reduce public tastes to their lowest common denominator. Following Supreme Court precedent, today's ruling delineates an area in which private individuals, particularly parents, must assume an important responsibility for maintaining a decent society. The first amendment puts "the decision as to what views shall be voiced largely into the hands of each of us, in the hope that the use of such freedom will ultimately produce a more capable citizenry and more perfect polity and in the belief that no other approach would comport with the premise of individual dignity and choice upon which our political system rests."

Because the Utah law was found to regulate "according to content," the district court rejected arguments that it was a legitimate time, place, or manner restriction. Upon review, the court of appeals affirmed the decision for reasons stated in the district court opinion. The Supreme Court affirmed without opinion. Although the ruling distinguishes cable from broadcasting for purposes of indecency control, the points of distinction illustrate the inherent treacheries of medium-specific analysis. Like receipt of cable, broadcast viewing or listening requires affirmative acts of purchasing necessary equipment, installation, activation, and selection. Program guides and blocking devices also are available for broadcast service. At most, therefore, the distinguishing factors rest not upon immutably different characteristics but upon shades of relativity. Left for consideration is whether these somewhat fine distinctions will or should continue to outweigh the broad functional similarities of media.

REFERENCES

CASES

Berkshire Cablevision of Rhode Island, Inc. v. Burke, 571 F. Supp. 976 (D.R.I. 1983), *vacated as moot*, 773 F.2d 382 (1st Cir. 1985).
Century Communications Corp. v. Federal Communications Commission, 835 F.2d 292 (D.C. Cir. 1987), *cert. denied*, 108 S. Ct. 2015 (1988).
Chicago Cable Communications v. Chicago Cable Commission, 879 F.2d 1540 (7th Cir. 1989).
City of Los Angeles v. Preferred Communications, Inc., 476 U.S. 689 (1986).
Community Television of Utah, Inc. v. Wilkinson, 611 F. Supp. 1099 (D. Utah 1985), *aff'd*, 800 F.2d 989 (10th Cir. 1986), *aff'd*, 107 S. Ct. 1559 (1987).
Federal Communications Commission v. Midwest Video Corp., 440 U.S. 689 (1979).

Federal Communications Commission v. Pacifica Foundation, 438 U.S. 726 (1978).

Fortnightly Corp. v. United Artists Television, Inc., 392 U.S. 390 (1968).

Quincy Cable TV, Inc. v. Federal Communications Commission, 768 F.2d 1434 (D.C. Cir. 1985), cert. denied, 476 U.S. 1169 (1986).

Teleprompter Corp. v. CBS, Inc., 415 U.S. 394 (1974).

United Video, Inc. v. Federal Communications Commission, 890 F.2d 1173 (D.C. Cir. 1989).

PUBLICATIONS

Knecht and Grinonneau, *Challenging the Constitutionality of Must-Carry*, 8 Com. & L. 3 (1986).

Schmidt, Freedom of the Press vs. Public Access (1976).

Chapter 12

Common Carriers

[I]t is not at all inconceivable that electronic publishing with its speed and convenience will eventually overshadow the more traditional news media.

United States v. American Telephone and Telegraph Co.,
552 F. Supp. 131 (D.D.C. 1982), *aff'd*, 460 U.S. 1001 (1983)

First Amendment issues concerning common carriers are less common than with other media because of their duty to provide equal access on a nondiscriminatory basis. Constitutional issues are not entirely absent, however, given judicial exclusion of AT&T from electronic publishing and some sentiment that common carriers are not obligated to carry indecent messages. Content diversification policies responding to AT&T's dominance have justified what essentially amounts to a prior restraint. Less well tolerated, for constitutional reasons, have been content controls governing use of their facilities for dissemination of sexually explicit expression.

I. PROMOTION OF CONTENT DIVERSIFICATION

Terms of the modified final judgment discussed in Chapter 8 that enabled AT&T to commence new business activities contain a significant restriction. Pursuant to concern with "potential dangers to competition and to First Amendment values," the company was prohibited from engaging in electronic publishing. Given AT&T's existing interexchange network, the district court worried that the company could discriminate against competing electronic publishers by giving priority to its own traffic and obtaining proprietary information concerning its rivals. Because "[t]he electronic publishing industry is still in its infancy" but has the potential to become "a very significant part of the American communications system," the court determined that AT&T's "resources would dwarf any efforts of its competitors" and that its "mere presence . . . would be likely to deter other potential competitors from even entering the market."

Beyond mere competitive concerns, the district court tied its decision to First Amendment values. Although a constitutional claim of freedom of the press was not present, the court chose to emphasize "the goal of the First Amendment . . . to achieve 'the widest possible dissemination of information from diverse and antagonistic sources.'" What essentially constituted a prior restraint thus was implemented on the premise that the "risks to the public interest" otherwise were too profound.

The electronic publishing industry is still in its infancy. Although this business may some day be a very significant part of the American communications system, at present, and most likely for the next several years, a small number of relatively small firms will be experimenting with new technology to provide services to an American public that is, for the most part, still almost totally unfamiliar with them. There can be no doubt that, if AT&T entered this market, the combination of its financial, technological, manufacturing, and marketing resources would dwarf any efforts of its competitors. In fact, AT&T's mere presence in the electronic publishing area would be likely to deter other potential competitors from even entering the market.

It is also readily apparent that competitors in the electronic publishing industry—far more so than competitors in any other industry—could easily be crushed were AT&T to engage in the types of anticompetitive behavior described above. Unlike most products and services, information in general and news in particular are by definition especially sensitive to even small impediments or delays. Information is only valuable if it is timely; by and large it is virtually worthless if its dissemination is delayed. This quality is especially important in electronic publishing because up-to-date information and constant availability are the features likely to be sought by subscribers. . . .

The goal of the First Amendment is to achieve "the widest possible dissemination of information from diverse and antagonistic sources." *Associated Press v. United States*, 326 U.S. 1, 20 (1945). See also *FCC v. National Citizens Committee for Broadcasting*, 436 U.S. 775, 795 (1978). This interest in diversity has been recognized time and again by various courts. In *Red Lion Broadcasting v. FCC*, 395 U.S. 367, 390 (1969), for example, the Supreme Court observed that

[i]t is the purpose of the First Amendment to preserve an uninhibited marketplace of ideas in which truth will ultimately prevail, rather than to countenance monopolization of that market.

See also *New York Times Co. v. Sullivan*, 376 U.S. 254, 270 (1964). Judge Learned Hand, speaking for the Court of Appeals for the Second Circuit, similarly noted that the media serve "one of the most vital of all general interests: the dissemination of news from as many different sources, and with as many different facets and colors as possible." *United States v. Associated Press*, 52 F. Supp. 362, 372 (S.D.N.Y.1943), *aff'd*, 321 U.S. (1945)....

Applying this diversity principle to the issue here under discussion, it is clear that permitting AT&T to become an electronic publisher will not further the public interest.

During the last thirty years, there has been an unremitting trend toward concentration in the ownership and control of the media. Diversity has disappeared in many areas; newspapers have gone out of business; others have merged; and much of the flow of news and editorial opinion appears more and more to be controlled and shaped by the three television networks and a handful of news magazines and metropolitan newspapers.

This concentration presents obvious dangers even today. Unless care is taken, both the concentration and the attendant dangers will be significantly increased by the new technologies. Indeed, it is not at all inconceivable that electronic publishing, with its speed and convenience will eventually overshadow the more traditional news media, and that a single electronic publisher would acquire substantial control over the provision of news in large parts of the United States....

The concentration that now exists in the media has presumably been brought about by impersonal economic and technological forces, and it is obviously beyond the concern of this or any other court. But the particular concentration that may emerge from the proposed decree is subject to the Court's jurisdiction in this antitrust case as part of the instant proceeding. Not only is AT&T a regulated company, and not only does the proceeding stem directly from serious charges of anticompetitive conduct, but the Court has been mandated not to approve the proposed decree unless it finds it to be in the public interest. AT&T's ability, described above, to use its control of the interexchange network to reduce or eliminate competition in the electronic publishing industry is the source of this threat to the First Amendment principle of diversity.

In sum, for a variety of reasons, the entry of AT&T into electronic publishing involves risks to the public interest that are greater than those which would be involved by that company's entry into other markets. Since under the Sherman Act, it is appropriate to bar a company from a market if the restriction is necessary to permit the development of competition in that market (*Ford Motor Co. v. United States, supra*, 405 U.S. at 577–78, and since First Amendment values, too, support a ban on electronic publishing by AT&T, the Court will require that the company be prohibited from entering that market.

II. CONTENT RESTRICTION

Congress in 1988 enacted legislation that entirely prohibited obscene and indecent telephone transmissions. The measure responded to "sexually-oriented pre-recorded messages (popularly known as 'dial-a-porn')" which were provided on special lines leased from the telephone company. Although finding no constitutional barrier to the prohibition of obscene communications, since they are beyond the First Amendment's concern, the Supreme Court in *Sable Communications of California, Inc. v. Federal Communications Commission* concluded that the indecency ban was unconstitutional. In so doing, the Court distinguished private telephone communications from what it referred to as the uniquely pervasive nature of broadcasting justifying indecency controls in that medium. It also dismissed a suggested captive audience rationale and noted the affirmative acts required to obtain access to the service. With respect to concerns about accessibility by children, the Court noted that FCC rules required use of credit cards, access codes, and scrambling devices. Absent evidence of the effectiveness of that "technological approach," the Court concluded that the law represented "another case of 'burn[ing] up the house to roast the pig.' "

There is no doubt Congress enacted a total ban on both obscene and indecent telephone communications. But aside from conclusory statements during the debates by proponents of the bill, as well as similar assertions in hearings on a substantially identical bill the year before, H. R. 1786, that under the FCC regulations minors could still have access to dial-a-porn messages, the Congressional record presented to us contains no evidence as to *how* effective or ineffective the FCC's most recent regulations were or might prove to be. It may well be that there is no fail-safe method of guaranteeing that never will a minor be able to access the dial-a-porn system. The bill that was enacted, however, was introduced on the floor; nor was there a committee report on the bill from which the language of the enacted bill was taken. No Congressman or Senator purported to present a considered judgment with respect to how often or to what extent minors could or would circumvent the rules and have access to dial-a-porn messages. On the other hand, in the hearings on H. R. 1786, the committee heard testimony from the FCC and other witnesses that the FCC rules would be effective and should be tried out in practice. Furthermore, at the conclusion of the hearing, the chairman of the subcommittee suggested consultation looking toward "drafting a piece of legislation that will pass constitutional muster, while at the same time providing for the practical relief which families and groups are looking for." Hearings, at 235. The bill never emerged from Committee.

For all we know from this record, the FCC's technological approach to restricting dial-a-porn messages to adults who seek them would be extremely effective, and only a few of the most enterprising and disobedient young people will manage to secure access to such messages. If this is the case, it seems to us that § 223(b) is not a narrowly tailored effort to serve the compelling interest of preventing minors from being exposed to indecent telephone messages. Under our precedents, § 223(b), in its present form, has the invalid effect of limiting the content of adult telephone conversations to that which is suitable for children to hear. It is another case of "burn[ing] up the house to roast the pig." *Butler* v. *Michigan*, 352 U. S., at 383.

Because the statute's denial of adult access to telephone messages which are indecent but not obscene far exceeds that which is necessary to limit the access of minors to such messages, we hold that the ban does not survive constitutional scrutiny.

Justice Scalia, in a concurring opinion, noted that the Constitution may foreclose the ban on indecent speech but does not "require[] public utilities to carry it." Justice Brennan, for reasons stated in earlier decisions, would have invalidated the prohibition with respect to obscene communications as well.

If the ruling is viewed strictly as a medium-focused decision, the consequent irony would be the elevation of editorial discretion for a medium with no pertinent First Amendment interest to a higher level than that afforded other constitutionally protected media. The result may be understandable, however, on grounds that it is the protected nature of the speech rather than the medium disseminating it that is dispositive. What is effectively demonstrated, nonetheless, is the interaction between speech and media that must be accounted for in factoring actual First Amendment guarantees.

REFERENCES

CASES

Sable Communications of California, Inc. v. Federal Communications Commission, 109 S. Ct. 2829 (1989).
United States v. American Telephone and Telegraph Co., 552 F. Supp. 131 (D.D.C. 1982), *aff'd*, 460 U.S. 1001 (1983).

Appendix A

New Technologies

Broadcasting and cable for contemporary purposes are the dominant electronic media. Although newer communications technologies have emerged, their potentiality so far exceeds their actuality. This appendix will identify those media that have evolved at least to the point of capturing regulatory attention. Also noted are technologies that, although not independent means for disseminating information, enhance the process in one way or another.

I. SATELLITE MASTER ANTENNA SYSTEMS

Satellite master antenna systems (SMATVs) in basic principle are not unlike early community antenna systems. An SMATV essentially is a mini–cable system that sets up a satellite receiving station in an office or residential complex and carries signals by wire to subscribers. The technology differs from larger cable systems only insofar as no public easements or rights of way are used. Although SMATV functions side by side with locally franchised cable systems, it has escaped comparable state and local regulation. Efforts to assert local control have been preempted by the FCC, which "based its authority over SMATV upon the federal interest in 'the unfettered development of interstate transmission of satellite signals.' " The Commission itself has refused to impose restrictions upon the medium on grounds "that open entry policies in the satellite field would create a more diverse and competitive telecommunications environment." The FCC's preemption order was upheld by the court of appeals in *New York State Commission on Cable Television v. Federal Communications Commission.*

II. HOME SATELLITE DISHES

Private reception of satellite signals is less a traditional medium than a way of intercepting signals for personal use. In 1979, the FCC determined that licensing of receive-only satellite dishes was not mandated by the Communications Act. At that time, the devices were in use primarily in rural areas that were unserved or underserved by broadcasting or cable. Soon after the deregulatory order, however, the cost of the technology began to drop to the point that receive-only dishes became widely affordable. Their accessibility proved distressing to broadcasters and cablecasters alike, who saw a segment of their respective audiences obtaining new programming minus commercials or a monthly fee. Responding to these concerns, the Cable Communications Policy Act of 1984 prohibits unauthorized reception of encrypted signals to the extent that they are marketed to the public. The industry thus has commenced scrambling many of its signals to prevent unauthorized reception. The FCC's position is that because encryption protects copyright and other economic concerns of programmers, it also serves the public interest. Despite arguments that the cable industry has used its influence to make program services for home satellite dish owners artificially high, the FCC has concluded that no specific evidence of such practices exists and thus has recommended against regulation of home satellite program prices.

III. MULTIPOINT DISTRIBUTION SERVICE

Multipoint distribution service (MDS) provides service especially in areas that have yet to receive cable and sometimes where broadcasting is underdeveloped or inaccessible. MDS essentially transmits microwave signals that, upon being received, are converted to a lower television frequency and carried by wire to an empty VHF channel. Traditionally, MDS operators have been licensed as common carriers. As operators began expanding their service from general data transmission to program distribution, however, MDS attracted increasing interest from potential regulators. The FCC, with judicial approval, has preempted state and local regulation. More recently, the Commission altered MDS's status as a common carrier insofar as the actual nature of service provided may determine how the medium will be regarded. Multichannel multipoint distribution service offers program diversification at a much lower start-up cost than, and without the lengthy construction process of, cable. Although MDS does not yet compete with cable in terms of the total number of channels available, technology is expanding its carriage capacity. The medium thus has been touted as a needed source of competition for cable.

IV. DIRECT BROADCAST SATELLITES

Direct broadcast satellites (DBSs) constitute a communications technology that so far has failed to meet expectations. The concept of transmitting programming directly from studio to home is simple and attractive. The service would cover large geographical areas and reach areas that would be unprofitable for cable. In the early 1980s, the FCC set up a licensing process for DBS operators, required compliance with international standards, and for the most part governed the service under the broadcast provisions of the Communications Act of 1934. Soon thereafter, international proceedings set aside a band for DBS, and specific assignments were made. So far, however, DBS has proved in large part economically infeasible because of the cost of launching satellites, the relatively lower price of cable service, and inadequate subscriber bases in areas that cable is unlikely to penetrate.

REFERENCES

CASES

New York State Commission on Cable Television v. Federal Communications Commission, 749 F.2d 804 (D.C. Cir. 1984).
Regulation of Domestic Receive-Only Satellite Earth Stations, 74 F.C.C.2d 205 (1979).

Appendix B

Communications Act of 1934

TITLE I—GENERAL PROVISIONS

§ 151. Purposes of chapter; Federal Communications Commission created

For the purpose of regulating interstate and foreign commerce in communication by wire and radio so as to make available, so far as possible, to all the people of the United States a rapid, efficient, Nation-wide, and world-wide wire and radio communication service with adequate facilities at reasonable charges, for the purpose of the national defense, for the purpose of promoting safety of life and property through the use of wire and radio communications, and for the purpose of securing a more effective execution of this policy by centralizing authority heretofore granted by law to several agencies and by granting additional authority with respect to interstate and foreign commerce in wire and radio communication, there is created a commission to be known as the "Federal Communications Commission," which shall be constituted as hereinafter provided, and which shall execute and enforce the provisions of this chapter. . . .

§ 152. Application of chapter

(a) The provisions of this chapter shall apply to all interstate and foreign communication by wire or radio and all interstate and foreign transmission of energy by radio, which originates and/or is received within the United States, and to all persons engaged within the United States in such communication or such transmission of energy by radio, and to the licensing and regulating of all radio stations as hereinafter provided; but it shall not apply to persons engaged in wire or radio communication or transmission in the Canal Zone, or to wire or radio communication or transmission wholly within the Canal Zone. The provisions of this chapter shall apply with respect to cable service, to all persons engaged within the United States in providing such service, and to the facilities of cable operators which relate to such service, as provided in subchapter V-A of this chapter....

§ 154. *Federal Communications Commission*

(a) *Number of commissioners; appointment; chair-*
man

The Federal Communications Commission (in this chapter referred to as the "Commission") shall be composed of five commissioners appointed by the President, by and with the advice and consent of the Senate, one of whom the President shall designate as chairman....

(i) *Duties and powers*

The Commission may perform any and all acts, make such rules and regulations, and issue such orders, not inconsistent with this chapter, as may be necessary in the execution of its function....

TITLE II—COMMON CARRIERS

§ 201. *Service and charges*

(a) It shall be the duty of every common carrier engaged in interstate or foreign communication by wire or radio to furnish such communication service upon reasonable request therefor; and, in accordance with the orders of the Commission, in cases where the Commission, after opportunity for hearing, finds such action necessary or desirable in the public interest, to establish physical connections with other carriers, to establish through routes and charges applicable thereto and the divisions of such charges, and to establish and provide facilities and regulations for operating such through routes.

(b) All charges, practices, classifications, and regulations for and in connection with such communication service, shall be just and reasonable, and any such charge, practice, classification, or regulation that is unjust or unreasonable is declared to be unlawful: *Provided,* That communications by wire or radio subject to this chapter may be classified into day, night, repeated, unrepeated, letter, commercial, press, Government, and such other classes as the Commission may decide to be just and reasonable, and different charges may be made for the different classes of communications: *Provided further,* That nothing in this chapter or in any other provision of law shall be construed to prevent a common carrier subject to this chapter from entering into or operating under any contract with any common carrier not subject to this chapter, for the exchange of their services, if the Commission is of the opinion that such contract is not contrary to the public interest: *Provided further,* That nothing in this chapter or in any other provision of law shall prevent a common carrier subject to this chapter from furnishing reports of positions of ships at sea to newspapers of general circulation, either at a nominal charge or without charge, provided the name of such common carrier is displayed along with such ship position reports. The Commission may prescribe such rules and regulations as may be necessary in the public interest to carry out the provisions of this chapter.

§ 202. *Discriminations and preferences*

(a) *Charges, services, etc.*

It shall be unlawful for any common carrier to make any unjust or unreasonable discrimination in charges, practices, classifications, regulations, facilities, or services for or in connection with like communication service, directly or indirectly, by any means or device, or to make or give any undue or unreasonable preference or advantage to any particular person, class of persons, or locality, or to subject any particular person, class of persons, or locality to any undue or unreasonable prejudice or disadvantage.

(b) *Charges or services included*

Charges or services, whenever referred to in this chapter, include charges for, or services in connection with, the use of common carrier lines of communication, whether derived from wire or radio facilities, in chain broadcasting or incidental to radio communication of any kind.

(c) *Penalty*

Any carrier who knowingly violates the provisions of this section shall forfeit to the United States the sum of $6,000 for each such offense and $300 for each and every day of the continuance of such offense. . . .

§ 223. *Obscene or harassing telephone calls in the District of Columbia or in interstate or foreign communications*

(a) Whoever—
(1) in the District of Columbia or in interstate or foreign communication by means of telephone—
(A) makes any comment, request, suggestion or proposal which is obscene, lewd, lascivious, filthy, or indecent;
(B) makes a telephone call, whether or not conversation ensues, without disclosing his identity and with intent to annoy, abuse, threaten, or harass any person at the called number;
(C) makes or causes the telephone of another repeatedly or continuously to ring, with intent to harass any person at the called number; or
(D) makes repeated telephone calls, during which conversation ensues, solely to harass any person at the called number; or
(2) knowingly permits any telephone facility under his control to be used for any purpose prohibited by this section,
shall be fined not more than $50,000 or imprisoned not more than six months, or both.
(b)(1) Whoever knowingly—
(A) within the United States, by means of telephone, makes (directly or by recording device) any obscene communication for commercial purposes to any person, regardless of whether the maker of such communication placed the call; or

(B) permits any telephone facility under such person's control to be used for an activity prohibited by subparagraph (A), shall be fined in accordance with Title 18, or imprisoned not more than two years, or both.

(2) Whoever knowingly—

(A) within the United States, by means of telephone, makes (directly or by recording device) any indecent communication for commercial purposes which is available to any person under 18 years of age or to any other person without that person's consent, regardless of whether the maker of such communication placed the call; or

(B) permits any telephone facility under such person's control to be used for an activity prohibited by subparagraph (A), shall be fined not more than $50,000 or imprisoned not more than six months, or both.

(3) It is a defense to prosecution under subparagraph (2) of this subsection that the defendant restrict access to the prohibited communication to persons 18 years of age or older in accordance with subsection (c) of this section and with such procedures as the Commission may prescribe by regulation.

§ 224. *Pole attachments*

(a) *Definitions*

As used in this section:

(1) The term "utility" means any person whose rates or charges are regulated by the Federal Government or a State and who owns or controls poles, ducts, conduits, or rights-of-way used, in whole or in part, for wire communication. Such term does not include any railroad, any person who is cooperatively organized, or any person owned by the Federal Government or any State.

(2) The term "Federal Government" means the Government of the United States or any agency or instrumentality thereof.

(3) The term "State" means any State, territory, or possession of the United States, the District of Columbia, or any political subdivision, agency, or instrumentality thereof.

(4) The term "pole attachment" means any attachment by a cable television system to a pole, duct, conduit, or right-of-way owned or controlled by a utility.

(b) *Authority of Commission to regulate rates, terms, and conditions; enforcement powers; promulgation of regulations*

(1) Subject to the provisions of subsection (c) of this section, the Commission shall regulate the rates, terms, and conditions for pole attachments to provide that such rates, terms, and conditions are just and reasonable, and shall adopt procedures necessary and appropriate to hear and resolve complaints concerning such rates, terms, and conditions. For purposes of enforcing any determinations resulting from complaint procedures established pursuant to this subsection, the Commission shall take such action as it deems appropriate and necessary, including issuing cease and desist orders, as authorized by section 312(b) of this title.

(2) Within 180 days from February 21, 1978, the Commission shall prescribe by rule regulations to carry out the provisions of this section.

(c) State regulatory authority over rates, terms, and conditions; preemption; certification; circumstances constituting State regulation

(1) Nothing in this section shall be construed to apply to, or to give the Commission jurisdiction with respect to rates, terms, and conditions for pole attachments in any case where such matters are regulated by a State.

(2) Each State which regulates the rates, terms, and conditions for pole attachments shall certify to the Commission that—

(A) it regulates such rates, terms, and conditions; and

(B) in so regulating such rates, terms, and conditions, the State has the authority to consider and does consider the interests of the subscribers of cable television services, as well as the interests of the consumers of the utility services.

(3) For purposes of this subsection, a State shall not be considered to regulate the rates, terms, and conditions for pole attachments—

(A) unless the State has issued and made effective rules and regulations implementing the State's regulatory authority over pole attachments; and

(B) with respect to any individual matter, unless the State takes final action on a complaint regarding such matter—

(i) within 180 days after the complaint is filed with the State, or

(ii) within the applicable period prescribed for such final action in such rules and regulations of the State, if the prescribed period does not extend beyond 360 days after the filing of such complaint.

(d) Determination of just and reasonable rates; definition

(1) For purposes of subsection (b) of this section, a rate is just and reasonable if it assures a utility the recovery of not less than the additional costs of providing pole attachments, nor more than an amount determined by multiplying the percentage of the total usable space, or the percentage of the total duct or conduit capacity, which is occupied by the pole attachment by the sum of the operating expenses and actual capital costs of the utility attributable to the entire pole, duct, conduit, or right-of-way.

(2) As used in this subsection, the term "usable space" means the space above the minimum grade level which can be used for the attachment of wires, cables, and associated equipment.

TITLE III—PROVISIONS RELATING TO RADIO

§ 301. License for radio communication or transmission of energy

It is the purpose of this chapter, among other things, to maintain the control of the United States over all the channels of radio transmission; and to provide for the use of such channels, but not the ownership thereof, by persons for limited periods of time, under licenses granted by Federal authority, and no such license shall be construed to create any right, beyond the terms, conditions, and periods of the license. No person shall use or operate any apparatus for the transmission of energy or communications or signals by radio (a) from one place in any State, Territory, or possession of the United States or in the District of Columbia to another place in the same State, Territory, possession, or District;

or (b) from any State, Territory, or possession of the United States, or from the District of Columbia to any other State, Territory, or possession of the United States; or (c) from any place in any State, Territory, or possession of the United States, or in the District of Columbia, to any place in any foreign country or to any vessel; or (d) within any State when the effects of such use extend beyond the borders of said State, or when interference is caused by such use or operation with the transmission of such energy, communications, or signals from within said State to any place beyond its borders, or from any place beyond its borders to any place within said State, or with the transmission or reception of such energy, communications or signals from and/or to places beyond the borders of said State; or (e) upon any vessel or aircraft of the United States (except as provided in section 303(t) of this title); or (f) upon any other mobile stations within the jurisdiction of the United States, except under and in accordance with this chapter and with a license in that behalf granted under the provisions of this chapter....

§ 303. Powers and duties of Commission

Except as otherwise provided in this chapter, the Commission from time to time, as public convenience, interest, or necessity requires, shall—

(a) Classify radio stations;

(b) Prescribe the nature of the service to be rendered by each class of licensed stations and each station within any class;

(c) Assign bands of frequencies to the various classes of stations, and assign frequencies for each individual station and determine the power which each station shall use and the time during which it may operate;

(d) Determine the location of classes of stations or individual stations;

(e) Regulate the kind of apparatus to be used with respect to its external effects and the purity and sharpness of the emissions from each station and from the apparatus therein;

(f) Make such regulations not inconsistent with law as it may deem necessary to prevent interference between stations and to carry out the provisions of this chapter: *Provided, however,* That changes in the frequencies, authorized power, or in the times of operation of any station, shall not be made without the consent of the station licensee unless, after a public hearing, the Commission shall determine that such changes will promote public convenience or interest or will serve public necessity, or the provisions of this chapter will be more fully complied with;

(g) Study new uses for radio, provide for experimental uses of frequencies, and generally encourage the larger and more effective use of radio in the public interest;

(h) Have authority to establish areas or zones to be served by any station;

(i) Have authority to make special regulations applicable to radio stations engaged in chain broadcasting;

(j) Have authority to make general rules and regulations requiring stations to keep such records of programs, transmissions of energy, communications, or signals as it may deem desirable: ...

(m)(1) Have authority to suspend the license of any operator upon proof sufficient to satisfy the Commission that the licensee—

(A) has violated, or caused, aided, or abetted the violation of, any provision of any Act, treaty, or convention binding on the United States, which the Commission is authorized to administer, or any regulation made by the Commission under any such Act, treaty, or convention; or...

(D) has transmitted superfluous radio communications or signals or communications containing profane or obscene words, language, or meaning, or has knowingly transmitted—

(1) false or deceptive signals or communications, or

(2) a call signal or letter which has not been assigned by proper authority to the station he is operating: or

(E) has willfully or maliciously interfered with any other radio communications or signals; or

(F) has obtained or attempted to obtain, or has assisted another to obtain or attempt to obtain, an operator's license by fraudulent means...

(r) Make such rules and regulations and prescribe such restrictions and conditions, not inconsistent with law, as may be necessary to carry out the provisions of this chapter, or any international radio or wire communications treaty or convention, or regulations annexed thereto, including any treaty or convention insofar as it relates to the use of radio, to which the United States is or may hereafter become a party.

(s) Have authority to require that apparatus designed to receive television pictures broadcast simultaneously with sound be capable of adequately receiving all frequencies allocated by the Commission to television broadcasting when such apparatus is shipped in interstate commerce; or is imported from any foreign country into the United States, for sale or resale to the public...

§ 307. Licenses

(a) Grant

The Commission, if public convenience, interest, or necessity will be served thereby, subject to the limitations of this chapter, shall grant to any applicant therefor a station license provided for by this chapter.

(b) Allocation of facilities

In considering applications for licenses, and modifications and renewals thereof, when and insofar as there is demand for the same, the Commission shall make such distribution of licenses, frequencies, hours of operation, and of power among the several States and communities as to provide a fair, efficient, and equitable distribution of radio service to each of the same.

(c) Terms

No license granted for the operation of a television broadcasting station shall be for a longer term than five years and no license so granted for any other class of station (other than a radio broadcasting station) shall be for a longer term than ten years, and any license granted may be revoked as hereinafter provided. Each license granted for the operation of a radio broadcasting station shall be for a term of not to exceed seven years. The term of any license for the operation of any auxiliary broadcast station or equipment which can be used only in conjunction with a primary radio, television, or translator station shall be concurrent with the term of the license for such primary radio, television, or translator station. Upon the expiration of any license, upon application therefor, a renewal of such license may be granted from time to time for a term of not to exceed five years in the case of television broadcasting licenses, for a term of not to exceed seven years in the case of radio broadcasting station licenses, and for a term of not to exceed ten years in the case of other licenses, if the Commission finds that public interest, convenience, and necessity would be served thereby. In order to expedite action on applications for renewal of broadcasting station licenses and in order to avoid needless expense to applicants for such renewals, the Commission shall not require any such applicant to file any information which previously has been furnished to the Commission or which is not directly material to the considerations that affect the granting or denial of such application, but the Commission may require any new or additional facts it deems necessary to make its findings. Pending any hearing and final decision on such an application and the disposition of any petition for rehearing pursuant to section 405 of this title, the Commission shall continue such license in effect. Consistently with the foregoing provisions of this subsection, the Commission may by rule prescribe the period or periods for which licenses shall be granted and renewed for particular classes of stations, but the Commission may not adopt or follow any rule which would preclude it, in any case involving a station of a particular class, from granting or renewing a license for a shorter period than that prescribed for stations of such class if, in its judgment, public interest, convenience, or necessity would be served by such action.

§ 308. Requirements for license . . .

(b) Conditions

All applications for station licenses, or modifications or renewals thereof, shall set forth such facts as the Commission by regulation may prescribe as to the citizenship, character, and financial, technical, and other qualifications of the applicant to operate the station; the ownership and location of the proposed station and of the stations, if any, with which it is proposed to communicate; the frequencies and the power desired to be used; the hours of the day or other periods of time during which it is proposed to operate the station; the purposes for which the station is to be used; and such other information as it may require. The Commission, at any time after the filing of such original application and during the term of any such license, may require from an applicant or licensee further written statements of fact to enable it to determine whether such original application should be granted or denied or such license revoked. Such application and/or such statement of fact shall be signed by the applicant and/or licensee. . . .

§ 309. Application for license

(a) Considerations in granting application

Subject to the provisions of this section, the Commission shall determine, in the case of each application filed with it to which section 308 of this title applies, whether the public interest, convenience, and necessity will be served by the granting of such application, and, if the Commission, upon examination of such application and upon consideration of such other matters as the Commission may officially notice, shall find that public interest, convenience, and necessity would be served by the granting thereof, it shall grant such application. . . .

(d) Petition to deny application; time; contents; reply; findings

(1) Any party in interest may file with the Commission a petition to deny any application (whether as originally filed or as amended) to which subsection (b) of this section applies at any time prior to the day of Commission grant thereof without hearing or the day of formal designation thereof for hearing; except that with respect to any classification of applications, the Commission from time to time by rule may specify a shorter period (no less than thirty days following the issuance of public notice by the Commission of the acceptance for filing of such application or of any substantial amendment thereof), which shorter period shall be reasonably related to the time when the applications would normally be reached for processing. The petitioner shall serve a copy of such petition on the applicant. The petition shall contain specific allegations of fact sufficient to show that the petitioner is a party in interest and that a grant of the application would be prima facie inconsistent with subsection (a) of this section. Such allegations of fact shall, except for those of which official notice may be taken, be supported by affidavit of a person or persons with personal knowledge thereof. The applicant shall be given the opportunity to file a reply in which allegations of fact or denials thereof shall similarly be supported by affidavit.

(2) If the Commission finds on the basis of the application, the pleadings filed, or other matters which it may officially notice that there are no substantial and material questions of fact and that a grant of the application would be consistent with subsection (a) of this section, it shall make the grant, deny the petition, and issue a concise statement of the reasons for denying the petition, which statement shall dispose of all substantial issues raised by the petition. If a substantial and material question of fact is presented or if the Commission for any reason is unable to find that grant of the application would be consistent with subsection (a) of this section, it shall proceed as provided in subsection (e) of this section.

(e) Hearings; intervention; evidence; burden of proof

If, in the case of any application to which subsection (a) of this section applies, a substantial and material question of fact is presented or the Commission for any reason is unable to make the finding specified in such subsection, it shall formally designate the application for hearing on the ground or reasons then obtaining and shall forthwith notify the applicant and all other known parties in interest of such action and the grounds and reasons therefor, specifying with particularity the matters and things in issue but not including issues or requirements phrased generally. When the Commission has so designated an application for hearing, the parties in interest, if any, who are not notified by the Commission of such action may acquire the status of a party to the proceeding thereon by filing a petition for intervention showing the basis for their interest not more than thirty days after publication of the hearing issues or any substantial amendment thereto in the Federal Register. Any hearing subsequently held upon such application shall be a full hearing in which the applicant and all other parties in interest shall be permitted to participate. The burden of proceeding with the introduction of evidence and the burden of proof shall be upon the applicant, except that with respect to any issue presented by a petition to deny or a petition to enlarge the issues, such burdens shall be as determined by the Commission.

(h) Form and conditions of station licenses

Such station licenses as the Commission may grant shall be in such general form as it may prescribe, but each license shall contain, in addition to other provisions, a statement of the following conditions to which such license shall be subject: (1) The station license shall not vest in the licensee any right to operate the station nor any right in the use of the frequencies designated in the license beyond the term thereof nor in any other manner than authorized therein; (2) neither the license nor the right granted thereunder shall be assigned or otherwise transferred in violation of this chapter; (3) every license issued under this chapter shall be subject in terms to the right of use or control conferred by section 606 of this title.

(i) Certain initial licenses and permits; random selection procedure; significant preferences; rules

(1) If there is more than one application for any initial license or construction permit which will involve any use of the electromagnetic spectrum, then the Commission, after determining that each such application is acceptable for filing, shall have authority to grant such license or permit to a qualified applicant through the use of a system of random selection.

(2) No license or construction permit shall be granted to an applicant selected pursuant to paragraph (1) unless the Commission determines the qualifications of such applicant pursuant to subsection (a) of this section and section 308(b) of this title. When substantial and material questions of fact exist concerning such qualifications, the Commission shall conduct a hearing in order to make such determinations. For the purpose of making such determinations, the Commission may, by rule, and notwithstanding any other provision of law—

(A) adopt procedures for the submission of all or part of the evidence in written form;

(B) delegate the function of presiding at the taking of written evidence to Commission employees other than administrative law judges; and

(C) omit the determination required by subsection (a) of this section with respect to any application other than the one selected pursuant to paragraph (1).

(3)(A) The Commission shall establish rules and procedures to ensure that, in the administration of any system of random selection under this subsection used for granting licenses or construction permits for any media of mass communications, significant preferences will be granted to applicants or groups of applicants, the grant to which of the license or permit would increase the diversification of ownership of the media of mass communications. To further diversify the ownership of the media of mass communications, an additional significant preference shall be granted to any applicant controlled by a member or members of a minority group.

(B) The Commission shall have authority to amend such rules from time to time to the extent necessary to carry out the provisions of this subsection. Any such amendment shall be made after notice and opportunity for hearing.

(C) For purposes of this paragraph:

(i) The term "media of mass communications" includes television, radio, cable television, multipoint distribution service, direct broadcast satellite service, and other services, the licensed facilities of which may be substantially devoted toward providing programming or other information services within the editorial control of the licensee.

(ii) The term "minority group" includes Blacks, Hispanics, American Indians, Alaska Natives, Asians and Pacific Islanders.

(4)(A) The Commission, not later than 180 days after September 13, 1982, shall, after notice and opportunity for hearing, prescribe rules establishing a system of random selection for use by the Commission under this subsection in any instance in which the Commission, in its discretion determines that such use is appropriate for the granting of any license or permit in accordance with paragraph (1).

(B) The Commission shall have authority to amend such rules from time to time to the extent necessary to carry out the provisions of this subsection. Any such amendment shall be made after notice and opportunity for hearing.

§ 310. License ownership restrictions

(a) Grant to or holding by foreign government or representative

The station license required under this chapter shall not be granted to or held by any foreign government or the representative thereof.

(b) Grant to or holding by alien or representative, foreign corporation, etc.

No broadcast or common carrier or aeronautical en route or aeronautical fixed radio station license shall be granted to or held by—

(1) any alien or the representative of any alien;

(2) any corporation organized under the laws of any foreign government;

(3) any corporation of which any officer or director is an alien or of which more than one-fifth of the capital stock is owned of record or voted by aliens or their representatives or by a foreign government or representative thereof or by any corporation organized under the laws of a foreign country;

(4) any corporation directly or indirectly controlled by any other corporation of which any officer or more than one-fourth of the directors are aliens, or of which more than one-fourth of the capital stock is owned of record or voted by aliens, their representatives, or by a foreign government or representative thereof, or by any corporation organized under the laws of a foreign country, if the Commission finds that the public interest will be served by the refusal or revocation of such license. . . .

(d) Assignment and transfer of construction permit or station license

No construction permit or station license, or any rights thereunder, shall be transferred, assigned, or disposed of in any manner, voluntarily or involuntarily, directly or indirectly, or by transfer of control of any corporation holding such permit or license, to any person except upon application to the Commission and upon finding by the Commission that the public interest, convenience, and necessity will be served thereby. Any such application shall be disposed of as if the proposed transferee or assignee were making application under section 308 of this title for the permit or license in question; but in acting thereon the Commission may not consider whether the public interest, convenience, and necessity might be served by the transfer, assignment, or disposal of the permit or license to a person other than the proposed transferee or assignee.

§ 311. *Requirements as to certain applications in the broadcasting service*

(a) *Notices of filing and hearing; form and contents*

When there is filed with the Commission any application to which section 309(b)(1) of this title applies, for an instrument of authorization for a station in the broadcasting service, the applicant—

(1) shall give notice of such filing in the principal area which is served or is to be served by the station; and

(2) if the application is formally designated for hearing in accordance with section 309 of this title, shall give notice of such hearing in such area at least ten days before commencement of such hearing.

The Commission shall by rule prescribe the form and content of the notices to be given in compliance with this subsection, and the manner and frequency with which such notices shall be given. . . .

(c) *Agreement between two or more applicants; approval of Commission; pendency of application*

(1) If there are pending before the Commission two or more applications for a permit for construction of a broadcasting station, only one of which can be granted, it shall be unlawful, without approval of the Commission, for the applicants or any of them to effectuate an agreement whereby one or more of such applicants withdraws his or their application or applications.

(2) The request for Commission approval in any such case shall be made in writing jointly by all the parties to the agreement. Such request shall contain or be accompanied by full information with respect to the agreement, set forth in such detail, form, and manner as the Commission shall require.

(3) The Commission shall approve the agreement only if it determines that (A) the agreement is consistent with the public interest, convenience, or necessity; and (B) no party to the agreement filed its application for the purpose of reaching or carrying out such agreement.

§ 312. *Administrative sanctions*

(a) *Revocation of station license or construction permit*

The Commission may revoke any station license or construction permit—

(1) for false statements knowingly made either in the application or in any statement of fact which may be required pursuant to section 308 of this title;

(2) because of conditions coming to the attention of the Commission which

would warrant it in refusing to grant a license or permit on an original application;

(3) for willful or repeated failure to operate substantially as set forth in the license;

(4) for willful or repeated violation of, or willful or repeated failure to observe any provision of this chapter or any rule or regulation of the Commission authorized by this chapter or by a treaty ratified by the United States;

(5) for violation of or failure to observe any final cease and desist order issued by the Commission under this section;

(6) for violation of section 1304, 1343, or 1464 of Title 18; or

(7) for willful or repeated failure to allow reasonable access to or to permit purchase of reasonable amounts of time for the use of a broadcasting station by a legally qualified candidate for Federal elective office on behalf of his candidacy.

(b) Cease and desist orders

Where any person (1) has failed to operate substantially as set forth in a license, (2) has violated or failed to observe any of the provisions of this chapter, or section 1304, 1343, or 1464 of title 18, or (3) has violated or failed to observe any rule or regulation of the Commission authorized by this chapter or by a treaty ratified by the United States, the Commission may order such person to cease and desist from such action.

(c) Order to show cause

Before revoking a license or permit pursuant to subsection (a) of this section, or issuing a cease and desist order pursuant to subsection (b) of this section, the Commission shall serve upon the licensee, permittee, or person involved an order to show cause why an order of revocation or a cease and desist order should not be issued. Any such order to show cause shall contain a statement of the matters with respect to which the Commission is inquiring and shall call upon said licensee, permittee, or person to appear before the Commission at a time and place stated in the order, but in no event less than thirty days after the receipt of such order, and give evidence upon the matter specified therein; except that where safety of life or property is involved, the Commission may provide in the order for a shorter period. If after hearing, or a waiver thereof, the Commission determines that an order of revocation or a cease and desist order should issue, it shall issue such order, which shall include a statement of the findings of the Commission and the grounds and reasons therefor and specify the effective date of the order, and shall cause the same to be served on said licensee, permittee, or person....

(e) Procedure for issuance of cease and desist order

The provisions of section 558(c) of title 5 which apply with respect to the institution of any proceeding for the revocation of a license or permit shall apply also with respect to the institution, under this section, of any proceeding for the issuance of a cease and desist order.

(f) Willful or repeated violations

For purposes of this section:

(1) The term "willful", when used with reference to the commission or omission of any act, means the conscious and deliberate commission or omission of such act, irrespective of any intent to violate any provision of this chapter or any rule or regulation of the Commission authorized by this chapter or by a treaty ratified by the United States.

(2) The term "repeated", when used with reference to the commission or omission of any act, means the commission or omission of such act more than once or, if such commission or omission is continuous, for more than one day.

§ 313. *Application of antitrust laws to manufacture, sale, and trade in radio apparatus*

(a) Revocation of licenses

All laws of the United States relating to unlawful restraints and monopolies and to combinations, contracts, or agreements in restraint of trade are declared to be applicable to the manufacture and sale of and to trade in radio apparatus and devices entering into or affecting interstate or foreign commerce and to interstate or foreign radio communications. Whenever in any suit, action, or proceeding, civil or criminal, brought under the provisions of any of said laws or in any proceedings brought to enforce or to review findings and orders of the Federal Trade Commission or other governmental agency in respect of any matters as to which said Commission or other governmental agency is by law authorized to act, any licensee shall be found guilty of the violation of the provisions of such laws or any of them, the court, in addition to the penalties imposed by said laws, may adjudge, order and/or decree that the license of such licensee shall, as of the date the decree or judgment becomes finally effective or as of such other date as the said decree shall fix, be revoked and that all rights under such license shall thereupon cease: *Provided, however,* That such licensee shall have the same right of appeal or review as is provided by law in respect of other decrees and judgments of said court.

(b) Refusal of licenses and permits

The Commission is hereby directed to refuse a station license and/or the permit hereinafter required for the construction of a station to any person (or to any person directly or indirectly controlled by such person) whose license has been revoked by a court under this section.

§ 315. *Candidates for public office*

(a) Equal opportunities requirement; censorship prohibition; allowance of station use; news appearances exception; public interest; public issues discussion opportunities

If any licensee shall permit any person who is a legally qualified candidate for any public office to use a broadcasting station, he shall afford equal opportunities to all other such candidates for that office in the use of such broadcasting station: *Provided,* That such licensee shall have no power of censorship over the material broadcast under the provisions of this section. No obligation is imposed under this subsection upon any licensee to allow the use of its station by any such candidate. Appearance by a legally qualified candidate on any—

(1) bona fide newscast,

(2) bona fide news interview,

(3) bona fide news documentary (if the appearance of the candidate is incidental to the presentation of the subject or subjects covered by the news documentary), or

(4) on-the-spot coverage of bona fide news events (including but not limited to political conventions and activities incidental thereto),

shall not be deemed to be use of a broadcasting station within the meaning of this subsection. Nothing in the foregoing sentence shall be construed as relieving broadcasters, in connection with the presentation of newscasts, news interviews, news documentaries, and on-the-spot coverage of news events, from the obligation imposed upon them under this chapter to operate in the public interest and to afford reasonable opportunity for the discussion of conflicting views on issues of public importance.

(b) Broadcast media rates

The charges made for the use of any broadcasting station by any person who is a legally qualified candidate for any public office in connection with his campaign for nomination for election, or election to such office shall not exceed—

(1) during the forty-five days preceding the date of a primary or primary runoff election and during the sixty days preceding the date of a general or special election in which such person is a candidate, the lowest unit charge of the station for the same class and amount of time for the same period; and

(2) at any other time, the charges made for comparable use of such station by other users thereof.

(c) Definitions

For purposes of this section—

(1) the term "broadcasting station" includes a community antenna television system; and

(2) the terms "licensee" and "station licensee" when used with respect to a community antenna television system mean the operator of such system.

(d) Rules and regulations

The Commission shall prescribe appropriate rules and regulations to carry out the provisions of this section....

§ 317. Announcement of payment for broadcast

(a) Disclosure of person furnishing

(1) All matter broadcast by any radio station for which any money, service or other valuable consideration is directly or indirectly paid, or promised to or charged or accepted by, the station so broadcasting, from any person, shall, at the time the same is so broadcast, be announced as paid for or furnished, as the case may be, by such person: *Provided,* That "service or other valuable consideration" shall not include any service or property furnished without charge or at a nominal charge for use on, or in connection with, a broadcast unless it is

so furnished in consideration for an identification in a broadcast of any person, product, service, trademark, or brand name beyond an identification which is reasonably related to the use of such service or property on the broadcast....

§ 325. False, fraudulent, or unauthorized transmissions

(a) False distress signals; rebroadcasting programs

No person within the jurisdiction of the United States shall knowingly utter or transmit, or cause to be uttered or transmitted, any false or fraudulent signal of distress, or communication relating thereto, nor shall any broadcasting station rebroadcast the program or any part thereof of another broadcasting station without the express authority of the originating station....

§ 326. Censorship

Nothing in this chapter shall be understood or construed to give the Commission the power of censorship over the radio communications or signals transmitted by any radio station, and no regulation or condition shall be promulgated or fixed by the Commission which shall interfere with the right of free speech by means of radio communication.

TITLE V—PENAL PROVISIONS—FORFEITURES

§ 501. General penalty

Any person who willfully and knowingly does or causes or suffers to be done any act, matter, or thing, in this chapter prohibited or declared to be unlawful, or who willfully and knowingly omits or fails to do any act, matter, or thing in this chapter required to be done, or willfully and knowingly causes or suffers such omission or failure, shall, upon conviction thereof, be punished for such offense, for which no penalty (other than a forfeiture) is provided in this chapter, by a fine of not more than $10,000 or by imprisonment for a term not exceeding one year, or both; except that any person, having been once convicted of an offense punishable under this section, who is subsequently convicted of violating any provision of this chapter punishable under this section, shall be punished by a fine of not more than $10,000 or by imprisonment for a term not exceeding two years, or both.

§ 502. Violation of rules, regulations, etc.

Any person who willfully and knowingly violates any rule, regulation, restriction, or condition made or imposed by the Commission under authority of this chapter, or any rule, regulation, restriction, or condition made or imposed by any international radio or wire communications treaty or convention, or regulations annexed thereto, to which the United States is or may hereafter become a party, shall, in addition to any other penalties provided by law, be punished, upon conviction thereof, by a fine of not more than $500 for each and every day during which such offense occurs.

§ 503. Forfeitures

(b) Activities constituting violations authorizing imposition of forfeiture penalty; amount of penalty; procedures applicable; persons subject to penalty; liability exemption period

(1) Any person who is determined by the Commission, in accordance with paragraph (3) or (4) of this subsection, to have—

(A) willfully or repeatedly failed to comply substantially with the terms and conditions of any license, permit, certificate, or other instrument or authorization issued by the Commission;

(B) willfully or repeatedly failed to comply with any of the provisions of this chapter or of any rule, regulation, or order issued by the Commission under this chapter or under any treaty, convention, or other agreement to which the United States is a party and which is binding upon the United States;

(C) violated any provision of section 317(c) or 509(a) of this title; or

(D) violated any provision of section 1304, 1343, or 1464 of Title 18;

shall be liable to the United States for a forfeiture penalty. A forfeiture penalty under this subsection shall be in addition to any other penalty provided for by this chapter; except that this subsection shall not apply to any conduct which is subject to forfeiture under subchapter II of this chapter, part II or III of subchapter III of this chapter, or section 507 of this title.

(2)(A) If the violator is (i) a broadcast station licensee or permittee, (ii) a cable television operator, or (iii) an applicant for any broadcast or cable television operator license, permit, certificate, or other instrument or authorization issued by the Commission, the amount of any forfeiture penalty determined under this section shall not exceed $25,000 for each violation or each day of a continuing violation, except that the amount assessed for any continuing violation shall not exceed a total of $250,000 for any single act or failure to act described in paragraph (1) of this subsection.

(B) If the violator is a common carrier subject to the provisions of this chapter or an applicant for any common carrier license, permit, certificate, or other instrument of authorization issued by the Commission, the amount of any forfeiture penalty determined under this subsection shall not exceed $100,000 for each violation or each day of a continuing violation, except that the amount assessed for any continuing violation shall not exceed a total of $1,000,000 for any single act or failure to act described in paragraph (1) of this subsection.

(C) In any case not covered in subparagraph (A) or (B), the amount of any forfeiture penalty determined under this subsection shall not exceed $10,000 for each violation or each day of a continuing violation, except that the amount assessed for any continuing violation shall not exceed a total of $75,000 for any single act or failure to act described in paragraph (1) of this subsection.

(D) The amount of such forfeiture penalty shall be assessed by the Commission, or its designee, by written notice. In determining the amount of such a forfeiture penalty, the Commission or its designee shall take into account the nature, circumstances, extent, and gravity of the violation and, with respect to the violator, the degree of culpability, any history of prior offenses, ability to pay, and such other matters as justice may require....

§ 509. Prohibited practices in contests of knowledge, skill, or chance

(a) Influencing, prearranging, or predetermining outcome

It shall be unlawful for any person, with intent to deceive the listening or viewing public—

(1) To supply to any contestant in a purportedly bona fide contest of intellectual knowledge or intellectual skill any special and secret assistance whereby the outcome of such contest will be in whole or in part prearranged or predetermined.

(2) By means of persuasion, bribery, intimidation, or otherwise, to induce or cause any contestant in a purportedly bona fide contest of intellectual knowledge or intellectual skill to refrain in any manner from using or displaying his knowledge or skill in such contest, whereby the outcome thereof will be in whole or in part prearranged or predetermined.

(3) To engage in any artifice or scheme for the purpose of prearranging or predetermining in whole or in part the outcome of a purportedly bona fide contest of intellectual knowledge, intellectual skill, or chance.

(4) To produce or participate in the production for broadcasting of, to broadcast or participate in the broadcasting of, to offer to a licensee for broadcasting, or to sponsor, any radio program, knowing or having reasonable ground for believing that, in connection with a purportedly bona fide contest of intellectual knowledge, intellectual skill, or chance constituting any part of such program, any person has done or is going to do any act or thing referred to in paragraph (1), (2), or (3) of this subsection. . . .

TITLE VI—CABLE COMMUNICATIONS

§ 521. Purposes

The purposes of this subchapter are to—

(1) establish a national policy concerning cable communications;

(2) establish franchise procedures and standards which encourage the growth and development of cable systems and which assure that cable systems are responsive to the needs and interests of the local community;

(3) establish guidelines for the exercise of Federal, State, and local authority with respect to the regulation of cable systems;

(4) assure that cable communications provide and are encouraged to provide the widest possible diversity of information sources and services to the public;

(5) establish an orderly process for franchise renewal which protects cable operators against unfair denials of renewal where the operator's past performance and proposal for future performance meet the standards established by this subchapter; and

(6) promote competition in cable communications and minimize unnecessary regulation that would impose an undue economic burden on cable systems. . . .

§ 531. Cable channels for public, educational, or governmental use

(a) Authority to establish requirements with respect to designation or use of channel capacity

A franchising authority may establish requirements in a franchise with respect to the designation or use of channel capacity for public, educational, or governmental use only to the extent provided in this section.

(b) Authority to require designation for public, educational, or governmental use

A franchising authority may in its request for proposals require as part of a franchise, and may require as part of a cable operator's proposal for a franchise renewal, subject to section 546 of this title, that channel capacity be designated for public, educational, or governmental use, and channel capacity on institutional networks be designated for educational or governmental use, and may require rules and procedures for the use of the channel capacity designated pursuant to this section.

(c) Enforcement authority

A franchising authority may enforce any requirement in any franchise regarding the providing or use of such channel capacity. Such enforcement authority includes the authority to enforce any provisions of the franchise for services, facilities, or equipment proposed by the cable operator which relate to public, educational, or governmental use of channel capacity, whether or not required by the franchising authority pursuant to subsection (b) of this section.

(d) Promulgation of rules and procedures

In the case of any franchise under which channel capacity is designated under subsection (b) of this section, the franchising authority shall prescribe—

(1) rules and procedures under which the cable operator is permitted to use such channel capacity for the provision of other services if such channel capacity is not being used for the purposes designated, and

(2) rules and procedures under which such permitted use shall cease.

(e) Editorial control by cable operator

Subject to section 544(d) of this title, a cable operator shall not exercise any editorial control over any public, educational, or governmental use of channel capacity provided pursuant to this section. . . .

§ 532. *Cable channels for commercial use*

(a) Purpose

The purpose of this section is to assure that the widest possible diversity of information sources are made available to the public from cable systems in a manner consistent with growth and development of cable systems.

(b) Designation of channel capacity for commercial use

(1) A cable operator shall designate channel capacity for commercial use by persons unaffiliated with the operator in accordance with the following requirements:

(A) An operator of any cable system with 36 or more (but not more than 54) activated channels shall designate 10 percent of such channels which are not otherwise required for use (or the use of which is not prohibited) by Federal law or regulation.

(B) An operator of any cable system with 55 or more (but not more than 100) activated channels shall designate 15 percent of such channels which are not otherwise required for use (or the use of which is not prohibited) by Federal law or regulation.

(C) An operator of any cable system with more than 100 activated channels shall designate 15 percent of all such channels.

(D) An operator of any cable system with fewer than 36 activated channels shall not be required to designate channel capacity for commercial use by persons unaffiliated with the operator, unless the cable system is required to provide such channel capacity under the terms of a franchise in effect on October 30, 1984.

(E) An operator of any cable system in operation on October 30, 1984, shall not be required to remove any service actually being provided on July 1, 1984, in order to comply with this section, but shall make channel capacity available for commercial use as such capacity becomes available until such time as the cable operator is in full compliance with this section.

(c) Use of channel capacity by unaffiliated persons; editorial control; restriction on service

(1) If a person unaffiliated with the cable operator seeks to use channel capacity designated pursuant to subsection (b) of this section for commercial use, the cable operator shall establish, consistent with the purpose of this section, the price, terms and conditions of such use which are at least sufficient to assure that such use will not adversely affect the operation, financial condition, or market development of the cable system.

(2) A cable operator shall not exercise any editorial control over any video programming provided pursuant to this section, or in any other way consider the content of such programming, except that an operator may consider such content to the minimum extent necessary to establish a reasonable price for the commercial use of designated channel capacity by an unaffiliated person.

(3) Any cable system channel designated in accordance with this section shall not be used to provide a cable service that is being provided over such system on October 30, 1984, if the provision of such programming is intended to avoid the purpose of this section.

(d) Right of action in district court; relief; factors not to be considered by court

Any person aggrieved by the failure or refusal of a cable operator to make channel capacity available for use pursuant to this section may bring an action in the district court of the United States for the judicial district in which the cable system is located to compel that such capacity be made available. If the court finds that the channel capacity sought by such person has not been made available in accordance with this section, or finds that the price, terms, or conditions established by the cable operator are unreasonable, the court may order such system to make available to such person the channel capacity sought, and further determine the appropriate price, terms, or conditions for such use consistent with subsection (c) of this section, and may award actual damages if it deems such relief appropriate. In any such action, the court shall not consider any price, term, or condition established between an operator and an affiliate for comparable services.

(e) Petition to Commission; relief

(1) Any person aggrieved by the failure or refusal of a cable operator to make channel capacity available pursuant to this section may petition the Commission for relief under this subsection upon a showing of prior adjudicated violations of this section. Records of previous adjudications resulting in a court determination that the operator has violated this section shall be considered as sufficient for the showing necessary under this subsection. If the Commission finds that the channel capacity sought by such person has not been made available in accordance with this section, or that the price, terms, or conditions established by such system are unreasonable under subsection (c) of this section, the Commission shall, by rule or order, require such operator to make available such channel capacity under price, terms, and conditions consistent with subsection (c) of this section.

(2) In any case in which the Commission finds that the prior adjudicated violations of this section constitute a pattern or practice of violations by an operator, the Commission may also establish any further rule or order necessary to assure that the operator provides the diversity of information sources required by this section.

(3) In any case in which the Commission finds that the prior adjudicated violations of this section constitute a pattern or practice of violations by any person who is an operator of more than one cable system, the Commission may also establish any further rule or order necessary to assure that such person provides the diversity of information sources required by this section.

(f) Presumption of reasonableness and good faith

In any action brought under this section in any Federal district court or before the Commission, there shall be a presumption that the price, terms, and conditions for use of channel capacity designated pursuant to subsection (b) of this section are reasonable and in good faith unless shown by clear and convincing evidence to the contrary. . . .

(h) Cable service obscene, lewd, etc., or otherwise unprotected by Constitution

Any cable service offered pursuant to this section shall not be provided, or shall be provided subject to conditions, if such cable service in the judgment of the franchising authority is obscene, or is in conflict with community standards in that it is lewd, lascivious, filthy, or indecent or is otherwise unprotected by the Constitution of the United States.

§ 533. *Ownership restrictions*

(a) Persons owning or controlling television station licensees

It shall be unlawful for any person to be a cable operator if such person, directly or through 1 or more affiliates, owns or controls, the licensee of a television broadcast station and the predicted grade B contour of such station covers any portion of the community served by such operator's cable system.

(b) Common carriers; provision of direct video programming; exception; waiver

(1) It shall be unlawful for any common carrier, subject in whole or in part to subchapter II of this chapter, to provide video programming directly to subscribers in its telephone service area, either directly or indirectly through an affiliate owned by, operated by, controlled by, or under common control with the common carrier.

(2) It shall be unlawful for any common carrier, subject in whole or in part to subchapter II of this chapter, to provide channels of communications or pole line conduit space, or other rental arrangements, to any entity which is directly or indirectly owned by, operated by, controlled by, or under common control with such common carrier, if such facilities or arrangements are to be used for, or in connection with, the provision of video programming directly to subscribers in the telephone service area of the common carrier.

(3) This subsection shall not apply to any common carrier to the extent such carrier provides telephone exchange service in any rural area (as defined by the Commission).

(4) In those areas where the provision of video programming directly to subscribers through a cable system demonstrably could not exist except through a cable system owned by, operated by, controlled by, or affiliated with the common carrier involved, or upon other showing of good cause, the Commission may, on petition for waiver, waive the applicability of paragraphs (1) and (2) of this subsection. Any such waiver shall be made in accordance with section 63.56 of title 47, Code of Federal Regulations (as in effect September 20, 1984) and shall be granted by the Commission upon a finding that the issuance of such waiver is justified by the particular circumstances demonstrated by the petitioner, taking into account the policy of this subsection.

(c) Promulgation of rules

The Commission may prescribe rules with respect to the ownership or control of cable systems by persons who own or control other media of mass communications which serve the same community served by a cable system.

(d) Regulation of ownership by States or franchising authorities

Any State or franchising authority may not prohibit the ownership or control of a cable system by any person because of such person's ownership or control of any media of mass communications or other media interests.

(e) Holding of ownership interests or exercise of editorial control by States or franchising authorities

(1) Subject to paragraph (2), a State or franchising authority may hold any ownership interest in any cable system.

(2) Any State or franchising authority shall not exercise any editorial control regarding the content of any cable service on a cable system in which such governmental entity holds ownership interest (other than programming on any channel designated for educational or governmental use), unless such control is exercised through an entity separate from the franchising authority....

§ 541. General franchise requirements

(a) Authority to award franchises; construction of cable systems over rights-of-way and through easements; conditions for use of easements; equal access to service

(1) A franchising authority may award, in accordance with the provisions of this subchapter 1 or more franchises within its jurisdiction.

(2) Any franchise shall be construed to authorize the construction of a cable system over public rights-of-way, and through easements, which is within the area to be served by the cable system and which have been dedicated for compatible uses, except that in using such easements the cable operator shall ensure—

(A) that the safety, functioning, and appearance of the property and the convenience and safety of other persons not be adversely affected by the installation or construction of facilities necessary for a cable system;

(B) that the cost of the installation, construction, operation, or removal of such facilities be borne by the cable operator or subscriber, or a combination of both; and

(C) that the owner of the property be justly compensated by the cable operator for any damages caused by the installation, construction, operation, or removal of such facilities by the cable operator.

(3) In awarding a franchise or franchises, a franchising authority shall assure that access to cable service is not denied to any group of potential residential cable subscribers because of the income of the residents of the local area in which such group resides....

(c) Status of cable system as common carrier or utility

Any cable system shall not be subject to regulation as a common carrier or utility by reason of providing any cable service....

(e) State regulation of facilities serving subscribers in multiple dwelling units

Nothing in this subchapter shall be construed to affect the authority of any State to license or otherwise regulate any facility or combination of facilities which serves only subscribers in one or more multiple unit dwellings under common ownership, control, or management and which does not use any public right-of-way.

§ 542. *Franchise fees*

(a) Payment under terms of franchise

Subject to the limitation of subsection (b) of this section, any cable operator may be required under the terms of any franchise to pay a franchise fee.

(b) Amount of fees per annum

For any twelve-month period, the franchise fees paid by a cable operator with respect to any cable system shall not exceed 5 percent of such cable operator's gross revenues derived in such period from the operation of the cable system. For purposes of this section, the 12-month period shall be the 12-month period applicable under the franchise for accounting purposes. Nothing in this subsection shall prohibit a franchising authority and a cable operator from agreeing that franchise fees which lawfully could be collected for any such 12-month period shall be paid on a prepaid or deferred basis; except that the sum of the fees paid during the term of the franchise may not exceed the amount, including the time value of money, which would have lawfully been collected if such fees had been paid per annum.

(c) Increases passed through to subscribers

A cable operator may pass through to subscribers the amount of any increase in a franchise fee, unless the franchising authority demonstrates that the rate structure specified in the franchise reflects all costs of franchise fees and so notifies the cable operator in writing....

(e) Decreases passed through to subscribers

Any cable operator shall pass through to subscribers the amount of any decrease in a franchise fee....

(g) "Franchise fee" defined

For the purposes of this section—
(1) the term "franchise fee" includes any tax, fee, or assessment of any kind imposed by a franchising authority or other governmental entity on a cable operator or cable subscriber, or both, solely because of their status as such;
(2) the term "franchise fee" does not include—
(A) any tax, fee, or assessment of general applicability (including any such tax, fee, or assessment imposed on both utilities and cable operators or their services but not including a tax, fee, or assessment which is unduly discriminatory against cable operators or cable subscribers);
(B) in the case of any franchise in effect on October 30, 1984, payments which are required by the franchise to be made by the cable operator during the term of such franchise for, or in support of the use of, public, educational, or governmental access facilities;
(C) in the case of any franchise granted after October 30, 1984, capital costs which are required by the franchise to be incurred by the cable operator for public, educational, or governmental access facilities;
(D) requirements or charges incidental to the awarding or enforcing of the franchise, including payments for bonds, security funds, letters of credit, insurance, indemnification, penalties, or liquidated damages; or
(E) any fee imposed under Title 17.

(h) Uncompensated services; taxes, fees and other assessments; limitation on fees

(1) Nothing in this chapter shall be construed to limit any authority of a franchising authority to impose a tax, fee, or other assessment of any kind on any person (other than a cable operator) with respect to cable service or other communications service provided by such person over a cable system for which charges are assessed to subscribers but not received by the cable operator.

(2) For any 12-month period, the fees paid by such person with respect to any such cable service or other communications service shall not exceed 5 percent of such person's gross revenues derived in such period from the provision of such service over the cable system.

(i) Regulatory authority of Federal agencies

Any Federal agency may not regulate the amount of the franchise fees paid by a cable operator, or regulate the use of funds derived from such fees, except as provided in this section.

§ 543. *Regulation of rates*

(a) *Limitation on regulatory power of Federal agencies, States, or franchising authorities*

Any Federal agency or State may not regulate the rates for the provision of cable service except to the extent provided under this section. Any franchising authority may regulate the rates for the provision of cable service, or any other communications service provided over a cable system to cable subscribers, but only to the extent provided under this section.

(b) *Promulgation of regulations; scope; contents; periodic review and amendment*

(1) Within 180 days after October 30, 1984, the Commission shall prescribe and make effective regulations which authorize a franchising authority to regulate rates for the provision of basic cable service in circumstances in which a cable system is not subject to effective competition. Such regulations may apply to any franchise granted after the effective date of such regulations. Such regulations shall not apply to any rate while such rate is subject to the provisions of subsection (c) of this section.

(2) For purposes of rate regulation under this subsection, such regulations shall—

(A) define the circumstances in which a cable system is not subject to effective competition; and

(B) establish standards for such rate regulation.

(3) The Commission shall periodically review such regulations, taking into account developments in technology, and may amend such regulations, consistent with paragraphs (1) and (2), to the extent the Commission determines necessary.

(c) *Regulation by franchising authority during initial two-year period*

In the case of any cable system for which a franchise has been granted on or before the effective date of this subchapter, until the end of the 2-year period beginning on such effective date, the franchising authority may, to the extent provided in a franchise—

(1) regulate the rates for the provision of basic cable service, including multiple tiers of basic cable service;

(2) require the provision of any service tier provided without charge (disregarding any installation or rental charge for equipment necessary for receipt of such tier); or

(3) regulate rates for the initial installation or the rental of 1 set of the minimum equipment which is necessary for the subscriber's receipt of basic cable service. . . .

(e) *Additional increases; reduction by amount of increase under franchise provisions*

(1) In addition to any other rate increase which is subject to the approval of a franchising authority, any rate subject to regulation pursuant to this section

may be increased after the effective date of this subchapter at the discretion of the cable operator by an amount not to exceed 5 percent per year if the franchise (as in effect on the effective date of this subchapter) does not specify a fixed rate or rates for basic cable service for a specified period or periods which would be exceeded if such increase took effect.

(2) Nothing in this section shall be construed to limit provisions of a franchise which permits a cable operator to increase any rate at the operator's discretion; however, the aggregate increases per year allowed under paragraph (1) shall be reduced by the amount of any increase taken such year under such franchise provisions.

Nothing in this subchapter shall be construed as prohibiting any Federal agency, State, or a franchising authority, from—

(1) prohibiting discrimination among customers of basic cable service, or

(2) requiring and regulating the installation or rental of equipment which facilitates the reception of basic cable service by hearing impaired individuals.

(f) Nondiscrimination; facilitation of reception by hearing-impaired individuals

Nothing in this title shall be construed as prohibiting any Federal agency, State, or a franchising authority, from—

(1) prohibiting discrimination among customers of basic cable service, or

(2) requiring and regulating the installation or rental of equipment which facilitates the reception of basic cable service by hearing impaired individuals.

. . .

§ 544. Regulation of services, facilities, and equipment

(a) Regulation by franchising authority

Any franchising authority may not regulate the services, facilities, and equipment provided by a cable operator except to the extent consistent with this subchapter.

(b) Requests for proposals, establishment and enforcement of requirements

In the case of any franchise granted after the effective date of this subchapter the franchising authority, to the extent related to the establishment or operation of a cable system—

(1) in its request for proposals for a franchise (including requests for renewal proposals, subject to section 546 of this title), may establish requirements for facilities and equipment, but may not establish requirements for video programming or other information services; and

(2) subject to section 545 of this title, may enforce any requirements contained within the franchise—

(A) for facilities and equipment; and

(B) for broad categories of video programming or other services.

(c) Enforcement authority respecting franchise effective under prior law

In the case of any franchise in effect on the effective date of this subchapter, the franchising authority may, subject to section 545 of this title, enforce requirements contained within the franchise for the provision of services, facilities, and equipment, whether or not related to the establishment or operation of a cable system.

(d) Cable service obscene, indecent or otherwise unprotected by Constitution

(1) Nothing in this subchapter shall be construed as prohibiting a franchising authority and a cable operator from specifying, in a franchise or renewal thereof, that certain cable services shall not be provided or shall be provided subject to conditions, if such cable services are obscene or are otherwise unprotected by the Constitution of the United States.

(2)(A) In order to restrict the viewing of programming which is obscene or indecent, upon the request of a subscriber, a cable operator shall provide (by sale or lease) a device by which the subscriber can prohibit viewing of a particular cable service during periods selected by that subscriber....

(e) Technical standards

The Commission may establish technical standards relating to the facilities and equipment of cable systems which a franchising authority may require in the franchise.

(f) Limitation on regulatory powers of Federal agencies, States, or franchising authorities; exceptions

(1) Any Federal agency, State, or franchising authority may not impose requirements regarding the provision or content of cable services, except as expressly provided in this sub-chapter....

§ 545. *Modification of franchise obligations*

(a) Grounds for modification by franchising authority; public proceeding; time of decision

(1) During the period a franchise is in effect, the cable operator may obtain from the franchising authority modifications of the requirements in such franchise—

> (A) in the case of any such requirement for facilities or equipment, including public, educational, or governmental access facilities or equipment, if the cable operator demonstrates that (i) it is commercially impracticable for the operator to comply with such requirement, and (ii) the proposal by the cable operator for modification of such requirement is appropriate because of commercial impracticability; or
>
> (B) in the case of any such requirement for services, if the cable operator demonstrates that the mix, quality, and level of services required by the franchise at the time it was granted will be maintained after such modification.

(2) Any final decision by a franchising authority under this subsection shall be made in a public proceeding. Such decision shall be made within 120 days after receipt of such request by the franchising authority, unless such 120 day period is extended by mutual agreement of the cable operator and the franchising authority.

(b) Judicial proceedings; grounds for modification by court

(1) Any cable operator whose request for modification under subsection (a) of this section has been denied by a final decision of a franchising authority may obtain modification of such franchise requirements pursuant to the provisions of section 555 of this title.

(2) In the case of any proposed modification of a requirement for facilities or equipment, the court shall grant such modification only if the cable operator demonstrates to the court that—

(A) it is commercially impracticable for the operator to comply with such requirement; and

(B) the terms of the modification requested are appropriate because of commercial impracticability.

(3) In the case of any proposed modification of a requirement for services, the court shall grant such modification only if the cable operator demonstrates to the court that the mix, quality, and level of services required by the franchise at the time it was granted will be maintained after such modification.

(c) Rearrangement, replacement or removal of service

Notwithstanding subsections (a) and (b) of this section, a cable operator may, upon 30 days' advance notice to the franchising authority, rearrange, replace, or remove a particular cable service required by the franchise if—

(1) such service is no longer available to the operator, or

(2) such service is available to the operator only upon the payment of a royalty required under section 801(b)(2) of Title 17 which the cable operator can document—

(A) is substantially in excess of the amount of such payment required on the date of the operator's offer to provide such service, and

(B) has not been specifically compensated for through a rate increase or other adjustment.

(d) Rearrangement of particular services from one service tier to another or other offering of service

Notwithstanding subsections (a) and (b) of this section, a cable operator may take such actions to rearrange a particular service from one service tier to another, or otherwise offer the service, if the rates for all of the service tiers involved in such actions are not subject to regulation under section 543 of this title.

(e) Requirements for services relating to public, educational, or governmental access

A cable operator may not obtain modification under this section of any requirement for services relating to public, educational, or governmental access.

(f) "Commercially impracticable" defined

For purposes of this section, the term "commercially impracticable" means, with respect to any requirement applicable to a cable operator, that it is commercially impracticable for the operator to comply with such requirement as a result of a change in conditions which is beyond the control of the operator and the nonoccurrence of which was a basic assumption on which the requirement was based.

§ 546. Renewal

(a) Commencement of proceedings; time; public notice and participation; purpose

During the 6-month period which begins with the 36th month before the franchise expiration, the franchising authority may on its own initiative, and shall at the request of the cable operator, commence proceedings which afford the public in the franchise area appropriate notice and participation for the purpose of—

(1) identifying the future cable-related community needs and interests; and

(2) reviewing the performance of the cable operator under the franchise during the then current franchise term.

(b) Submission of renewal proposals; contents; time

(1) Upon completion of a proceeding under subsection (a) of this section, a cable operator seeking renewal of a franchise may, on its own initiative or at the request of a franchising authority, submit a proposal for renewal.

(2) Subject to section 544 of this title, any such proposal shall contain such material as the franchising authority may require, including proposals for an upgrade of the cable system.

(3) The franchising authority may establish a date by which such proposal shall be submitted.

(c) Notice of proposal; renewal; preliminary assessment of nonrenewal; administrative review; issues; notice and opportunity for hearing; transcript; written decision

(1) Upon submittal by a cable operator of a proposal to the franchising authority for the renewal of a franchise, the franchising authority shall provide prompt public notice of such proposal and, during the 4-month period which begins on the completion of any proceedings under subsection (a) of this section, renew the franchise or, issue a preliminary assessment that the franchise should not be renewed and, at the request of the operator or on its own initiative, commence an administrative proceeding, after providing prompt public notice of such proceeding, in accordance with paragraph (2) to consider whether—

(A) the cable operator has substantially complied with the material terms of the existing franchise and with applicable law;

(B) the quality of the operator's service, including signal quality, response to consumer complaints, and billing practices, but without regard to the mix, quality, or level of cable services or other services provided over the system, has been reasonable in light of community needs;

(C) the operator has the financial, legal, and technical ability to provide the services, facilities, and equipment as set forth in the operator's proposal; and

(D) the operator's proposal is reasonable to meet the future cable-related community needs and interests, taking into account the cost of meeting such needs and interests.

(2) In any proceeding under paragraph (1), the cable operator shall be afforded adequate notice and the cable operator and the franchise authority, or its designee, shall be afforded fair opportunity for full participation, including the right to introduce evidence (including evidence related to issues raised in

the proceeding under subsection (a) of this section), to require the production of evidence, and to question witnesses. A transcript shall be made of any such proceeding.

(3) At the completion of a proceeding under this subsection, the franchising authority shall issue a written decision granting or denying the proposal for renewal based upon the record of such proceeding, and transmit a copy of such decision to the cable operator. Such decision shall state the reasons therefor.

(d) Basis for denial

Any denial of a proposal for renewal shall be based on one or more adverse findings made with respect to the factors described in subparagraphs (A) through (D) of subsection (c)(1) of this section, pursuant to the record of the proceeding under subsection (c) of this section. A franchising authority may not base a denial of renewal on a failure to substantially comply with the material terms of the franchise under subsection (c)(1)(A) of this section or on events considered under subsection (c)(1)(B) of this section in any case in which a violation of the franchise or the events considered under subsection (c)(1)(B) of this section occur after the effective date of this subchapter unless the franchising authority has provided the operator with notice and the opportunity to cure, or in any case in which it is documented that the franchising authority has waived its right to object, or has effectively acquiesced.

(e) Judicial review; grounds for relief

(1) Any cable operator whose proposal for renewal has been denied by a final decision of a franchising authority made pursuant to this section, or has been adversely affected by a failure of the franchising authority to act in accordance with the procedural requirements of this section, may appeal such final decision or failure pursuant to the provisions of section 555 of this title....

§ 553. Unauthorized reception of cable service

   (a) Unauthorized interception or receipt or assistance in intercepting or receiving service; definition

(1) No person shall intercept or receive or assist in intercepting or receiving any communications service offered over a cable system, unless specifically authorized to do so by a cable operator or as may otherwise be specifically authorized by law.

(2) For the purpose of this section, the term "assist in intercepting or receiving" shall include the manufacture or distribution of equipment intended by the manufacturer or distributor (as the case may be) for unauthorized reception of any communications service offered over a cable system in violation of subparagraph (1).

   (b) Penalties for willful violation

(1) Any person who willfully violates subsection (a)(1) of this section shall be fined not more than $1,000 or imprisoned for not more than 6 months, or both.

(2) Any person who violates subsection (a)(1) of this section willfully and for purposes of commercial advantage or private financial gain shall be fined not

more than $25,000 or imprisoned for not more than 1 year, or both, for the first such offense and shall be fined not more than $50,000 or imprisoned for not more than 2 years, or both, for any subsequent offense....

§ 555. *Judicial proceedings*

(a) Any cable operator adversely affected by any final determination made by a franchising authority under section 545 or 546 of this title may commence an action within 120 days after receiving notice of such determination, which may be brought in—

(1) the district court of the United States for any judicial district in which the cable system is located; or

(2) in any State court of general jurisdiction having jurisdiction over the parties.

(b) The court may award any appropriate relief consistent with the provisions of the relevant section described in subsection (a) of this section.

§ 556. *Coordination of Federal, State, and local authority*

(a) *Regulation by States, political subdivisions, State and local agencies, and franchising authorities*

Nothing in this subchapter shall be construed to affect any authority of any State, political subdivision, or agency thereof, or franchising authority, regarding matters of public health, safety, and welfare, to the extent consistent with the express provisions of this subchapter.

(b) *State jurisdiction with regard to cable services*

Nothing in this chapter shall be construed to restrict a State from exercising jurisdiction with regard to cable services consistent with this subchapter.

(c) *Preemption*

Except as provided in section 557 of this title, any provision of law of any State, political subdivision, or agency thereof, or franchising authority, or any provision of any franchise granted by such authority, which is inconsistent with this chapter shall be deemed to be preempted and superseded....

§ 558. *Criminal and civil liability*

Nothing in this subchapter shall be deemed to affect the criminal or civil liability of cable programmers or cable operators pursuant to the Federal, State, or local law of libel, slander, obscenity, incitement, invasions of privacy, false or misleading advertising, or other similar laws, except that cable operators shall not incur any such liability for any program carried on any channel designated for public, educational, governmental use or on any other channel obtained under section 532 of this title or under similar arrangements.

§ 559. *Obscene programming*

Whoever transmits over any cable system any matter which is obscene or otherwise unprotected by the Constitution of the United States shall be fined not more than $10,000 or imprisoned not more than 2 years, or both....

§ 605. Unauthorized publication or use of communications

(a) Practices prohibited

Except as authorized by chapter 119, Title 18, no person receiving, assisting in receiving, transmitting, or assisting in transmitting, any interstate or foreign communication by wire or radio shall divulge or publish the existence, contents, substance, purport, effect, or meaning thereof, except through authorized channels of transmission or reception, (1) to any person other than the addressee, his agent, or attorney, (2) to a person employed or authorized to forward such communication to its destination, (3) to proper accounting or distributing officers of the various communicating centers over which the communication may be passed, (4) to the master of a ship under whom he is serving, (5) in response to a subpena issued by a court of competent jurisdiction, or (6) on demand of other lawful authority. No person not being authorized by the sender shall intercept any radio communication and divulge or publish the existence, contents, substance, purport, effect, or meaning of such intercepted communication to any person. No person not being entitled thereto shall receive or assist in receiving any interstate or foreign communication by radio and use such communication (or any information therein contained) for his own benefit or for the benefit of another not entitled thereto. No person having received any intercepted radio communication or having become acquainted with the contents, substance, purport, effect, or meaning of such communication (or any part thereof) knowing that such communication was intercepted, shall divulge or publish the existence, contents, substance, purport, effect, or meaning of such communication (or any part thereof) or use such communication (or any information therein contained) for his own benefit or for the benefit of another not entitled thereto. This section shall not apply to the receiving, divulging, publishing, or utilizing the contents of any radio communication which is transmitted by any station for the use of the general public, which relates to ships, aircraft, vehicles, or persons in distress, or which is transmitted by an amateur radio station operator or by a citizens band radio operator.

(b) Exceptions

The provisions of subsection (a) of this section shall not apply to the interception or receipt by any individual, or the assisting (including the manufacture or sale) of such interception or receipt, of any satellite cable programming for private viewing if—
(1) the programming involved is not encrypted; and
(2)(A) a marketing system is not established under which—
(i) an agent or agents have been lawfully designated for the purpose of authorizing private viewing by individuals, and
(ii) such authorization is available to the individual involved from the appropriate agent or agents; or
(B) a marketing system described in subparagraph (A) is established and the individuals receiving such programming has obtained authorization for private viewing under that system.

(c) Scrambling of Public Broadcasting Service programming

No person shall encrypt or continue to encrypt satellite delivered programs included in the National Program Service of the Public Broadcasting Service and intended for public viewing by retransmission by television broadcast stations; except that as long as at least one unencrypted satellite transmission of any program subject to this subsection is provided, this subsection shall not prohibit additional encrypted satellite transmissions of the same program.

(d) Definitions

For purposes of this section—

(1) the term "satellite cable programming" means video programming which is transmitted via satellite and which is primarily intended for the direct receipt by cable operators for their retransmission to cable subscribers;

(2) the term "agent", with respect to any person, includes an employee of such person;

(3) the term "encrypt", when used with respect to satellite cable programming, means to transmit such programming in a form whereby the aural and visual characteristics (or both) are modified or altered for the purpose of preventing the unauthorized receipt of such programming by persons without authorized equipment which is designed to eliminate the effects of such modification or alteration;

(4) the term "private viewing" means the viewing for private use in an individual's dwelling unit by means of equipment, owned or operated by such individual, capable of receiving satellite cable programming directly from a satellite;

(5) the term "private financial gain" shall not include the gain resulting to any individual for the private use in such individual's dwelling unit of any programming for which the individual has not obtained authorization for that use; and

(6) the term "any person aggrieved" shall include any person with proprietary rights in the intercepted communication by wire or radio, including wholesale or retail distributors of satellite cable programming, and, in the case of a violation of paragraph (4) of subsection (d) of this section shall also include any person engaged in the lawful manufacture, distribution, or sale of equipment necessary to authorize or receive satellite cable programming.

(e) Penalties; civil actions; remedies; attorney's fees and costs; computation of damages; regulation by State and local authorities

(1) Any person who willfully violates subsection (a) of this section shall be fined not more then $2,000 or imprisoned for not more than 6 months, or both.

(2) Any person who violates subsection (a) of this section willfully and for purposes of direct or indirect commercial advantage or private financial gain shall be fined not more than $50,000 or imprisoned for not more than 2 years, or both, for the first such conviction and shall be fined not more than $100,000 or imprisoned for not more than 5 years, or both, for any subsequent conviction.

(3)(A) Any person aggrieved by any violation of subsection (a) of this section or paragraph (4) of subsection (e) of this section may bring a civil action in a United States district court or in any other court of competent jurisdiction.

(B) The court—

(i) may grant temporary and final injunctions on such terms as it may deem reasonable to prevent or restrain violations of subsection (a) of this section;

(ii) may award damages as described in subparagraph (C); and

(iii) shall direct the recovery of full costs, including awarding reasonable attorneys' fees to an aggrieved party who prevails....

(f) Universal encryption standard

Within 6 months after November 16, 1988, the Federal Communications Commission shall initiate an inquiry concerning the need for a universal encryption standard that permits decryption of satellite cable programming intended for private viewing. In conducting such inquiry, the Commission shall take into account—

(1) consumer costs and benefits of any such standard, including consumer investment in equipment in operation;

(2) incorporation of technological enhancements, including advanced television formats;

(3) whether any such standard would effectively prevent present and future unauthorized decryption of satellite cable programming;

(4) the costs and benefits of any such standard on other authorized users of encrypted satellite cable programming, including cable systems and satellite master antenna television systems;

(5) the effect of any such standard on competition in the manufacture of decryption equipment; and

(6) the impact of the time delay associated with the Commission procedures necessary for establishment of such standards.

(g) Rulemaking for encryption standard

If the Commission finds, based on the information gathered from the inquiry required by subsection (f) of this section, that a universal encryption standard is necessary and in the public interest, the Commission shall initiate a rulemaking to establish such a standard.

Appendix C

Glossary

Absolutism. The notion, never fully subscribed to by the Supreme Court, that the First Amendment is indefeasible under any circumstances.

Access. (1) The right of a person or entity to use a medium that he, she, or it does not own or operate. (2) The right to be present at a government activity or obtain official information.

Actual malice. A state of mind characterized by prior knowledge of falsehood or the entertaining of serious doubt concerning the truth of a publication. Unless actual malice is established, a public official or public figure may not prevail in a defamation action.

Allocation. The distribution of the electromagnetic spectrum into bands of frequencies for specific services (e.g., radio, television, marine services, microwave, cellular telephones).

Allotment. The distribution to geographical areas of electromagnetic spectrum use within an allocated band.

Amplitude modulation (AM). Radio-wave propagation characterized by variation of wavelength and constancy of frequency. AM service occupies frequencies from 535 to 1605 kilohertz.

Antitrust laws. Legislation protecting industry and commerce against unlawful restriction and monopolies.

Appropriation. Unauthorized use of a name or likeness for profit—also known as right of publicity.

Areopagitica. John Milton's tract, published in 1644, attacking the English licensing system and projecting the imagery of what later would be denominated the marketplace of ideas.

Assignment. The awarding of a license to a user of the electromagnetic spectrum.

Blackstone, Sir William. A prominent eighteenth-century English jurist who advanced the notion that the central meaning of press liberty is freedom from prior restraint.

Broadcasting. Propagation by electromagnetic radiation that is converted into sound (radio) or picture and sound (television) at the point of reception.

Cable Communications Policy Act of 1984. Title VI of the Communications Act of 1934, which bifurcated responsibility for cable television regulation by assigning separate roles to federal and state governments.

Cable television. A communications technology that propagates signals along a closed transmission path and converts them into video at the point of reception.

Chain ownership. Ownership of multiple media of the same type by a single individual, group, or entity.

Clear and present danger. A constitutional standard permitting regulation of speech to the extent that the expression is intended and likely to produce imminent harm. The test is used primarily in connection with speech advocating illegal action, including insurrection.

Commercial speech. A classification of expression that includes speech relating to economic self-interest proposing a commercial transaction.

Common carrier. A medium, including telephones and telegraph service, obligated to provide equal access in a nondiscriminatory fashion.

Communications Act of 1934. A comprehensive federal regulatory scheme governing broadcasting, cable, and common carriers.

Consent decree. A judicial order reflecting a negotiated agreement between or among adverse parties that resolves a case or controversy and is contractually enforceable.

Copyright. A means of protecting intellectual property by defining and securing usage rights.

Cross-ownership. Ownership of different media in the same community or market area by a single individual, group, or entity.

Defamation. Expression, spoken or published, that injures reputation. Traditionally, spoken defamation is characterized as slander and written defamation is regarded as libel.

Direct broadcast satellite (DBS). The technology of broadcasting directly from point of origination to a home satellite dish.

Distant importation. A cable system's carriage of a television signal from outside the local broadcast service area.

Duopoly. Ownership of more than one of the same type of broadcast service in a given service area.

Duplication. A cable system's carriage of a distantly imported signal providing the same network programming as a local broadcast station.

Electronic publishing. Propagation by closed transmission path of textual or visual information to a television set or computer display screen.

Fairness doctrine. Regulation obligating broadcasters to provide coverage of controversial issues of public importance and ensure that such programming is balanced.

Fairness regulation. A regulatory concept that includes the fairness doctrine, the political editorial rule, and the personal attack rule.

False light privacy. Publication of a falsehood about a person, the harm of which is not damage to reputation but invasion of privacy.

Federal Communications Commission. The governmental agency that, under the Communications Act of 1934, is charged with executing and enforcing the act's provisions concerning broadcasting, cable, and common carriers.

Franchise. An agreement between state or local government authorizing a cable company to provide service in a designated area pursuant to specific terms and conditions.

Frequency modulation (FM). Radio-wave propagation characterized by variation in wave frequency and constancy of wavelength.

Gag order. A prior restraint upon speech or publication entered by a court.

Indecent speech. A classification for expression that is sexually explicit or vulgar but not obscene and thus is not without constitutional status.

Injunction. A court order prohibiting a person or entity from engaging in certain action or, less frequently, requiring affirmative conduct.

Intrusion. Invasion of privacy by breaching a person's environment or solitude.

Joint operating agreement (JOA). A partial merger by which newspapers combine their business operations but maintain separate editorial departments. JOAs are exempt from antitrust law, provided they satisfy terms of the Newspaper Preservation Act.

Leapfrogging. A cable system's importation of distant signals. Until 1976, leapfrogging was prohibited in an effort to protect local broadcasters who would have to compete against identical programming at risk to market base.

Libel. Traditionally, defamation by publication. *See* Defamation.

License. A limited use right granted by the Federal Communications Commission to broadcast on an assigned frequency.

Lower-power television (LPTV). A broadcast service characterized by its limited transmission range (usually ten to fifteen miles), which may operate on any available channel provided it does not interfere with primary television service.

Meiklejohn, Alexander. Legal scholar whose writings emphasizing the value of political speech have profoundly influenced modern reading of the First Amendment.

Multipoint distribution service (MDS). Transmission of microwave signals over a short range, usually in urban areas, which are received, converted, and displayed on an open VHF channel.

Must carriage. Regulation obligating a cable system to pick up and distribute to its subscribers specified broadcast signals. Must-carry rules have been invalidated in each instance when challenged.

Obscenity. A classification of expression that appeals to the prurient interest, is patently offensive as measured by contemporary community standards, and is without redeeming political, artistic, literary, or scientific value. Obscenity is constitutionally unprotected.

Overbroad. A term applied to regulation of expression that sweeps protected speech into its purview.

Personal attack rule. A conditional right of access that affords an opportunity to respond to a broadcast attack upon a person's or group's honesty, character, integrity, or like qualities. A similar rule for print media was declared unconstitutional.

Piracy. Unauthorized receipt of a broadcast, cable, or satellite signal.

Preemption. Displacement of state law by federal law pursuant to the supremacy clause of the Constitution.

Prime Time Access Rule (PTAR). A rule limiting network control over prime-time programming by requiring, subject to certain exemptions, affiliates to restrict network programming in prime time to three hours.

Prior restraint. A governmental action that prohibits speaking or publication.

Public figure. For defamation purposes, a person who has achieved pervasive fame or notoriety (public figure for all purposes) or who voluntarily injects himself or herself into a public controversy to influence its outcome (public figure for limited purposes). A public figure, to prevail in a defamation action, must show that the falsehood was propagated with actual malice.

Public official. For defamation purposes, a person whose status in a government position of responsibility is sufficient to require that a falsehood was propagated with actual malice.

Reporter's privilege. The notion that the First Amendment protects journalists from having to disclose sources in a grand jury or judicial proceeding.

Right of publicity. *See* Appropriation.

Right of reply. Right of access contingent upon a specified event, such as a personal attack appearance of a political candidate.

Satellite master antenna television system (SMATV). Essentially a miniaturized cable system that receives satellite signals and distributes them in a building or small-community leg wire.

Sedition Act. A law enacted by the Federalist Congress and administration in 1798 that criminalized criticism of the government or government officials. The Sedition Act lapsed after two years.

Seditious libel. Speech that criticizes government or a government official in a way proscribed by law.

Siphoning. A cable system's presentation of programming that traditionally has been broadcast on commercial television.

Slander. Traditionally, defamation by spoken word. *See* Defamation.

Spectrum scarcity. The notion that the electromagnetic spectrum has a finite capacity and thus more demand for its use than can be accommodated.

State action. Action or policy attributable to a government rather than private source and thus having constitutional significance.

Subscription Television (STV). A broadcast service that transmits encoded signals that are deciphered at the point of reception.

Superstation. A television station that transmits its programming by satellite and distributes its programming nationally or globally by means of cable, home satellite dish, or other means.

Symbolic speech. Nonverbal expression communicating a viewpoint.

Syndicated exclusivity. Regulation that prohibits a cable system from importing and distributing syndicated programming for which a local broadcaster has exclusive broadcasting rights.

Teletext. An electronic publishing format characterized by the one-way transmission of signals, which are converted at the point of termination into text and images.

Time, place, and manner regulation. A restriction upon the scheduling, location, or methodology of expression pursuant to a significant governmental interest and providing the availability of alternative opportunities for expression is not foreclosed.

Tying arrangement. A condition imposed by a seller which requires purchase of an additional good or service as a condition for receiving the desired good or service.

Ultrahigh frequency (UHF). A band of television service comprising 56 channels from fourteen through 69.

Vagueness. A term applied to regulation that lacks precision to the point that a reasonable person is uncertain about what is prohibited. Vagueness is a special concern of the First Amendment insofar as protected expression may be chilled.

Very high frequency (VHF). A band of television service comprising twelve channels. VHF service consists of channels two through thirteen.

Videotext. An electronic publishing service characterized by two-way transmission of signals, which enables subscribers to receive text and image upon a display screen.

Voir dire. The process of selecting a jury.

Table of Cases

Index

About the Author

DONALD E. LIVELY is Professor of Law at the University of Toledo, College of Law, in Ohio, where he teaches and writes on constitutional law and communications law. He has also authored *Modern Communications Law* (Praeger, 1991) and has published extensively on First Amendment issues in law reviews and journals.